This book presents a new view of Jean Sibelius as composer and man, a figure of national and international significance, patriot, husband and father. Three introductory articles explore Sibelius reception in Finland, performance practice and recording history, and Sibelius's aesthetic position with regard to modernity. The second group of essays examines issues of ideology, sexuality, and mythology, and their relationship to musical structure and compositional genesis. Studies of the Second, Fourth, Sixth, and Seventh Symphonies are presented in the concluding section. Collectively, these articles address historical, theoretical and analytical issues in Sibelius's most important works. The analyses are supported by new investigations of Sibelius's compositional process as documented by the manuscripts and sketches primarily in the Sibelius Collection of the Helsinki University Library. Exploring Sibelius's innovative approach to tonality, form, and texture, the book delineates his unique brand of modernism, which has proven highly influential in the late twentieth century.

TIMOTHY L. JACKSON is Assistant Professor of Music at the University of North Texas at Denton. He is the author of *Tchaikovsky: Symphony No. 6 (Pathétique)* (1999), in the series Cambridge Music Handbooks, and coeditor of *Bruckner Studies* (1997).

VEIJO MURTOMÄKI is Professor of Music History at the Sibelius Academy in Helsinki. He is the author of *Symphonic Unity: The Development of Formal Thinking in the Symphonies of Sibelius* (1993).

Sibelius Studies

Sibelius Studies

EDITED BY

Timothy L. Jackson
College of Music, University of North Texas

AND

Veijo Murtomäki
Sibelius Academy

PUBLISHED BY THE PRESS SYNDICATE OF THE UNIVERSITY OF CAMBRIDGE
The Pitt Building, Trumpington Street, Cambridge, United Kingdom

CAMBRIDGE UNIVERSITY PRESS
The Edinburgh Building, Cambridge CB2 2RU, UK
40 West 20th Street, New York, NY 10011–4211, USA   www.cup.org
10 Stamford Road, Oakleigh, Melbourne 3166, Australia
Ruiz de Alarcón 13, 28014 Madrid, Spain
Dock House, The Waterfront, Cape Town 8001, South Africa

http://www.cambridge.org

First published 2001

Printed in the United Kingdom at the University Press, Cambridge

Typeset in Adobe Minion 10.75/14pt, using QuarkXpress™ [SE]

A catalogue record for this book is available from the British Library

Library of Congress cataloguing in publication data

Sibelius studies / edited by Timothy L. Jackson and Veijo Murtomäki.
      p.   cm.
    Includes bibliographical references and index.
    ISBN 0 521 62416 9 (hardback)
      1. Sibelius, Jean, 1865–1957. I. Jackson, Timothy L. II. Murtomäki, Veijo. III. Title.
    ML410.S54 S54 2000
    780′.92–dc21   00-03608

ISBN 0 521 62416 9 hardback

Contents

Plates

Preface

In a 1996 *New York Times* review of the world première recording of Sibelius's incidental music to Hofmannsthal's *Everyman*, Alex Ross called attention to the controversy surrounding the music of the Finnish composer:

> The collective scorn heaped on the music of Sibelius over the years could fill a companion volume to Nicolas Slonimsky's famous *Lexicon of Musical Invective*. What is unusual about anti-Sibelius bile is that it has often stemmed from fellow composers. Virgil Thomson called the Second Symphony "vulgar, self-indulgent, and provincial beyond all description." Benjamin Britten looked at the Fourth Symphony and said that its composer must have been drunk. René Leibowitz, a disciple of Schoenberg, called the Fifth "the worst symphony ever written." Theodor Adorno, typically venturing farther than most, accused Sibelius of fascistic nature worship.[1]

On the other hand, as Ross observes, Sibelius has not lacked defenders among other important twentieth-century composers:

> Alban Berg, breaking from the Schoenberg party line, found things to like in several Sibelius pieces. Morton Feldman loved the opening of the Fourth Symphony, its long and obsessive scrutiny of four ambiguous notes. Contemporary figures from John Adams to Wolfgang Rihm to Magnus Lindberg . . . have admired Sibelius not as a painter of pictures but as an original thinker, one who evolved radical methods of interweaving orchestral sonorities and mobilized harmonies at the edge of conventional tonality.[2]

This book attempts to present a new, more accurate picture of Jean Sibelius, the composer and man, a figure of national and international significance, patriot, husband, and father. Three introductory chapters explore Sibelius reception in Finland (Eero Tarasti), performance practice and recording history (Robert Layton), and Sibelius's aesthetic position with regard to modernity (Timothy Howell). The second group of essays (by Peter Franklin, Eija Kurki, Veijo Murtomäki, Timo Virtanen and Timothy Jackson) examines issues of ideology, sexuality, and

---

[1] Alex Ross, "A Serious Image Made Up of Bold Even Weird Strokes," *New York Times*, Arts Section, 23 June, 1996, p. 30.

[2] Ibid. And the list of Sibelius's avant-garde admirers continues: to it we may add Sorabji, the young Estonian composer Erkki-Sven Tüür, and the French, Tristan Murail.

mythology, and their relationship to musical structure and compositional genesis. Analytical studies of the Second, Fourth, Sixth, and Seventh Symphonies (by Tapio Kallio, Elliott Antokoletz, James Hepokoski, and Edward Laufer) are presented in the book's concluding section.

Adorno's attack on Sibelius is multi-pronged. Equating modernism with both novelty and quality, he argues that only by achieving the most advanced "state of the musical material" ("den Stand des musikalischen Materials") can music be simultaneously "modern" and "good." For Adorno, Mahler and the Second Viennese School participate in a continuous evolution towards post-tonality; therefore, these composers represent the one "true" modernism and pinnacle of quality. Because Sibelius remains tonal and outside "mainstream" modernism, he cannot be a modernist, nor can his music be any good.

Interestingly – the "Schoenberg party line" notwithstanding – Schoenberg himself was careful to dispute Adorno's overly simplistic equation of post-tonal modernism with innovation and quality. Asserting that "great music is still to be written in the key of C major," Schoenberg, in his late essay "Criteria for the Evaluation of Music" (1949), reaffirmed his admiration for both Sibelius and Shostakovich, writing that "[earlier in my career] I said something which did not require the knowledge of an expert. Every amateur, every music lover could have said: 'I feel they have the breath of symphonists.'"[3] Schoenberg clearly acknowledged the quality – and the validity – of Sibelius's own brand of modernism.

Alluded to by Ross, another prong of Adorno's attack in his 1938 article "Glosse über Sibelius" associates Sibelius – as *the* paragon of musical conservatism – with Nazi ideology: "The song [of Sibelius's supporters] hinges on the refrain 'everything is Nature, everything is Nature.' The great Pan, yearning for 'blood and soil' (*Blut und Boden*) quickly installs itself. The trivial passes for the elemental, the unarticulated for the noise of unconscious creation."[4] Adorno's contemporaries would have immediately recognized the phrase "Blut und Boden" as the slogan

---

[3] Arnold Schoenberg, "Criteria for the Evaluation of Music" (1949), in *Style and Idea. Selected Writings of Arnold Schoenberg*, ed. Leonard Stein, trans. Leo Black (London: Faber, 1975), p. 136.

[4] "Ihr Lied hört auf den Refrain ''s ist alles Natur, 's ist alles Natur'. Der grosse Pan, je nach Bedarf auch Blut und Boden, stellt prompt sich ein. Das Triviale gilt fürs Ursprüngliche, das Unartikulierte für den Laut der bewusstlosen Schöpfung." (This and the following original text is taken from Theodor Adorno's book review "Törne, B. de, Sibelius; A Close Up" published in *Zeitschrift für Sozialforschung* 7 [1938], pp. 460–63, and reprinted with the title "Glosse über Sibelius" first in Adorno, *Impromptus* [Frankfurt am Main: Suhrkamp, 1968], pp. 88–92, and thereafter in his *Gesammette Schriften* vol. XVII [Frankfurt am Main: Suhrkamp, 1982], pp. 247–32.)

of Goebbels' propaganda campaign to return culture to "its native soil." Indeed, Adorno correctly interprets the "spin" the Nazis had put on Sibelius: for them, he becomes the paragon of the "Nordic" composer: virile, manly, nature-oriented, and nationalistic.

After 1918, Finland became generally hostile towards Soviet Bolshevism and, like many Finnish intellectuals, Sibelius remained German-oriented, especially because of his early training under German-speaking musicians. For all of these reasons, in 1934, Sibelius accepted Goebbels' invitation to serve as vice-president of the Council of Composers' International Cooperation (of which Richard Strauss was then president). In 1935, on his seventieth birthday, at Hitler's personal recommendation, Sibelius received the Goethe prize, the highest honor for artistic achievement in the Third Reich. Goebbels went on, in 1941, to found the first German Sibelius Society, the only such society dedicated to a foreign composer. But despite such seemingly close relationships, whereby Sibelius's eminence was exploited by politicians to cement Finnish–German "brotherhood-in-arms," the composer himself remained aloof; his diary entries from the 1940s unequivocally disclose his aversion to Nazi ideology.[5] After the war, Sibelius's popularity declined somewhat in Central Europe, probably as a result of his prominence in the Third Reich, where, along with Respighi, he had been the most-played foreign composer.[6]

In retrospect, Adorno's critique of Sibelius's compositional technique has proven the most damaging – more harmful even than his allusion to the Nazi connection. Composers' unsavory political affiliations – real or imagined – may be excused as long as they are *good composers* (Richard Strauss especially comes to mind); but if they are *bad composers*, they will be forgiven nothing. Adorno sets out to prove that Sibelius's music is "amateurish," characterized by "the asceticism of impotence." Sibelius's "asceticism," as constructed by Adorno, is "the originality of incapacity" (*die Originalität der Hilflosigkeit*), as "it was denied to him to write either a chorale or a proper counterpoint [against it]" (*ihm weder einen Choral auszusetzen, noch einen ordentlichen Kontrapunkt zu schreiben vergönnt war*). Furthermore, in its representation of Nature, Sibelius's music reveals – contrary to French Impressionism as epitomized by Debussy – no sense of color, but only "dull, rigid, and accidental orchestral color" (*das stumpfe, steife und zufällige Orchesterkolorit*), in which there is "no palette: everything is only tints." Seventeen years later, in 1955, Adorno's influential apprentice and "representative" of the New Vienna School in

---

[5] See Eero Tarasti's discussion of Ilmari Krohn, pp. 9–10 below.

[6] Erik Levi, *Music in the Third Reich* (London etc: Macmillan Press, 1994), pp. 217–18.

France, René Leibowitz, published a pamphlet entitled "Sibelius, le plus mauvais compositeur du monde," which, essentially, recapitulates Adorno's allegations in French.[7]

Tarasti argues that Adorno could not forgive Sibelius his distinctly Finnish voice in the teeth of German hegemony in music. To be sure, this feat of originality has granted Sibelius "cult" status in Finnish society – with its concomitant excesses – but Tarasti still considers Sibelius a hero in Finland's struggle to throw off the stigma of colonialism, both political and cultural. Perhaps in no small measure because Sibelius's music played such an important role in Finland's ultimately successful bid for independence, to this day his work remains central to Finland's cultural life. A small nation of only five million inhabitants, Finland nevertheless boasts today a significant number of composers, conductors, theorists, and musicologists of international stature, almost twenty symphony orchestras (many world class), and more than one hundred music schools or conservatories – all thanks, in no small measure, to Sibelius's enduring influence.

In fact, numerous exercises in harmony and counterpoint worked for Martin Wegelius, Albert Becker, and Robert Fuchs during Sibelius's school and student years in Hämeenlinna, Helsinki, Berlin, and Vienna (c. 1881–91) disclose that the young Finn acquired solid technical grounding in harmony and counterpoint, which reinforced his extensive early compositional efforts. These exercises and early compositions document his thorough grounding in Viennese classical and romantic compositional technique. The young Sibelius was also a capable practical musician: as a violinist, he performed chamber music and served as the concertmaster in one of the two orchestras in Helsinki, in which he also played the viola. That Sibelius was offered the chair in composition at the Vienna Music Academy in 1912, and a similar position at the Eastman School of Music in 1921, shows that he was widely considered an accomplished composer with impressive technical equipment. Although Sibelius would reject these later offers, he did accept a number of composition students; for example, Leevi Madetoja and Toivo Kuula, two prominent Finnish composers, numbered among his composition students in the early years of the twentieth century.

Ironically, Sibelius's radical works composed at the turn of the century fulfill Adorno's central criterion for modernism by achieving the most advanced "state of the musical materials." His harmonic language in *En saga*, *Skogsrået* and the *Lemminkäinen Suite* may be judged "modern" by

---

[7] Ilkka Oramo's article "Sibelius, le plus mauvais compositeur du monde" discusses the relationships between Adorno's and Leibowitz's pamphlets; see BOREALES, Colloque international Jean Sibelius, 1993 (54/55), pp. 51–58.

any criterion of the 1890s, containing inversions of ninth chords before Schoenberg's *Verklärte Nacht*. Sibelius's *Kullervo* is an amazing achievement, comparable only to Mahler's *Das klagende Lied*, but still more innovative in its overall concept. The dynamic "minimalism" of the dwarves' music in *Skogsrået*, which prolongs a half-diminished (*Tristan*) chord built on A for over two hundred measures, adumbrates the minimalism of the 1960s. Carl Dahlhaus in his *Neues Handbuch der Musikwissenschaft (Band 6)* groups Sibelius with Zemlinsky, Schreker, Busoni, Mahler, Reger, Strauss, and the young Schoenberg among the representatives of "die Moderne." Furthermore, one could argue that Sibelius's late music is equally innovative in its formal, rhythmic, and tonal organization, albeit in less obvious ways.

To be sure, Sibelius's oeuvre as a whole includes pieces employing "old-fashioned" musical languages and genres of the nineteenth century, sometimes recalling salon-like entertainment and domestic music. But, in its combination of progressive and conservative aspects, his music becomes as Janus-faced as that of Schoenberg, where conservatism in rhythmic or formal dimensions sometimes counterbalances radicalism in the post-tonal harmonic language. As Howell observes, Sibelius's formal thinking and orchestral technique, superimposition of different textures and temporal processes, and extensions of modal language are distinctly progressive features, recognized and further developed by present-day composers. If the melodic and harmonic idioms of his *Gebrauchsmusik* seem to be regressive, they do not deny it the charm of *autrefois*, a quality shared with comparable music by Rakhmaninov or Richard Strauss.

The above-cited debate among composers is symptomatic of a troubled – almost schizophrenic – Sibelius reception history. With the general public, Sibelius has enjoyed the kind of international success – even adulation – of which most composers can only dream. Charting the vicissitudes of Sibelius's popularity and its consequences for recordings and performance practice, Layton's survey of "Sibelius on record" offers an overview of the enormous Sibelius discography. Paradoxically, in spite of this enthusiastic promotion by musicians and the recording industry, academics outside of Finland have taken Sibelius seriously only recently. Perhaps the public's favor has proven to be Sibelius's undoing, since in the eyes of many arbiters of taste, what remains popular cannot, by definition, be good. Even Bruckner, still a "controversial" figure in academe, has been accorded the dignity of a scholarly edition of the first versions of his symphonies. But not Sibelius; a scholarly edition of the first versions of his major works is still years away. However, publication of this book, *The Sibelius Companion* in 1996, *Jean Sibelius. A Guide to Research*, and the *Proceedings* of the 1990 and 1995 International

Symposia in Helsinki shows that Sibelius research is increasingly recognized as a legitimate field of inquiry.[8]

The present, improved, situation is due, in part, to access to new sources of information. The Sibelius Collection, donated in 1982 by the Sibelius Family to the Helsinki University Library and containing over 10,000 manuscript pages, is fueling new research. Providing the basis for the new Complete Works, begun in 1996 with the first volume published in 1999, it also includes some 120 early compositions (1881–91), the majority of which will be published for the first time. Drawn from this collection, Sibelius's music for solo piano, and solo violin with piano accompaniment, dating from the 1880s, is now being performed, possibly for the first time. Performance, publication, and scholarly evaluation of Sibelius's early music – suppressed by the composer himself – will encourage a more accurate assessment of his total oeuvre and its comparison with that of his contemporaries, most notably Strauss and Mahler. Sorely needed, this new edition will not only correct misprints and errors in the old printed scores, it will make many scores available for the first time.

The Collection has enabled musicologists and music theorists to trace the evolution of Sibelius's compositional ideas from their initial manifestation in preliminary sketches through to their final form. The sketches reveal Sibelius to be a "constructivist," a conscious manipulator of musical material who may forge and elaborate his themes and sections of pieces in his numerous sketchbooks years before the actual compositions come to fruition.[9] He referred to motives and themes as "mosaic pieces," which could be rearranged within a work, and even migrate from one piece to another. As Virtanen and Jackson suggest with regard to *Pohjola's Daughter* and the Third and Seventh Symphonies, this "migration" may have a deeper programmatic significance connected with Sibelius's relationship with his wife Aino and daughter Ruth. When working on his Fifth Symphony, Sibelius remarked in his diary: "The arrangement, make-up and grouping of the themes: with all its mystery and fascination, this is the important thing. It is as if God the Father had thrown down mosaic pieces from the floor of the heavens and asked me to put them back as they were. Perhaps that is a good definition of composition – perhaps not?"

Sibelius biography is also making significant strides with the discovery

[8] *The Sibelius Companion*, ed. Glenda Dawn Goss (Westport, CT: Greenwood Press, 1996); Glenda Dawn Goss, *Jean Sibelius. A Guide to Research* (New York and London: Garland, 1998); *Proceedings from the First International Jean Sibelius Conference*, Helsinki, August 1990, ed. Eero Tarasti (Helsinki: Sibelius Academy, 1995); *Proceedings from the Second International Jean Sibelius Conference*, Helsinki November 25–29, 1995, ed. by Veijo Murtomäki, Kari Kilpeläinen, and Risto Väisänen (Helsinki: Sibelius Academy, 1998).

[9] In this way of composing, Sibelius has much in common with Beethoven.

of new documents and access to sources that have remained "off limits." The Hämeenlinna letters, recently published by Glenda Dawn Goss, portray the composer in his formative years, intimating his future development.[10] A catalogue of Sibelius's complete correspondence now in preparation will shed new light on his contacts with the leading cultural personalities of his time. Perhaps most importantly, Sibelius's diaries will probably be opened – at least to scholars – in 2000, and, it is to be hoped, later published. This wealth of primary source material will supplement and correct Tawaststjerna's five-volume biography. Furthermore, Fabian Dahlström's *Thematisch-bibliographisches Verzeichnis*, slated to be published by Breitkopf und Härtel in late 2000, will serve as "the Sibelius Köchel," providing a complete accounting of all of Sibelius's music.

The essays by Franklin, Virtanen, Murtomäki, and Jackson initiate a new chapter in the Sibelius literature by exploring the connection between personal – especially sexual – issues and structure in Sibelius's music. In his daily life, Sibelius chafed against bourgeois values as he struggled with alcoholism and Don Juanism. The striking appearance of his wife's name – "Aino" – in the sketches for a number of major works (especially *Pohjola's Daughter* and the Seventh Symphony) discloses that his relationship with her – albeit often strained – remained of central importance, not only for his personal life but also his music. Although Sibelius's symphonies are much lauded as "absolute music," essays in "symphonic logic," these personal graffiti in the sketches intimate that he conceived his work as "confessional." Kurki further proposes that Sibelius cites passages from his theatrical music in his symphonies to transfer their semantic from the dramatic to the putatively "absolute" musical context.

The colloquy on the Second, Fourth, Sixth, and Seventh Symphonies presents contrasting yet complementary views of a cross-section of Sibelius's symphonic oeuvre. Kallio focuses on the opening of the Second Symphony, observing that the notation seems to be strangely at odds with the way the music actually sounds: in particular, the placement of the barlines appears to contradict the perceived meter. An earlier draft of the symphony reveals that the notated and heard meters correspond much more closely with each other; in the final version, some – but not all – of the musical elements have been metrically shifted. Kallio proposes that, by moving originally separate events closer together, Sibelius creates a more intensified and dramatic continuation. In his study of the Fourth Symphony, Antokoletz posits that Sibelius's innovative tonal language is

[10] Jean Sibelius, *The Hämeenlinna Letters.*
Jean Sibelius ungdomsbrev, ed. Glenda Dawn
Goss (Helsinki: Schildts Förlag, 1997).

"hybrid" – more specifically, that the harmony is "semi-functional," pitch formations being conditioned by *both* traditional voice-leading and non-traditional pitch collections, modal, whole-tone, and octatonic. Employing two analytical constructs developed in prior work on Sibelius – "rotational form" and "teleological genesis" – Hepokoski offers a new view of the formally innovative finale of the Sixth Symphony. From different perspectives, Kallio, Antokoletz, and Hepokoski all refute Adorno's claim that Sibelius fails to achieve the "state of the musical material."

Perhaps Adorno's most damaging technical critique of Sibelius concerns lack of organic unity: "'themes,' some completely unplastic and trivial successions of pitches, are put forth, most of the time never once harmonized, instead *unisono* with organ points, stationary harmonies and whatever else the five-line staff will produce in order to avoid logical harmonic progression."[11] Instead of musical coherence, Sibelius's scores are ruled by "the configuration of the banal and the absurd":

> Each detail sounds hackneyed and familial. The motives are common linking elements from the common language of tonality. One has heard them so often that one believes one has understood them. But they are brought into a senseless juxtaposition: as when one hears the words gas station, lunch, death, Greta, plowshare cobbled together with verbs and particles in a senseless way. An incomprehensible whole built from the most trivial details produces the deceptive picture of the unfathomable.[12]

"If Sibelius is good," Adorno concludes, "this invalidates the standards of musical quality that have persisted from Bach to Schoenberg: the richness of inter-connectedness, articulation, unity in diversity, the 'multi-faceted' in 'the one.'"[13]

It is, perhaps, then, *the* crowning irony of Sibelius reception history that – *pace* Adorno – Schenkerians have lionized Sibelius as their own, precisely on account of his "organic unity" and "symphonic logic." Laufer's detailed analysis of *continuity* in the design of the Seventh Symphony demonstrates that the motivic material evolves logically, one

[11] Das sieht so aus: es werden, als "Themen," irgendwelche völlig unplastischen und trivialen Tonfolgen aufgestellt, meistens nicht einmal harmonisiert, sondern unisono mit Orgelpunkten, liegenden Harmonien und was sonst nur die fünf Notenlinien hergeben, um logischen akkordischen Fortgang zu vermeiden.

[12] Es ist die Konfiguration des Banalen und des Absurden. Alles Einzelne klingt alltäglich und vertraut. Die Motive sind Bruchstücke aus dem kurrenten Material der Tonalität. Man hat sie so oft gehört, daß man sie zu verstehen meint. Aber sie sind in einen sinnlosen Zusammenhang gebracht: wie wenn man die Worte Tankstelle, Lunch, Tod, Greta, Pflugschar mit Verben und Partikeln wahllos zusammenkoppelt. Ein unverständliches Ganzes aus den trivialsten Details produziert das Trugbild des Abgründigen.

[13] Wenn Sibelius gut ist, dann sind die Maßstäbe der musikalischen Qualität als des Beziehungsreichtums, der Artikulation, der Einheit in der Mannigfaltigkeit, der Vielfalt im Einen hinfällig, die von Bach bis Schönberg perennieren.

theme being wonderfully transformed into another, thereby providing both unity and contrast, complexity within simplicity. Laufer's graphs lay bare the underlying middleground connections – the line of continuity – that Sibelius creates through concealed motivic transformations, enlargements, and recomposed restatements. From a technical point of view, Laufer's analysis confirms Sibelius's own perception of "that wonderful artistic logic that I seldom notice as I compose but can recognize afterwards."

The essays by the Finnish analysts (Murtomäki, Virtanen, and Kallio) bespeak an important development in music theory, namely the "internationalization" of the Schenkerian approach through its return to ⟶ Europe. Originally developed in Vienna before the Second World War, in the second half of the twentieth century Schenkerian analysis metamorphosed in the American Academy, an experience eloquently described by William Rothstein in his article "The Americanization of Heinrich Schenker."[14] Thanks to the efforts of Eero Hämeenniemi, Veijo Murtomäki, and Matti Saarinen, who invited leading Schenkerians to teach at the Sibelius Academy in the eighties and nineties (most notably David Beach, Carl Schachter, Edward Laufer, and Timothy L. Jackson), Schenkerian analysis has taken firm root in Finland; today, Lauri Suurpää, the most important representative of the Finnish Schenkerian school, currently offers courses in Schenkerian analysis at the Sibelius Academy. This successful transplantation was facilitated by the music of Sibelius. For, while Adorno's *aperçu* concerning the "commonness" and "disparateness" of Sibelius's "foreground" thematic materials may contain a kernel of truth, his music attains synthesis precisely by attenuating a compensating coherence in the middle- and background. Since Schenkerian analysis offers the best explanation of this kind of deeper-level synthesis, it has been recruited by the defenders of Sibelius – both Finnish and North American – to provide a potent weapon against the gainsayers (like Adorno). This book testifies to the coming of age of a new generation of Finnish Schenkerians, who take their place with distinction alongside the North Americans. But comparison of graphs of the same pieces (e.g. *Skogsrået*, *Pohjola's Daughter*, the Seventh Symphony) reveals that all of these analysts speak different personal and national "dialects"; contrasting – even diametrically opposed – analyses of the same pieces are placed in apposition, and the reader is left to glean the more compelling insights from each.

Many of the essays in this book suggest that Sibelius speaks to us with the troubled voice of the twentieth century. If the *per aspera ad astra* narrative was central to nineteenth-century discourse with its belief in

---

[14] William Rothstein, "The Americanization of Heinrich Schenker," in *Schenker Studies*, ed.
Hedi Siegel (Cambridge: Cambridge University Press, 1990), pp. 193–203.

"infinite progress," this essential optimism dissipates in Sibelius's twenti-eth-century equivocation. In his analysis of the finale of the Sixth Symphony, for example, Hepokoski speaks of "the thematizing of absence and loss." The Sibelian discourse "mourns" the passing of faith and in its ineffable grief resides its irreducible modernism: in the end, it must withdraw into silence.

The cover reproduction is from the Sibelius Collection in the Helsinki University Library, HUL 0354, pp. 101–02, showing an earlier ink draft of the conclusion of the Seventh Symphony (revised in the final version).

The editors wish to express their gratitude to a number of Sibelius schol-ars who have assisted with this project. By organizing and cataloguing the Sibelius Collection, Kari Kilpeläinen has laid the foundation for all future Sibelius research. Markku Hartikainen, who has been working on Sibelius's letters, provided transcriptions of the letters from Bayreuth and Munich cited in Murtomäki's article. Fabian Dahlström checked many details in his as yet unpublished *Sibelius Werkverzeichnis*. Matti Saarinen and Hannu Apajalahti, successive heads of the Department of Composition and Theory at the Sibelius Academy; Eero Tarasti, Professor of Musicology at the University of Helsinki; Rollie Schafer, Vice-President for Research at the University of North Texas; and Lester Brothers, Chair of the Division of Musicology, Music Theory, and Ethnomusicology at the University of North Texas generously provided funding for this project. The Finnish National Theater and The Swedish Theater in Helsinki have granted permission to publish photographs from their archives, and the Sibelius Family has graciously allowed us to reproduce manuscripts from the Sibelius Collection. We wish to thank Timo Virtanen, Jennifer Sadoff, and Dan Badnjar for type-setting the complicated musical-analytical examples. Risto Väisänen read some of the articles and made many valuable comments; in addition to this, his technical expertise with computers proved invaluable in solving difficult communication problems half-way across the globe. The editors are grateful to William Colson (Southwestern Baptist Theological Seminary), Allen Gimbel (Lawrence University), Christoph Walton (Zentralbibliothek Zurich), and Gregory Straughn (doctoral candidate, UNT) for their help in correcting the proofs. Finally, we would like to express our profound gratitude to Penny Souster, Music Editor at Cambridge University Press, for her unwavering support of this project.

Timothy L. Jackson, University of North Texas
Veijo Murtomäki, Sibelius Academy

PART I

Reception history and aesthetics

1 An essay in post-colonial analysis: Sibelius as an icon of the Finns and others

Eero Tarasti

Introduction to the topics

In the twentieth century all Finns – not just musicologists – grew up amidst a Sibelius cult. In the 1970s and 1980s, attention focused on yet another Finnish "icon," the Sibelius biographer Erik Tawaststjerna, the very incarnation of the Sibelius cult. When he spoke, one got the impression that the great master still dwelt among us, for Tawaststjerna appeared to be a direct link to the composer. When Tawaststjerna's Sibelius biography was finally completed, Seppo Heikinheimo, the chief music critic for the *Helsingin Sanomat*, wrote that Sibelius was now a "picked bone." But subsequent events have proven him wrong, for after Tawaststjerna came a new flurry of Sibelius studies, including many doctoral dissertations. The initial versions of many of the composer's works were recorded for the first time, and there were Sibelius symposia, at first only in Finland, but soon in other important centers such as Paris, London, Berlin, and New York.

On their own, musicologists, record companies, and even illustrious conductors can neither create a national cult nor revive one. While Finland has always had a Sibelius cult, it has recently gained fresh momentum from the national turning inward of the 1990s. Patriotism has become fashionable, along with its accompanying national spectacles and ceremonies. A timely example of the renewed Sibelius cult was the concert series entitled "Sibelius in Memoriam" held in the fall of 1997 at the Kallio Church in Helsinki to commemorate the fortieth anniversary of the composer's death. For that event, Osmo Vänskä conducted the Lahti Symphony Orchestra in performances of all seven symphonies.

For a semiotician, the occasion had two significant dimensions. On the one hand, the musical signifiers afforded the ear a new and fresh experience; on the other, at the level of signifieds, one experienced a national spectacle of sorrow, as if Sibelius had just recently passed away. Newspapers publicized the concerts on black-gilt pages. The audience was placed before an altar above which hung a huge, candle-lit picture of the composer. Thus, the social-semiotic aspect bracketed the purely musical qualities in the signifiers, placing greatest emphasis on the signified, namely Sibelius as an iconic figure. The audience's identification with Sibelius simultaneously reinforced its sense of "Finnishness."

The fact is that we find ourselves at the center of a Sibelius cult. The reasons for this phenomenon, as I shall attempt to show, can be traced to colonialism – and post-colonialism as its continuation.[1] I first encountered ideas about colonialism years ago when studying the "Brazilian Sibelius," Heitor Villa-Lobos. One treatise on Latin American literature employs the term "the colonialized imagination" to indicate that Third-World people do not know how to appreciate their own achievements, leaders, and "icons"; instead, they put stock only in the values and models imported from outside their native lands (for example, from Europe). I believe that the term "colonialized" accurately describes certain phenomena in Finland, particularly the Finnish sense of national inferiority and worship of everything foreign. Since Europe can be divided into colonizers and colonized, there is no doubt to which category a country like Finland belongs. Thus, post-colonial theories apply not only to the so-called "Third World" but also to highly developed countries like Finland – a country that has been spiritually "colonialized" or trapped within a "colonialized imagination."

Colonialist models, which have profound implications for semiotics, are essentially based on the opposition between dominator and dominated. Taking discursive practices captive, the dominators occupy the *langue* of communication while the dominated are permitted to produce new *paroles* only within specified limits. Thus the dominator/dominated categories decisively influence the *langue* and *parole* of a culture. Since *parole* consists of signifiers and signifieds, the only way to erase the aforementioned dominance relationship is to create radically new signifiers and signifieds capable of "exploding" the colonialist scheme of communication.

The foregoing reflections have a place in my new theory of existential semiotics. The word "icon" in recent usage may refer to "cultural icons," who are persons or phenomena that have attained the status of "concepts" inasmuch as they have assumed a permanent place and signification in people's everyday thinking. In what follows, I present my own theory of the formation of icons in the recent, popularized sense of the term, believing that the Sibelius cult might yield itself to study from this perspective.

[1] "Post-colonialism" is a term used by Jean Franco in *A Literary History of Spain* (London: Barnes and Noble, 1973), p. 3; see my discussion in Tarasti, *Heitor Villa-Lobos. The Life and Works, 1887–1959* (Jefferson, North Carolina: McFarland, 1995), p. 4.

Analysis of the Sibelius cult

The Finnish Sibelius cult began with the first performance of the *Kullervo* Symphony in 1892. Although this cult became an essential part of Finnish national history, it has not been studied systematically.[2] The objective of Philip Donner and Juhani Similä was not to analyze the Sibelius myth as such, but only to investigate the composer as an ethno-musicological and musico-cultural phenomenon, since "his personality accumulates the crucial values of Finnish art music."[3] Yet their essay did not constitute a probing analysis, but rather a general mapping of the phenomenon.[4] Among later studies, one finds Anni Heino's analysis of the public image of Sibelius as represented in Finnish newspapers, and Matti Huttunen's articles on Sibelius as a national figure.[5] Naturally, the monumental history of music in Finland by Dahlström, Heiniö, and Salmenhaara discusses this side of Sibelius. The centrality of Sibelius is undeniable, and therefore the third volume of the history, written by Erkki Salmenhaara, presents a story in which the central plot consists of the composer's various phases. Deviations into side plots occur, concerning events between Sibelius's "heroic acts." In the fourth volume, written by Mikko Heiniö, however, the narrative no longer focuses on Sibelius.[6] The main protagonists are now other Finnish composers over whom Sibelius casts his "shadow." Heiniö employs the word "shadow" in three contexts: first, when discussing Sibelius as the object of national reverence; second, his influence on Finnish composers; and third, the new Sibelius reception.

[2] Among efforts to do so was the project by Philip Donner and Juhani Similä on Sibelius as an idol, in which the authors used a method developed by the Finnish folklorist Matti Kuusi; see Donner and Similä, "Jean Sibelius – teollistumisajan musiikkimurroksen idolihahmo" (Jean Sibelius – an Idol Figure in the Transition of Music in the Period of Industrialism), in *Musiikkikulttuurin murros teollistumisajan Suomessa* (*The Transition of Music Culture in the Period of Industrialism*), ed. Vesa Kurkela and Riitta Valkeila (Jyväskylä: Jyväskylä University Dept. of Music, series A: tutkielmia ja raportteja no. 1, 1982), pp. 33–49. According to Kuusi who is quoted on p. 18, "idols are wish figures, real or fictive, which personify what we dream of, admire, appreciate, aspire after, desire (or fear)."
[3] Ibid., p. 1.
[4] Furthermore, it irritated, among others, Erik

Tawaststjerna, who viewed the authors' work as an attack on his own Sibelius biography.
[5] See Anni Heino's MA Thesis, "Kansallinen ja kansainvälinen Sibelius suomalaisessa julkisuudessa" (Tampere: Tampere University, 1999). Among studies by Matti Huttunen note the following: "'The Canon' of Music History and the Music of a Small Nation," in *Music History Writing and National Culture*, ed. Urve Lippus (Tallinn: Institute of Estonian Language, 1995), and "How Sibelius Became a Classic in Finland," in *Sibelius Forum. Proceedings from the Second International Jean Sibelius Conference. Helsinki, November 25–29, 1995*, ed. Veijo Murtomäki, Kari Kilpeläinen, and Risto Väisänen (Helsinki: Sibelius Academy, 1998).
[6] See Mikko Heiniö, *Suomen musiikin historia, osa 4: Aikamme musiikki* (*Music History in Finland*, vol. 4: *Contemporary Music*) (Porvoo: WSOY, 1995), p. 64.

In recent Finnish Sibelius reception, the personality cult metamorphosed into "abstract" form by focusing on the "immortal idea of the symphony." In this, the dominated Finns directly adopted the canonized view of the dominating central European culture: the symphony was the summit of art music, it was "absolute" and hence of a higher order than programmatic music, and it was based upon immortal supra-historical thinking. Consequently, the "myth of the symphony" was transformed into the myth of "organicism," which to date no one has analyzed in detail. The notion of organicism plays a central role in the writings of Joonas Kokkonen, and has increasingly informed academic discussions of the musical texts themselves.[7]

My primary focus is the reception of the composer in Finnish texts that portray him as an icon and idol. These sources often do not include visual "texts," whose existence is laudably mentioned, however, by Donner and Similä.[8] In what follows, I draw on certain verbal "topics" in texts dealing with Sibelius as an icon, examine them in the light of postcolonial musicology and semiotics, and conclude by briefly indicating how new perceptions of the signifiers might liberate us from the dominating/dominated relationships of post-colonial discourse.

Sibelius icons in Finland

Typical expressions of Sibelius iconization can be found in texts by Sulho Ranta, Martti Similä, Ilmari Krohn, and other contemporaries.[9] In my view, it is crucial to perceive these icons in the dialectics of the categories "Sameness/Otherness." Who are the "we" of music and arts, and who are the "others"? Ranta, a Finnish composer and fervent, Europe-oriented modernist in the 1920s, writes on Sibelius's birthday in 1945 in a style understandable in the context of that memorial event:

> We Finns are always aware of the greatness of Sibelius as the national composer . . . we understand as well his breadth as a composer, his universal view that recognizes no limits. Yet only the Finnish Sibelius is our Sibelius.[10]

[7] See Joonas Kokkonen in his essay collection *Ihminen ja musiikki* (*Man and Music*), ed. Kalevi Aho (Helsinki: Gaudeamus, 1992), p. 59.
[8] Well known is their analysis of a photograph that shows the baby Sibelius and his mother in a Madonna and child pose, made possible by retouching the photo to remove Sibelius's sister! We do find exciting visual iconizations, such as the painting by Eemu Myntti that represents Sibelius as Väinämöinen, in which the composer's

features are blended with those of the ancient Finnish god.
[9] See Sulho Ranta's essay "Jean Sibelius eurooppalaisena ja yleismaailmallisena ilmiönä" ("Jean Sibelius as a European and global phenomenon"), in *Sävelten valoja ja varjoja: toinen kirja musiikista ja muusikoista* (Porvoo: WSOY, 1946), pp. 13–18, and Martti Similä's booklet *Sibeliana* (Helsinki: Otava, 1945).
[10] Ranta, "Jean Sibelius eurooppalaisena," p. 11.

In terms of the *langue* and *parole* of music, Ranta elsewhere recognizes the difficulty of transforming *parole* into a new *langue*. The dominated does not alter its subordinate position by creative acts solely within the framework of the dominant *langue*. Ranta writes about the difficulty of penetrating to the area of *langue*; typically, he underlines the nationality of the dominated:

> Every nation, every country sees the great men of its art mostly as national artists and fighters . . . Nevertheless, the domains of the great artists are limitless. Shakespeare, Goethe, and Beethoven are great world citizens of art. Purely national art . . . does not easily become such a common property. Such an art has its own atmosphere, in which it grows in the easiest way and breathes most naturally. Yet even it has . . . possibilities of being accepted in very broad areas.[11]

In Ranta's essay "Jean Sibelius as a European and global phenomenon" the life of the composer-hero follows a narrative scheme whereby the initial phase is constituted by the assumption of the dominant *langue*; the second phase is the production of one's own *parole* within its limits; and the last phase the creation of one's own *langue*. Ranta observes that "Fifty years ago Finland needed a Finnish composer, and Sibelius knew his place . . . the result was Finnish, national art. Only when we had been able to show Europe that distant Finland is a country that has its own culture, only then could even Sibelius be relieved [from bearing the national standard], sink his thoughts inward, and let the goals of his art carry him still further away."[12]

In Ranta's text, the most crucial act of the hero-idol is the legitimizing of his home country ("only when we had been able to show Europe," i.e. "the Other"). Throughout, Europe appears as the Other of the Finns – the Other which determines what is valuable and what is not. The acceptance of the German view of culture as innate Spirit (*Geist*), as a matter of inwardness (*Innigkeit*), is revealed by the conclusion that the new *langue* emerges only from a sinking into oneself. The new *langue* is not created by means of external activities such as manifestoes, schools, or outwardly dramatic acts, but by a turning or looking inward.[13]

---

[11] Ibid., p. 13.
[12] Ibid.
[13] See Richard Taruskin in his broad and brilliantly written study *Defining Russia Musically. Historical and Hermeneutical Essays* (Princeton: Princeton University Press, 1997). In his treatise, Taruskin also utilizes the concept of "the semiotic," by which he understands corporeal meanings in music, especially when they reflect some oriental stereotypes. Similar "corporeality" in Sibelius could be sketched reflecting the Nordic or Finno-Ugric version of masculinity and virility in musical discourse – not to be confused with the Wagnerian sense of the term.

Another *topos* is formed by personal meetings with the iconized figure, when even the slightest signifiers assume great iconic significance. Such was the case with Ranta, but more particularly with Martti Similä in his *Sibeliana*, published in 1945. In this book, every statement by the composer assumes monumental proportions, along with his every gesture and expression. When Similä, a pianist and conductor devoted to Sibelius's music, played the Piano Sonata (perhaps somewhat overdramatically) at Sibelius's home in Ainola, the master looked keenly at him and said: "I wonder whether you understand me when I say that my style is ascetic."[14] The story continues:

> We sipped mocha and smoked our Havanas in all quietness. Then suddenly, almost as if mid-thought, [Sibelius] stood up and walked vehemently, sometimes from one corner of the room to the other. This was truly not the jovial pondering of an old priest. No, like a lion did he step.[15]

Similä spins out the mythologization of Sibelius's music with a type of discourse that was very common at that time:

> As the background of his seven symphonies there is the deserted nature of the North, and at the same time an austere and mild, autumnal gray, or the reflections of the calm beauty of a summer day. In the First and Second, and even in the Third Symphony, from this soil arises the heroic figure of the young master-composer, in the first two [symphonies] as strong, in the Third already much acquiesced, and in its final hymn, one might say, in the serenity of antiquity.[16]

Similä had no doubt that the hero of the symphony was the composer himself. Such a view was espoused not only in popular texts such as this, but also in academic discourse, as is well illustrated by the analyses of Ilmari Krohn.[17]

Krohn, a composer and musicologist, was the first to hold the chair of musicology at the University of Helsinki. His study *Der Stimmungsgehalt der Symphonien von Jean Sibelius* (1945) can be interpreted in the light of both colonialism and iconization. Krohn experiences the Second Symphony in particular as depicting Finland's struggle for independence and proposes that it be called the "Finlandia" or the "Suomi Symphony." He interprets motifs and tone colours as musical signifiers for the political battle in which "the Russian dominant power tried to deprive Finland of its autonomy and free cultural development." In Krohn's reading, the sym-

---

[14] Similä, *Sibeliana*, p. 36.
[15] Ibid.
[16] Ibid., p. 19.
[17] Ilmari Krohn was the leading Finnish musicologist until the 1950s. See particularly his *Der Stimmungsgehalt der Symphonien von Jean Sibelius*, 2 vols. (Helsinki: Suomalaisen tiedeakatemian toimituksia, Sarja B, nos. 57–58, 1945–46).

phony predicts the liberation of the Fatherland with the help of German brothers-in-arms. For Krohn, music thus has the ability to forecast social events, a view nowadays held by many.[18]

According to Krohn the main key of D major, "As the dominant of the dominant . . . represents higher activity than the general referential key of C major, and its symbolic color, intensified yellow [*potenzierte gelbe Farbe*], fits well with the [symphony's] expression, which depicts fervent patriotism."[19] Thus, Krohn views musical signifiers as if they existed within a ready-made framework. Elsewhere, he compares the Second Symphony with the First, noting that when Sibelius adopts the necessary compositional technique – the *langue*, as we would say – then the difference in his subsequent symphonies must appear on the level of the contents – or in the *parole*. Every master achieves more certainty in the technical sense by mastering the *langue*. The better he can handle it, the less effort the work of composition requires.[20]

In Krohn's writings there is no doubt about what constitutes the *langue* of music, which he describes in his monumental treatise on musical form. Musical *langue*, in his view, is a neutral way to express ideological and aesthetic ideas. By taking this position, he assumes an anti-colonialist stance. But when he reduces the Sibelian text to a Wagnerian *leitmotif* table and a straitjacket of strictly metrical analysis, he betrays a very "Germanic" attitude. In other words, what he wins in content, at the level of the signified, he loses elsewhere, at the level of his own discourse. In sum, despite his efforts to be an anti-colonialist, his logic follows that of the dominating German culture. This impression is intensified by his dry, Germanic style of writing that allows no intuitive flights of fantasy. The very manner of unfolding the analysis in Krohn's writing – or as the French put it, his *écriture* – that alone and in itself constitutes the taking of a certain position or standpoint. Krohn's analysis of the Second Symphony culminates in a diagram in which every theme and section of the symphony is provided with its "signified":

Introduction: *treues Tagewerk der tiefen Volksschichten* (*Strebemotiv*)
(faithful daily work of the lower classes, striving motive); the main phrase:

[18] See Krohn's discussion of Sibelius's Second Symphony (ibid., pp. 120–227); also Jacques Attali, in his treatise *Noise. The Political Economy of Music*, trans. Brian Massumi (Minneapolis: Minnesota University Press, 1985).

[19] Krohn published in 1911–37 his monumental treatise of music theory, which established his method of music analysis for several decades in Finland; it was based on the idea of musical form stemming from the smallest rhythmic units to large-scale musical forms, leading into similar schemes bar-by-bar, as in Alfred Lorenz's analyses of the same time. See Krohn, *Musiikinteorian oppijakso* (*A Course in Music Theory*) (Porvoo: WSOY, 1911, 1916, 1923, 1927 and 1937).

[20] See Krohn, *Der Stimmungsgehalt der Symphonien*, pp. 125 and 149.

Fremde Kultur der Oberschicht (*Ziermotiv und Blütemotiv*) (alien culture of
the upper classes, decoration motif and blossoming motif); transition:
vereinigende Liebe zum Vaterland (*Mahnmotiv und Vaterlandsmotiv*)
(unifying love for the Fatherland, exhortation motif and Fatherland
motif); subordinate theme: national awakening (*Weckrufmotiv und
Funkenmotiv*)(awakening call motif and spark motif) [...] Development:
awakening of the national consciousness (*Aufbruchsmotiv*)("surging forth"
motif) into the diligent striving in all disciplines of the cultural life, etc.[21]

By contrast, in retrospect, some texts seem to be completely free from
the iconization of their object, although they were interpreted as such in
their time. One of them is Bengt von Törne's *Sibelius: A Close Up*, published
in English in 1937.[22] Törne's work sparked one of the most (in)famous
anti-iconizations of Sibelius, Theodor Adorno's review of Törne's book,
(1938).[23] What in von Törne's tiny book could have ignited Adorno's rage?
In fact, Törne's style is astonishingly objective compared to the overt
mythologizing of other Finns. The book relates encounters between von
Törne and Sibelius, and these reports do not idolize Sibelius more than is
usual when a young composer meets an older *maestro*. Von Törne writes:

> I had had the unique opportunity of being in touch with a man who at
> every moment gives one the impression of a great genius. But Sibelius has
> nothing of the rigidity which is peculiar to the characters of Corneille's or
> Racine's tragedies. He is more akin to Shakespeare's heroes: at the same
> time human, great and humorous.[24]

One of Adorno's primary arguments was directed against the notion
that Sibelius's closeness to nature could dictate his compositional style.
When von Törne, arriving in Finland from the Baltic sea, described the
landscape, Sibelius replied: "And when we see those granite rocks, we
know why we are able to treat the orchestra as we do."[25] Later, this statement would be transmuted into an iconizing form in the obituary by Yrjö
Kilpinen: "So is Jean Sibelius's life-work like a mighty lighthouse standing
on the solid granite rock of Finland, a lighthouse whose bright radiance is

[21] Ibid., pp. 152–53.
[22] Bengt von Törne was one of the very few
pupils of composition Sibelius ever had.
Therefore his remarks have a certain value
although they were modified by his own
aesthetic views. See Törne, *Sibelius: A Close
Up* (London: Faber, 1937); in Finnish *Sibelius:
Lähikuvia ja keskusteluja* (Helsinki: Otava,
1945/65).
[23] Theodor Adorno's hostility toward Sibelius
was ideological (basing his views on the
"progressive" in music history), practical (he

was a friend of Alma Mahler and wanted to
promote Mahler as the great proponent of the
symphonic tradition in the twentieth
century), and musical (he was unable to grasp
Sibelius's radically new musical language).
His critique appears without a title in the
Zeitschrift für Sozialforschung 7 (1938), pp.
460–63; repr. in two further collections; see
note 4 on page xii.
[24] Törne, *Sibelius: A Close Up*, p. 100.
[25] Ibid., p. 97.

seen everywhere in the world."[26] According to such "musical progressivists" as Adorno, music could not be based on a return to "nature," since in music even nature is negated by culture to become a *zweite Vermittlung*, i.e., a form of mediation. His reasoning approaches the position of semiotics, in the sense that cultural texts are always arbitrary and conventional "social constructions" that cannot be based upon or justified by appeals to a "nature" that motivates compositions in a directly indexical way. The problem is that Adorno employs Hegelian-semiotic logic tendentiously, in the manner of the dominating culture, as did his ideal composer, Schoenberg. He did not accept the proposition that for any composer, even Stravinsky, nature could provide the source of aesthetics. In his shortsighted conjectures about aesthetics, Adorno proves himself to be an adherent of colonialist discourse, although his persuasive rhetorical style often conceals this fact.

What probably irritated Adorno even more was Sibelius's negative judgements about those other "gods," Richard Wagner and Gustav Mahler, who had been canonized by the dominant German tradition. Von Törne (presumably reflecting Sibelius's opinion) says about Mahler: "He certainly aspired at vast epic perspectives, and his intentions are supported by an unfailing technical skill and experience. Yet all these undoubtedly great qualities avail him nothing, for there is no life in these gigantic works, conceived as they are without inspiration."[27] Additionally, he quotes Sibelius's criticisms of Wagner's heavy-handed rhetorical style, adding that there is in music nothing further removed from the character of Sibelius than Wagner's overloaded baroque: "Sibelius's personal dislike of him is further increased by the conviction that the influence of that master and his whole school has been disastrous to the evolution of music."[28] Sibelius even said, according to von Törne, that "Wagner reminds me of his former friend and later antagonist Nietzsche, who always suggests a butler who has been created a baron."[29] These anti-Wagner statements anticipate later negative Wagner reception in Finland, many composers considering it their duty to take the same position as Sibelius (see, e.g., Kokkonen's writings). Even the third volume of the new *Music History in Finland* echoes Sibelius's position: "Wagner fever was a disease from which only a few musicians of the turn of century were spared. Likewise, Sibelius had his own Wagner crisis."[30]

[26] The Finnish Lieder composer Yrjö Kilpinen in his obituary of Jean Sibelius in the newspaper *Uusi Suomi*, 1 October 1957.
[27] Törne, *Sibelius: A Close Up*, pp. 74–75.
[28] Ibid., p. 60.

[29] Ibid.
[30] Erkki Salmenhaara in his part of the *Suomen musiikin historia* vol. 3 (Helsinki: WSOY, 1995), p. 98.

"Post-colonial" musical signifiers

When the colonizer wishes to deny sanctuary to any colonials who aspire to enter, then he looks to those signifiers of *parole* that do not fit with the *langue* but rather break from it. These signifiers may be greatly admired by the dominating culture, which focuses on their great originality and uniqueness. But at the same time this kind of admiration guarantees their exclusion from the "Pantheon" as exotic peculiarities. While errant musical signifiers can satisfy the consumer's need for variety and novelty, for this very reason they cannot represent the discourse of Power and Sameness.

To establish Sibelius as a subject for post-colonial musicology, we should explore the music's spontaneous metaphors. At this level of "Firstness," signifiers would be the gestures in themselves. And at this level, they have not yet been sublimated to serve a "spiritual" – i.e., colonialized – discourse in the Adornian sense (for colonial discourse has given itself the right to define what is spiritual, profound, beautiful or generally "universal" in art). Gestures in music are always to some extent corporeal. What kind of body, then, speaks in Sibelius's music? Is it a virile, Wagnerian body? Or is it an androgynous one, inclined to Nordic melancholy and Arctic hysteria? Certainly it is often a relatively slow-moving, frequently cumbrous body, with rare flashes of quick motion. Joseph Gingold has spoken about the "brooding quality" in Sibelius, but added that it was a noble, sublime brooding.[31] Excessive repetition that approaches the per- suasive powers of incantation forms one of the most constant features of Sibelius's music. Leo Normet uses the term "driving force" to describe this trait, which could be defined as but one variant of desire. Normet also finds an "arabesque" quality in Sibelius's music, which links it to another artistic phenomenon of the time, art nouveau.[32] Moreover, Sibelius's music transforms itself over time, particularly in his symphonies, becoming more and more of a linear art, a "linear counterpoint" (precisely during those years when musicologist Ernst Kurth coined the term).

Although the term comes from the visual arts, *chiaroscuro* – or the play of light and darkness – is another phenomenal quality of Sibelius's music. For instance, the timbre of the violins in the upper register in the *Andante festivo* is quickly recognized as a type of "*Lohengrin* sound." Although a

[31] Joseph Gingold as interviewed by the author in the spring of 1987 at Indiana University, Bloomington.

[32] Leo Normet was a leading Estonian musicologist and Sibelius specialist. His fascinating notion of Sibelius's "synthetic style" and its "driving force" is presented in his essay "The Sibelian Driving Force of Development as Expressed in his Symphonies," in *Proceedings from The First International Jean Sibelius Conference, Helsinki, August 1990*, ed. Eero Tarasti (Helsinki: Sibelius Academy, 1995), pp. 145–49.

"cultural unit" in Western art music, this timbre is simultaneously an immediately experienced quality, a "Firstness," which penetrates our senses with unquestionable certainty. Likewise, darkness has its place in Sibelius's music, which one "hears," among other places, in the brooding timbre of the opening of *Kullervo* and the overall dark sonority of the Fourth Symphony.

To the light/dark opposition we may add the dichotomy of lightness/heaviness. Sibelius's music is seldom light in the sense of playing with ambivalence such as parody, irony, and the grotesque. The signifiers in his music usually represent what they stand for to an astonishing degree. His skill was put to the test in salon music, which is "light" by definition; but even there his specialty was the *Valse triste* and other topics of death. Yet Sibelius's texture is not invariably heavy. Enacting Ruskinian ideas of power, Sibelius's themes rise up and surge forward, always meeting heavy resistance, their final elevation and dispersal invariably earned by a previous struggle now sanctified by a reward.[33] To speak in such terms leads us "naturally" to another category of Sibelius's music, that of "desire."

So well conceptualized by recent gender analysis, desire is a quality directly experienced in music. In Sibelius's music, one may detect this quality in the actorial "desires" of the themes themselves, a discourse charged with masculine virility or feminine "softness." But for Sibelius, desire is also neutralized by a process of sublimation that transmutes it into something else altogether. This is not the straightforward repression of desire, but rather a stymying, freezing, depersonalization and de-actorialization of it. In *The Swan of Tuonela*, for instance, the English horn sounds "neutrally," as if its original feminine-erotic connotations have been neutralized (perhaps this phenomenon is related to the linguistic fact that Finnish has only one word, "hän," to indicate both he and she, *il* and *elle*, or *er* and *sie*). This neutralization of the subject of desire in Sibelius's music is associated with the phenomenal category of presence/absence. The music often creates the impression of a bare landscape without a living soul (consider, for example, the beginning of the Violin Concerto). And concomitant gender neutrality becomes increasingly pronounced in the later works. The category of desire further manifests itself through euphoric/dysphoric aspectual *semes* that are especially noticeable in the shift from dysphoria to euphoria, as occurs in the simple but effective narrative program of *Finlandia*.

[33] John Ruskin, the British nineteenth-century art historian and founder of the art education movement, proposes in his series *Modern Painters* (5 vols., 1843–1860; ed. and abridged David Barrie [London: André Deutsch, 1987]) that art expresses certain "ideas" like those of "power," "relation," "beauty," "imitation," and "truth."

2 From Kajanus to Karajan: Sibelius on record

Robert Layton

Few composers of Sibelius's generation took the gramophone seriously. In the early years of the century the gramophone (or phonograph) was more about nostalgia than a serious vehicle for repertoire. True, Sibelius mentions it as early as 1888 in a letter to his uncle Pehr in Åbo,[1] which shows awareness of its emergence on to the technological arena. But when discs arrived, the 78 rpm format with its four-minute side naturally imposed constraints that discouraged large-scale symphonic works. Busoni was not alone in his dismissive response to the medium. Although he made piano rolls, he recorded only a derisory four 78 rpm discs. Indeed, who in the days of acoustic recording could imagine the rich orchestral sonorities of Strauss and Skryabin being adequately served by acoustic recording! The advent of electrical recording changed all that. It enabled Elgar, an early enthusiast for the gramophone, to record his major works in sound of remarkable fidelity for its period; and Rakhmaninov to give us his four concertos, the *Rhapsody on a Theme of Paganini* and two major orchestral masterpieces, the Third Symphony and *Isle of the Dead*. Even Sibelius's exact contemporary Glazunov made a record of his ballet *The Seasons*. But apart from a 1939 broadcast of the *Andante festivo* nothing survives from Sibelius's baton.[2] Electrical recording came too late to capture him or his great contemporary Carl Nielsen in their prime. In Nielsen's case we have to rely on conductors like Thomas Jensen, Launy Grøndahl, and Erik Tuxen, who played under him to divine his artistic intentions. Even so the Danes remained surprisingly indifferent to the need to promote Nielsen's cause.

The Finns, on the other hand, recognized the importance of presenting their greatest composer to the world right from the start. In 1930,

---

[1] Jean Sibelius, *The Hämeenlinna Letters. Jean Sibelius ungdomsbrev*, ed. Glenda Dawn Goss (Helsinki: Schildts Förlag, 1997), p. 98.
[2] For long the run-through for the performance, possibly under Toivo Haapanen, Martti Similä, Erkki Linko, or some other conductor, was in the public domain as being the actual broadcast. Of course, in the early days of LPs, Sibelius was invited to London by Walter Legge to conduct (or failing that supervise) the recordings of the symphonies with the Philharmonia Orchestra.

only five years after the first electrical recording had appeared,[3] the
Finnish Government sponsored recordings of the first two Sibelius symphonies on Columbia.[4] By 1934 all seven had been committed to disc
together with *Tapiola*, *Belshazzar's Feast*, and *Pohjola's Daughter*, mostly
under the ægis of the HMV Sibelius Society, the brainchild of Walter
Legge. By contrast the first Nielsen cycle was not completed until 1952,
when coarse-groove shellac was giving way to microgroove vinyl. The
next generation of composers did not doubt the importance of recording
and we are fortunate in having most of Stravinsky, Britten, Copland, and
Walton available under the composers' own direction.

It is a truism that premier recordings invariably reveal special insights.
They have a special concentration and intensity because they exhibit the
process of discovery. Now, some later performances can come close to that
but it is not so easy (indeed it is well nigh impossible) to recapture the
atmosphere of a period! There is a special aura about the wartime recordings of the Shostakovich symphonies under Stokowski and Toscanini, and
Mravinsky's 1947 recording of the Eighth; and the ambience we perceive
in Elgar's own recordings of his symphonies and *Falstaff* is not something
a modern conductor could readily reproduce. This cultural or spiritual
climate becomes more fleeting as we move away from the period. If the
gramophone was too primitive to record Sibelius's pioneering performances in the 1920s of his last three symphonies, we do at least know his
intentions concerning Nos. 1, 2, 3 and 5 at second hand from the conductor most associated with him, Robert Kajanus (1856–1933).

Kajanus's records of the first two symphonies were the very first to
reach the gramophone, and his account of the Second remains one of the
tautest on record. Yet from many Sibelian conductors – including some of
the very finest – we have been accustomed to a much broader, more
expansive approach. Nor is it as if this has happened as Kajanus's account
has gradually faded from view. It was a view that was already in currency
in Sibelius's lifetime.[5] It is hardly surprising that after forty years – from
En saga which Kajanus commissioned in 1892, through to his death –
there should be a complete sympathy, and though the playing he secured
from the London Symphony Orchestra was not always perfect (as in the
finale of the Fifth), he communicates overwhelmingly a sense of total

[3] Tchaikovsky's Fourth Symphony played by
the Royal Albert Hall Orchestra conducted by
Sir Landon Ronald was issued by HMV in
December 1925.
[4] Of course popular Sibelius works had
reached the gramophone much earlier: the
very first recording of *Valse triste* was made in
London as early as 1907 by the band of the

Coldstream Guards in an arrangement by
J. H. Matthey!
[5] Memory is notoriously deceptive but the
performances that I can remember in London
during and immediately after the war from
conductors like Basil Cameron, Sir Adrian
Boult and others adopted a relatively
leisurely approach.

identification with the composer's mind. These were all premier recordings: *Tapiola* had only been written eight years earlier and the Fifth Symphony six years before that. No one has taken the famous 'storm' in *Tapiola* as slowly as did Kajanus, and the effect is greatly to enhance its chilling terrors and majesty. Sibelius himself wrote concerning the First Symphony: "very many are the men who have conducted this Symphony during the last thirty years but there are none who have gone deeper and given them [*sic*] more feeling and beauty."[6]

When Armas Järnefelt was asked in a radio interview, not long after Sibelius's death, what he thought of his brother-in-law as a conductor, he replied whimsically, "Well, let's say he was better as a composer!" But if Järnefelt was condescending on this occasion Erik Tawaststjerna[7] quotes the German-born violinist, Ernst Märcke, who was a member of the Gothenburg Orchestra in the 1920s, saying that the composer conducted "flawlessly." Moreover Sibelius's first biographer, Erik Furuhjelm, writing after a concert in 1916, spoke of him as "a very fine conductor; he appears inspired and skilful on the concert podium and is instructive in rehearsal. It is a great pleasure to watch his preparation of his own works. He ... has an extraordinary capacity to draw playing of culture and nobility from the orchestra," and spoke of his "subtlety and finesse." The Second Symphony was given in

> a surprisingly brisk tempo. I don't remember whether the composer has ever conducted it at this pace on an earlier occasion. Kajanus performances – *which can generally be regarded as authoritative* [my italics] – have usually been much broader in character. In any event I was for my part very much taken with his reading yesterday. The outer movements were given with energy and speed and in the slow movement the tragic pathos communicated itself powerfully.[8]

Kajanus's account of the Second Symphony (Columbia LX50–54; US numbering: Columbia Masterworks Set 149, 67833–37) made fourteen years later in May 1930 is pretty brisk (he takes 38′44″ over it as opposed to Koussevitzky's 40′31″ in his 1935 Boston account.[9] One can observe a gradual relaxation of grip over the years, particularly in the first movement, which took 8′14″ under Kajanus, 8′22″ under Barbirolli in his 1940

---

[6] Sibelius's relationship with Kajanus was not untouched by feelings of paranoia but the suspicions often voiced in his diary entries do not seem to have swayed his artistic judgement on this occasion.

[7] Erik Tawaststjerna, *Sibelius. Vol. III, 1914–1957* trans. Robert Layton (London: Faber, 1997 [1978/88]), p. 163.

[8] In *Dagens Press*, 31 March 1916, quoted in ibid., p. 83.

[9] In his authoritative and exhaustive survey of *The Symphonies of Sibelius. A Discography and Discussion* (Bloomington: Indiana University, 1990), Guy Thomas gives it as 34′07″ but obviously has not included the seventh 78 rpm side (LX53).

New York Philharmonic performance (American Columbia 11403–7) and 8'51" in Toscanini's 1938 performance with the BBC Symphony Orchestra (EMI mono CDH7 63307-2) and 8'31" in his 1940 NBC broadcast (RCA GD 60294). Perhaps the most "sluggish" (the word is Guy Thomas's) is by a fellow Finn, Paavo Berglund, in the first of his recordings with the Bournemouth Orchestra (HMV ASD3497 – not issued in the USA) which the conductor Trevor Harvey, writing in *The Gramophone* magazine, called "lethargic." The first modern conductor to return to the urgent tempo of Kajanus was Neeme Järvi in 1984 (BIS-CD252).

Of course statistics can be misleading but they give at least some indication of tempo. No apology need be made for stressing tempo, for it is axiomatic that a conductor who finds the *tempo giusto* also gets most other things right. The right tempo enables detail to fall into the right place, phrases to take the right shape and to breathe life into the overall shape of a piece. Needless to say a few bars taken out of context and juxtaposed alongside another can give a wholly false impression. It is always the relationship of part to whole that is the touchstone of a performance.[10] Listening again to Kajanus in the first movement of the Second Symphony, one notes not just the brisk tempo but the flexibility: he pulls back for the horns to reply to the oboe theme more dramatically than one would expect. The slow movement, though brisk, is also full of striking contrasts: the entry of the F sharp major tune really is *andante* for once and *piano pianissimo*. And while never losing sight of their structural strength, Kajanus does not shrink from recognising their Tchaikovskian inheritance.

Once these records had appeared others were not slow to follow: Koussevitzky and the Boston Symphony recorded the Second in 1935 (HMV DB2599–2603 & DB2604S and in the USA RCA Victor Set 272, M2721–6S) and the Fifth in 1940 (HMV DB3168–71; US numbering: RCA Victor Set 474, M15019–22). Both are powerful accounts that won a wide following on both sides of the Atlantic.[11] Eugene Ormandy and the Minneapolis Orchestra recorded the First in 1936 (HMV DB2709–13; US numbering: RCA Victor Set 290 M8873–77). Like so many pioneering records it has a blazing intensity that he did not quite recapture in either of his subsequent remakes with the Philadelphia Orchestra in 1946 (US

[10] I am also aware that there can be more than just one *tempo giusto*: the role of the conductor is to find what is for him the most natural tempo and persuade the listener that there is no other.

[11] Koussevitzky re-recorded the Second in 1950 (RCA LM1172) and off-air recordings of the First and Seventh, and the Fifth and Sixth, obviously from the late 1940s or early 1950s, appeared on the Canadian Rococo label (Rococo 2103 – 2LPs). The Seventh is if anything more magisterial than his celebrated 1933 account, though the Sixth, which he never recorded commercially, is less convincing.

numbering: RCA M18499–502 or 1963 mono BRG stereo SBRG72111; US numbering: ML5795 stereo MS6395). Generally speaking, however, Ormandy's Sibelius on record has been underrated or rather "taken for granted." He recorded the Second with the Philadelphia Orchestra no fewer than three times: in 1949 (Columbia LX1175–79; US numbering: ML4131), in 1958 (Philips mono ABL3214; stereo SABL155; US numbering: ML5027 stereo MS6024), and finally and most impressively in quadrophony in 1973 (CD–4 ARD10018). Perhaps his most imposing performances though are the 1956 Fourth (Philips mono ABL3084; US numbering: ML5045), powerfully stark and concentrated, with a particularly inward-looking slow movement and the 1962 Seventh (CBS mono BRG stereo SBRG72026; US numbering: ML5675 stereo MS6275). Writing in *The Gramophone*, Lionel Salter spoke of the "extremely intense performance" of the Seventh ("by any reckoning one of the most masterly pieces of compressed organic thinking in the symphonic repertoire") as "more akin to Karajan in its slower tempi than to Beecham," and thought that "for stereo users there is no question about this leading the field."[12]

Other loyal Sibelians in the 1940s were Barbirolli, who in his days with the New York Philharmonic recorded the First in 1942 (Columbia 11923–27) and the Second in 1940 (Columbia 11403–7), re-recording the latter with the Hallé Orchestra in 1954 (HMV mono ALP1122) and in 1967 as part of a complete cycle (HMV ASD2308; US numbering: Angel 36425), but most memorably in 1962 with the Royal Philharmonic Orchestra – which did not gain wider circulation until 1976 (RCA Gold Seal GL25011; US numbering: Quintessence PMC7008). Barbirolli's love of the composer shone through almost every performance he recorded from his first Seventh (1949) with the Hallé Orchestra (HMV C3895–97; US numbering: LHMV1011) to his last eighteen years later (HMV ASD2326). Over the chaotic middle section in the development of the first movement of the Fourth, it is perhaps kinder to draw a veil (HMV ASD2494).

The Sibelius Society records in which Kajanus's recordings of the Third and Fifth symphonies appeared were outstanding technically for their day. According to Thomas, the composer "could scarcely have hoped for a more auspicious debut on record than that provided in England by the Society. Together with the Beecham recording of the Sixth issued in 1950 . . . they remain essential listening for Sibelians sixty years later."[13] As we have seen, Nos. 1, 2 and 5 were available in alternative versions during the 1930s, but the Third, Fourth and Sixth were only to be had in

---

[12] *The Gramophone* 40 (August 1962), p. 101.   [13] Thomas, "Discography," p. 6.

the volumes of HMV's Sibelius Society. Stokowski's 1932 set of the
Fourth (Victor M7683–6) was not made available in England until
1970.[14] The Fourth was recorded during the Finnish National Orchestra's
visit to London[15] in June 1934 with Georg Schnéevoigt. Ten years earlier
Sibelius had promised him the dedication of the Eighth Symphony
whose ideas were then beginning to surface in his mind. Sibelius did not
approve the test pressings and Walter Legge did not issue it.[16] It was
on this same visit that they programmed the Sixth Symphony, which
HMV also recorded. Axel Carpelan, writing as early as 1915, thought
Schnéevoigt "stupid and crude," and went so far as to say that he "should
be forbidden to conduct any Sibelius work in public."[17] Listeners in the
1930s would have been approaching this symphony in a completely
different climate and from a totally different perspective from our own. It
was some twenty years old, little-known and considered difficult. Hence
Sibelius's anxiety concerning a performance that fell short of the ideal.
The very existence of these 78 rpms was known to very few people until
the 1970s. When I was staying in Karelia with Professor Tawaststjerna I
was shown a file of correspondence between Sibelius and Sir Thomas
Beecham from which it transpired that the test pressings of the
Schnéevoigt performance had been sent to Sir Thomas when he was preparing his own recording together with a detailed list of the composer's
comments concerning tempi, phrasing, note durations, and so on. The
notion that Beecham re-recorded it in 1937 not long after his sessions
with the LPO in October (HMV DB3351–5; US numbering RCA Victor
Masterworks set 446, M12215–21) gained some currency as Sibelius had
sent further criticisms. The matter is resolved in the last chapter of Erik
Tawaststjerna's magisterial Sibelius biography.[18] Sibelius's anxieties were
not wholly misplaced as I am sure that the cause of the Sixth was not
advanced by the scrappy, rough-and-ready Schnéevoigt performance
(HMV DB2321–3; US numbering RCA Victor Masterworks set 344;
M14386–92). Sir Thomas recorded it in 1947 though HMV did not
release it until June 1950 (HMV DB6640–42), possibly on account of
contractual problems with RCA. Sibelius is said to have spoken of

---

[14] Stokowski also recorded an electrifying
account of the Seventh Symphony in
September 1940 with the All-American Youth
Orchestra (The Leopold Stokowski Society of
the USA, LSSA-6).

[15] The orchestra was so called on this
occasion but was, of course, the Helsinki
orchestra, now known as the Helsinki
Philharmonic, which Kajanus had founded
and which Schnéevoigt "inherited" on his

death. They gave two concerts, and the one on
4 June was recorded. It included the Fourth
Symphony and *Luonnotar* with Helmi
Liukkonen, neither of which was passed for
release.

[16] It was eventually published in 1976 (World
Records/EMI mono SH237).

[17] Tawaststjerna, *Sibelius Vol. III*, p. 93–94.

[18] Ibid., p. 322.

Beecham's 1947 account of the Sixth as his favorite recording of any of his symphonies,[19] and it deservedly enjoys a classic status.

Apart from the Fourth and Sixth, Beecham recorded the Second with the RPO in 1946 (HMV DB6588–92) and again in 1954 with the BBC Symphony Orchestra, and there are three accounts of the Seventh with the New York Philharmonic in 1940 (American Columbia 11890–92), the Helsinki Philharmonic in 1954 (Ondine mono ODE809–2), and with the Royal Philharmonic in 1956 (HMV ASD468). The Finnish version of the Seventh Symphony has a higher voltage than his later account and there is a sense of occasion and of an orchestra trying to surpass itself. One of the special things about Beecham's Sibelius was its sheer refinement of sonority: there was a fresh, vernal sheen on the strings quite different from the opulence of Koussevitzky or Karajan but with all their flexibility and plasticity of phrasing, and a magic that is easier to discern than define. Suffice it to say that his feeling for atmosphere in Sibelius was always matched by a strong grip on the architecture. But it is the poetic feeling that marks him off. This is at its most highly developed in the suite from *Pelléas et Mélisande* and *The Oceanides*, the latter recorded specifically at Sibelius's request. They may have been matched in atmosphere by later conductors but never surpassed. His account of the Second Symphony recorded at a birthday concert with the BBC Symphony Orchestra in 1954 and issued on LP eight years later (HMV mono ALP1947) is a prime example. "Spine-tingling" was Thomas's verdict and, as he rightly puts it, "few if any other Sibelius recordings have so great a sense of occasion."[20]

Along with Kajanus and Beecham, the third conductor most closely identified with Sibelius in the public mind during the 1930s and 40s was Serge Koussevitzky. He had been a relatively late convert to the cause and it was not until the mid-1920s that his enthusiasm was really fired. Koussevitzky did not conduct any Sibelius until 1916 (probably the First Symphony), though he would surely have heard quite a lot since his friend Alexander Siloti conducted the Third Symphony and *Night Ride and Sunrise* in St. Petersburg in the first decade of the century. It was not until 1926, two years after he had come to Boston, that he returned to Sibelius in earnest. That year Stokowski conducted the Seventh Symphony in Philadelphia, Frederick Stock gave it in Chicago and Koussevitzky introduced it to Boston. It seems to have inspired his enthusiasm for Sibelius, for in 1928 he gave the Third Symphony to great acclaim ("Sibelius Third, much ahead of its time in 1907, now modern," ran one critical headline). Alas, he never committed it to records, though, as we have noted (see foot-

---

[19] The composer's eldest daughter, Eva Paloheimo, confirmed this when I asked her to verify the matter in 1959.

[20] Thomas, "Discography," p. 15.

note 11), performances of Nos. 1, 5, 6 and 7 given in Boston were briefly in circulation. In 1929 he wrote to the composer to ask if there was a new symphony, and for the next few months they corresponded frequently. Sibelius promised him the Eighth[21] (as indeed he did Beecham, Basil Cameron and Schnéevoigt) to crown the complete cycles of the symphonies he gave. Alas, this was never realised but Koussevitzky did go on to record a number of Sibelius works in Boston in the 1930s: the Second Symphony in 1935 – he recorded it again in 1950 – and in the following year, *Pohjola's Daughter* (May 1936), the Fifth Symphony (December 1936), which appeared with a movement, "Tärnorna med rosor" (The Maidens with Roses), from *Swanwhite* (in his hands it possesses a silky allure) – and finally, an electrifying *Tapiola* (1939).

Perhaps the most famous of Koussevitzky's recordings is of the Seventh Symphony, made during his guest appearances in May 1933 with the then newly-formed BBC Symphony Orchestra – which remains arguably the most concentrated and highly-charged performance ever committed to disc. The Seventh was barely a decade old (Sibelius himself had conducted its first performance in Stockholm in March 1924). It has a seemingly inexhaustible capacity for evolving new material from the same basic germinal ideas and is masterly in its control of contrasting tempi. Koussevitzky's performance has an extraordinary white-hot intensity, though he professed himself not to be wholly satisfied with the results: "some of it is good but some details and phrasings are not as clear as they should be,"[22] he told the composer. He had, incidentally, added a trumpet at the very end to strengthen the strings. Sibelius had every reason to be overjoyed by the recordings: "everything was so full of life and natural and I cannot thank you sufficiently."[23] Koussevitzky's account of the Second is very different: his opening *allegretto* is far more measured than Kajanus's, and has the greater breadth; the orchestral playing of the Boston Symphony is in a different league from Kajanus's LSO, which, incidentally, could not be identified for contractual reasons. With the great Russian conductor there is a sustained feeling for line, a *tenuto* of remarkable quality. The Second Symphony, with its combination of Italianate warmth and Nordic intensity, must have gone some way to dispel Koussevitzky's initial impressions of Sibelius's music as "dark."[24]

Of course apart from the symphonies the Sibelius Society volumes included other important works that were otherwise not available: Beecham's superb accounts of movements from *The Tempest* and his

[21] Erik Tawaststjerna, "The Mystery of Sibelius's Eighth Symphony I–II," *Finnish Music Quarterly* 1–2 (1985), pp. 61–70, and 3–4 (1985), pp. 92–101.

[22] Tawaststjerna, *Sibelius Vol. III*, p. 314.
[23] Ibid.
[24] Ibid., p. 276.

stunning *Lemminkäinen's Return* and in 1935 the Violin Concerto with Heifetz as soloist.[25] The Violin Concerto is not only the most frequently recorded major work of Sibelius but itself holds the record of being the most recorded concerto of the twentieth century.[26] The concerto did not reach as large a public as it should have: it was part of a seven-78 rpm set. It was not until Legge re-recorded it with Ginette Neveu and the newly-founded Philharmonia Orchestra under Issay Dobrowen (DB6244–47) that it scored its breakthrough with the wider record-buying public. There were other wartime recordings by Guila Bustabo and the Städtisches Orchester, Berlin under Fritz Zaun in the early 1940s, and another by Anja Ignatius, the first Finnish violinist to record it. There is no shallow glamour about her playing and a certain nobility that more than offsets any technical shortcomings. She was certainly a fine musician, albeit not a virtuoso in the present-day meaning of the word like an Oistrakh, Perlman or Cho-Liang Lin. Part of the interest of this issue is the presence of Armas Järnefelt, who gets playing of considerable warmth from the Städtisches Orchester, Berlin. Wartime conditions prevented the wide dissemination of these records and apparently only four copies were taken out of Germany.

None of the great conductors of the 1930s recorded a complete cycle of the symphonies. This distinction fell to the Swedish conductor and pianist Sixten Ehrling, who recorded a generally well-paced survey in 1952–53 with the Stockholm Radio Orchestra for Mercury in America (Metronome in Scandinavia), but his survey was rather overshadowed by Anthony Collins's cycle with the London Symphony Orchestra on Decca (1952–55). I would not dissent from Thomas's verdict that his great asset is his "near-infallible sense of pace, finding the *tempo giusto* and shaping musical incident without distorting the all-embracing pulse. Only in his brisk, chirpy account of the second movement of the Third and his cautious finale of the Fourth is he wide of the mark."[27] As with the Second Symphony, Kajanus's tempi fell from view with the advent of vinyl. True, he "reveals the granite beneath a deceptively gentle exterior in the first movement of the Third," but the urgency of the onward flow seems to me misplaced. He gallops through the symphony in just under 25′00″ as opposed to Kajanus's 29′40″ and set an example that, broadly speaking, became the norm in the 1960s until it was replaced by Okko Kamu's 1974 DG recording with the Helsinki Radio Orchestra (DG2530 426) and Colin Davis's 1977 Boston set (Philips 9500 142).

[25] A year earlier Heifetz had made the premier recording of its near contemporary, the Glazunov A minor Concerto with John Barbirolli.

[26] See Martti Haapakoski, "The Concerto that Holds a Record," *Finnish Music Quarterly* 3–4 (1990), pp. 32–35.

[27] Thomas, "Discography," p. 14.

Sibelius's strong profile on records was to prove of vital importance to his cause when the pendulum eventually swung against him in the Anglo-Saxon countries in the late 1950s and more or less throughout the 1960s. Having played a role of crucial importance in furthering his art when the public appetite was at its greatest in the 1930s, recordings sustained that interest once the vogue had peaked. Mahler and Bruckner were both rarities in the early 1950s and by the end of that decade had begun to make serious inroads into the catalogue. Of course, the gramophone to a certain extent *reflects* rather than *creates* changes in public taste, whereas radio – at least during the post-war period – was more concerned with pushing back the boundaries. In the autumn of 1946 the advent of the BBC Third Programme served to introduce the British musical public to repertoire from which it had hitherto been cut off. A complete cycle of the Mahler symphonies, the first ever undertaken in Britain, kindled a flame that was to burn ever more brightly in the succeeding years and a Bruckner cycle soon followed. Yet it was only when LPs had become firmly established that either composer came into his own. LPs enabled a whole range of repertoire to reach a wider public that would have found it burdensome to cope with countless side changes and fibre-needle sharpening. Act III of *Die Meistersinger* had been recorded before the war on thirty sides,[28] Mahler's Ninth on twenty sides,[29] and Bruckner's Fifth on eighteen.[30] Even so, it was still some time before either a Bruckner or Mahler canon was complete.

But 1960s London, in whose concert halls and broadcasting studios Sibelius had been staple fare for the best part of the 1930s, turned to other things. Sibelius's dominance had not only been at the expense of Mahler and Bruckner: Nielsen was virtually unplayed until the 1950s. Against this background it is ironic that Hans Rosbaud encountered opposition to his proposed inclusion of the Fourth Symphony during his guest appearance with the BBC Symphony Orchestra in the early 1960s. Rosbaud, who was generally thought of as an apostle of the second Viennese school and contemporary music, was no mean Sibelian. He recorded an intensely felt and remarkably powerful account of *Tapiola* with the Berlin Philharmonic in late 1950 (DG LPEM19185).[31] As Deryck Cooke put it, "Although he lacks Karajan's ultra-sensitivity to beauty of sound, he has all his drama and precision, and does not make the fatal error of jamming on the brakes after the final climax; moreover the intensity of the final pages is something to marvel at."[32] In its evocation of the terrors

[28] Recorded in Dresden under Karl Böhm on HMV DB4562–76.
[29] Recorded in Vienna under Bruno Walter on HMV DB3613–22.
[30] Recorded in Dresden under Karl Böhm on HMV DB4486–94.

[31] Reissued in 1996 after a lapse of almost four decades on DG The Originals mono 447 453-2GOR.
[32] *The Gramophone* 37 (December 1959), p. 288.

of the forest it has few rivals and can stand alongside the great *Tapiola*s of Koussevitzky, Beecham, Karajan, and Kajanus. My memories of Rosbaud's Fourth Symphony are of a performance of far greater poetic intensity and depth of feeling even than Klemperer's. Moreover at about the same time Eugen Jochum made a little-known recording of *Night Ride and Sunrise, The Oceanides,* and the Prelude to *The Tempest* with the Bavarian Radio Orchestra which shows an extraordinarily strong feeling for the Sibelius idiom (DG17075).[33] The transition in *Night Ride and Sunrise* from the trochaic pattern of the ride to the glowing and majestic movement of the sunrise has scarcely been managed with greater artistry. Neither recorded a symphony commercially, though there were a number of German or German-born maestros who did – most notably Kurt Sanderling.

But Sibelius's cause had its champions – among them Robert Simpson, who published his *Sibelius and Nielsen: A Centenary Essay* and produced an ambitious series of music by these composers for the BBC Third Programme. By the end of the 1960s things had already improved on radio.[34] But the yardstick of his public following (and our concern here) is the gramophone. During the 1960s Sir John Barbirolli with the Hallé Orchestra (HMV), Leonard Bernstein and the New York Philharmonic (CBS), and perhaps most importantly on account of its technical excellence, Lorin Maazel and the Vienna Philharmonic (Decca) embarked on cycles. Apart from major maestros like Pierre Monteux (No. 2 with the LSO), Ernest Ansermet (Nos. 2 and 4 with the Orchestre de la Suisse Romande) or Yevgeni Mravinsky (No. 7 with the Leningrad Philharmonic), there were others from as far afield as Alexander Gibson in Scotland and Akeo Watanabe in Tokyo. Sibelius's profile, though lower in the 1960s, never sank below a respectable level though he was less exposed both on record and radio than Mahler. It is a pity that George Szell recorded so little Sibelius commercially. His sterling account of the Second Symphony with the Concertgebouw Orchestra (Philips SAL3515; US numbering Philips 500092) appeared in the centenary year at the time when Sibelius's star was not in the ascendant. Its first movement is distinguished by great concentration and economy, and throughout there is the integrity and intellectual power which marked all his work. (No doubt

---

[33] Reissued in 1998 on DG The Originals mono 449 178-2GOR.

[34] In 1969 the BBC broadcast the Fifth and Seventh Symphonies eight times each – four from records and four live studio performances – and the Violin Concerto nine times. In 1976 there were ten performances of the Seventh Symphony, seven of the Fifth, six each of the First and Second, five of the Fourth, and only one of the Sixth, while the Violin Concerto scored nine, as against the Grieg Piano Concerto, which had only four. (Just for the record there were six performances of Roussel's Third Symphony, four of Bruckner's Ninth Symphony, and four of Nielsen's Sixth Symphony.)

his feeling for Sibelius would have been sparked by his years with the BBC Scottish Orchestra before the war.) Recordings of concert performances in Cleveland of the Third, Fourth and Seventh symphonies as well as *En saga* have been included in two Cleveland Orchestra CD boxes but, apart from the Second, he was never asked to record any of them commercially.

Shifts in taste do not always have one single explanation: one generation of critics reacts against another, and Sibelius's unprecedented success in England and America may indeed have *ensured* his neglect in Germany[35] and France. Of course Sibelius was not the only composer of his generation who had difficulty in regaining acceptance in German concert halls: Elgar, Stenhammar and Delius also disappeared as early as the 1920s. However, one German advocate of Sibelius was the youthful Herbert von Karajan. Already in the late 1930s he was perceived as a star in the ascendant, and he had recorded Tchaikovsky's *Symphonie pathéthique* with the Berlin Philharmonic when he had just turned thirty years of age – and more remarkably within six months of Furtwängler's classic recording with the same orchestra, which may not be uncommon now but was altogether unprecedented then. During his time as conductor in Aachen when he was still in his twenties, he was invited to Stockholm and persuaded by Per Lindfors of the Swedish Radio to learn the Sixth Symphony, which was then still new music. Sibelius had set down firmer roots in Sweden than in either Norway or Denmark, thanks to the championship of the composer-conductor Wilhelm Stenhammar and the fact that both Armas Järnefelt, Sibelius's brother-in-law, and another Finn, Georg Schnéevoigt, held conducting appointments in Stockholm. Indeed, during the very week that Karajan was due to conduct the symphony on Swedish Radio it was being performed under Simon Pergament-Parmet with the *Konsertförenings Orkester* (now the Royal Stockholm Philharmonic). Karajan went along to hear it. Sibelius himself had conducted the work both in Stockholm and Gothenburg in 1923. The Sixth was to inaugurate what was to prove a life-long attachment to Sibelius on Karajan's part, one which grew and deepened with the years. Not only was he conducting Sibelius in 1936 but was doing so almost fifty years later in 1984. In fact, with the possible exception of Kajanus, who conducted his countryman's music from 1893 through to 1932, Sibelius enjoyed no more committed an advocate.

A stroke of fate ensured that he was able to continue to do so, for it was thanks to the intervention of Walter Legge, who as we have seen had founded the pioneering HMV Sibelius Society in the 1930s, that Karajan

---

[35] Moreover the fact that Sibelius's music was enlisted by Nazi ideologists (during 1941–45 Finland and Germany were common enemies of the Soviet Union) cannot have helped his cause in the immediate post-war climate even if (or particularly as) it had no effect in the English-speaking world.

was enabled to emerge into prominence in the post-war musical scene. At that time Karajan was under a cloud and awaiting clearance by the Allied authorities concerned with de-Nazification, but though he was forbidden to conduct publicly he was not forbidden to record.[36] Legge, by now in charge of EMI's dark-blue Columbia label, seized his chance and in the late 1940s made a number of celebrated records with Karajan and the Vienna Philharmonic. In the early 1950s Legge had written to Sibelius to invite him to come to London and conduct (or at least supervise) a new cycle of the symphonies with the Philharmonia Orchestra which he had founded in 1946 – but to no avail.

The first three symphonies were recorded by the Philharmonia under Paul Kletzki (though for some reason the Third was never issued in England) but the remainder, plus *Tapiola*, were entrusted to Karajan. These evidently enjoyed Sibelius's imprimatur. Legge wrote to Sibelius in September 1954 to say that he had already recorded the Fourth together with *Tapiola* (Columbia 33CX1125) and the Fifth (Columbia 33CX1047) and added that in his view Karajan "of all the important conductors of the present time, goes deepest into the heart of your music." If he approved these performances he would record all seven in good time for Sibelius's ninetieth birthday at the end of 1955. He added that Sibelius had probably forgotten that he had sent new metronome markings to Sir Thomas Beecham in 1937 for the ending of the Fourth Symphony, which had proved invaluable, and that he had been particularly gratified by the reaction of some American critics. They had written that they had now seen the last two pages of the symphony in a completely new light. Sibelius later told Legge, "Karajan is the only one who really understands my music."[37] There is no record as to whether or not Sibelius actually heard the Stockholm broadcast of the Sixth Symphony in the 1930s but his friend, the writer Adolf Paul, had drawn his attention to him in December 1938. "Watch out for the name Herbert von Karajan. He is, for all his thirty years, the most phenomenal conductor they have in this country."[38]

But, of course, Karajan was not the only German maestro who conducted Sibelius. Before the war, on the occasion of his seventieth birthday in 1935, along with telegrams from composers like Strauss, Vaughan Williams, and Respighi, and such conductors as Furtwängler, Weingartner, and Toscanini, came one from Otto Klemperer which hailed Sibelius as

[36] See Richard Osborne, *Herbert von Karajan. A Life in Music* (London: Chatto & Windus, 1998), pp. 221ff.

[37] Tawaststjerna, *Sibelius Vol. III*, p. 330.

[38] Erik Tawaststjerna, *Jean Sibelius. Åren 1920–1957* (Keuru: Söderström Förlags, 1997 [1988]), p. 328.

one of the purest and most heart-warming phenomena among living
composers. Without glancing to left or right, without regard to fashions or
trends, he goes his own way . . . He follows the classical symphony
traditional forms but always builds upon them with living, life-enhancing
musical material. We conductors thank him from our hearts for the great
works he has given us.[39]

When, during the latter part of the 1950s, Karajan's energies were
increasingly absorbed by his engagements in Vienna and Berlin, Legge
looked for a successor with whom to record the central classical repertoire, and thus began Klemperer's association with the Philharmonia. No
Sibelius recordings were forthcoming but Klemperer did conduct a
memorable account of the Fourth Symphony at London's Royal Festival
Hall in the late 1950s, no doubt at the prompting of Legge. I remember it
as a reading of total integrity, starkly powerful and full of intensity. No
doubt with the advent of stereo recording Legge still hoped to re-record
the symphonies: for at about this time, in the early 1960s, Karajan re-
recorded the Fifth with the Philharmonia (Columbia 33CX1750 stereo
SAX2392) and recorded the Second for the first time (Columbia
33CX1730 stereo SAX2379).

The 1961 Fifth Symphony was not quite as well received as the earlier
version or either of its subsequent versions with the Berlin Philharmonic.[40] One of the central problems that the Fifth Symphony poses to
any interpreter is the transition from *Andante* to *Allegro*, where the first
and second movements become one. There is something primordial
about this, like two huge heavenly bodies being merged over the aeons
into one. And the transition is difficult to judge even for the
Koussevitzkys and Karajans, let alone lesser maestros.[41] It was in his 1966
account with the Berlin Philharmonic that Karajan judged this most perfectly – even better, I think, than in his very first Philharmonia and subsequent 1977 Berlin recording. In all Karajan recorded the Fifth no fewer
than four times.

In the early 1980s, when he was recording the First Symphony for the
first time, I was able to talk to him about his feeling for the Finnish
master. We talked for a time about the all-pervasive influence of Wagner,
not just on those who adored him like Chausson or Vincent d'Indy, but
those who turned their back on him like Debussy and Sibelius. Karajan
said, "In a sense no composer, not even Beethoven, has influenced others
more deeply or more radically than has Wagner – and his influence is

[39] Tawaststjerna, *Sibelius Vol. III*, p. 319.
[40] Recorded in 1965 on DG SLPM 138973
and in 1976 HMV ASD3409.
[41] Two of the finest were Sir Malcolm

Sargent's 1959 account with the BBC
Symphony Orchestra (HMV ALP1730) and
Simon Rattle's with the Philharmonia
Orchestra in 1982 (EMI ASD4168).

visible even on those who have consciously rejected him."[42] Sibelius's rejection was really a gloss that disguised the enormous impact Bayreuth made on him when he made his pilgrimage there in the summer of 1894. But what Karajan felt, interestingly enough, was "a much deeper influence, affinity, kinship – call it what you like – with Bruckner. There is this sense of the *Ur-Wald*, the primæval forest, the feeling of some elemental power, that one is dealing with something profound. Although they are very different, I know, there are important musical similarities too." The obvious ones are string *tremolandi* and long pedal points, and there are Brucknerian echoes in the very early *Kullervo* Symphony. (We know that Sibelius was overwhelmed by the Bruckner he heard in his student days in Vienna and retained a lifelong admiration for him.) Karajan also recorded that great evocation of the *Ur-Wald*, *Tapiola*, on four occasions: Beecham did it only twice. The last of these performances from 1984 strikes me as being as great as any ever committed to disc (DG413 755-2GH) – and I do not forget the other Ks, Koussevitzky and Kajanus. I can only regret that he did not turn to *Pohjola's Daughter*, which came up in our conversation and which he said he did not really know, but some months later I had a message from his DG producer asking for suggestions he should consider for an appropriate coupling for *Peer Gynt* which he was recording for the nth time. This prompted my thoughts – among other things – to turn to the complete *Pelléas* music, on which his choice eventually fell. The result is every bit as magical and intense as Sir Thomas's superb record of the late 1950s.

What distinguishes the finest of Karajan's records is their firm sense of direction. One always feels that the momentum is irresistible, that one could not stop the symphonic journey even if one wanted to – a vital ingredient in Sibelius. For Karajan, as he has said on numerous occasions, sheer beauty of sound is a *sine qua non*, whereas for conductors like Klemperer it was not a primary consideration. This surface beauty has rarely been equalled, let alone surpassed – Beecham, Koussevitzky and Mravinsky were also artists of this calibre. But beauty excites suspicion and uneasiness among Northern Puritans who feel that if music sounds sumptuous it can't possibly be "improving." I regret my own glib response to the Fourth Symphony when it first appeared:

> The sheer beauty of sound quality only serves to cushion the
> uncomfortable impact of this extraordinary work and diminish the
> intensity of its desolation. This music offers no false consolation, and like
> many great works of art it has a forbidding serious exterior that dispenses

[42] Layton, "Karajan's Sibelius," *The Gramophone* 59 (October 1981), p. 523.

with any gesture towards the listener . . . Orchestral opulence is not a useful tool in uncovering the secrets of this strange work: instead of the well-modulated rich tone of the Berlin strings, one longs for the cold disembodied sound Beecham drew in his famous Sibelius performances.

I spoke of it "as insulating the listener from the cold reality as if one were perceiving the icy landscape from the comfort of a well-heated limousine."[43] Three decades later I hope I know better. Over the years I have come to discern the depths of this performance; its beauty of sound *heightens* the impact of the music and after coming closer to it, one realizes that there is no protective insulation: the beauty of sonority is never there to attract attention to itself but to bring one as close to the ideal conception of the Fourth Symphony as possible.

In a broadcast for CBC Toronto, Karajan told his interlocutor, Robert Chesterman, that there were three works that exhausted him both physically and spiritually: Strauss's *Elektra*, Berg's *Drei Orchesterstücke*, Op. 6, and the Fourth Symphony of Sibelius. He made his feelings for the last of these abundantly clear when he insisted on it being on the first program he gave on his appointment as chief conductor of the Berlin Philharmonic. The 1960s were a time of the greatest hostility towards Sibelius in the German-speaking world: Adorno, whose *Glosse über Sibelius* had somehow legitimized the natural resistance of German-speaking music-lovers towards the thought of there being a great symphonist outside the immediate German-central European tradition, exercised his greatest influence at this time.

If his feeling for the Fourth Symphony is transparent in all three of his recordings (Philharmonia, 1954; Berlin Philharmonic, 1966 and 1977), it was the Sixth which launched his Sibelian voyage way back in 1936, that drew out something special. Whether or not this was the case, the three accounts that Karajan committed to disc (in 1954, 1966 and 1980 respectively) serve to underline the composer's words spoken to Legge that Karajan "really understands my music." All three go to its heart and the last strikes me as one of the greatest Sibelius performances on record – along with Koussevitzky's Seventh with the BBC Symphony Orchestra and Beecham's *Tempest* music and *The Oceanides*. Alas, Karajan never conducted the Third, so one will never know whether it would be numbered among the triumphs like 4, 5 and 6 or have been perhaps like his less imposing Sevenths.

During the 1960s there was a constituency arguing that Finnish performers brought special insights to bear on Sibelius.[44] Tauno Hannikainen's set of

[43] Robert Layton, "Quarterly Retrospect," *The Gramophone* 44 (August 1966), p. 107.
[44] I distinctly recall some measure of resentment in the mid-1960s when the

Helsinki Philharmonic Orchestra came to London with Sir John Barbirolli rather than a Finnish conductor at the helm.

the *Four Legends* acquired a cult status, though it was difficult to discern any superiority to the pioneering set by Thomas Jensen and the Danish State Radio Orchestra (Decca LXT2831). It was certainly no match for the later recording by Eugene Ormandy and the Philadelphia Orchestra (HMV ASD3644). That partnership served Sibelius well throughout the microgroove era. It seems to me, however, that for all the advantages that Finnish-born conductors would have in their familiarity with the music of the Finnish[45] and Swedish languages, which inevitably is a contributory factor in shaping the melodic language, their success is primarily related to their grasp of architecture, the relation of part to whole and all the other interpretative factors that face any conductor. With Berglund one can rely on an approach that is selfless and dedicated with no playing to the gallery. He has recorded the Fourth Symphony no fewer than four times already, first in 1968 with the Finnish Radio Symphony Orchestra (Decca SXL6431)[46] and later with the Bournemouth and Helsinki Philharmonic Orchestras (both HMV) as part of complete cycles, and yet again most recently with the Chamber Orchestra of Europe.[47] There is a lot to be said for Sibelius plain and unadorned, and that is perhaps to be preferred to the idiosyncratic Sibelius which his countryman Leif Segerstam has given us during his tenure with the Danish Radio Symphony Orchestra (Chandos). His sophisticated feeling for texture is offset by curious interpretative touches: an abrupt and completely inorganic change of tempo at the second group of the first movement of the Third Symphony or an account of *In memoriam* that takes almost twice as long as any other.

With the mid-1970s we come to another chapter in the Sibelius discography with the recording of the works which Sibelius had (to use a euphemism) "discouraged" in his lifetime: first and foremost, his early masterpiece, the *Kullervo* Symphony, which Paavo Berglund pioneered in 1971. Now almost all conductors who have embarked on a cycle – Berglund, Sir Colin Davis, Neeme Järvi, Osmo Vänskä,[48] Jukka-Pekka Saraste, and Leif Segerstam – have also gone on to record this remarkable and masterly score. Other areas of his output followed, perhaps most notably the songs, only a quarter of which were put on to record in the days of 78s and mono LPs. The first songs to appear were as early as 1904–06 with Ida Ekman (*Var det en dröm, Se'n har jag ej frågat mera, Svarta rosor,* and *Sehnsucht*), Alexandra Ahnger (*Demanten på marssnön;*

---

[45] See Simon Parmet, *The Symphonies of Sibelius. A Study of Musical Appreciation,* trans. Kingsley A. Hart (London: Cassell, 1959 [1955]).

[46] Recorded in 1968 and licensed to Decca in Britain who released it in February 1973.

[47] In comparing Berglund's earlier accounts with those of Rattle, Guy Thomas speaks of them as "earthbound" (1990, p. 24), and despite the enthusiasm and dedication of his younger players, these remain as selfless and literal as his earlier sets.

[48] In preparation.

Säv, säv, susa, and *Men min fågel märks dock icke*), and Sibelius's brother-in-law's wife, Maikki Järnefelt (*Flickan kom ifrån sin älsklings möte,* as well as *Säv, säv, susa* and *Svarta rosor*) – duplication was already beginning in the gramophone industry! An unfortunate omission, however, is Aino Ackté, celebrated as the founding mother of Finnish opera. A legendary Marguérite in *Faust* at the Paris Opéra and Beecham's Salome in 1910, it was she who commissioned an orchestral song from Sibelius, a commission which he admittedly did not immediately fulfill (the thematic material found its way into the finale of the Fourth Symphony) but which eventually took wing in *Luonnotar.* No one listening to the all-too-few recordings she made can doubt that her *Luonnotar* must have been extraordinary! With the arrival of electric recording the song repertoire began to expand. The celebrated Marian Anderson recorded five songs in 1936–37, including one of Sibelius's finest to words of Tavaststjerna, *Långsamt som kvällskyn* with Kosti Vehanen (HMV DA1517). Indeed this is the song that haunts the listener with its concentration of mood and atmosphere, but the success of her record rests rather more on the thrilling sound she produced than her interpretative insights. For these one must turn to Aulikki Rautavaara, aunt of the composer Einojuhani Rautavaara, who had caused a stir at Glyndebourne as the Countess in the 1934 *Figaro* under Fritz Busch.

As with the Grieg songs, the very popularity of the few served to hinder many music-lovers from exploring the greatest. Although twenty-eight songs were recorded on 78 rpm or coarse-groove records (some like *Säv, säv, susa* in numerous duplications),[49] the advent of LPs dramatically increased Sibelius's representation. Even so, the great Lieder singers of the LP era, Schwarzkopf, Fischer-Dieskau, Souzay, and the late Hermann Prey have fought shy of this repertoire, though Schwarzkopf did record some Grieg as well as Sibelius. To the best of my knowledge, no non-Nordic singer has recorded *Höstkväll,* and Flagstad's, the first on record (Decca SXL2030), remains unsurpassed. The voice was still glorious and she enters the heart of this extraordinary miniature tone poem with its wide compass and almost Wagnerian grandeur and breadth. Birgit Nilsson by comparison has a wonderfully cool magnificence that is equally valid (Decca SXL6185). Tom Krause's recording of the Lieder in the complete set is one of his less successful endeavors. It is always intelligent and atmospheric – but much is lost when we hear it in the monochrome of the piano, and it does not match the wide-spanned seemingly

---

[49] Rautavaara with Gerald Moore (Parlophone RO20575), and with the Berlin Philharmonic and an unnamed conductor (Telefunken A2519); Anderson (HMV DA5171); Björling (HMV DA1791); Wiese (Decca M503); and the American singer Mme Charles Cahier (Walker Odeon D-4836).

effortless line of Flagstad. Kim Borg's mid-1950s anthology of sixteen songs with Erik Werba for Deutsche Grammophon (DGM 19113) is one of the pinnacles of the Sibelius song discography. It was somewhat over-shadowed by Kirsten Flagstad's classic set, which was a pity as no one has given a more affecting account of the simple Finnish settings *Souda, souda, sinisorsa* (*Swim, Duck, Swim*) and *Illalle* (*To Evening*), which Flagstad sings in Swedish. Made at the very height of his powers, Borg gives all the songs on this record with rich sonority and a marvellously variegated tonal palette, and above all with the artistry that conceals art: it all sounds so completely natural and effortless, and the sense of line in the Finnish settings is quite masterly.

Sibelius's setting of Rydberg's *Höstkväll* is among his very greatest and most self-revealing songs, and in the hands of a Flagstad encompasses an enormous range of feeling. Not all of Sibelius's poets are of Rydberg's stature but most of them are of quality, and all are linked by their highly developed feeling for the northern landscape and its desolate melan-choly and grandeur. Runeberg was undoubtedly the poet Sibelius loved most deeply, an enthusiasm shared by Brahms, no less, and roughly a quarter of Sibelius's output in the genre are Runeberg settings. The chal-lenge posed by language did not deter Astra Desmond from recording Grieg for Decca and championing Sibelius in the concert hall (and in a perceptive essay in Gerald Abraham's 1947 *Sibelius Symposium*). The poem *Säv, säv, susa* (*Sigh, Sedges, Sigh*) by Gustav Fröding is so rich in verbal music that setting it must have been a daunting task, and Flagstad's poignant account still reigns supreme. It was recorded by Björling on 78s (HMV DA1797) and then later at a concert in Gothenburg conducted by the legendary Nils Grevillius only a few weeks before his death (RCA RB6620), a glorious but operatic account that really misses much of the intimacy and melancholy of the poem. Nicolai Gedda's 1969 recording (ASD2574) is less histrionic but conveys the character and poignancy of its closing bars to excellent effect. Even so, in terms of vocal beauty it is no match for Tom Krause in 1963 (SXL6046) as far as poetic insight is concerned. I am tempted to say that Hynninen's 1975 account (Harmonia Mundi HMC5142) is perhaps the most affect-ing of all.

Kim Borg's performances are the epitome of style in that one never questions whether it is even possible to sing these songs in any other way! Although the two anthologies from Tom Krause (Decca SXL6046 and SXL6314) brought a number of marvellous songs such as the setting of Bertel Gripenberg's *Narcissen* into circulation, it was the appearance of the Complete Songs on Decca's Argo label that must be accounted the great event of the 1980s in this field (Argo 411 739-1ZH5). In its different way this was as important for Sibelians as were the pre-war volumes of the Hugo Wolf Society. Many of the songs, including two of the very greatest, *Jubal* and *Teodora*, had, amazingly enough, never been recorded on LP before. *Teodora* must have come as a revelation to many collectors, for in its over-heated expressionism it comes close to the Strauss of *Salome* and *Elektra*. Tom Krause is superb here: the subtlety with which he prepares the Empress's entrance, "hon kommer, kejsarinnan, hon nalkas, Teodora" (she comes, the Empress, she is drawing near, Theodora) is masterly. The vast majority of the songs falls to his lot, the remaining dozen or so coming from Elisabeth Söderström and Vladimir Ashkenazy.

For the wider musical public the appearance of these songs brought a shift in perspective, for Sibelius emerges as not merely a minor master of the *romans* but a major song composer. Composers who have channelled their inspiration exclusively or predominantly in this medium, like Othmar Schoeck or Yrjö Kilpinen are, of course, a special case, but among those whose creative energies have sought diverse outlets and for whom song is only one facet of their genius, Sibelius can more than hold his own. In a lifetime in which the greatest masters of the genre were recognised as Wolf, Mahler and Strauss, Grieg,[50] Fauré, Debussy, Britten, Schoeck and Kilpinen, Sibelius's claims may not have been thought particularly strong. True, Kim Borg and Jorma Hynninen were active in expanding their representation in the 1960s and 70s, but the complete Argo set remains a great achievement. Together with Anne-Sofie von Otter and Bengt Forsberg on BIS, it is Krause and Gage who have enriched our understanding of them.

In Britain Vladimir Ashkenazy and the Philharmonia Orchestra (Decca), Alexander Gibson and the Scottish National Orchestra (Chandos), Simon Rattle at Birmingham (EMI) and most recently Sir Colin Davis with the London Symphony Orchestra (RCA) have given us performances whose merits are too well known to need further exegesis. However in the late 1980s and 90s the boundaries have been extended in a way that would have been scarcely imaginable even after *Kullervo* entered the repertory. In the days of the HMV Sibelius Society the only chamber work to represent Sibelius was the mature *Voces intimae* Quartet. Sibelius had discouraged performances of the B flat Quartet, Op. 4, and for long only the first violin part of an earlier Quartet in A minor survived. The discovery of a set of parts in Christian Sibelius's library restored this piece to us. Both these and the Piano Quintet in G minor which Busoni premièred in Leipzig are now

---

[50] Nor had there been a complete recording of Grieg's songs. This was not achieved until 1993.

on compact disc and serve to fill in the picture of Sibelius's developing musical personality. Even earlier pieces, some only in fragmentary form from his student years, have been recorded. Given the fact that Sibelius suppressed *Kullervo* and the Op. 4 Quartet, his views about the publication of these pieces can only be imagined!

However, it is one small Swedish-based label, BIS, and its driving force, Robert von Bahr, who have pushed back the boundaries farthest.[51] They have explored such rarities as *Everyman*, *Scaramouche*, the complete *Tempest* music, the original *Swanwhite* music and the first 1892 version of *En saga*, the 1915 four-movement version of the Fifth Symphony, and the recently discovered tone-poem, *Skogsrået* (*The Wood Nymph*). None of these has been in the public domain before. The music to *Everyman* does not lend itself to being turned into a suite in the same way as *Belsazars gästabud* (*Belshazzar's Feast*), but it is one of the boons of Robert von Bahr's goal to record every note that Sibelius penned, that music which would not sit comfortably in the concert hall can enter the repertoire. The score to *Scaramouche* on which Sibelius embarked with such reluctance is another case in point. With its fleeting hints of the "scherzo" section of the Seventh Symphony it conveys the sense of music from another world as does *The Tempest*, and offers music of the highest poetic inspiration, albeit alongside passages of thinner invention. The merits of the first and rejected version of the Fifth Symphony have been authoritatively discussed elsewhere,[52] but having recorded it successfully, the Lahti Symphony Orchestra under Osmo Vänskä has gone on to complete another cycle. Theirs are thoughtful and deeply-felt performances that belong only in the most exalted company. Sibelius calls for playing of great concentration and poetic intensity that must put you completely under its spell. Each of the seven links in the Alpine chain poses its own interpretative problems and there is no one way of viewing them any more than there is one overview of the real Alps. Each shift of light enables us to observe new contours and colors. In the seven decades in which so many great conductors and their musicians have scaled these peaks, the majesty of this great music never loses its power to put us completely under its spell.

[51] One of Robert von Bahr's antecedents was the Finnish critic Wasenius, who wrote under the pseudonym "Bis": hence the record label's name!

[52] James Hepokoski, *Sibelius. Symphony No. 5* (Cambridge: Cambridge University Press, 1993).

3 "Sibelius the Progressive"

Tim Howell

The past

My adaptation of the title of Schoenberg's famous essay on Brahms is intentional.[1] All the resonances that it evokes, the associations of compositional misunderstanding, historical reassessment, and a subtle balance between old and new, are useful to the current debate. While this essay does not seek to explore precise parallels between Brahms and Sibelius, the idea that both have been dismissed as rather anachronistic figures and subsequently reconsidered as "progressive" composers is of central concern. There is, of course, an irony in all of this: Schoenberg the musicologist discerning the modernism of Brahms's music while Schoenberg the composer was setting the standard against which others, including Sibelius, were to be measured – and found wanting. However, it was always with regard to issues of style, rather than idea, that such a case was made. Today, with atonality and serialism being only a part of contemporary musical thought, which also embraces (neo-) tonality and preoccupations with formal process and time scale, it seems as if this trend has finally been reversed, or at least seriously undermined. The whole issue of what is "progressive" has moved with the times alongside the notion and value of originality, which now may include those who seek to reinterpret the past rather than just those who try to overturn it.

But what did Schoenberg mean by "progressive" and how far is his view relevant to Sibelius? Michael Musgrave is right to assert that "Brahms the Progressive" was written with a clear purpose: "to rectify the traditional view of Brahms on the occasion of the centenary of his birth – and it is extreme in many ways."[2] That Schoenberg had a specific agenda, which sought to link Brahms's position in music history with his own, is also a factor here; his choice of examples is extremely selective and partial. As Musgrave concludes, "what interested Schoenberg was not rounded analysis, but historical tendency

---

[1] See "Brahms the Progressive," in *Style and Idea. Selected Writings of Arnold Schoenberg*, ed. Leonard Stein, trans. Leo Black (London: Faber, 1975).

[2] Michael Musgrave, "Schoenberg's Brahms," in *Brahms Studies*, ed. George S. Bozarth (Oxford: Clarendon, 1990), p. 125.

and, to be more precise, tendency towards his own music."[3] It was Brahms's ability to manipulate musical material, especially through the organicism of developing variation, that Schoenberg discerned and found relevant to his own "free" – and indeed serial – contexts. Such progressive elements enabled him to chart a link with the past in order to legitimize the future; "style" became a transient feature, "idea" the true historical continuity.[4] Fundamentally, Schoenberg wanted to prove that beneath the apparently conservative surface of Brahms's music lay a compositional process of great originality and inventiveness that was advanced and challenging, relevant and up to date. From this perspective, Schoenberg's view of the "progressive" in Brahms is directly relevant to any assessment of Sibelius.

A central theme of Schoenberg's essay concerns the view that Brahms and Wagner were complementary as well as independent figures and that the so-called Brahms/Wagner divide cannot be summarized merely as the distinction between Apollonian and Dionysian art. By now we realize that elements of both characteristics are present in each composer's style; indeed a corresponding balance, between classical control and romantic freedom, is manifest within Sibelius's music. This balance exists on different, but related, levels within the composer's output as a whole. It is reflected within the series of symphonies themselves: consider the stylistic pairing of, respectively, Symphonies Four and Six and that of Five and Seven; in the relative degrees of formal restraint and freedom as seen through the genres of symphony and tone poem; and in the contrast between "private" and "public" music which emanates from Sibelius's personality. This Apollonian/Dionysian distinction seems to originate from the composer's own relationship to the music of Wagner, the strong influence that it had upon him, and the ensuing struggle to find an individual voice. Ultimately driven by a desire to produce first-rate Sibelius rather than second-hand Wagner, this idea of a mingling of extremes, a balance between fantasy and vision – even exploiting the creative interplay between the intuitive and the rational – are all significant in any assessment of his historical position.

Of course the twentieth-century equivalent of the Brahms/Wagner polemic (and one that was equally artificial) did not directly involve Sibelius, though it retains a degree of relevance. Both the pro-Stravinsky and pro-Schoenberg camps of the 1930s and those who championed their causes, Virgil Thomson and Theodor Adorno respectively, were united in their dismissal of Sibelius as a reactionary figure. Critical orthodoxy has always remained suspicious of composers who

---

[3] Ibid., p. 134   [4] Ibid., p. 136

are immensely popular in their own lifetime and there is no doubt that Sibelius suffered from the accessibility and immediate appeal of much of his work. An enthusiastic following had emerged in Britain due to the well-intentioned efforts of Gray, Lambert, Abraham, and even Tovey.[5] Their traditional analytical approach had emphasized the "traditional" aspects of this music; there was no question of the "progressive" to be found here since conservatism has always been a peculiarly endearing trait to the British. A parallel situation arose in America with the committed advocacy of Olin Downes and others, with Sibelius's music becoming entangled in an on-going debate about the relative merits of original art and mass appeal. Essentially, whether you promoted or castigated Sibelius's music it appeared to be for the same reasons: the traditional, conservative features of compositional style and genre. Neither side submitted this oeuvre to a balanced, critical assessment which might reveal its progressive tendencies. On the other hand, the modernism of Sibelius's music was equally misunderstood, and labels of "cubist music," "futurist music," "ultra-modern" emerging from reviews of the Fourth Symphony were all presented in a derogatory fashion; of supreme irony in the current context was the comment: "We do not think that Sibelius has any business in the pasture of Schoenberg."[6]

It is against this background of misunderstanding, and a persistently prevalent view of Sibelius as just another nineteenth-century national-romantic composer, that any consideration of the progressive elements in his music should be placed. In fact, much that is original – progressive – about Sibelius's composition comes not from a rejection of earlier practice but from its reinterpretation. Of course, part of that reinterpretation involves an acknowledgement of that past and the associations to which it gives rise. One of the reasons why the Sibelian method remains so effective is the agility of this composer in playing on listeners' expectations to highly dramatic effect. Assessing the discrepancy between the anticipated course of events as predicted and their actual progress as presented is especially significant in this music. Unlike the selectivity and partiality of Schoenberg's Brahms, a deliberate attempt at providing a "rounded analysis" of the symphonies and tone-poems characterized my initial work on Sibelius.[7] As the first comprehensive survey to apply

[5] See Cecil Gray, *Sibelius* (London: Oxford University Press, 1931) and *Sibelius. The Symphonies* (London: Oxford University Press, 1935); Constant Lambert, *Music Ho!. A Study of Music in Decline* (London: 1934); Gerald Abraham, ed., *Sibelius. A Symposium* (London: Oxford University Press, 1947); Donald Francis Tovey, *Essays in Musical Analysis.*

Symphonies and other Orchestral Works (London: Oxford University Press, 1935–39).
[6] Nicholas Slominsky, *Lexicon of Musical Invective* (Seattle: University of Washington Press, 1935).
[7] Tim Howell, *Jean Sibelius: Progressive Techniques in the Symphonies and Tone-Poems* (New York: Garland Press, 1989).

modern analytical methodology to this repertoire, its conclusions – that Sibelius should be viewed as neither a reactionary nor a revolutionary but as a progressive composer – still seem relevant. A very brief summary of those findings can provide a useful starting point for the present discussion; indeed, this may convey something of how the "progressive" in Sibelius actually originated.

Aspects of formal compression, directly discernible in the Fifth Symphony[8] and originating from the Second Symphony,[9] culminate in the single-movement entity of the Seventh Symphony.[10] Here is a work that amounts to something of a celebration of the composer's command of material which *appears* to function in one respect (at the time) yet *actually* assumes a different structural role (in retrospect). Segmenting this music *horizontally* into layers of activity (rather than dividing it *vertically* into blocks of material) reveals the true secrets as to the function of these elements. This is not, after all, a succession of symphonic movements welded together; instead, implicit multi-movement contrasts are simultaneously presented, like geological strata.[11] Questions of extended tonality are especially pertinent to any consideration of Symphonies Four and Six and their respective emphasis on whole-tone and modal organization. To explore the conflict between the hierarchical qualities of diatonicism and the anti-hierarchical situation established by the whole-tone scale – in *symphonic* terms – is another particularly progressive aspect of Sibelius's compositional technique. The Fourth Symphony stands as the most extreme example of tonal experimentation within the whole series of seven symphonies and its effectiveness arises from a

[8] For a more detailed and specific discussion, see Howell, "Two Versions of the Fifth Symphony: A Study in Compositional Process," in *Proceedings from the First International Sibelius Conference, August 1990*, ed. Eero Tarasti, Sibelius Academy Publications (Helsinki, 1995), pp. 74–85.

[9] The Second Symphony contains a far greater degree of structural originality than the mere *attacca* indication between its scherzo and finale might at first suggest. The cycle of mediant relationships that characterize the formal compression of the opening *Allegro moderato* reaches its structural goal in the major-third conflict of the finale; the F♯ minor secondary key of the opening movement (a major third above the tonic) is directly counterbalanced by the emphasis on B♭ major (a major third below) in the closing movement. However, such a re-balancing of the prevailing tonal

equilibrium is only part of the story; there is a sense of an accumulation of tension leading to eventual release, operating on differing yet related structural levels, throughout the piece as a whole.

[10] For additional supporting material see Howell, "Sibelius Studies and Notions of Expertise," *Music Analysis* 14/2–3 (1995), 315–40.

[11] A variety of analytical interpretations of the structural ambiguity within Sibelius's music is to be encouraged; for an alternative segmentation of the Seventh Symphony, which is equally valid and a further example of "rounded analysis," see Veijo Murtomäki, *Symphonic Unity. The Development of Formal Thinking in the Symphonies of Sibelius*, trans. Henry Bacon, Studia Musicologica Universitatis Helsingienis 5 (Helsinki: University of Helsinki, 1993).

considerable economy of expression. Tonal ambiguity (which in this piece occasionally verges on the atonal) arises from a lack of information, a deliberate policy of understatement. At the opening of the work, for example, it is almost as if pitch-class material is revealed on a need-to-know basis. An equivalent degree of tonal ambiguity is present in the Sixth Symphony since its initial D-based dorian mode is merely a hierarchical reordering of a (whole-tone related) C major scale. Consequently, the minimal collection change associated with traditional modulation results in a range of alternatives which feel as though they are "variants" on their original model (sometimes only using a *reordering* of content), rather than offering tonic/dominant polarity. Much of the prevailing mood and nature of the Sixth Symphony arises from this sense that its different collections ultimately complement rather than conflict with one another. In both instances, the exploration of whole-tone potential in relation to diatonic organization is a significant compositional feature.

Examples of thematic process, a technique that may be defined as the continuous development of material, are also relevant to any assessment of the progressive in Sibelius. His manipulation of thematic material is a highly ingenious procedure. An ability to generate large-scale musical structures, through the logical and systematic exploration of the inherent compositional potential of small motivic cells, characterizes this method. Above all lies an instinctive grasp of an overall shape, ensuring that local events eventually subscribe to a larger structure. While the process in itself may be traced on the surface by way of observing specific intervallic patterns, it is the implications of these cells as subsets of larger collections – diatonic, modal, chromatic, whole-tone – that are important. This, in turn, needs to be viewed alongside the resultant ambiguity to which the selection of a few pitch classes, or the restriction of their deliberately limited interval content, ultimately gives rise. Patterns of tension and release, of large-scale conflict and resolution, are reflected within this surface process. Contrasting shapes associated with different harmonic/tonal/formal areas, that is, local details of long-term structural effect, are typically shown to be related. The underlying basic shapes from which such thematic material was originally generated are, during the progress of a piece, gradually revealed: the implicit becomes explicit as diversity gives way to unity. As is so often the case with Sibelius's music, there is a paradox here: while the surface workings of continuous development convey a sense of accumulation or accretion of material, this is ultimately geared towards a moment of synthesis – as discrete elements come together – resulting in the complete opposite. A process of expansion reveals a product of distillation: a simplification. Finally, an underlying pattern representing the unity of resolution is revealed; in this respect, Sibelius's music may be regarded as self-revelatory, almost self-analytical.

The present

While the "progressive" elements discerned so far – formal compression, extended tonality, and thematic process – provide a useful background and are, in themselves, reflective of issues of timescale, they are all concerned with pitch-class organization. What seems necessary now is a consideration of other areas – tempo, meter, rhythm, repetition patterns, texture, articulation, dynamics, register, even timbre – if we are to appreciate the degree of independence with which these so-called "secondary" parameters can be seen to operate, thereby fully understanding the extent of Sibelius's originality. To be able to convey a sense of musical expansiveness through a reductionist attitude to the material being processed is a singular achievement. The interplay between a maximum of effect set against a minimum of constituent parts is a characteristic which Sibelius makes uniquely his own. Understanding the relevant underlying patterns of pitch-class relationships will explain something of an overall level of unity within a given piece and this is undoubtedly reassuring for both listener and analyst alike. But it does not fully account for elements of *diversity*, for the effect of music that seems, at one and the same time, to be both static and dynamic, slow- and fast-moving, repetitive yet varied: in short, music that involves contradictory perceptions of time.

We need to address the complex question of how Sibelius manipulates our perception of musical time and, as a starting point, Jonathan Kramer's categorization of various types of time perception provides a useful background.[12] The categories of "linear" and "non-linear" time are quite fundamental to his thesis and approximately correspond to the philosophical distinction between "becoming" and "being."[13] His definitions are as follows:

> Let us identify linearity as the *determination of some characteristic(s) of music in accordance with implications that arise from earlier events of the piece*. Thus linearity is processive. Nonlinearity, on the other hand, is nonprocessive. It is *the determination of some characteristic(s) of music in accordance with implications that arise from principles or tendencies governing an entire piece or section.*[14]

[12] Jonathan Kramer, *The Time of Music* (New York: Schirmer, 1988).

[13] Ibid., p. 16.

[14] Ibid., p. 20.

Given the obvious links between linear and non-linear time with, respectively, tonal and atonal contexts (though Kramer is at pains to explore the overlaps of such a distinction), his category of non-linearity is not especially relevant to Sibelius's music. But, by adapting these considerations, it is possible to adopt a more appropriate terminology that is reflective of the music itself: a distinction between time that is "linear" and that which is "circular." Definitions may be kept quite simple. Linear time is perceived as progressive and developmental, and circular time as repetitive and static. Sibelius's music contains a subtle mix of these categories, be they separated, juxtaposed, or superimposed: a kind of counterpoint of time segments. The remaining principle to keep in mind is the issue of subjective time – musical time as experienced by the listener – as distinct from absolute time – a rationalization into abstract duration(s) as "clock" time.

Duality is the starting point here. From the outset, even as early as *En saga*, Sibelius was able to present two (or more) types of musical material simultaneously. Unified in terms of pitch-class content yet diversified in terms of their metrical independence, the slow-moving, background pedal points act as an anchor against which faster, apparently more dynamic, surface events exert an inexorable pull. Thus, by the simplest of means, two levels of activity co-exist, and the inherent tension within a musical surface becomes all the more cogent when measured against the potential resolution offered by the background pedal. Of course, due to the passing of time, any pedal in itself appears to demand resolution (it feels like the equivalent of a dominant), and this sets up an additional level of tension; gradually, the pedal is transformed from being perceived as a static element into a more dynamic one. From such relatively uncomplicated beginnings, a more sophisticated control of pitch-class structures permitted greater experimentation within these metrical levels. By the time of the Seventh Symphony and *Tapiola*, the same principle of juxtaposing differing temporal layers – essentially involving slow and fast music – had developed into multi-level structures open to a range of interpretations; duality becomes plurality in mature Sibelius. In both these pieces, a balance between illusion and reality arises from the apparent distinction – yet very real relationship – between tempo and articulation. While the prevailing tempo, the underlying metrical pulse, may be slow moving and part of a large-scale pattern governing the overall unity of the piece, the surface articulation of events may suggest greater energy, speed and motion. Collectively, these suggestions threaten to undermine that unity – at the time these events are unfolding; but retrospectively, they come to be seen and understood as actually subscribing to that fundamental structural pattern. The passing of time in itself has an effect on our perceptions of the passing of time. Texture and the rate of change, a narrowing of the interval in time between successive events, contribute to a sense of "faster" music, however superficial this eventually proves to be. It is a highly-skilled control of material that allows Sibelius to create the illusion of time passing more quickly than actually proves to be the case.

However, there is (yet again) a paradox in all of this and one which Sibelius is all too ready to exploit. Music that appears to contain a greater number of events,[15] though fast in itself due to its articulatory subdivision of the metrical pulse, also seems to continue for longer: there is a cumulative effect which arises from so much happening within a given time span. An immediate sense of speed and an intermediate feeling of expansiveness arise from the same source, due to the sheer wealth of events being projected. On the other hand, slow music, because of a lack of activity, may appear to take a long time and be even more expansive. However, if projected for long enough, the concept of "slowness" eventually gives way to a more fundamental sense of timelessness; the listener begins to lose any real sense of the passing of time. Additionally, if the so-called "events" of "faster" music prove to be merely *surface* activity, that is to say that they are not associated with articulating deeper structural levels, they may ultimately be experienced as rather static. Textural articulation may certainly be "busy," but it becomes merely decorative and non-functional if disassociated from goal-directed motion. The adroit use of repetition patterns and metrical articulation can mitigate these two extremes; such patterns may, in themselves, suggest eventfulness and therefore a quickness of pace, but the cumulative effect of their repetition may result in stasis. Again, it is the functional distinction between what is ornamental and what is fundamental – and the potential to switch from one to the other – that is crucial to our perception of musical time.

The use of repetition patterns is a highly characteristic feature of Sibelius's music and one which demonstrates his compositional resourcefulness and ingenuity. Again, it seems as if our understanding of these constructs stems from (and is limited to) a consideration of pitch- or interval-class patterning, yet it is possible to view things from a different perspective by considering the placing of events in time, rather than merely in relation to pitch. Indeed, the extent to which these parameters work together, or are at variance with one another, is of significant compositional potential. The distance between motivic statements, the idea of "interval" in terms of duration (rather than pitch class) and the timings of

[15] What Kramer terms its "information content."

these patterns merit individual investigation. This is not to ignore pitch entirely but perhaps to consider it less in relation to prevailing collections and tonal (or non-tonal) centers, but more globally in terms of register, transposition levels, and contour. Repetition patterns in Sibelius range from ostinati (associated with circular time) to continuous development of material (associated with linear time); they encompass the literal, the varied, and the sequential presentation of particular cells, with elements of immediate or delayed, metrically regular or irregular, repetition thrown in for good measure in a range of permutations. Combinations of these different kinds of "repetition," pursuing the relative degree of variety or relatedness between successions of such units, are skilfully deployed. Musical continuity (or, indeed, discontinuity) emerges from such patterning and a balance between essentially what is static and what is dynamic (and a play on the illusion and reality of both of these) is carefully exploited. The timing of such patterns of expectation and denial and the effect to which they give rise has been carefully calculated even though there is an apparent spontaneity – sometimes verging on the improvisatory – about all of this. Any sense of the improvisatory, however slight, makes the task of analysis and exemplification a more complex one. Nevertheless, it is time to consider some specific examples as illustrative of the general observations outlined above. With the Seventh Symphony and *Tapiola* standing, respectively, as the peak of symphonic (Apollonian) and tone-poetical (Dionysian) achievement, these works provide the most appropriate contexts for further investigation.

A symphonic fantasy?

It was after a considerable amount of rewriting and revision that Sibelius, in the Fifth Symphony, fused two traditionally discrete symphonic movements into a single organic structure. The key to his success lies in Sibelius's adroit recognition and exploitation of the distinction between the function and nature of essentially the same material: once again, a duality of purpose. Here the listener experiences (in a direct precursor of what would now be termed "metrical modulation") the sense of earlier material almost imperceptibly taking on the characteristics of a scherzo (see mm. 106–14). Thus the nature of what is recognizably the "same" material *evolves* – in temporal terms, changing from that of an opening *Tempo molto moderato* movement into that of a scherzando *Allegro moderato*. However, despite this metamorphosis, its function is actually quite static: it is ultimately concerned with large-scale repetition. The same passage therefore has a double meaning: *at the time*, its scherzo-like gestures suggest further development of material, *while in retrospect* their clear sense of (varied) restatement offers structural resolution. The Seventh Symphony marks a further stage in this progressive evolution in formal compression, though to such an extreme extent that Sibelius wondered what he had actually created: a symphonic fantasy or a new kind of symphony.[16]

The passage generally referred to as the "first scherzo" (beginning thematically at m. 134 but not adopting its full characteristics until the *Vivacissimo* from m. 156) is a useful starting point. This is the first extensive passage of "fast" music within the symphony and it conveys all the attendant implications of multi-movement diversity inherent in such a tempo change. At the time it suggests a direct move away from the prevailing slow tempo of the piece while, viewed from the reality of retrospect, it ultimately prepares for the *Adagio* central statement of the trombone theme. Here is a pattern of events of an explicitly dual function: fast surface activity giving the sense of an independent scherzo movement that overlies background projections which subscribe to the overall tonal scheme of the piece as a whole.[17] Relevant to the current discussion is the idea that within this scherzo passage the organization and timing of a series of repetition patterns is equally important.

The use of large-scale transposed repetition immediately conveys the balance between illusion and reality; "transposition" suggests motion away from a prevailing center (as if part of a discrete symphonic "movement") but the choice of pitch levels here is carefully counterbalanced so that ultimately events are static (part of a single-movement entity). Thus the passage in mm. 147–55 reappears transposed *up* a perfect fourth (mm. 169–80), while that of mm. 155–69 is restated *down* a perfect fourth (see mm. 181–94). With cycle of fifths motion being neutralized by its use in opposite directions, the passage simultaneously conveys sense of motion (exploring linear time), as immediately perceived, and stasis (suggesting circular time), as understood in retrospect; the listener is required to look both forwards and backwards in time.

Such principles also operate on the largest time scale and thereby offer particular analytical significance. The basic concept that temporal organ-

---

[16] For a full discussion of this issue see Veijo Murtomäki, "Symphonic Fantasy, a Synthesis of Symphonic Thinking in Sibelius's Seventh Symphony and *Tapiola*," in *The Sibelius Companion*, ed. Glenda Dawn Goss (Westport CT: Greenwood Press, 1996), pp. 147–63.

[17] Tonal issues have been discussed elsewhere (see Howell, *Progressive Techniques* and "Two Versions") but in summary these involve the progressively less ambiguous establishment of an A♭-minor "centre" reflective of the same dual function: initially in conflict with the prevailing C major tonality, the A♭ eventually proves to be its complement by functioning as a Neapolitan to the dominant. This, in turn, prepares for the C *minor* of the central trombone statement as the next stage in the large-scale tonal diversification.

ization plays an important part in the structural articulation of this unique symphonic solution can be immediately illustrated by considering the scherzo material in question (mm. 147–55) and comparing it with an extract from the coda (mm. 500–10). Events presented at one tempo represent the first significant stage of contrast and diversity within the piece while essentially the same material – at a notably slower pace – forms part of a climactic resolution and confirmation of great intensity. Such a large-scale cross reference arises from the preservation of pitch- and interval-class identity: this is recognizably the "same" material. Its reversal of function emerges from these events being placed in a new context, but the issue here concerns the means by which they are adapted in order to fit that context. The process is essentially one of variation involving the parameters of tempo and articulation in particular but also including aspects of rhythm and, of course, internal repetition patterns. These transformational procedures contribute significantly to the sense of resolution and it is Sibelius's adroit recognition of how much to preserve in order to provide large-scale correspondences of underlying unity – a balance between old and new – that is so carefully achieved. Taken in isolation, this single example may not amount to a convincing case but it is offered simply to illustrate the principle, since it is part of an entire network of such transformational cross-references. Tempo is a crucially significant structural force in the Seventh Symphony since it is extremes of pace that convey the concept of multi-movement contrast, and the mitigation and integration of such extremes that ultimately confirm single-movement unity. Form is, therefore, perceived as a temporal process, rather than the composing-out of a pre-existent scheme.[18]

The concept of Sibelius using the same material placed in differing temporal contexts as part of an underlying variation process within the Seventh Symphony is certainly one of the most progressive features of his technique. However, given the tonal preoccupations of the piece in its diversification of a C major unity, it is difficult and potentially artificial to discuss the manipulation of material divorced from its harmonic and tonal position. The final return of the trombone theme (mm. 475ff.) is a useful example in this respect, since the passage that prepares for this hugely arresting structural moment (from m. 450 onwards) encompasses

[18] Kramer's single reference to Sibelius places the Seventh Symphony alongside pieces like the Liszt B minor Sonata and Schoenberg's First Chamber Symphony as "one-movement compositions that incorporate multi-movement structural logic . . . It is only by thinking of form as a mold, rather than as a process, that these composers invented their many-in-one forms." (Kramer, *The Time of Music*, p. 47). It seems as if misunderstandings with regard to Sibelius's formal *process* seem to persist; the Seventh Symphony is a very different kind of musical structure from the other works with which it is grouped by Kramer.

one of the most dramatic temporal transitions of the work. Moving from *Presto*, as a peak of temporal activity, back to the original *Adagio*, it involves a texture which simultaneously presents two types of activity: a fast string background and a slow brass foreground, though crucially they are both playing essentially the same, scalar material – but at different tempi. The use of varied and sequential repetition plays an important role in the musical continuity of this passage and helps prepare for the exact moment of "return" by building up a pattern and, therefore, our expectations. While all of this significantly contributes to this structural moment, the most crucial element of all is the presence of 26 measures of dominant pedal! Nevertheless, the fact that this harmonic tension is subject to a prolonged *rallentando* and that the moment of release is not merely a return to any kind of C major – but C major *at the original, slow tempo* – underlines the fact that it is a combination of tempo and tonality which is responsible for the structural articulation of the Seventh Symphony. It is only in a context where the articulatory role of tonality has been reduced to secondary importance that a consideration of Sibelius's control of musical time scale may be fully addressed. *Tapiola* provides us with just such an example.

A frozen landscape

In its extreme concentration on a single idea, *Tapiola* encapsulates issues of time and space in its depiction of a frozen landscape. In summary, its pitch organization revolves around a single collection (the ascending melodic minor scale on B) which is obsessively varied such that the generation of contrasting whole-tone and chromatic passages may be shown to emerge from that variation process.[19] *Tapiola* is not a conventionally tonal piece; there are no conflicting tonal areas, secondary keys, no sense of fundamental collection change, nothing of the machinery of modulation – not even a perfect cadence – despite its being based on a diatonic collection. Given such an absence, the contrast of whole-tone and chromatic organization is analogous to traditional tonal conflict and is generated in an equivalent manner. However, while this may offer a degree of dynamic friction, both whole-tonality and chromaticism, by

[19] Some of the preliminary ideas for this discussion were drawn from a paper given at the Second International Sibelius Conference, Helsinki, November 1995. For further details see Howell, "Sibelius's *Tapiola*: Issues of Tonality and Timescale," in *Sibelius Forum*. *Proceedings from the Second International Sibelius Conference, November 1995*, ed. Veijo Murtomäki, Kari Kilpenäinen, and Risto Väisänen (Helsinki: Sibelius Academy, 1998), pp. 237–46.

symmetrically dividing the octave into equidistant steps, are non-directional and essentially static. Thus any sense of *directed* motion has to be generated by other means, through levels which operate beyond pitch organization in itself and concern the control of musical time. By removing from tonality its power to articulate the passage of time, Sibelius explores ways of changing the parameters that control the pacing of surface events, elevating traditionally secondary forces to a primary role, in order to give a sense of direction to this music.

While the pitch organization of *Tapiola* is demonstrably that of an organic process form, its truly progressive characteristics stem from a new attitude towards the very concept of "variation." If the piece is to be viewed as a series of variations, then these are primarily temporal and involve aspects of speed, meter, rhythm, repetition patterns, texture, and articulation – rather than pitch relationships and intervals. What is significant is the way in which these elements work together in different combinations to create a variety of effects even though, in terms of pitch class, it is essentially the same material that is being manipulated. Of further significance is the extent to which these structural principles work from the most local level right up to the largest scale. Example 3.1 shows the overall layout of material (defined by relative "contrasts" within the pitch organization) and alongside this is a scheme of tempo changes, alternating between *Allegro moderato* and *Allegro*. In addition to these tempo changes, indications of underlying temporal perceptions (to be discussed later) are also provided and, collectively, these levels give both a dynamic shape and a sense of continuity to that arch-form outline. Instability of pitch and tempo clearly work together in that the most extreme passages of whole-tone and chromatic organization occur at the faster (*Allegro*) speed. Local recurrences of material suggest an immediate sense of varied repetition within each (letter-named) block while these sections, despite elements of contrast which account for their different labels, constitute a succession of variations.

Much of the local continuity of the piece is generated through repetition patterns, exploring perpetual variation of a limited number of shapes, which are used to create a sense of musical progress – of movement through time – to compensate for the stasis of pitch-class organization. To begin to explore this process, it is useful to consider section A. While issues of pitch organization have been covered elsewhere,[20] it is worth summarizing these as a background to the current discussion. In this example, mm. 26–52, subsection (a) and its "large-scale" repetition

[20] Ibid., pp. 240–41.

Ex. 3.1   Sibelius, *Tapiola*, formal and temporal schemes

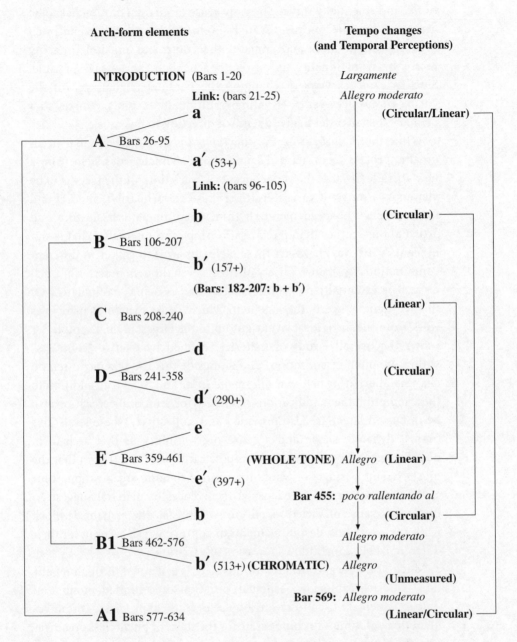

over mm. 53–84ff. (a′), numerous repetitions of a B minor triad/*Tristan* chord alternation (both immediately [vertically] and as part of larger arpeggiations [horizontally]) occur. Thus, in terms of pitch organization, this passage concerns a partitioning of the collection upon which *Tapiola* is based being projected to static effect.

What gives a sense of dynamism to this passage is, essentially, a series of temporal variations. Fundamentally this is a metrical issue; it concerns the placing of these events, the distance between motivic statements, their duration, the use of literal and/or sequential repetition, whether or not this is immediate or delayed: in short, the placing and timing of these patterns of expectation and denial have been carefully worked out. Of particular interest are the different ways in which repetition patterns are deployed, the different effects they generate and the large-scale sense of continuity they impart to the piece as a whole. Example 3.2 begins to explore this by showing such patterns operating over bars 26–52. Its findings may be summarized as follows:

> there are seven motivic statements (labeled I–VII), although IV–VII are subject to elision resulting, effectively, in five blocks of material to consider;
>
> the phrase structure, calculated in numbers of measures, is shown at the bottom of the example;
>
> a more precise listing of the duration of these statements and the delays (rests) between them is given in terms of the number of quarter-note beats involved;
>
> these basic measurements reveal both an underlying metrical pattern and a distortion to that framework: issues of symmetry and asymmetry;
>
> overall, a balance between triple and duple metrical patterns emerges in units of 4+4 or 4+3 measures; this 27-measure passage amounts to a total of 108 quarter-note beats which can be grouped in either triple ($3 \times 36 = 108$) or duple ($2 \times 54 = 108$) patterns.

Collectively, these features result in a sense of unpredictability which, in turn, gives temporal dynamism to an otherwise static effect of motivic repetition.

That unpredictability stems from the construction of the opening gesture (mm. 26–27), which establishes the temporal issues to be explored during this passage as a whole (see Ex. 3.2a). This six-beat figure is metrically unstable and aurally its structure is much more complex than when viewed on the page. Its six-beat duration is symmetrically positioned within an eight-beat framework (given the quarter-note rest on either side), and this raises ambiguities regarding duple (eight-beat)

Ex. 3.2a–d   Sibelius, *Tapiola*, section A (mm. 26–52), repetition patterns, temporal perceptions

a)

b)

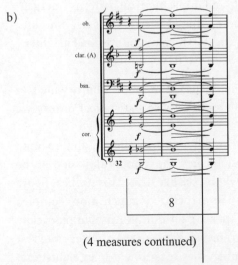

(4 measures continued)

Ex. 3.2 (*cont.*)

c)

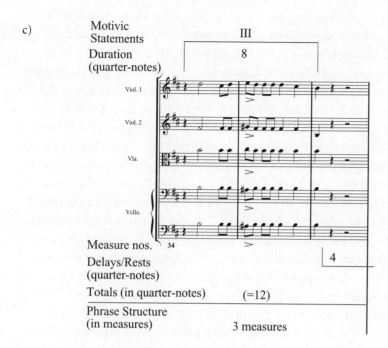

| Motivic Statements | III |
| Duration (quarter-notes) | 8 |

Measure nos. 34

Delays/Rests (quarter-notes) — 4

Totals (in quarter-notes) — (=12)

Phrase Structure (in measures) — 3 measures

d)

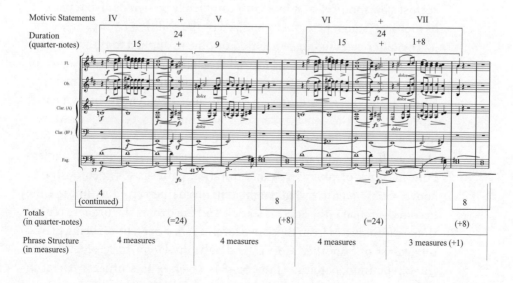

| Motivic Statements | IV | + | V | | VI | + | VII |
| Duration (quarter-notes) | 15 | 24 + | 9 | | 15 | 24 + | 1+8 |

Measure nos. 37   41   45   49

4 (continued)   8   8

Totals (in quarter-notes): (=24)   (+8)   (=24)   (+8)

Phrase Structure (in measures): 4 measures   4 measures   4 measures   3 measures (+1)

or triple/duple (six-beat [3×2 or 2×3]) meter with a disguised sense of upbeat/downbeat. Just how clearly does the listener perceive the rests? Such metrical uncertainty, alongside the rhythmic shape of this motive, gives it a sense of dynamism which counteracts the static nature of its pitch-class content; five (2+3) of its six beats project a B minor triad. A sense of unpredictability is heightened by the duration and placing of this statement in relation to subsequent repetition patterns, enabling us to perceive it as the initiator of later events. Looking again at Ex. 3.2, this figure is the shortest motivic statement of the entire passage (six beats) and it is followed by the longest period of delay (rests of ten beats) before the process of sequential and varied repetition gets underway. Although asymmetrical as a unit of 6+10 beats, sixteen-beat patterns become the norm thereafter: eight beats of statement II are followed by an eight-beat delay before the third statement; this makes the woodwind *Tristan* chord of mm. 32–33 (Ex. 3.2b), in its verticalization of the linear pitch organization, all the more striking. Thereafter, the eight-beat duration of statement III (Ex. 3.2c) apparently pursues the pattern, so that only having a four-beat delay prior to Statement IV is all the more dramatic. Statements IV and V (Ex. 3.2d) capitalize on that drama: not only are they "early" but they are elided, in a neatly balanced pattern of 15+9 beats (given the prevailing sixteen-/eight-beat model). This 24-beat sequence continues with statements VI and VII. From now on, the calculated unpredictability of either when (in time) or where (in register, given a mixture of transposed and literal repetition) events will occur changes further with the structural repetition of material: compare mm. 53–84 with this model of mm. 26–52. Motivic statements are now presented against a bassoon/cello ostinato in a completely regular, four-bar pattern; its metrical "squareness" is emphasized by the additional timpani pedal.

The differences in our perception of time as applied to these two passages of essentially the same material are significant, and establish one of the most fundamental and far-reaching principles of temporal manipulation in the piece. Measures 26–52, in their deployment of sequential repetition, seem to convey a sense of something progressive, even developmental. But, given the static nature of the pitch organization, this effect is illusory and, moreover, the "sequence" itself is unpredictable – both in terms of pitch levels and duration patterns – as demonstrated above. Consequently, what might initially be perceived as linear time becomes circular – the effect is static – and the dynamism of these repetition patterns arises from those two levels of time perception being played off against one another. Correspondingly, the larger-scale repetition of these repetition patterns (mm. 53–84) reverses this process. Here, in abstract, such a consistency in metrical placing suggests that events are more static, but the regularity of phrase structure and pulse arouses feelings of anticipation, which might suggest a faster pace at this stage. By providing a clear background meter against which the listener may plot a sense of motion, what was fundamentally perceived as circular time (due to further repetition) becomes much more linear (given a "measure" of progress). Additionally, such deliberate (underlying) monotony (of temporally varied repetition patterns) actually forces the listener to draw different sensations from (essentially) the same music.

Although "essentially" the same, events are not identical and the additional ostinato figure (on bassoon and lower strings) is correspondingly elevated in our perception since everything else is all too familiar. An ostinato with its own repetition pattern might appear merely to add to the prevailing sense of this being static music. But gradually, almost imperceptibly, this ostinato shifts from the background to the foreground, its significance being elevated due to the passing of time. This change of focus, a new perspective on apparently consistent material, is an important and radical feature of Sibelius's control of time scale. From m. 85 onwards, the ostinato comes to dominate the texture due to its registral expansion, which creates a sense of progress, and acts as a link into the next section; by this stage there has been a shift in our perception of this ostinato: from circular to linear time. Thereafter, it is reduced to a single whole-tone interval, becomes a background feature once more, and perceptions are reversed from linear to circular time. Here, from section B (letter C, mm. 106ff.), two clearly-defined textures, each with its own metrical terms of reference, are simultaneously presented. When, from letter E (mm. 157ff.), this material is reworked (subsection b′), its metrical contrasts are even more acute in these extremes of pace that are texturally segregated yet juxtaposed in time: a kind of counterpoint of time segments. Is this slow or fast music? While the articulation of the woodwind figures suggests speed and motion (linearity), especially offset against the static string ostinato, this is really an illusion. The woodwind sequences prove to be completely non-directional in any conventional harmonic sense (suggesting circularity) and are, therefore, slow if not static.

These examples, like many other instances in *Tapiola*, involve the use of a very specific kind of repetition pattern: the ostinato. Conventionally, an ostinato might be deployed to provide a driving force of motoric, rhythmic propulsion, especially in contexts where pitch organization is static and lacking any sense of linear motion. In fact, such contexts in *Tapiola* are relatively rare and most ostinati explore the opposite effect, using patterns to create a sense of stasis, lacking any driving force and being devoid of motoric rhythm. Section B (mm. 106ff., as mentioned above) presents material in two stages and these are unified by the continuous presence of a whole-tone based ostinato which imparts a degree of continuity. However, such a prolonged ostinato is extremely static and, although it presents a background against which other levels of activity stand in strong relief, it does not provide sufficient metrical regularity to convey a sense of temporal motion. True, its rhythmic shape may help clarify a sense of pulse, but such a high incidence of uniformity ultimately contributes to the perception of its temporal effect as being circular. In complete contrast, the whole-tone ostinato within section E (from letter N, mm. 417ff.) is fundamentally motoric. Its regular subdivision of the beat in a heterophonic presentation of material gives a strong metrical impulse to music which, in terms of its pitch organization, would otherwise be static. While the effect concerns the progression of linear time and, correspondingly, events are perceived as moving rather faster than earlier within this *Allegro* episode, ironically, the ostinato is subject to a *rallentando* (from mm. 455) leading to a return of the prevailing *Allegro moderato* tempo and the first large-scale architectural restatement of material (section B1, m. 462). Of course, the ability to perceive a slowing down in tempo – crucial to the overall formal articulation of the piece – is only possible because the ostinato is of a linear, rather than circular, type.

Structurally, these passages counterbalance one another, section B representing relative contrast with the original model and section B1 forming part of the overall sense of an arch-form outline through a process of restatement. Yet all this music is unified by the same, fundamentally whole-tone, apparently static, ostinato figuration. It is the temporal variation – firstly circular and secondly linear – to which this material is subjected that conveys its differing formal function within the overall shape of *Tapiola*. A variety of temporal organization is not just apparent within local repetition patterns, but is used to articulate large-scale structural effects as well.

A brief survey of the "progress" of one motivic shape will serve as a final summary of the cumulative effect of the variation procedures operating throughout *Tapiola*. The passage from letter K (mm. 290ff. subsection (d′)) isolates a turn-figure shape from much earlier in the piece and subjects it to a series of local repetition patterns of the kind discussed above (in relation to section A). Its final climactic statement at letter L (mm. 353ff.) comes as something of a surprise, as the twelve previous versions of this figure, for all their variety of harmonization and orchestration, convey a consistency of expression. Dynamics, register, reorchestration, and metrical displacement – the rhythmic diminution of the end of this figure – all contribute to the dramatic effect here.

This moment of arrival in fact proves to be the opposite: it precipitates the first major tempo change of the piece as the *Allegro moderato* (established since m. 21) gives way to *Allegro* (from m. 359) and one of the greatest degrees of contrast so far. Variants of this material may be traced from now on but its direct recurrence forms the main climax of the entire work (from letter Q, mm. 552ff.). The relative instability of a faster tempo (*Allegro* mm. 513ff.), coupled with the most extreme and extensive use of chromaticism in the piece, results in a kind of temporal chaos: that of unmeasured time. The dynamics, register, texture, and articulation all contribute to a sense of heightened expectation, but the repetition patterns here create an effect that is beyond circular time: essentially, this texture is atemporal. As the listener becomes unable to perceive any metrical downbeats, the passing of time is, effectively, suspended. Against this background, the woodwind/brass motives (from letter Q) comprise three statements, sequential in pitch but also in time (since they involve a regular pulse), built to cumulative effect. This is the most extreme example of the juxtaposition of measured and unmeasured time and thus marks a peak in an overall scheme of temporal variations. During this passage, in the absence of traditional functional harmony, a sense of motion is generated by other means; a combination of register, dynamics, and stepwise sequential repetition (which outlines, on the large scale, local interval patterns common to *all* of the material at this point) creates the effect of progress. The momentous sense of anticipation experienced by the listener arises from recollection of earlier events and, although the material may be the "same," its context and the passage of time result in a hugely effective climax.

The future

Sibelius's control of musical time scale is perhaps the single most progressive aspect of his compositional technique. In its extreme concentration of material, the workings of *Tapiola* have had a direct influence on later twentieth-century composers, perhaps ultimately finding something of a corollary in the minimalist aesthetic. This is not to suggest that Sibelius's music is, in any direct sense, an example of minimalist composition, though it may help place his achievements, in terms of the manipulation of time perception, within an historical continuum; that was, after all, part of Schoenberg's notion of a "progressive" composer. The forward-looking characteristics of *Tapiola* are numerous and collectively significant: the use of a single idea to derive multi-level music; repeated music, placed in different contexts, which alters the focus and perspective for the listener; repetition patterns which force the listener to draw different perceptions from the same material; a uniformity of pitch relationships which elevates a sense of diversity amongst traditional "secondary" parameters; the articulation of linear and circular time and the cross-connections between the two; the notion of temporal variations as a structural force.

From a list such as this, it is easy to see parallels with the manipulation of sound masses in the music of Ligeti (consider *Atmosphères*, 1965, for example), and comparisons between the formal processes of the Seventh Symphony and Elliot Carter's *Concerto for Orchestra* (1969) can also be made. The fact that Philip Glass, in "Floe" from the album *Glassworks* (1982), uses the ostinato from the finale of the Fifth Symphony is perhaps the most direct example (albeit a rather superficial one) of an influence on minimalist thinking. Pinpointing specific examples or particular trends is less significant than acknowledging the more general influence on contemporary composers of the Sibelian method of manipulating material. To some extent, history may be repeating itself, though, appropriately in this context, it is a significantly varied repetition. Early enthusiasm for Sibelius's music in Britain unwittingly undermined any appreciation of its progressive features; today, it directly confirms them. The composer David Matthews, for example, acknowledges Sibelius as follows:

> Most of my works are symphonic in character, which for me means music that contrasts dynamic energy with passivity. True stasis is achieved through energy and movement. Sibelius's symphonies are fine examples of how to do this: I have learned a lot from his control of pace, his welding together of different kinds of movement, his imperceptible transitions from fast to slow or slow to fast.[21]

while George Benjamin, discussing his piece *At First Light*, cites *Tapiola* as a direct influence.[22] Meanwhile, Sir Peter Maxwell Davies has spoken frequently of his indebtedness to aspects of Sibelius's technique and the following provides an apt summary: "What I find interesting is the way he articulates his time and the way he transforms his material"; the resonances with Schoenberg's view of Brahms are strikingly clear.[23] Finally, it is surely no accident that the most extreme example of these issues of time and timelessness in Sibelius's music should occur in the depiction of a

[21] See *New Sounds, New Personalities: British Composers of the 1980s in Conversation with Paul Griffiths* (London: Faber, 1985), p. 97.

[22] Ibid., p. 29.

[23] See *Trackings: Composers Speak with Richard Dufallo* (New York: Oxford University Press, 1989), p. 154.

frozen landscape. Perhaps what is quintessentially Finnish about Sibelius is this manipulation of time scale, since it would appear to originate from his perceptions of landscape and the seasons working on that landscape and from the timeless quality evoked by extreme periods of darkness and light. The musical consequences of his native land constitute some of the most original aspects of both style and idea, making Sibelius a truly progressive composer.

PART II

Ideology and structure

4 Kullervo's problem – Kullervo's story

Peter Franklin

In one sense, the story of Sibelius's *Kullervo* is easily told. We can all tell it: it concerns an over-ambitious programmatic symphony on a Finnish national subject that is marked by undigested influences (Bruckner, Tchaikovsky, Kajanus) but which affords glimpses of future mastery – a work that Sibelius himself came to regard as a problematic product of his youth. Do we need to generate an alternative story by means of critical sleight-of-hand? It is easy to become jaded about the post-modern validation of multiple, divergent, and even apparently deviant readings of texts once bound by constructions of authenticity, greatness, or authorial intention. In Sibelius's case, post-modern license might cynically be construed as a way of evading the problems facing non-Finnish- and non-Swedish-speaking commentators' embarrassment at being unable to consult relevant sources (like the full original version of the Tawaststjerna biography or contemporary local journalism). Such license might also serve decent historical ends, however. A little indulgence in Barthesian *jouissance*, after exorcising the patriarchal author and his academic puppet-masters, may even assist in *re*constructing as much as deconstructing (in the popular sense) an historical artist at a particular historical moment. *That* author, arguably more subtle and even subversive than his interpreters, may tell a richer story than the fake's discredited manipulators, with their canons, theories of influence, and categories of greatness. In standard accounts of late nineteenth- and early twentieth-century music the term "nationalist," to begin with one such category, represents a favorite drop-curtain heading behind which complex creative and cultural-political strategies may lie hidden. Do national characteristics in music tarnish it with worldly specificity or mark it as an assertive statement of identity?

> I think it is important to understand the relationship of specifics to the world in general, to know what one has before oneself and to understand the concept of beauty. This is clearer in Schubert's art than in all subsequent music. It is true that he has something of the Bohemian about him but this does not affect his deeper character. There are Hungarian traits in Brahms. I must admit that I find his songs very beautiful but I must again emphasize

that nothing can be compared to Beethoven. The wonderful inner form, the highest lyricism.[1]

Academic discussion about nationalism and the national in music has echoed as much as it has illuminated the culturally institutionalized discourse about such matters. The young Wilhelm Furtwängler here rehearses a version of that discourse for a childhood sweetheart in a letter of 1901, in which he tries complicatedly to justify his belief that Schubert is a greater composer than Schumann or Brahms, but less great than Beethoven. That he does so in a way that anticipates words subsequently used by Sibelius leads me to wonder whether the aspiring young composer of *Kullervo*, who had studied in Germany and Austria, might not have been able to write a closely similar sort of letter when beginning his choral and orchestral symphony just ten years earlier in Vienna. Furtwängler was supported by a great tradition in reconciling distaste for the limiting worldliness of Hungarian and Bohemian traits in Brahms and even Schubert with admiration for the implicitly transcendent Germanness (read "deeper character"?) of Beethoven. Sibelius, however, came from somewhere significantly "else": a smaller country in thrall to another great Empire (the Russian); he would be symptomatically dismissed, with heavy irony, as a "national genius" by his great Viennese contemporary Gustav Mahler, for whom the most readily available imperial discourse of nationalism was inevitably negative, marginalizing ("the most hackneyed clichés . . . served up, with harmonizations in the 'Nordic style,' as a national dish"[2]). Sibelius significantly forged a career that seems deliberately, as if in response, to have replaced overt national manners and preoccupations with others more in accord with a belief in Furtwängler's "wonderful inner form"; he famously came to cherish the "wonderful logic" of an idealized classical style[3] which put beauty and inner form above the superficial emblems of national identity and political causes.

Here, in essence, we begin to see the problem he faced with *Kullervo*: that work of his youth whose celebrated "retraction" by Sibelius, after just a few performances, so neatly served the mobilization of another

[1] Wilhelm Furtwängler, *Briefe*, ed. Frank Thiess (Wiesbaden: Brockhaus, 1964; 4th edn, 1980), pp. 29–30. I am grateful to Furtwängler scholar Roger Allen, whose translation is used here, for drawing my attention to this passage.
[2] Alma Mahler, *Gustav Mahler, Memories and Letters*, ed. Donald Mitchell, 3rd edn (London: John Murray, 1973), p. 297. It is, incidentally, clear that Mahler heard only Sibelius's *Spring Song* and *Valse Triste* in a concert conducted by Kajanus; see Erik Tawaststjerna: *Sibelius. Vol. II. 1904–1914*, trans. Robert Layton (London: Faber, 1986), p. 76.
[3] The phrase comes from Sibelius's letter of 20 July 1909 to Axel Carpelan, quoted in Erik Tawaststjerna, *Sibelius. Vol. II*, pp. 129–30; see also James Hepokoski, *Sibelius. Symphony No.5* (Cambridge: Cambridge University Press, 1993), p. 12.

institutionalized category which post-modernity threatens: that of "juvenilia." Theories of intertextuality and a related suspicion of constructions of originality (supposed to mark the mature creations of originating genius) may help re-voice early works along with those of women composers – and even the so-called nationalists who were once condemned to strum folksy tunes when not aspiring vainly to emulate the "masters" of the dominant Germanic tradition: a tradition that was not their authentic cultural birthright (so the story ran). It says something, incidentally, about the power and hegemony of the cultural discourse of nationalism as a derogatory category that Mahler, of all people, could so readily mobilize it against Sibelius, even though he had himself suffered from a version of it for much of his career.

My aim here is deliberately to bracket the available interpretation of *Kullervo* as a symptom of youthful inexperience or symptomatic nationalism (in the negative sense). As a result we may no longer take it that the problem it posed Sibelius might be solvable on technical or stylistic grounds that could be established through systematic analysis. Instead, a pragmatic investment in critical post-modernity will lead me to follow an ostensibly more subjective path to celebrating the peculiar brilliance and vision of this early work, comparable in so many ways to Mahler's own, similarly misunderstood, *Das klagende Lied. Kullervo*'s problem was, I will suggest, the result of multiple and conflicting creative strategies in a world where music was a cultural practice like no other,[4] a world in which the needs of the local audience and the material conditions for the establishment of an international career as a composer were in complicatedly productive conflict – albeit one mediated by the more abstract terms of aesthetic debate. Interestingly, but hardly fortuitously, a reversed mirror image of just such a conflict conditions the symbolic performance of the hero of Sibelius's fragmented, technically versatile narrative symphony. *Kullervo*'s problem can only be understood fully in terms of Kullervo's story – which was in some serious sense an odd one for a young Finnish nationalist composer (if such he was[5]) to select from the otherwise obvious source of *The Kalevala*, even if it did figure in contemporary performances by Karelian singer Larin Paraske.[6] Colorful heroes abound

---

[4] This phrase is an intentional allusion to Lawrence Kramer's *Music as Cultural Practice* (Berkeley: University of California Press, 1990), whose implications and general approach were to be still more sharply focused in *Classical Music and Postmodern Knowledge* (Berkeley: University of California Press, 1995).

[5] Sibelius's position, as a member of Finland's Swedish-speaking minority who had to learn Finnish, underlines the complexity and constructedness of the "nationalism" that he was, for a time, publicly to affirm.

[6] I am indebted to Veijo Murtomäki for this information; see also below.

there. Why choose one who rapes his sister and subsequently falls upon his sword?

Before those terrible events, Kullervo's history was more relevantly tailored to the aspirations of the young nationalist audience whose hero Sibelius would become. It will be convenient to begin with the second movement: "Kullervo's Youth." Since the details of the *Kalevala* source are confusingly glossed in the available accounts (where musical influence-spotting predominates), it will be necessary to expand even upon the indications offered by Tawaststjerna in the most extensive treatment of the work available in English.[7] His intimation that Kullervo is "brought up by his uncle, whose warriors have killed his father and all his retinue"[8] fails to do justice to the circumstances that mark Kullervo's youth in Canto 31 of *The Kalevala*, or quite why Sibelius should have described this movement as a "lullaby" whose "theme will grow in intensity on each return."[9]

Programmatic source analysis might seem altogether opposed to any post-modern strategy for liberating the movement from restrictive interpretative orthodoxy. Yet no such orthodoxy exists here – perhaps for the reason that this extraordinary work demands a kind of interpretative and imaginative license that contradicts conventional constructions of both autonomous symphonic music *and* late nineteenth-century "programme music." Tawaststjerna's observation that the form of the movement is "A B A1 B1 A2"[10] clearly fails to tell us enough (he himself goes on to say more, of course). On the other hand, standard approaches to late nineteenth-century programmatic narrativity in music are restricted both by relative ignorance of *The Kalevala* outside Finland and by the curious technical character of its narrative style: an arcane, repetitive and even self-contradictory rhetorical practice that offered much more to the young Sibelius than mere "stories" – although those were striking enough.

Canto 31 of *The Kalevala* opens a new narrative strain, following immediately upon the tales of Lemminkäinen which would furnish Sibelius with later musical inspiration. A metaphorical conceit is used (a clutch of baby swans carried off in different directions by an eagle and a

[7] See Erik Tawaststjerna, *Sibelius. Vol. I. 1869–1905*, trans. Robert Layton (London: Faber, 1976), chapters 5 and 6, specifically pp. 93–123. Valuable passing references to *Kullervo* will also be found in Veijo Murtomäki, *Symphonic Unity. The Development of Formal Thinking in the Symphonies of Sibelius*, trans. Henry Bacon, *Studia Musicologica Universitatis Helsingiensis* 5 (Helsinki: University of Helsinki, 1993) and in a number of the contributions to *The Sibelius Companion*, ed. Glenda Dawn Goss (Westport, CT: Greenwood Press, 1996).

[8] Tawaststjerna, *Sibelius. Vol. I*, p. 110.
[9] Ibid., p. 100.
[10] Ibid., p. 112.

hawk) to introduce three originally related but subsequently separated individuals, or even peoples: one is carried off to Russia to become a trader, one, called Kalervo, to Karelia. The third, Untamo ("who would blight his father's days / who would break his mother's heart"[11]), is "left at home." The wider implications of the ensuing account of warfare between the rival clans of Kalervo and Untamo would have needed little interpretative license on the part of Sibelius's nationalist audience in Finland for it to have seemed to allegorize their own country's enslavement to Imperial Russia in its account of Untamo's sacking of Kalervo's house and the killing of all except Kalervo's pregnant wife. She is captured by Untamo's warriors and taken home with them as a slave. Her son – Kullervo – is born in captivity and rocked in a foreign cradle. Narrative time here tumbles forward in its eagerness to place the avenging adult hero before us:

> The child rocked in the cradle
> the child rocked, his locks wafted:
> he rocked one day, he rocked two
>   till by the third
>   when the boy kicked out –
>   kicked out, tensed himself
> he burst through his swaddling bands
> got on top of his cover
> smashed the rocker of limewood
>   ripped up all his rags.[12]

Just thirteen lines (and a mysterious "three months") later Kullervo begins to think for himself:

> Would I were to get bigger
> to grow stronger in body
> I'd avenge my father's knocks
> I'd pay back my mother's tears![13]

Thus is born the hero Kullervo whose threat to Untamo leads the latter to devise a series of Herculean tasks for the youth; their murderous intent is, of course, repeatedly thwarted.

What this narrative might offer, interpretatively, is not inspiration for the pointless task of elucidating the descriptive intention of contrasting episodes, like that at cue H. Instead, it might sanction a multi-layered

---

[11] This, like all subsequent passages from *The Kalevala*, is taken from the most recent translation by Keith Bosley, *The Kalevala. An Epic Poem after Oral Tradition by Elias Lönnrot* (Oxford: Oxford University Press, 1989), p. 432.
[12] Ibid., p. 434.
[13] Ibid., p. 435.

response to the initiating B minor music as a dark-hued lullaby of mourning, the lullaby of a captive mother for her surviving but fatherless child – perhaps even the runic singing of other women, women of Untamo's clan, sadly rocking the cradle of an infant with whose tragedy they sympathize, even as they are implicated in its cause. The "rocking" quality is emphasized by the almost choreographic gestural movement of the music, initially stressing and differentiating the first and second beats of the 3/2 measures as push and return, push and return.

The female, "maternal" subject-position thus figured, as in the dream-like or idyllic episodes that ensue, seems to reflect a standard affective trope for nineteenth-century symphonic slow movements – not least programmatic ones in the Russian and Austro-German traditions (one thinks, for example, of Tchaikovsky's Fourth, whose second-movement "recollection" of past happiness is implicitly set against the darkness of the fated present from which it escapes; the second movement of Mahler's Second Symphony offers a related example, designated "a mournful memory of youth and lost innocence."[14]) What is so extraordinary about the *Kullervo* movement are the coloristic, registral, and harmonic devices whereby Sibelius enabled the lullaby theme (as he put it) to "grow in intensity on each return,"[15] heightening the remembered tones of the muted strings and the strange, "keening" arabesque that repeatedly descends above them in the first violins (from one after cue A). But where the thematic outline of the rest of the lullaby melody evinces "runic" characteristics, possibly gleaned from Sibelius's meetings with the Karelian singer Larin Paraske in the summer of 1891,[16] the originary "folklike tone"[17] of its opening motive is progressively transformed into something threateningly and disruptively present: the initial rocking figure sheds its character as "music" (here feminine, maternal, lamenting . . . the timeless plaint of the oppressed) and becomes a heroic, "masculine" gesture, what Tawaststjerna calls "a cry of protest and revolt."[18] The climax comes before cue Ö (Breitkopf score pp. 61–62), where the rocking figure is turned into a full-orchestral, *fortissimo* B major call to arms. It is answered twice, in Wagnerian manner, by a quiet clarinet and bassoon chord of G minor that prefigures the reversion of the motive to its original form when the lullaby returns. The ancestral maternal rights

[14] See Alma Mahler, *Memories and Letters*, p. 213, for Mahler's 1901 program for the Second Symphony, from which this description is taken.

[15] See Tawaststjerna, *Sibelius. Vol. I*, p. 100.

[16] See ibid., p. 113, and William A. Wilson, "Sibelius, the *Kalevala* and Karelianism," in *Sibelius Companion*, pp. 43–60.

[17] The phrase is Dahlhaus's, after Mahler. See Carl Dahlhaus, "The Natural World and the 'Folklike Tone'," in his *Realism in Nineteenth-Century Music,* trans. Mary Whittall (Cambridge: Cambridge University Press, 1985), pp. 106ff.

[18] Tawaststjerna, *Sibelius. Vol.I*, p. 113.

of Music as a timeless source of consolation, solace, and support, are not only asserted in this movement, but also challenged by an expressive impulse that demands action, disruption, and change. The implications of the first movement, to which I will shortly turn, are thus consolidated and emphasized in a way that focuses the need for an altogether different kind of music in whatever might follow.

This sketched interpretation of "Kullervo's Youth" will appropriately suggest a community of purpose with James Hepokoski's analysis of "teleological genesis" in later Sibelius, linked to what he calls "rotational structure," with its underlying character as a maternal cradle rocking.[19] The movement might further be represented as a case study in the strategic multi-valency of musical meaning in the period. Its significance can be both shrouded and celebrated in "purely musical" accounts of it as an intensifying, returning lullaby with contrasting episodes, its form comfortingly reducible to Tawaststjerna's cipher "A B A1 B1 A2." It is no less interpretable (particularly to those who know their *Kalevala*) as a nationalist *cri de coeur* which has the added cultural-political implication of an exercise in the dominant discourse of Russo-Germanic symphonic form that is subjected to an internal, structural-expressive critique (although one whose threat to traditional form is conventionally, if inconclusively, thwarted by the last return of the lullaby). The first movement ostensibly engages in a similar, if more far-reaching "deformation" of conventional late nineteenth-century sonata practice.[20] But here Hepokoski's perhaps unintentionally negative term seems to merit replacement by the more positive one of *re*-formation. In the discourse of analysis, no less than that of nationalism, illuminating observations may also re-inscribe relations of power.

The tantalizingly understated title "Introduction" (*Einleitung* in the Breitkopf score) appears to accommodate the mores of "absolute" symphonic music in the Austro-German manner. Influence-spotters will appropriately find frequent allusions to Bruckner, along with a confusing structural profile that might be written off as inept or "immature" in the time-honored way. Viewed more favourably, and perhaps imaginatively, it might equally be interpreted as a carefully planned preparation for what follows (both in the second movement and the work as a whole), and one of unusual cogency and power. An interpretative key lies in the relative weakness of its references to what might be called the "rhetoric"

[19] See Hepokoski, *Symphony No. 5*, pp. 26–7, and "The Essence of Sibelius. Creation Myths and Rotational Cycles in *Luonnotar*" in *Sibelius Companion*, pp. 121–46.

[20] Hepokoski, *Symphony No. 5*, pp. 5ff.

of late nineteenth-century symphonic first-movement form.[21] The structure seems neither to rotate exactly, in Hepokoski's sense, nor to invest in any clearly defined *telos*. Its progress is marked by gestural interruptions that seem, in fact, to posit some other, as yet undefined greater *telos* whose clearest image is glimpsed in the C major episode at the climax of the development section, where a hitherto unheard and subsequently discarded *Abgesang* to the main first theme fleetingly scales triumphant heights (see cue O).

The movement's opening is already *echt*-Sibelius: an oscillating string ostinato is set up as the ground against which the heroic main theme of the movement (it positively demands to be called the "Kullervo" theme) unfolds with all the energetic muscularity of a painted figure by Gallén-Kallela. Where reference to a "development" section might appear to conflict with my point about the movement's weak sonata rhetoric, that observation is nevertheless explained and reinforced by the surprising absence of any contrasting "*Gesangsperiode*" that might fit the late nineteenth-century model of an almost inevitably feminized second subject to Kullervo's over-determinedly masculine first.[22] Instead, we are treated as if to the openings of a series of alternative narratives that are juxtaposed but unrelated, like the confusingly inter-cut elements of a certain kind of cinematic "titles" sequence, introducing characters and plot lines that will only later be contextualized and explained. First there is the expectant bustle of what might be the opening market scene of a Slavic opera (cue B) then, soon after cue C, a long-breathed horn melody, static and portentous. At cue D a newly animated, fanfare-like figure seems to open a new and more forcefully extended narrative episode, but the returning "Kullervo" theme stalls its progress and insists upon another general pause before a cryptic flute and bassoon motif (four before cue I) initiates yet another kind of forward momentum whose short-term goal is the *pianissimo* version of the Kullervo theme, now in three flats, which sounds at last unequivocally like the beginning of a "development" section.

The recapitulation will begin no less quietly with the Kullervo theme in the woodwinds, now back in the home modality of E minor. But conventional tonal rhetoric is entirely eclipsed by thematic and affective characteristics of the *narrative* rhetoric in what now proceeds as a unified

---

[21] By "rhetoric" I refer here to thematic and gestural signification, linked to representational or narrative implications. It is my implicit contention that the tonal and harmonic indicators of Germanic sonata structure are subordinate to this rhetoric.
[22] It is significant that Sibelius himself, referring to his earlier attempt at a symphony, had written to his wife-to-be explaining that the first movement's "second theme represents you, melancholy, feminine and yet passionate." See Tawaststjerna, *Sibelius. Vol.I*, p. 88.

peroration whose subject-position is that of "Kullervo" himself, that of the main opening theme of the movement. The point is splendidly made when its initial climax, ten bars before cue W, is newly extended by what proves to be an augmented version of the first, bustling episode from cue B in the exposition. From this point onwards, all the previously disconnected narrative gambits are drawn together in what might be read as a composite "portrait" of the hero. Thematic connections with the symphony's closing movement suggest that he even glimpses and emotionally surmounts a vision of his own death. The defiant, *fortissimo* last statement of the Kullervo theme is followed by a series of daring silences, punctuated by hushed gestures of brooding, reluctant acceptance that nevertheless harbor the impulse from which the rest of the symphony will grow.

This Kullervo comfortably fits the bill of national hero, his story implicitly an allegorical version of Sibelius's own, as the aspiring symphonist seeking to avoid marginalizing himself as a "mere" nationalist while nevertheless turning the master narrative to his own ends. He may subsequently have felt that he had gone too far, even in the opening movements; that the work would appear "merely" nationalist, in Mahler's derogatory sense, if played in Berlin or Vienna. This reactivates questions about Sibelius's desire to keep both his national and international options open, to speak to both local and foreign audiences. Did the implicit requirement of compromise subsequently shade into an aim to write himself into the master narrative of the Germanic symphony, with its "inner form" and transcendent "concept of beauty"?

It would, of course, not be difficult further to ironize those notions; the very symphonic master narrative to which I refer has come in for a good deal of critical attention recently. Might Sibelius's worry that his *re*formation of it would be taken negatively as *de*formation indicate that he, like any other young non-German symphonist at the end of the nineteenth century, was in an impossible position with respect to its underlying ideological character, which he might thus have been forced to reinscribe? Its usual focal nexus of sexual politics and gender representation – alluded to by Hepokoski and explored more forthrightly by Susan McClary[23] – is clearly relevant to the story of *Kullervo*, whose first two

[23] The most relevant texts here are Susan McClary, "Sexual Politics in Classical Music," in *Feminine Endings. Music, Gender and Sexuality* (London: University of Minnesota Press, 1991; repr. 1994), pp. 53–79; "Narrative Agendas in 'Abstract' Music. Identity and Difference in Brahms's Third Symphony," in *Musicology and Difference. Gender and Sexuality in Music Scholarship*, ed. Ruth Solie (Berkeley: University of California Press, 1993) pp. 326–44; and "Constructions of Subjectivity in Schubert's Music," in *Queering the Pitch. The New Gay and Lesbian Musicology*, ed. Philip Brett, Gary Thomas and Elizabeth Wood (London: Routledge, 1994), pp. 205–33.

movements invest powerfully in masculine-heroic characteristics which are even thematically developed "out of" (and in opposition to?) the maternal lullaby of the second movement. The story's most remarkable turn is taken neither in the fine choral account of Kullervo's death, with which the work ends, nor in the effective, but slighter, fourth movement ("Kullervo goes to war"). It is in the central third movement where Sibelius first invokes the mighty tradition of the Beethovenian choral symphony[24] and calls in a specifically *male*-voice choir – but not to sing a collective anthem of rebellious or revolutionary brotherhood so much as to narrate a story of incest that problematizes the hero's masculinity in the most disturbing manner possible. The Wagnerian precedent for treating brother–sister incest (in *Die Walküre*) is relevant here only as a "revolutionary" model which Sibelius rejects in favour of a version that reinvests the transgressive act with terrifying destructive power. This should not be taken to signify a straightforward reinstatement of bourgeois moral values. Sibelius's problematization of heroic masculinity here, using a musical language of boldly uncompromising originality, finds its nearest echo in the 1912 symphonic poem *Stanisław i Anna Oswiecymowie* by the Polish composer Miecysław Karłowicz.[25] Both works depict brother–sister incest, reinforcing the self-destructive implication that, in an age of militaristic imperialism, the apparent acquisition of "mastery" back-handedly confirms the feminization of the marginalized.

The treatment of the incest episode from Canto 35 of *The Kalevala* seems to have played a significant part in Sibelius's maturing plans for *Kullervo*. It caused him difficulties that bear revealingly upon uncertainties he had about what music might be permitted to express, and how. Where cultural politics may have conditioned what he felt he could be *explicit* about, they appear no less subverted by his concern to treat the theme at all. Even the double concealment of textual omission and the "purely musical" representation of the sexual encounter in the final version in no way hides what the music blatantly conveys – particularly (once again) for those who know their *Kalevala*. Before addressing that, however, we must consider how the movement begins and initially progresses.

The agogic bustle and breathless excitement of the opening first violin melody in 5/4 is immediately arresting. Its stagily communal quality is

---

[24] In April 1891, just when ideas for *Kullervo* were developing, Sibelius had been greatly moved by a performance of the Ninth Symphony under Richter in Vienna (see Tawaststjerna, *Sibelius. Vol. I*, p. 93).

[25] For an account of this work, see Alistair Wightman, *Karłowicz, Young Poland and the Musical Fin-de-siècle* (Aldershot: Scholar Press, 1996), pp. 71–78.

reinforced by the male-voice choir that soon embarks with emphatic relish upon the now verbalized narrative. Verbalized, and in the process distanced as "story" in the enthusiastic act of "telling:"

> Kullervo, Kalervo's son,
> the blue-stockinged gaffer's child
> > yellow-haired, handsome
> > fair of shoe-upper
> went to take in the taxes
> > to pay in the tithes.[26]

It is worth pointing out that by this stage of his life history in *The Kalevala*, Kullervo has been presented not only as overdeterminedly masculine (his beauty, strength, and wilfulness matched by the only half-deliberate clumsiness that had caused Untamo maliciously to sell him as a servant to Ilmarinen the Smith). He has also been the subject of a confusingly self-regenerating narrative: after causing the death of Ilmari's woman, he escapes with the intention of returning to wreak vengeance upon Untamo, only to be told that his father had not, in fact, been killed and that he and his mother have been reunited. Kullervo finds them and returns to live with them, troubled only by the absence of his sister. She, his mother informs him, had disappeared after going to pick berries in the forest. After further manifestations of the clumsiness that had exasperated Untamo and Ilmari, his father sends Kullervo on the fateful journey to pay their taxes, after which he settles into his sledge and makes for home. His epic journey becomes a search for sexual conquest as he encounters a series of three young women. With the last he is successful, although as much by force as by effective seduction. The following day he discovers that the girl is his lost sister. She laments her fate and drowns herself. Kullervo, distraught, is left with no goal but finally to wreak vengeance upon Untamo before seeking his own death.

It is above all the vehemence and commitment with which Sibelius's music presents and "performs" the story that emphasizes the movement's problematic significance as defining a kind of anti-*telos*, the opposite of all that such a promising symphonic hero might have been expected to achieve. The long-delayed confrontation by the masculine subject of his female "other" proves startlingly to be just that: an encounter with his own sister, whose conquest they both bitterly regret. The reversal is made all the more shocking in *The Kalevala* by the fact that the seduction and conquest are narrated, in thoroughly laddish fashion, as a coarsely humorous "men's story." This is particularly obvious in the section of text which

---

[26] Bosley, *The Kalevala*, p. 437.

Sibelius omitted, following the passage where Kullervo, having pulled the girl into his sledge, dazzles her with a chest full of coins and fine clothes:

> Kullervo, Kalervo's son
> the blue-stockinged gaffer's child
> there flattered the maid
> he took hold, tickled
> one hand on the stallion's reins
> the other on the maiden's tits:
> there he sported with the maid
> touched up the tin-breast
> under the copper-bright cloak
> on top of the speckled fur.[27]

It is hardly surprising that Sibelius thought long and hard about how to depict the conquest – "the scene where he actually takes her," as he had referred to it.[28] In a subsequent letter to his wife-to-be (March 1892) he even appears to suggest that the movement had once been scored for *full* chorus (he refers to a friend to whom he had played it; the relevant text is that quoted above):

> he thinks the women will be embarrassed and won't sing. You, darling, would understand! There is a passage perhaps which could be less vividly portrayed in the orchestra after the words "Verat veivät neien mielen" and where the orchestra goes on. In case the ladies are troubled by this I shall give it to the male choir.[29]

Sibelius thus accommodates the conventional sexual-political discourse of his day in a manner that only heightens the startling implications of what happens here. Up to, and through, the orchestral "passage" mentioned, the music reinforces the constructed gender characteristics of both narrative subject and choral narrators in music whose phallic and penetrative implications require no McClaryesque interpretative daring.

The key to understanding the movement must be that this most fundamental goal of patriarchal power marks only an approximate mid-point in its progress, a catastrophic event after which nothing is as it was before. The graphic, final sexual climax at cue M crashes the hitherto unbroken 5/4 metre out of gear into compound triple time (3/2, then 9/4, with an internal section in 6/4). The conventionally less "masculine" character of triple metre is here accompanied by a no less significant shift of narrative subject-position from male to female. The dystopic implications of the relationship between the two "halves" of the movement[30] bear careful consideration.

[27] Ibid., p. 479.
[28] Tawaststjerna, *Sibelius. Vol. I*, p. 104.
[29] Ibid., p. 105.

[30] On the conventionally utopian impications of bi-partite structures in the Romantic period, see Kramer, *Music as*

Apart from the briefly spotlighted solo voices of Kullervo and the Sister ("sisar") – in which her role is emphatically rewritten as that of *one* woman who assertively resists Kullervo's first two advances – the communal masculinity of the choral narration receives further confirmatory determination. This comes both from the "journeying" metaphor, sanctioned by the poetic image of Kullervo dashing across country in his sledge in search of women, and the exotic-originary effect of the Finnish language and appropriately stylized "runic" music that Sibelius seems to have adapted from the performances of Larin Paraske. Three large, musically comparable narrative sections each conclude with an attempted sexual conquest: three blocks of patriarchal "*Ur*-narrative," as uncompromising in their Finnish national costume as in their ostensibly "universal" implications.

The post-coital second half of the movement casts the blackest shadow on all of this. The shift in subject-position is strikingly emphasized in the original *Kalevala* text by the fact that the Sister, previously a figure in the men's story, now becomes a narrator in her own right, directly telling the story we had previously been told by others. In the process Kullervo's own two extended solo performances are structurally marginalized. While the Sister's initial self-description is a (devastating) mirror image of Kullervo's response to her question about his identity, her subsequent monologue finds its own decisive *telos* in death (although Sibelius omits the description of it in *The Kalevala*), leaving Kullervo now as the tragically unmanned responder to what *he* has heard and seen. His concluding, "masculine" 4/4 tempo emphatically lacks all the drive of his 5/4 heroics. She turns him from a naive hero into the agent of a tragedy whose only outcome can be death.

The key central episode in the Sister's narrative (not all sopranos are responsive to its peculiar demands) comes at the point in her story where, having become lost on her berry-picking expedition, she had found her way to a "lofty peak" from whose summit she had "shouted and yelled out." In the fourteen bars preceding cue R, she recalls what the echoing backwoods and heaths had answered:

> Do not shout mad girl
> mindless one, don't make a din!
> It won't be heard anyway
> the shout won't be heard at home.[31]

Cultural Practice chap. 2, "Beethoven's Two-Movement Piano Sonatas and the Utopia of Romantic Aesthetics," pp. 21ff.

[31] Bosley, *The Kalevala*, p. 481.

In music corresponding to what Mahler might have called a *Naturlaut*, an unsentimentally naturalistic bird chirrups unresponsively (flutes) above her eerie line that at first winds obsessively up and down through the interval of a major third (D and F♯). The "voice of nature," so often gendered female in *fin-de-siècle* poetic discourse, is here mimicked by a woman who presents it as the uncaring patriarchal misogynist that feminist theory would later accuse it of having always been. Small wonder that the shocked and fractured threnody with which Kullervo concludes the movement after her death should insist on the bleak minor mode of the bright F major with which it had opened.

Read with the license of post-modernity to attend to details of sexuality, gender representation, and narrative techniques, this movement explodes into meaning of a kind that is as much grounded in musical and textual detail as it is subversive of *Kullervo*'s more traditional or conventional interpretation as an exercise in "nationalism." The work's actual conclusion is more than just anticipated here. It is made musically and emotionally unavoidable by the end of the third movement, which has turned assertiveness against political oppression into a story of sexual trauma that threatens the stability of culturally constructed gender roles and their symbolic reflection in patriarchal narrative (concerning Nature and the heroic "quest" in particular). Elements of that patriarchal narrative are presented in the first part of "Kullervo and his Sister," and elsewhere in the work, with sufficiently determined energy to account for regressive interest in Sibelius in the Third Reich, for example (or at least in that strain of his subsequent symphonic output that is initiated here). But the movement's closing sections assert something deeply contradictory to male-voice-choral heroics and the "national genius" they might seem to resound.

The grim misogynist implications of another early work of Sibelius, *Skogsrået* (*The Wood Nymph*, c. 1894), are similarly problematized by *Kullervo*'s subject-position slippage towards the feminine. The handsome Björn (in the source poem by Rydberg), is depicted by Sibelius with what sounds like a prototypically muscular national hymn, but is then spoiled for "normal" sexual relations by a *femme fatale* of the forest in a way that marks him out as a standard trope of *fin-de-siècle* misogyny. In the light of *Kullervo*, and its third movement in particular, *Skogsrået*, too, may be read in a quite different way as a work that similarly transforms its hero into a socially dysfunctional figure for the very reason that his ideal *telos* is a fantasy, a "fairy-story." Björn's belief in it condemns him to become a brooding function of the natural world (listening "with inconsolable grief to the sigh of the woods"[32]), where Nature itself, often invoked as a trope for the unfolding of symphonic form in Sibelius's later works, is reconstructed as a process with no clear outcome, a journey without a comprehensible goal. The dark underside of Sibelius's subsequent quest to solve the puzzle of the "wonderful logic" implicit in the divine fragments that were the stuff of symphonic mastery to him[33] was to be glossed in a remarkable way in a 1910 diary entry where he considered his position *vis à vis* the innovations of European "new music" and consoled himself that he, like Björn, would have his "small, modest place" as an "*Erscheinung aus den Wäldern*," an apparition from the forests.[34] By offering us a key to the problematic intensity of Sibelius's questioning of the terms of the narrative in which he sought to inscribe his own story, *Kullervo* helps us to understand how relevant that "small, modest place" was to the intersecting cultural and historical aims of European symphonic music in the decades before the 1914–18 war. The problem of Kullervo's "nationalist" story was hardly the exclusive property of one aspiring young composer brooding on questions of power, gender, and "Nature" in the forests of Russian-dominated Finland.

---

[32] I quote from William Jewson's translation of Viktor Rydberg's poem (in the form used by Sibelius) printed in the notes accompanying the first recording of *The Wood Nymph* under Osmo Vänskä, BIS-CD-815, 1996.

[33] Rosa Newmarch quoted Sibelius as having described musical inspiration as being "like the children's game of *Word-taking* and *Word-making*. A spiritual force (call it God) throws down to one a handful of letters – a message – and a voice says: 'make what you can of this.' Alas we cannot always make the best of it." Rosa Newmarch, *Jean Sibelius* (London: Goodwin and Tabb, 1944), p. 56.

[34] Tawaststjerna, *Sibelius. Vol. II*, pp. 139–40.

5 Sibelius and the theater: a study of the incidental music for Symbolist plays

Eija Kurki

During the autumn of 1904, Sibelius wrote to his friend Axel Carpelan: "Of course, I have not been able to resist composing for the theater. My old bad habit! *Pelléas et Mélisande*."[1] Incidental music forms a central part of Jean Sibelius's oeuvre, and many well-known works, such as *Finlandia* and *Valse triste*, originated as incidental music. Sibelius's collaboration with dramatists began in the 1890s, encompassing scenic music for tableau performances (1893 and 1899),[2] a one-act opera (1896), music for Adolf Paul's play *King Christian II* (1898) and concluded with Hugo von Hofmannsthal's *Everyman* (1916), and finally, in 1926, the *Tempest* music to Shakespeare's last play. In the first years of the twentieth century, Sibelius composed incidental music for a group of dramatists who belonged to the Symbolist school in vogue at the time, and who were influenced by late nineteenth-century French poets including Stéphane Mallarmé, Arthur Rimbaud, and Paul Verlaine. Their plays incorporating fairy tales, dreams, death, mysticism, and the exotic included Arvid Järnefelt's *Kuolema* (*Death*, 1903), Maurice Maeterlinck's *Pelléas et Mélisande* (1905), Hjalmar Procopé's *Belshazzar's Feast* (1906), August Strindberg's *Swanwhite* (1908), and Mikael Lybeck's *Ödlan* (*The Lizard*, 1909). The association of artists called "Euterpe," centered in Helsinki at the turn of the century, included playwrights, architects and theater critics. Their aim was to expose Finland to contemporary international artistic developments, as is evident from the group's keen interest in, for example, the works of Oscar Wilde and Maeterlinck. Sibelius is known to have participated in the group's functions and celebrations.[3]

The opening nights of the plays in question attracted considerable attention in Helsinki and, judging by the number of performances, many

[1] Sibelius's letter to Axel Carpelan, 21 September 1904. National Archives, Sibelius Collection, Helsinki. Regarding Sibelius's incidental music, see Eija Kurki, *Satua, kuolemaa ja eksotiikkaa. Jean Sibeliuksen vuosisadan alun näyttämömusiikkiteokset* (Helsinki: Kurki, 1997).

[2] *Scenic music for a festival and lottery in aid of education in the province of Viipuri* (1893) and *Music for the Press Celebrations* (1899).

[3] Olof Mustelin, *Euterpe. Tidskriften och kretsen kring den* (Åbo, 1963), pp. 81, 113; Erik Tawaststjerna, *Sibelius , Vol. I, 1865–1905*, trans. Robert Layton (London: Faber, 1976), pp. 270–71.

of them achieved popularity. Undoubtedly, their success owed a great deal to Sibelius's music. *Swanwhite* was one of the most performed Strindberg plays at the Swedish Theater in Helsinki, and Sibelius's incidental music for the play must have contributed to its box office attraction. Sibelius later compiled orchestral suites (*Pelléas et Mélisande*, *Belshazzar's Feast*, and *Swanwhite*) and individual concert pieces (*Valse triste* and *Scene with Cranes* from the music of *Death*) from the incidental music for these plays. While the later arrangements are well known, the original scores remain unpublished.

How does Sibelius's music relate to the text of the play? If the text evokes musical ideas, how are they realized? Does the orchestration describe characters and impressions? Is the music always in harmony with the text? In addition to broaching these questions, the present essay also addresses particular issues such as the exact placement of Sibelius's music in the play (as accompaniment to pantomime, background music for the dialogue, singing, or intermezzos without scenic action). My primary focus will be the music for Järnefelt's *Death*, Hjalmar Procopé's *Belshazzar's Feast*, and August Strindberg's *Swanwhite*. I conclude with some remarks concerning the significance of Sibelius's incidental music for his symphonies: although the symphonies are often considered to be "absolute music," by borrowing from his incidental music in some of his symphonies, he seems to transfer to the strictly instrumental medium semantic elements drawn from the plays.[4]

According to Marcel Schneider "the Wagnerian influence, the Mallarméan notion of suggestion, the lessons that can be extracted from Debussy's work and diffuse mysticism founded more on spiritual and esthetic intuitions than on religious dogma contribute towards forming what we can call: 'symbolistic music.'"[5] And what of the symbolism in Sibelius's music? According to Schneider, Sibelius's music – in this context he mentions *Finlandia*, *The Swan of Tuonela*, and *Tapiola* – unites Wagner and Debussy. In particular, Schneider associates Sibelius's *Kalevala*-inspired works with symbolism, and hereby makes a connection between symbolism and the mythological themes in these works.[6] In his description of *The Swan of Tuonela*, "Tuonela is the Isle of Avalon of this Ultima Thule – just as melancholy as Arnold Böcklin's famous *Isle of the Dead* – there swims Sibelius's swan, symbolized by a beautiful *cor anglais* melody."[7] In this way, Schneider defines the *cor anglais* and its

[4] See the chapters by Virtanen and Jackson in this book (on pp.139ff and 175ff).

[5] Marcel Schneider, "Symbolist movement," trans. by Edouard Roditi, in *The Symbolist Movement in the Literature of European* *Languages. A Comparative History of Literatures in European Languages*, ed. Anna Balakian (Budapest: Akadémiai Kiadó, 1982), p. 474.

[6] Ibid., pp. 475–76.

[7] Ibid., p. 476.

melody in symbolist terms. Erik Tawaststjerna, too, considers *The Swan of Tuonela* a symbolist work. In his view, this piece is the most remarkable manifestation of symbolism in Finnish music of the 1890s.[8] Detecting the influence of Wagner (especially of *Lohengrin* and *Tristan*), he sees *The Swan of Tuonela* as incorporating the swan symbolism popular at the time: "In Sibelius's piece flows the water of death's mysticism; there the current of Tuoni flows darkly; there the swan sings."[9]

Swan symbolism features prominently in many works from the turn of the century. A swan appears in Wagner's *Parsifal* and *Lohengrin*; Arnold Böcklin depicted swans in his pictures and, among Finnish artists, Akseli Gallén-Kallela and Magnus Enckell used them in their work. The swan was considered to symbolize the most profoundly human spirituality and poets' most elevated thoughts. Additionally, it figures in Russian music in such pieces as Rimsky-Korsakov's *Sadko* and Tchaikovsky's ballet *Swan Lake*, and also in the pictures of Alexander Vrubel.[10]

What, then, makes *The Swan of Tuonela* a symbolist work? According to Tawaststjerna the symbolist atmosphere is created by the orchestral sonority, both the tone colors of the instruments and the choice of register:

> By omitting flutes, clarinets and trumpets and including parts for *cor anglais*, bass clarinet and bass drum Sibelius darkens the palette in such a way that the music becomes akin to some sort of symbolistic half-light. In the opening bars, the chord of A minor is gradually (and most magically) moved through the whole string section, *divisi con sordini*, producing a continuous but ever-changing sonority.

As Tawaststjerna observes, Wagner had already pioneered this idea in his *Lohengrin* prelude.[11] As the music rises up from darkness into light – towards infinity – its dark sonority and low register gradually change to something brighter symbolizing the transition from the natural to the supernatural. The *cor anglais* solo in *The Swan of Tuonela* may also be related to the Shepherd's "alte Weise" recitative in the third act of *Tristan und Isolde*. As Tawaststjerna observes, in both works the atmosphere of death is associated with the tone color of the wind instruments.[12] If, in *The Swan of Tuonela*, Sibelius refers to other contemporary artists – Puvis de Chavannes and Böcklin, Edvard Munch and Wagner[13] – the *Lemminkäinen* Suite's coloration is nevertheless essentially Wagnerian.[14]

[8]   Tawaststjerna, *Sibelius. Vol. I*, p. 171.

[9]   Ibid.

[10]   Edouard Roditi, "The Spread and Evolution of Symbolist Ideals in Art," in *The Symbolist Movement*, p. 504.

[11]   Tawaststjerna *Sibelius. Vol. I*, p. 171.

[12]   Ibid., p. 172.

[13]   When Felix Weingartner conducted *The Swan* in Berlin in 1901, critics compared it to Böcklin's *Isle of the Dead*. See Tawaststjerna, *Sibelius. Vol. I*, pp. 161, 242–43.

[14]   Ibid., p. 159.

As György M. Vajda observes concerning the symbolist style, works of art rather than the artists themselves belong to stylistic movements.[15] Stylistic direction can therefore change within the oeuvre of a given artist, and pieces can belong to various periods. While Sibelius was actively composing, i.e., from the 1890s until the 1920s, one can distinguish varied stylistic directions and periods. A more important factor than the period, however, is the character of the work. Essentially, a clear, individual compositional style can be discerned in Sibelius's music which, at the beginning of the century, combined influences from the world of symbolist drama with other elements then in vogue, such as exoticism.

Kuolema (Death)

In the late autumn of 1903 Sibelius was working on his Violin Concerto, and he composed his music for *Kuolema* around the same time. Sibelius's brother-in-law Arvid Järnefelt asked him to compose a score for his new play *Kuolema*. In the play many elements are combined: idealism, symbolist thought, dreams, death, and a fairy-tale atmosphere. The origins of the incidental music are described in memoirs of the playwright's son Eero:

> Once my father [Arvid Järnefelt] said to him [Sibelius]:
>   "I've written a play; will you write music for it?" – "I'll think about it," Sibelius replied. So one sunny morning he came to see us and sat down by the piano. My father sat beside him and explained the play to him. Sibelius began to play. Suddenly he exclaimed: "Good Lord, what bright sunshine! I should be wearing tails, then I'd be able to play better!" And he carried on playing. The melody of *Valse triste* rang out for the first time. I was present to hear its birth.[16]

Sibelius composed six musical numbers, Op. 44, for *Kuolema*. The movements are essentially scored for strings, although there are vocal parts in the second and third movements, the fifth scene calls for bass drum, and the final piece incorporates the ringing of church bells. At the beginning of the play, a sick woman lies asleep in bed, and her small son Paavali is sitting at her bedside. In her dream, the Mother sees dancers, represented

[15] György Vajda, "The Structure of the Symbolist Movement," in *The Symbolist Movement*, p. 29.
[16] Pekka Häkli, *Arvid Järnefelt ja hänen lähimaailmansa* (Porvoo-Helsinki: WSOY,

1955), p. 337. See also Eija Kurki, "Sibelius's Music for the Play *Kuolema*," trans. Andrew Barnett, in *Jean Sibelius. Karelia, Kuolema*, BIS-CD-915 (Djursholm, 1997), pp. 9–11.

Plate 5.1   A scene from Arvid Järnefelt's *Kuolema* (*Death*) in a National Theater production of 1911 at the point in the drama immediately after Sibelius's *Valse triste* was played. Photo: Finnish National Theater archives.

in the play by a separate dance scene. According to the stage directions, "we begin to hear the quiet playing of orchestral violins which, as the lights go up, becomes clearer and finally becomes a graceful waltz." The dancers fill the room and dance with the Mother. But the dance exhausts her and, here according to the directions, "then the playing ceases as well," and the dancers start to leave the room. Waking up as the dancers are departing, the Mother dances again, as the music recommences with renewed vigor, and the room is once again filled with dancers. The music stops when Death knocks three times at the door; at that moment, the dancers disappear. Death, in the guise of her deceased husband, arrives to claim the Mother (Pl. 5.1).

Sibelius's music begins pizzicato, the chromaticism of the main theme creating a dreamy, unreal mood. The "waltz tune" mentioned in Järnefelt's report probably refers to this waltz. Some of the musical material was later to find a place in Sibelius's Seventh Symphony.[17] Sibelius later reworked this first musical number as *Valse triste*. To the

[17] Compare the printed score of the *Valse triste* (Breitkopf & Härtel, 1904), four measures before rehearsal C (mm. 37–41) with the concluding page (mm. 518–521) of the score of the Seventh Symphony (Hansen, 1925), in which the melodic lines and harmonies are almost the same.

original material he added a stretto before the final bars, and expanded the scoring to include flute, clarinet, two horns, and timpani. In the process of revision, he also made various melodic and harmonic changes. In the play, Death knocks three times at the door; in the revised *Valse triste*, these knocks are transformed into three concluding chords played by four solo violins. *Valse triste* was published in 1904 and achieved worldwide acclaim.

In the second act, Paavali has grown into a young man. Outside, a winter storm is raging, and he arrives at the cottage of an old witch, who is lying ill in bed. In the witch's cottage, Paavali does good deeds: he lights the fire, bakes bread, and so on. As a token of gratitude, the witch gives him a ring through which he can see his future bride. The scene immediately changes to a forest in summer, with the young maiden Elsa singing to herself. Sibelius's music is divided into three sections: *Moderato assai– Moderato–Poco adagio*. The first section consists of smoothly flowing harmonies assigned to muted strings. The middle section is Elsa's song, a vocalise to the syllables "eilaa, eilaa." As far as we know, Sibelius chose this "text" at the suggestion of Arvid Järnefelt, but he had used it before in his *Rakastava* suite for male choir and baritone soloist, which had been premiered in 1894.[18] The image of Elsa in the forest in Järnefelt's play and the atmosphere evoked by her song conform to the ethos of Finnish national romanticism. Paavali and Elsa fall asleep side by side in the forest. When they awake Paavali intends to continue his journey, but Elsa asks him to stay with her. At that moment a flock of cranes flies past. A single bird detaches itself from the flock and brings a baby to Elsa and Paavali, this part of the scene being reminiscent of a fairy-tale. The manuscript of the play also contains a second version in which the cranes acquire a sinister meaning: in the call of the cranes, Paavali recognizes the voice of his deceased mother. The music Sibelius provided for this scene is short, a mere nine bars; in it, the violins imitate the calls of the cranes.

The events of the third act take place some years later. Paavali's idealistic principles have conflicted with his family life with Elsa and the children. Suddenly Paavali's and Elsa's house catches fire. Paavali remains in the burning structure where, amid the flames, he reflects on his past deeds. In the fire, the ghost of his mother appears with a scythe in her hand. She has come to fetch Paavali in the same way that Paavali's father had summoned his mother at the beginning of the play. Sibelius composed this musical number for strings with bass drum. The music is characterized by the

---

[18] See Jussi Jalas, "Valse triste och Musiken till *Kuolema*," *Musikvärlden* 4 (Stockholm, 1948), p. 140.

strings' insistent rapid triplets, heard throughout the movement; fragments of a cello solo theme are heard against this agitated dramatic texture. Paavali remains in the burning house, which eventually collapses upon him. Sibelius's music at this point is brief, a mere eight bars (plus repeat). It consists of arpeggio figurations on muted violins, violas and cellos, combined with pizzicati on double basses. Once the house has collapsed in ruins, Sibelius's music – in accordance with the instructions in Järnefelt's text – calls for church bells ("campanelli di chiesa"). The stage direction reads: "the whole house crashes down with a roar. When, after a moment – once the dust has settled – the air gradually clears, a distant church bell is heard."

Järnefelt's *Kuolema*, with Sibelius's music, was premiered at the Finnish National Theater in Helsinki on 2 December 1903 with the composer himself conducting the first performance.[19] In 1906 Sibelius fashioned another independent piece from the *Kuolema* music: *Scene with Cranes* (*Scen med tranorna*). In this piece Sibelius combined the string passages which frame Elsa's "eilaa eilaa" vocalise with the calls of the cranes. The violins, which had imitated the cries of the cranes in the original incidental music, are replaced by clarinets, the tone quality being closer to the sound of cranes.[20] Sibelius conducted the *Scene with Cranes* at a concert of his own works in Vaasa on 14 December 1906 but the piece remained unpublished until 1973. When Järnefelt substantially revised the play in 1911, Sibelius's music for the 1903 production could no longer be used. Only the first act remained virtually unchanged; the second act was completely different and the third act too was subjected to major alterations. For the dance scene in the first act of the 1911 production, the published version of *Valse triste* was used. Järnefelt's revised play contains two further dance scenes to be performed by young girls. For the first dance scene in Act 2, Sibelius composed the *Valse romantique* (Op. 62b), and for the latter scene he wrote the *Canzonetta* (Op. 62a).

Belsazars gästabud (*Belshazzar's Feast*)

Hjalmar Procopé's *Belshazzar's Feast*, which appeared in 1905, revels in the type of exotic oriental themes from the Old Testament that were in vogue at the turn of the century. Based upon the feast of Belshazzar described in chapter 5 of the *Book of Daniel*, the linguistic form of Procopé's play is

[19] The premiere was a remarkable event, with both theater and music enthusiasts in the audience; see Hjalmar Lenning, "Finska teatern," *Hufvudstadsbladet* (3 December 1903). Järnefelt's *Kuolema* was performed a total of six times in 1903.

[20] In addition, the revised score calls for timpani.

Biblical, the lines themselves and the stage directions being borrowed directly from the *Book of Daniel*. The holy vessels used at the feast and the text which appeared on the wall in the middle of the celebration ("mene, mene, tekel parsin"), all are taken from the Biblical account; in accordance with the *Book of Daniel*, Belshazzar is killed on the night following the feast.[21]

The Jewish girl Leschanah, who has been chosen as Belshazzar's assassin, emerges as the principal character in Procopé's play. Another important figure is the dancing girl Khadra, who is replaced as the object of Belshazzar's affections by Leschanah. These two women competing for Belshazzar's favor are the main protagonists. Khadra – who is strikingly reminiscent of Oscar Wilde's Salomé – falls in love with the prophet (Ben Oni) and wishes to kiss him. A dancer, she performs the *Dance of Life* and *Dance of Death*, which recall Salomé's *Dance of the Seven Veils*. In terms of chronology, it is noteworthy that Wilde's play appeared in 1892; it was staged at the Finnish National Theater in 1905, and attracted much attention. 1905 was also the year in which Richard Strauss's opera *Salome* was premiered. Procopé's play was published that year and produced in the following year, 1906. Sibelius composed his music for *Belshazzar's Feast* Op. 51 in the autumn of that year.[22]

Located in Babylon, the play opens with a scene set in the middle of the city square dominated by an idol before which all must prostrate themselves. Elieser, the King's Jewish adviser, explains that the young Jewish woman Leschanah is God's choice to carry out an important task: the assassination of King Belshazzar. The Jewish prophet Ben Oni walks past the idol without bowing, and is arrested. Also present is Belshazzar's favorite slave-girl, the dancer Khadra, who falls in love with the prophet and wants him for herself, if only for one night. Khadra admires Ben Oni for his good looks and wishes to kiss him, but the prophet refuses to accept the kiss. Leschanah, the one chosen to kill Belshazzar, arrives, and Belshazzar himself also appears with a procession, carrying idols. The first musical number accompanies the procession's arrival, which is depicted by an increase in dynamic level. In this march, while the bass

[21] Hjalmar Procopé, *Belsazars gästabud*, a play in four acts (Helsingfors: Helios, 1905); see Thomas Warburton, *Åttio år finlandssvensk litteratur* (Helsingfors: Holger Schilds förlag, 1984), p. 55. With regard to *Belshazzar's Feast*, see Eija Kurki, "Belshazzar's Feast," trans. Andrew Barnett, *Jean Sibelius, Jedermann, Belshazzar's Feast,* BIS-CD-735 (Djursholm, 1995), pp. 8–10.
[22] The incidental music is scored for flute, two clarinets, two horns, various percussion instruments (bass drum, cymbals, tambourine, and triangle), and strings. In all, there are eleven musical numbers, some of which are repeated; Jean Sibelius, *Belsazar's gästabud*, manuscript, Sibelius Collection (Helsinki University Library, HYK 0881, 1906); Jean Sibelius, *Belsazar's gästabud*, copyist's score (Archives of the Swedish Theater in Helsinki, 1906).

drum, cymbals, tambourine, and triangle maintain the beat, the strings' quintuplets create an oriental atmosphere, which is intensified by the woodwind solos and the piccolo's shrill squeals. Sibelius's music evokes the oriental atmosphere of the paintings of Gustave Moreau, which, according to Philippe Jullian, dream "of an Alexandrian Orient, Hebraic or even Brahmin, bristling with domes and cabochon gems, peopled with elephants, lands over which criminal queens and perverse gods reign."[23]

The second act is set in the King's palace. In the bright, starlit night, Leschanah rests on the bed surrounded by the other slave girls. They watch the stars moving through the sky; it is as though the stars were speaking to each other, their words being like gold sparkling in the night sky. The solo flute glitters like the stars above an accompaniment from the strings. The third act is set in the King's hall, where a great banquet is taking place, the scene overflowing with fine robes, jewels, fruit, wine, and roses. Khadra then dances the *Dance of Life* on roses and tiger skins. In the incidental music, a duo of flute and clarinet alternate charmingly. Belshazzar, delighted by the dance, grants Khadra's request to drink a toast from the holy beaker of Moses. In gratitude for the granting of her wish, Khadra dances the *Dance of Death*. She opens a box, from which a glistening, writhing cobra begins to emerge; winding the snake around her neck, she dances slowly. During the dance she makes powerful move-ments as a result of which the snake wakens from its trance, bites her in the chest, and she collapses. To represent this musically, a sinuous melody in the clarinet's low register moves in a serpentine manner. At the end of the play, Leschanah assassinates Belshazzar with the sword. Leschanah then reveals to the party-goers in the neighboring hall that the Jews were behind this deed. The Jewish adviser Elieser claims that Leschanah alone is responsible for it. He pulls the sword from Belshazzar's chest and murders Leschanah with it.

In toto, the incidental music encompasses eleven musical numbers, including repetitions (Khadra's *Dance of Life* is played three times during the play, and her *Dance of Death* occurs twice). The score also contains one song in the second act: in the distance a Jewish girl is rowing a boat on the river, and her song carries through the air to the palace. Upon hearing this song, Leschanah remembers Jerusalem. The incidental music is closely bound to the text of the play, and its oriental atmosphere is clearly dis-cernible. Sibelius compiled an orchestral suite from the theater score, which he himself conducted at a concert on 25 September 1907.[24]

---

[23] Philippe Jullian, "The Esthetics of Symbolism in French Art and Belgian Art," trans. Edouard Roditi, in *The Symbolist Movement*, p. 542.

[24] The first number in the theater score is also the first item in the concert suite (*Oriental Procession*), the second number corresponds to the *Nocturne* in the suite and the original

Svanevit (Swanwhite)

In 1901 the Swedish author August Strindberg (1849–1912) wrote *Swan-white* (*Svanevit*), a symbolist fairy-tale about love, as an engagement present for the Norwegian-born actress Harriet Bosse, who was to become his third wife. In 1906, she made a guest appearance at the Swedish Theater in Helsinki, playing the role of Mélisande in Maurice Maeterlinck's symbolist play *Pelléas et Mélisande*. Sibelius had composed the incidental music for that play, and Bosse later reminisced that "As I lay on my deathbed during the last act, the orchestra played *The Death of Mélisande*. I was so moved that I cried – at every performance."[25]

In the context of these performances, Bosse made Sibelius's acquaintance and, impressed by his music for *Pelléas*, proposed to Strindberg that Sibelius write a score for *Swanwhite*, which had not yet been performed on stage.[26] Strindberg replied favorably.[27] The premiere was planned for 1907 in Stockholm, but when this proved impossible, the Swedish Theater in Helsinki decided to mount the premiere of *Swanwhite*, and commissioned Sibelius to write the music. The first performance of both Strindberg's play and Sibelius's incidental music took place in Helsinki on 8 April 1908.[28]

The central character in Strindberg's play, the fifteen-year-old Princess Swanwhite, lives in a medieval fairy-tale castle with her father (the Duke) and wicked Stepmother, who is a witch. The castle is also home to a number of the Stepmother's fantasy animals such as a peacock, and the

Jewish Girl's Song appears in the concert suite in a purely instrumental version entitled *Solitude*. Khadra's original *Dance of Life* and *Dance of Death* were combined in the movement *Khadra's Dance*, which concludes the four-movement orchestral suite. The orchestral suite thus omits three numbers from the original score: the music from the banquet scene (number 3), the music from the beginning of the fourth act where Leschanah hesitates to complete her task (number 7), and the music accompanying the dialogue between Belshazzar and his advisor Aspenasi (number 8). See Jean Sibelius, *Belsazar's Gastmahl* (Berlin: Robert Lienau, 1907).

[25] Carla Waal, *Harriet Bosse. Strindberg's Muse and Interpreter* (Carbondale and Edwardsville: Southern Illinois University Press, 1990), p. 59. See also Eija Kurki, "Swanwhite," trans. Andrew Barnett, in *Jean Sibelius, The Wood Nymph*, BIS-CD-815 (Djursholm. 1996), pp. 6–8.

[26] Letter from Harriet Bosse to Sibelius, 31 April 1906. National Archives, Helsinki.
[27] Strindberg replied in a letter to Harriet Bosse, "Sibelius is welcome to write music for Swanwhite"; see August Strindberg, *August Strindbergs Brev 15. April 1904–April 1907*, ed. Torsten Eklund, in *Strindbergssällskapets skrifter, Strindbergssällskapet* (Stockholm: Albert Bonniers Förlag, 1976), p. 147.
[28] Sibelius's original incidental music to *Swanwhite* contains fourteen musical numbers for small orchestra. The score requires flute, clarinet, two horns, triangle, timpani, organ, and strings; Jean Sibelius, *Svanehvit av Jean Sibelius*, copy of the musical manuscript (Sibelius Museum at Turku: Åbo Akademi, 1908 [original manusript is located at the Library of Congress, Washington D.C]); Jean Sibelius, *Svanehvit*, copyist's score written by Gottfried Bjurha (Sibelius Collection, HYK 0892, 1908). Only when he had reworked it into a seven-movement orchestral suite was it given the opus number 54.

Stepmother's three servant girls. When she was small, Swanwhite was promised in marriage to the Young King in the neighboring principality. When the King's ambassador, the youthful Prince, arrives to instruct Swanwhite in regal etiquette, she falls in love with him. The Young King discovers the lovers and, in his wrath, threatens to burn down the Duke's castle and kill the Prince. To avoid the Young King's revenge, the Prince flees by boat. The Duke resolves the dispute and decides that Swanwhite should be united with the Prince instead. While sailing to safety, the Prince decides to swim back to Swanwhite, but on the way he is drowned; his body is brought to Swanwhite and, with God's help, she brings the Prince back to life.

Strindberg's *Swanwhite* breathes an air of medieval fairy-tale romance, which is reminiscent of Maeterlinck's *Pelléas et Mélisande*. Both of these plays are clearly influenced by the story of Tristan and Isolde – Wagner was, after all, greatly admired by the symbolists. In Maeterlinck's play, Golaud kills Pelléas out of jealousy, and Mélisande dies after giving birth to a daughter. In Strindberg's text the Prince (who corresponds to Tristan and Pelléas) is drowned at sea, but Swanwhite (Isolde/Mélisande) restores him to life. Unlike the lovers in *Tristan und Isolde* or *Pelléas et Mélisande*, the protagonists in *Swanwhite* are united in this world, not the next.

Swanwhite was inspired by various literary sources. In a letter, Strindberg acknowledges that he was influenced by Maeterlinck, observing that "There are princes and princesses everywhere; I have long found the stepmother motif to be a constant feature in fairy-tales; and in such tales we also find dead people coming back to life."[29] *Swanwhite*'s plot is also strongly reminiscent of Maeterlinck's play *Princess Maleine*, which Strindberg had read in early Ferbuary 1901 just prior to commencing work on *Swanwhite*.[30] In Maeterlinck's play, there is also an evil Stepmother who disrupts the Prince and Princess's romance so that the Prince might marry the Stepmother's own daughter.[31] Additionally, *Swanwhite* was influenced by Rudyard Kipling's tale *The Brushwood Boy*, in which two characters meet each other only in a dream. In *Swanwhite*, the lovers also go hand in hand into the land of dreams.[32] As in Wagner's *Tristan und Isolde*, Isolde is supposed to become the wife of King Mark, who is King of a foreign power; in *Swanwhite*, too, the heroine is

[29] August Strindberg, *Öppna Brev till Intima Teatern. Samlade skrifter femtionde delen* (Stockholm: Albert Bonniers Förlag, 1919), pp. 300–301.
[30] Michael Meyer, *Strindberg. A Biography* (London: Secker & Warburg, 1985), p. 417.
[31] Ibid; see also August Strindberg, *Ur ockulta Dagboken. Äktenskapet med Harriet Bosse*, ed. Torsten Eklund (Stockholm: Albert Bonniers Förlag, 1963), p. 20.
[32] Strindberg, *August Strindbergs Brev 14. 1901–Mars 1904*, ed. Torsten Eklund (Stockholm: Albert Bonniers Förlag, 1974), pp. 31–32.

betrothed to the king of a neighboring country. In *Tristan und Isolde*, great significance is attached to the sea journey and maritime environment; likewise, in *Swanwhite*, the Prince comes from across the sea and drowns towards the end of the play. Perhaps Strindberg also borrowed this motif from the Swedish folk-song *Konungabarnen* (*The King's Children*), in which a prince sinks beneath the waves and a princess kisses the mouth of the drowned prince.[33] To bring the Prince back to life, Swanwhite also intends to kiss him but, on the advice of the Stepmother, whispers in his ear and thereby resurrects him. In Wagner's opera, Tristan and Isolde are finally united in death. In Strindberg's play, too, Swanwhite wishes to die with the Prince. But the Duke tells Swanwhite that death cannot join lovers, and that she and the Prince can be together only in life. Then, Swanwhite petitions God's help in sparing the Prince's life, and thereby realizes Strindberg's concept of love, which combines romantic with divine love, i.e., with Christian fellowship, *agape*.

At the beginning of the play, the deceased mothers of Swanwhite and the Prince appear before Swanwhite in the form of swans, their assumption of swan form recalling Wagner's *Lohengrin*.[34] Another important connection between *Swanwhite* and *Lohengrin* concerns the secret of the Prince's name. Lohengrin forbids Elsa to ask about his origins; similarly, Swanwhite asks her father what the Prince's name is, and he answers: "My child, you must not ask him or anybody else, for it has been foretold that whoever can say his name must love him." Swanwhite's mother combs her daughter's hair, washes her feet with tears and places a fresh white dress on her bed. The mothers of the Prince and Swanwhite arrange the forthcoming union of their children.[35]

The wicked Stepmother and her three servant girls arrive to interrupt the encounter between Swanwhite and the Prince. The Stepmother orders the Prince to sleep in the castle tower. Swanwhite's dead mother flies past the castle in the shape of a swan. In Sibelius's incidental music

[33] Gunnar Ollén, "Kommentarer: Tillkomst och mottagande Kronbruden-Svanevit," in *August Strindbergs Samlade Verk 45. Kronbruden. Svanevit* (Stockholm: Stockholm University, 1990), p. 251.

[34] The mothers are thus also in the form of angels, which are common in symbolist painting. The role of angels is significant in the pictures by the great French and Belgian symbolists. Angels had previously figured prominently in the work of Charles Baudelaire and Emanuel Swedenborg; see Jullian, *The Esthetics of Symbolism*, p. 541.

[35] The mothers' swan forms are also associated with the mythological theme of Zeus and Leda, which was subsequently incorporated into many folk tales; see Anna Birgitta Rooth, "Motive aus Griechischen Mythen in einigen Europäischen Märchen," in *Antiker Mythos in unseren Märchen*. Veröffentlichungen der Europäischen Märchengesellschaft, Band 6, ed. Wolgdietlich Siegmund (Kassel: Erich Röth-Verlag, 1984), p. 40. Leda was the wife of King Tyndareus of Sparta, of whose five children Zeus fathered two. Zeus approached Leda in the form of a swan and ravished her.

Plate 5.2   Sibelius's daughter Ruth Snellman in the role of Swanwhite in a 1930 Finnish-language production of *Swanwhite* at the National Theater in Helsinki. Photo: Finnish National Theater archives

(the third number), the Swan-mother's flight is represented musically by a sustained E major chord. At first, the chord is allocated to the strings and, by adding wind instruments on the last quarter note of the first bar, Sibelius creates the impression of something approaching. This effect is further emphasized by the dynamics. The chord begins pianissimo and gradually increases in intensity, and then, towards the end of the second bar, it returns to the original *pp* marking. In this way the music creates the illusion of the Swan-mother flying past. In the play, a few lines after the chord sounds, comes the following exchange:

PRINCE: Did you see the swan?
SWANWHITE: No, but I heard it! It was my mother!

Plate 5.2 shows one scene of the play; Sibelius's daughter Ruth Snellman in the role of Swanwhite in a 1930 Finnish-language production of *Swanwhite* at the National Theater in Helsinki. In this way, Sibelius's music associates the flight of the Swan-mother with the E major chord. This link having been established, when the chord recurs it refers to swans. Thus, the music depicting the Swan-mother's flight is integrated into the very fabric of the story; it belongs to the world of the characters' imagination, and they make remarks about it.

In the play there are a number of fairy-tale objects, among them musical instruments, a magic mirror, a poppy, a feather, a pumpkin, and moving walls. The musical instruments include a magic horn and a harp, which assist Swanwhite. She blows her magic horn to summon help from her father, the Duke. The central elements of Sibelius's music at this point are a clarinet solo and the horns' short signals. As Swanwhite blows her own horn, and another horn answers her, the timpani rumble in the background.[36]

The magic harp belongs to Swanwhite's Swan-mother. The heroine's wicked Stepmother has not allowed her to wash her feet, brush her hair, or wear clean clothes. At the beginning of the second act, while Swanwhite lies asleep, her Swan-mother arrives, carrying the magic harp that plays itself. She combs her daughter's hair, washes her feet, and brings her a fresh, white gown. The stage directions read:

> Now the swan flies over the rose grove outside. A trumpet chord is heard, just like the call of migrating swans. Then Swanwhite's mother is seen, dressed in white, outside the gates. On one arm she has a swan costume, and on the other a small golden harp. She hangs the swan costume on the gate, which opens and closes itself. The mother enters the room and places the harp on the table. She glances around the room and espies Swanwhite. Then the harp starts to play: the girls' lamps are extinguished one after another, the most distant first, and the chamber doors close, the most distant first. The golden clouds regain their lustre. The mother lights the candles and goes to the bed, where she falls to her knees. The harp plays during the following scene. The Mother rises, lifts Swanwhite from the bed, sits her down in a big chair without waking her.

Swanwhite's mother's harp is a miraculous instrument because when it begins to play itself remarkable things immediately happen: the lamps held by the girls watching over Swanwhite are extinguished and the chamber doors close. Sibelius's incidental music is based on rising arpeggiated pizzicato figures on muted strings. While the pizzicato figures support two short, high-pitched and easily distinguishable flute solos, at the end of the piece there is a brief clarinet solo in the lower register. Interestingly, Sibelius's musical number does not contain a harp; instead, the string pizzicato figures produce harp-like sonorities. According to the play's text, Swanwhite's mother cries while washing her daughter's feet, the short, melancholy flute solos and the clarinet solo effectively depicting the mother's mood.

[36] Number 12. (This and all further such references are to the copyist's score by Bjurha.)

In the quiet beginning of the play (Act 1, Scene 2), Swanwhite awaits the arrival of the Prince. This scene (without dialogue) contains indications of stage effects: the wind whistles outside, the peacock shakes its wings and tail. The recurring note E in the flute and clarinet parts represents the peacock's cries, and the transition-like string figurations depict the rosewood blowing in the wind.[37]

The Stepmother offers the Prince the hand of her own daughter Magdalena in marriage. As a result of the recent dispute, the Prince decides to accept her in the place of Swanwhite and, straight away, they celebrate the wedding. The stage directions read as follows:

STEPMOTHER: Have my powers failed me? Or what has happened? . . .
        Where is the bride?

(Four girls enter from behind; they are carrying baskets of white and pink roses; music is heard from above. The girls approach the bed and scatter the roses there. Behind them come two knights with their visors down. They take the Prince by the hand and lead him towards the background; from there the wrong Magdalena comes towards them, led by two women. The bride is thickly veiled. With a movement of her hand the stepmother tells everybody else to leave except the bride and groom; she herself is the last to exit, having first drawn the curtains and closed the gates.)

The stage directions call for the bride to be thickly veiled, this disguise leading the other characters and the audience to assume that the bride is Magdalena. But Magdalena does not in fact appear in the *dramatis personae*; instead, she is only alluded to by the other characters. For this wedding scene, Sibelius followed Strindberg's instructions and composed music for a scene without dialogue. Strindberg's directions indicate: "music is heard from above." The mood of the wedding scene between the Prince and his bride is dejected. The melody is reminiscent of a wedding waltz, but the "low-spirited" E flat minor key reveals that something is terribly amiss. The subdued atmosphere is created by the strings, which are muted throughout the movement, and by the *pianissimo* horns. The string texture is dominated by a syncopated waltz melody. Sibelius has, in consequence, interpreted Magdalena as an actual character in the play, even though – according to Strindberg's text – the bride is in fact "the wrong Magdalena," i.e., Swanwhite.

Before the planned premiere of *Swanwhite* in 1907, Strindberg added additional text at the beginning of the third act. In this scene, the young King, who is to become Swanwhite's husband, meets her but does not con-

---

[37] Number 2.

sider her to be a suitable candidate for a marriage. He finds Swanwhite unattractive, and he sets her free. Indeed, the King intends to explain his decision to the Prince, and he exits. Immediately, the Prince enters from a secret passage and Swanwhite runs to him. Sibelius's musical number is made up of two themes and the key alternates between A minor and C major. The first theme is assigned to the strings and is largely based on rising scale figures. The second theme consists of a note reiterated three times and followed by two quarters and an eighth. This theme, in the flute and violins, is gentle in character; its lightness comes especially from the flute's staccato figures. According to Strindberg's text, the magic harp plays itself. Sibelius's music follows Strindberg's instructions except that in this case, as before, he employs string pizzicato instead of a harp. The second theme's gentle staccato flute rhythms emphasize Swanwhite's happy reunion with the Prince. Very similar musical material was later to find a place in Sibelius's Fifth Symphony.[38]

The play ends with a scene in which all the characters fall on their knees in gratitude for this miraculous resurrection, praising God. The music Sibelius provided for the play's culmination is in C major, the use of simple thematic material effectively creating a mood of devotion. Just over a week after the first performance, Sibelius added an organ part to the last two numbers in his score.[39]

In the autumn of 1908, Sibelius reworked the incidental music to *Swanwhite* into a seven-movement orchestral suite for concert use.[40] Combining several numbers from the original score, the orchestral suite includes almost all of the material from that score. In addition, he expanded the orchestration: for example, the suite calls for a harp as well as four horns. In the suite, an entire movement is devoted to Swanwhite's mother's fantasy creature – the peacock – the rapping of whose beak is rendered musically by castanets. Although the suite is conceived for a symphony orchestra, Sibelius reduces the brass section to only four horns. Sibelius's use of the horns is inspired by Swanwhite's magic horn. Similarly, the castanets are explicitly mentioned in Strindberg's stage directions in the scene with the peacock:

[38] Compare the printed score of the *Swanwhite* Suite (Lienau, 1909), second movement *The Harp*, eight measures before rehearsal letter D (mm. 35–41) with the score of the Fifth Symphony (Hansen, 1921), second movement *Andante mosso, quasi Allegretto*, rehearsal A (mm. 20–27).

[39] Number 14.
[40] Kari Kilpeläinen, *Tutkielmia Jean Sibeliuksen käsikirjoituksista.* Studia Musicologica Universitatis Helsingiensis III (Helsinki: Helsingin Yliopiston Musiikkitieteen laitos, 1992), p. 48.

(The curtain behind which the peacock is sitting moves, and immediately a strange noise is heard, just like castanets.)

PRINCE: What was that?

SWANWHITE: It's Pavo [the peacock]. Do you think it can understand what we are saying?

PRINCE: Who knows?

SWANWHITE: Well, what's your name?

(The peacock raps with its beak once again.)

It is remarkable that, in the original theater score, Sibelius did not make use of the castanets, although he incorporated them in the concert suite. In the movement entitled "The Peacock," the castanets are combined with the pizzicato string chords, which depict the Prince.

Sibelius's process of composition

The incidental music for *Swanwhite* also illuminates Sibelius's process of composition in an interesting manner. Kari Kilpeläinen has shown that some motives derive from ideas that originated earlier. For example, one sketch for the second musical number ("Commodo. Tyst duvan min prins kommer") dates from 1903–04. In the tenth musical number, Sibelius used several sketches from the years 1892–93 and 1899–1903.[41] In view of Sibelius's synthetic way of composing, it is not unusual for musical ideas originally intended for one work to be employed in an another. Additionally, some themes were not originally intended for use in any specific work, but were simply drawn from the sketchbooks. In this way Sibelius was able to exploit usable motives when the opportunity arose. This manner of composing proved economical and also convenient for occasional pieces.[42]

This "migration" and "cross-pollination" of ideas naturally leads one to consider the relationship between Sibelius's theater music and his other works. As I have pointed out, there is a link between *Swanwhite* and the Fifth Symphony (see note 38). If his symphonic music was inspired by an extra-musical source (such as the text of a play), did Sibelius perceive his symphonies as embodying something extra-musical? More specifically, did Sibelius intend that the *Andante mosso* theme in the Fifth Symphony should evoke the scene in *Swanwhite* in which he employs this flute motive? The motive appears in the theater score precisely at the point where, in Strindberg's text, Swanwhite and the Prince are reunited after having been apart. Their reunion is joyful, a fact emphasized by the

[41] Ibid., p. 125.   [42] Ibid., p. 150.

light flute figures. Therefore, the alert and knowledgeable listener would tend to associate these motivically related passages, transferring the semantic of "joyful reunion" from the incidental music to the symphony.

It is noteworthy that the borrowing was unidirectional: Sibelius re-used material from stage works in his symphonies, but he did not re-cycle material from his symphonies in his stage works. Thus, from the functional music designed for the use in the theater, Sibelius derived themes for his major orchestral works, especially the Fifth and Seventh Symphonies. By deploying material from *Kuolema* – specifically the *Valse triste* with its connotations of death – in the Seventh Symphony, Sibelius may have been deliberately assigning this symphony a valedictory character (see note 17).

Nature was vitally important for Sibelius: the forests and various animals (especially cranes and swans) figure prominently in his life and work. This is apparent from various diary entries:

> Today, just before ten-to-eleven, I saw sixteen swans. One of the greatest experiences in life: Oh God, what beauty: they circled over me for a long time. Disappeared into the hazy sun like a silver ribbon, which glittered from time to time. Their cries were of the same woodwind timbre as the cranes but without any tremolo. The swans are closer to trumpets though there is an element of the sarrusophone. A low suppressed memory of a small child's cry. Nature's mystery and life's melancholy! The Fifth Symphony's finale theme. The trumpet will bind it together!! . . . This must now come to me which has so long resonated in the air. Have been transported today, 21st April 1915.[43]

Sibelius's thoughts on Nature's mystery and, in particular, the remark "Have been transported" bring to mind Charles Baudelaire's poem *Correspondance*: "Nature is a temple . . ." A few days later Sibelius expanded his previous comment:

> The swans are always in my thoughts and give life its lustre. It is curious that nothing in the whole world, be it art, literature or music, has anything like the same effect on me as these swans, cranes and wild geese. Their sound and their very being. – *Apropos* the symphonies. They are my *credo* as I perceived it at various stages in my life. Which is why they are all so different. *Nos mutamur in temporibus.* Or better still: *tempora mutantur et nos in illis mutamur.*[44]

And what was Sibelius's attitude to symbolism? The following remarks to Santeri Levas illuminate his approach. His comments betray his belief in the symbolist notion of a connection between symbols and the world at

---

[43] Tawaststjerna, *Jean Sibelius. Vol. III*, p. 49.   [44] Ibid., pp. 49–50.

large, and also the idea that, with the aid of symbols, one can achieve things that cannot be consciously understood:

> "As I get older, I see all the more clearly that everything is a symbol," Sibelius once said. "Whoever knows how to interpret the symbols will understand all the secrets of the world." He had told me previously that a man can further music more with the aid of symbols than with reason alone and that, for this very reason, Freemasonry had been of great value to him.[45]

[45] Santeri Levas, *Jean Sibelius. Muistelma suuresta ihmisestä* (Porvoo-Juva: WSOY, 1992 [1957/60]), p. 453.

6 Sibelius's symphonic ballad *Skogsrået*: biographical and programmatic aspects of his early orchestral music

Veijo Murtomäki

The performance in 1996 of Sibelius's two neglected and "rediscovered" works entitled *Skogsrået* – one a large-scale symphonic ballad and the other a melodrama – was a sensation.[1] It was clear that the orchestral ballad was a masterpiece whose inclusion in the canon of Sibelius's major orchestral works would decisively change our view of the composer. At the same time the obvious question was posed: why should a major work like *Skogsrået* have languished unperformed for decades?

With regard to his music from his student period in the 1880s and his early career in the 1890s, Sibelius's later position was both complicated and critical. Erik Furuhjelm's biography (1916), John Rosas's study (1961), and the first volume (1965) of Erik Tawaststjerna's magnificent five-volume biography of Sibelius provided some information about Sibelius's student works, although the composer himself prevented performances of these pieces during his lifetime.[2] But only when the huge collection of Sibelius's manuscripts, containing more than 10,000 pages, was donated by the Sibelius family to Helsinki University Library in 1982 was it finally possible to examine and evaluate these early pieces. The sheer volume of compositions – primarily chamber music – and their generally high quality was unexpected. Most of these pieces were composed during Sibelius's student years in Helsinki in 1885–89 and Berlin or Vienna in 1889–91.

Especially problematic was Sibelius's relation to his early orchestral and other works (1891–99), i.e., those pieces that predate the First Symphony. Sibelius's first orchestral pieces from his Vienna period, the

---

[1] The concert was given on 9 February 1996 by The Lahti Symphony Orchestra under its artistic director Osmo Vänskä, now also chief conductor of the BBC Scottish Symphony Orchestra.

[2] Erik Furuhjelm, *Jean Sibelius. Hans tondiktning och drag ur hans liv* (Borgå:

Holger Schildt, 1916); John Rosas, *Otryckta kammarmusikverk av Jean Sibelius* (Åbo: Åbo Akademi, 1961); Erik Tawaststjerna, *Jean Sibelius. Vol. I* (Helsinki: Otava, 1965), trans. Robert Layton in *Sibelius, Vol. I, 1865–1905* (London: Faber, 1976).

Overture in E Major and the *Scène de ballet* (both composed in 1891), were probably never played again after their initial performances; they remained unpublished and without opus numbers. Like these pieces, Sibelius's first large-scale work, *Kullervo* (1892), was never performed again in its entirety after its initial successes; it too remained unpublished but nevertheless retained its place in the canon of works assigned opus numbers as Opus 7. *En saga* Op. 9 (1892) was played a few times during the 1890s, but only its revision in 1902 saved it from the destiny of its predecessors. Scenic music to illustrate the history of Karelia in several tableaux (1893) was partly destroyed by the composer during the 1940s, whereas the *Karelia* Overture and a brief, yet extremely popular *Karelia* Suite of the original music were published in 1906 and assigned the opus numbers 10 and 11.[3] In spite of a half dozen well-received performances, *Skogsrået* (1894/5) was left without an opus number and languished unpublished.

The slow publication history of the four *Lemminkäinen* Legends Op. 22 suggests that Sibelius was unsure about the true value of these early works, especially since the leading music critic Karl Flodin had harshly attacked them.[4] Composed in 1893–95, and revised in 1897 and 1900, only the two last movements (*The Swan of Tuonela* and *Lemminkäinen's Return*) were published in 1901, whereas the longer and more substantial two first movements (*Lemminkäinen and the Maidens of the Island* and *Lemminkäinen in Tuonela*) were not published until 1954.[5] Sibelius's only

[3] Although Sibelius destroyed almost one half of the original orchestral score of the *Karelia* music, he "forgot" that the orchestral parts were still around, even if some of these, too, have been lost. The orchestral score was reconstructed by Kalevi Kuosa, the former general manager of the Turku Philharmonic, for the Sibelius centennial in 1965. However, the missing flute, viola, violoncello, and doublebass parts in tableaux 2, 3, 5, 6, and 7/8 had to be completed. This was accomplished in 1997 by two Finnish composers working independently, Kalevi Aho and Jouni Kaipainen. These two slightly different versions are both available on record: Aho's version has been released by BIS (CD-915), and that by Kaipainen by Ondine (ODE 913-2).

[4] Flodin wrote in *Nya Pressen* (3 November 1897) after having heard the revised version of the *Lemminkäinen* Legends that "it leaves mixed feelings, painful and difficult to put into words since they have so little in common with the aesthetic feelings of pleasure that all art and above all music should prompt . . . music like the *Lemminkäinen* portraits depresses me, makes me miserable, exhausted and apathetic"; quoted in Tawaststjerna–Layton, *Sibelius. Vol. I*, p. 196.

[5] In the original version of the *Lemminkäinen* Legends the movements were ordered by a rising key disposition in minor thirds: first movement, *Lemminkäinen and the Maidens of Saari* (E♭ major); second movement, *Lemminkäinen in Tuonela* (F♯ minor); third movement, *The Swan of Tuonela* (A minor); and fourth movement, *Lemminkäinen's Return* (C minor followed by E♭ major). However, when the complete score was published in 1954, Sibelius changed the order of the second and third movements, thus creating a symphony-like tempo structure following the standard movement pattern fast–slow–moderately fast–fast.

opera, *The Maiden in the Tower,* had to wait almost a century after its premiere in 1896 for its next performance; it remained unpublished and without opus number. Of the seven musical numbers composed in 1899 for the historical tableaux for the *Press Celebrations* illustrating Finnish history three were rejected. The last one was preserved with the new title *Finlandia* Op. 26 and three more numbers were published as the *Scènes historiques* No. I, Op. 25 (1912).[6]

Thus the history of those compositions stemming from the initial phase of Sibelius's career, often referred to as his "nationalist period," is chequered. In view of the vicissitudes of these early works, it is unsurprising, then, that there are different theories and explanations as to why it was so difficult for Sibelius to accept his output from the 1890s. Perhaps he denigrated the pieces of this period as initial "essays" in orchestral composition and, consequently, inferior to his more mature orchestral works. It is true, for instance in *Kullervo,* that his orchestral writing is occasionally unpractical or clumsy in comparison to his later masterful orchestration.

The second possible reason that Sibelius turned his back on his early works is that his style changed in the first decade of the twentieth century. With the revisions of *En saga* (1892/1902) and the Violin Concerto (1904/05), he was distancing himself from the nineteenth-century romantic style and trying to find a new, more classical way of composing. According to this explanation, Sibelius sought to reorient himself stylistically away from Wagnerism and the New German School;[7] those composers who had espoused these ideals in Bohemia, Russia and Scandinavia tended to be associated with national romantic schools and denigrated as folklorists. Although Sibelius's early career can be linked with Finnish national strivings for independence and his output associated with Finnish history, cultural tradition, and landscape, in his later period Sibelius wished to be appreciated as more than just a local hero (*Heimatkünstler*); by writing "absolute" symphonies, he wanted to be considered an international composer. He articulated this aspiration unequivocally in his now famous speech from 1896 written in connection with the competition for a lectureship at the University of Helsinki: "We see how fruitful an influence folk music is in a composer's upbringing . . . in this lies much of his

[6] *The Press Celebrations Music* is available in its original and complete form on Ondine record (ODE 913-2), and now also on BIS record (CD-1115).

[7] This explanation is given by Michael Mäckelmann, "Sibelius und die Programmusik. Eine Studie zu seinen Tondichtungen und Symphonien," in *Programmusik, Studien zu Begriff und Geschichte einer umstrittenen Gattung.* Hamburger Jahrbuch für Musikwissenschaft Band 6, ed. Constantin Floros, Hans-Joachim Marx and Peter Petersen (Hamburg: Laaber-Verlag, 1983), p. 127.

originality. In his work, however, he must free himself particularly as far as his expressive means are concerned from any suggestion of the parochial."[8]

In addition to his development as a composer and his stylistical evolution, biographical factors also influenced Sibelius's later attitude towards his early works. During his student period in Helsinki, Berlin, and Vienna (1885–91) and early career in Helsinki in the 1890s, Sibelius pursued a Bohemian life style, spending whole days and nights in restaurants and hotels, drinking excessively and succumbing to the temptations of the flesh. He was forced to confess to Aino, his fiancée, in a letter from Vienna (13 December 1890) that "I have all the propensities towards vice that most men have and perhaps more than most." In another letter from Vienna (8 February 1891) he reveals that "I am not an innocent, though this is the result of circumstances rather than wantonness."[9] When composing his only opera, *The Maiden in the Tower*, he wrote in the sketchbook (22 August 1896): "Tried to compose but it has not been with *schwung*... Perhaps my excesses *in Venere* or *in Baccho* have produced a spiritual paralysis."[10]

The autobiographical novel *En bok om en människa* (*A Book about a Man*) written in 1891 by Adolf Paul, one of Sibelius's closest friends, described the life of the composer Sillén (=Sibelius), who praised Woman in restaurants with numerous toasts – and spoilt his credit![11] Furthermore, the painting *Symposion* (1894) by Axel Gallén-Kallela, in which the famous young geniuses of Finnish culture (the artist himself, conductor Robert Kajanus, Sibelius, and probably composer Oskar Merikanto) were portrayed as drowsy after a heavy drinking bout, made an unfavorable impression. Now Sibelius was harshly criticised by Flodin, who early on recognized Sibelius's enormous talent but accused him of composing in a way which was too "pathological." He might have stigmatized this phase of Sibelius's career as the "Symposium period," thus echoing the criticism Albert Edelfet directed towards Gallén-Kallela's *Symposion* painting.[12] Also Richard Faltin, who had a much milder temperament and was more understanding of Sibelius, described Sibelius's compositions from that time as belonging to the "composer's *Sturm und Drang* period."[13]

---

[8] Tawaststjerna–Layton, *Sibelius. Vol. I*, p. 191.

[9] Ibid., pp. 82–83.

[10] Ibid., p. 183.

[11] Ibid., pp. 100–101. See also Adolf Paul, *En bok om en människa* (Stockholm: Albert B. Bonniers Förlag, 1891), especially pp. 193 and 197–200, where Sillén is characterized as the "most refined skirt-chaser of all of us" (den mest raffinerade flickjägare af alla) and Sillén proclaims, after proposing toasts, that "woman is for me like a frivolous book" (kvinnan är för mig detsamma som en lätsinnig bok).

[12] Tawaststjerna–Layton, *Sibelius. Vol. I*, p. 196.

[13] Quoted from Eija Kurki, "Sibeliuksen Metsänhaltijoiden tähänastiset seikkailut", *Musiikki* 26/3 (1996), p. 357.

But the image of a careless Bohemian, drunkard, and libertine was incompatible with Sibelius's increasing prominence as a national hero. Although he never completely abandoned his Bohemian way of life, he sought to make a more positive impression and settled down in 1904 outside of Helsinki in Tuusula in a new house built for his family, which was called Ainola. If the works from the 1890s were connected with libertinism and probably reflected some of the composer's more dubious adventures, it is not difficult to understand why Sibelius, now the husband and national hero, wished to distance himself from his earlier pieces. Perhaps, he had "revealed himself" too much, as he said about *En saga*.[14] As I will suggest in my study of its genesis and poetical-programmatic content, *Skogsrået* belongs to the same category of confessional works.

I

Although *Skogsrået* later fell into oblivion, Sibelius nevertheless continued to think highly of this symphonic ballad, which was, in its original form, perhaps his longest single orchestral work.[15] It was performed for the first time on 17 April 1895, and also a few days later. Sibelius planned further performances for 1897 in Helsinki, but they were cancelled for unknown reasons; instead, two performances were realized the same year in Turku (on 29 and 30 December 1897).[16] That Sibelius still valued this piece is revealed by the fact that he programmed it for the same concert held on 26 April 1899 in which his First Symphony was premiered together with the *Song of the Athenians*. He planned to revise the orchestral ballad in 1911 but abandoned the idea of reworking, assigning the opus number 15 to its sister work, a melodrama with the same title.[17]

It has been widely but incorrectly believed that the ballad was forgotten after 1899: Sibelius selected *Skogsrået* for a Pohjola-Norden ceremony

[14] Santeri Levas, *Jean Sibelius. Muistelma suuresta ihmisestä* (Porvoo, Helsinki, Juva: WSOY, 1986 [1957/60]), p. 116. Abbreviated English translation by Percy M. Young, *Jean Sibelius. A Personal Portrait* (London: J. M. Dent, 1972 [2nd edn.]).
[15] In the original part of Violin I (1895 or 1894?) there is a handwritten marking by a player: "23 minutes." See Kari Kilpeläinen, *The Jean Sibelius Musical Manuscripts at the* *Helsinki University Library. A Complete Catalogue* (Wiesbaden, Leipzig, Paris: Breitkopf & Härtel, 1991), p. 25.
[16] Kurki, "Sibeliuksen Metsänhaltijoiden," p. 353.
[17] Kari Kilpeläinen, *Tutkielmia Jean Sibeliuksen käsikirjoituksista*. Studia Musicologica Universitatis Helsingiensis 3 (Helsinki: Helsingin yliopiston musiikkitieteen laitos, 1992), p. 170.

held at the Helsinki Congress Center on 27 October 1936.[18] Why, when it had languished unplayed for thirty-seven years, did Sibelius choose this piece for the occasion, especially when he had been commissioned to write a new work for the festivities?[19] The explanation seems obvious: since he had stopped composing, it was reasonable to select a composition based on a Swedish text and treating Scandinavian mythology. Nothing had flowed from his pen after opus 117, the Suite for Violin and String Orchestra (composed in 1929), except some minor works: *Funeral* Op. 112, No. 2 in memory of his close friend Axel Gallén-Kallela in 1931; two further pieces, Op. 113, Nos. 8–9, were to be composed for *Masonic Ritual Music* in 1946. And there is still a further possible reason why Sibelius returned to *Skogsrået* later in life: at the age of seventy he might have been attracted to the piece because of its connection with his youth. Furthermore, by 1936, as a world-famous composer, Sibelius could now safely risk presenting one of his "youthful sins," just as he had released the first two movements of *Lemminkäinen*, allowing them to be played again in 1935 and revised later in 1939 for publication, which, however, was delayed by the war for a further fifteen years.[20]

The way in which the ballad was composed remains somewhat obscure. Since the melodrama version was given its first performance on 9 March 1895, more than one month before the ballad, some scholars have believed that the melodrama was finished first and then Sibelius quickly prepared the orchestral version, elongating and elaborating the melodrama's material.[21] Indeed, Sibelius later told Karl Ekman that he composed these two pieces in that order.[22] However, it seems improbable, if not totally impossible, that an orchestral composition of this length could have been written in such a short period of time; rather the melodrama seems to be a compressed version of the orchestral work, presenting the four different principal sections of the ballad in a compact and simplified form without any bridges and repetitions. Moreover, since Sibelius selected the melodrama version based on a poem by the Swedish writer Viktor Rydberg to

[18] See Kurki, "Sibeliuksen Metsänhaltijoiden," pp. 353–355; Pohjola-Norden, formed during the 1920s, was a society of Scandinavian countries for the purpose of maintaining and strengthening cultural and economic relationships between Sweden, Norway, Denmark, Finland, and Iceland and increasing common solidarity among them. At the ceremony in 1936 in Helsinki it was planned, in addition to speeches, to give performances of Nordic music and the national anthems of all the countries involved.

[19] Ibid.
[20] Tuomas Kinberg, "Jean Sibelius. Sinfoninen runo *Skogsrået* eli Metsänhaltija (*Ballade pour orchestre*)" (M.Mus thesis, Helsinki University, 1996), p. 135.
[21] Tawaststjerna–Layton, *Sibelius. Vol. I*, p. 163.
[22] Karl Ekman, *Jean Sibelius. Taiteilijan elämä ja persoonallisuus* (Helsinki: Otava, 1935), p. 126. English translation by Edward Birse, *Jean Sibelius. His Life and Personality* (Westport, CT: Greenwood Press, 1976 [1938]).

be performed at a lottery to benefit the Finnish Theater (which was a bastion of Finnish national ideology), this choice can be explained by the fact that it was easier for Sibelius to produce the melodrama version as an arrangement of a pre-existent large orchestral work, and not vice versa. Perhaps the strongest argument for the genetic priority of the ballad can be found in the manuscript: on the autograph piano part of the melodrama version there is a handwritten note by the composer, "Melodrama arr. [for] String Orchestra, 2 Horns . . ."; in addition to this, on the autograph fair copy of the orchestral score, Sibelius in old age wrote on both the title page and page 26 the year "1894."[23] Finally, Sibelius's diary entries and letters from Bayreuth and Munich to his wife Aino during the summer 1894 disclose, as we will see, that he began working on a symphonic poem, i.e. *Skogsrået*, in that period and the piece was finished probably by the end of 1894, or at the latest by early 1895.

Sibelius departed for Bayreuth at the beginning of July 1894; the first opera he heard was *Parsifal*. His report on this experience in a letter of 19 July 1894 was highly enthusiastic: "Heard *Parsifal*. Nothing in the world has ever made so overwhelming an impression on me. All my innermost heartstrings throbbed."[24] As we know, he was then in the midst of planning his own opera *The Building of the Boat* and had gone to Bayreuth seeking inspiration. The previous year, he had been an eager supporter of Wagner's ideas and expressed his faith in a letter to J. H. Erkko (on 8 July 1893) using phrases taken almost literally from Wagner's *Oper und Drama*: "I believe that music alone, that is to say absolute music, is in itself not enough . . . Music is like a woman, it is only through man that she can give birth and that man is poetry."[25] Before leaving for Bayreuth Sibelius had purchased the piano scores of *Tannhäuser* and *Lohengrin*, and borrowed the orchestral score of *Die Walküre* from Aino Ackté, the future Finnish star soprano of the Paris Grand Opéra and the favorite Salome of Strauss. During his one-month visit to Bayreuth and Munich he heard almost all of the Wagner operas.

At the same time, he was trying to compose his own opera, although on 10 August he had to confess to only "some progress in instrumentation" of the music that had already been written.[26] More significantly,

---

[23] Kilpeläinen, *The Jean Sibelius Musical Manuscripts*, p. 26; *Tutkielmia Jean Sibeliuksen käsikirjoituksista*, p. 170.

[24] Tawaststjerna–Layton, *Sibelius. Vol. I*, p. 153.

[25] Ibid., p. 141. Compare Sibelius's expression with Wagner's own words: "aller musikalische Organismus ist seiner Natur nach aber – ein weiblicher . . . die zeugende Kraft liegt außer ihm . . . Die Musik ist die Gebärerin, der Dichter der Erzeuger . . . Die Musik ist ein Weib." In Richard Wagner, *Oper und Drama* (Stuttgart: Philipp Teclam Jun., 1984 [1852]), pp. 116–18.

[26] Tawaststjerna–Layton, *Sibelius. Vol. I*, p. 156.

however, he had begun doubting Wagner's way of composing (letter on 28 July): "Wagner's music . . . is altogether too well calculated . . . Besides his musical ideas themselves strike me as manufactured (not fresh)."[27] By 22 August, Sibelius's Wagner crisis was over: "I am no longer a Wagnerite. . . . I must be led by my inner voices."[28] That Wagner's music strongly influenced Sibelius is more than obvious: Wagner's orchestral coloring, elements of his harmonic vocabulary, and above all the *Tristan* chord can be found in Sibelius's early works. *Skogsrået*, the *Lemminkäinen* Suite, and *Pohjola's Daughter* would have been different compositions if Sibelius had not been possessed by Wagner's music. As I shall attempt to show, *Skogsrået* with its eroticism and close connection between words and music betrays Wagner's influence.

But now Sibelius turned away from the opera to the symphonic poem and the ideas of Liszt. He wrote home (on 19 August): "I have found my old self again, musically speaking. Many things are now clear to me: really I am a tone painter and poet. Liszt's view of music is the one to which I am closest. Hence my interest in the symphonic poem. *I'm working on a theme that I'm very pleased with* [my emphasis]."[29] What was this new theme, which had sparked such enthusiasm? It has been generally believed that Sibelius was referring to his *Lemminkäinen* Legends.[30] This may be the case; however, there are three passages in his letters that suggest he was alluding to *Skogsrået* instead. In the midst of his opera crisis he had sketched another "libretto" or scenario for a *verismo* opera. The passage is worth quoting in full because of its importance for the genesis of *Skogsrået* and Sibelius's ideology at this point in his career (on 28 July):

> It [the libretto] is set in the seventeenth century. A young student is engaged to a peasant girl. *He takes himself off abroad* and there sees a dancer with whom he falls in love; *he is unfaithful* [my emphases]. On his return he describes the dance and the dancer so vividly that his fiancée suspects what has happened and is overcome by sorrow. However *they meet later on in the forest* [!?]. *In the last act he meets a funeral procession* [my emphases] and learns that it is his fiancée who is being buried. And her father turns on him and says: you are to blame![31]

On 10 August he wrote to Aino: "I have done *a piece in the style of a march* (quite new and short even though I don't know *what it will be like seen in its proper context*) [my emphases]. There you have a piece which in its own way is good (I like it anyway)."[32] Together these three letters provide

[27] Ibid., p. 155.
[28] Ibid., p. 160.
[29] Ibid., p. 158.
[30] Ibid., p. 158.
[31] Ibid., pp. 155–56.
[32] Ibid., p. 156.

invaluable information regarding the genesis of *Skogsrået*. The literary context of *Skogsrået* is foreshadowed by the opera plot: unfaithfulness or forbidden love and death. The piece in the style of a march would become the opening section of *Skogsrået*,[33] and the opera's funeral procession its conclusion. One can detect the influence of Wagner's Overture to *Die Meistersinger* in the march and hear distant echoes of *Siegfried's Funeral March* from *Götterdämmerung* in *Skogsrået*'s closing section. Between these two sections is the section where the protagonist "takes himself off (abroad)" and then the section with forbidden, sensual love (a Sibelian version of Wagnerian *Liebesseligkeit* in *Tristan*'s second act). Sibelius was indeed here "working on a theme that he was very pleased with," since he had already composed several years previously a solo song on Viktor Rydberg's *Skogsrået*.[34]

In total, then, Sibelius composed four different pieces entitled *Skogsrået*: the above-mentioned early solo song (1889?), the orchestral ballad (1894[–5?]), the melodrama (1895) and the piano transcription of the last section of the ballad (1895). Although the early song is based on the same poem as the melodrama and the ballad, musically it is separate from the other three works, which belong closely together.[35] In addition to these pieces, many of Sibelius's early orchestral and vocal works are concerned with the theme of forbidden or tragic love.[36] Perhaps most importantly, there is another factor linking these works: the ballad genre. Although the word "ballad" may not appear in the title, all of these pieces share balladic features. The following works are ballads either by title or are based on balladic poems: in addition to the four *Skogsrået* compositions, the *Ballad* from the *Karelia* Suite, *The Maiden in the Tower*, the ballad *The Ferryman's Brides*, the *Ballad* from *King Christian II* Suite, the cantata *The Captive Queen*, *The Bard* (as described as a ballad by Sibelius), and the *Ballade* for Violin and Piano Op. 115 No. 2.

Clearly the ballad concept is central to Sibelius in the 1890s, facilitating comprehension of his development both as a composer and as a person. First the composer represents himself as a youthful hero of the Don Juan type; then he acquires political conciousness and assumes responsibility for his own country and its strivings for independence,

[33] Kinberg, *Jean Sibelius. Sinfoninen*, pp. 15–16.

[34] The solo song is preserved only as an autograph fair copy without opus number and is located in the Sibelius collection at the Helsinki University Library; see Kilpeläinen, *The Jean Sibelius Musical Manuscripts*, p. 332.

[35] There is one apparent connection between the song and the ballad (and melodrama): the

third stanza of the poem describing the love scene is in Db/C♯ major in both the song and the ballad.

[36] These works include *Scène de ballet*, *Kullervo*, *En saga*, *Lemminkäinen and the Maidens of the Island*, the one-act opera *The Maiden in the Tower*, *The Ferryman's Brides*, the *Ballad* from the Incidental Music to *King Christian II*, and *Snöfrid*.

thus overcoming – at least partially – what I shall designate his personal, "balladic" problems (his excessive drinking, desire for sexual experiences, instability as a husband and father). Before discussing *Skogsrået* in the context of Sibelius's "ballad period" (c. 1891–1900[–1906]),[37] it is helpful to examine some of the basic principles and expressive modes of the ballad genre.

II

The ballad is rooted in ancient Nordic and medieval French poetry. As a genre, it has been defined as "a story told in simplest poetic manner . . . a popular form of poetry."[38] Romantic writers were attracted to the ballad because it is a poem treating the most important issues, namely love and death. Generally, the love portrayed in the ballad is absolute, and passion has a strong sensual, erotic, openly sexual undercurrent; however, this "*love can be directed towards the hero's own country or his ideology*" (my emphasis).[39] Passion proves stronger than religion or norms of social life and overcomes the fear of death. The ballad always depicts great emotions:

[37] I shall designate as the "ballad period" Sibelius's second period following the first "chamber music period" (1881–91).

[38] In modern times, the title "ballad" as a type of narrative folk poetry and song was established in eighteenth-century England. During the last half of the eighteenth century, the folk ballad and the new art of the ballad began to merge, firstly in the pseudo-folk collections by James Macpherson (*Ossian Songs*) and Thomas Percy (*Reliques of Ancient English Poetry*; both 1765). These two collections, in addition to those compiled and published by Johann Gottfried Herder containing Scandinavian and Scotch ballads (*Volkslieder*, 1778–79; later *Stimmen der Völker in Liedern*, 1807), inspired further ballad poetry by Gottfried August Bürger (1774, 1778), Johann Wolfgang von Goethe and Friedrich Schiller (both 1797) in Germany, William Wordsworth and Samuel Coleridge (both 1798) in England, Vassily Zukovsky (1808) in Russia, Adam Mickiewicz (1822) in Poland, Victor Hugo (1826) in France, Johann Ludvig Runeberg (1848) and August Ahlquist-Oksanen (1853) in Finland, and Viktor Rydberg (1882) in Sweden.

It is significant that the ballad as a literary genre came to the fore at the same time as

romanticism generally was becoming the dominating tendency in the arts. The ballad was a suitable vehicle for romantic writers to overcome the rationality of enlightened Classicism because the ballad was seen – thanks to its ancient heritage – as a genre of literary expression that allowed the narrator to exceed the limits of reason. According to Goethe the ballad should always possess "a tone of awe-inspiring mystery, which fills the reader's mind with the presence of supernatural powers, and contain strong dramatic elements"; he considered the ballad to be the "primary egg (*Ur-Ei*)" of literature, in which "the natural forms of poetry – epic, lyric, and drama – were not yet separated from each other." See Sydney Northcote, *The Ballad in Music* (London: Oxford University Press, 1942), pp. 4, 46; Satu Grünthal, *Välkkyvä virran kalvo. Suomalaisten kaunokirjallisten balladien motiivit* (Helsinki: SKS, 1997), pp. 18–20; Gottfried Weissert, *Ballade* (Stuttgart, Weimar: J. B. Metzler, 1993 [2nd rev. edn]), pp. 1–9; Florian Sauer, "Ballade," in *Die Musik in Geschichte und Gegenwart* 1, ed. Ludwig Finscher (Kassel: Bärenreiter, 1994), col. 1136.

[39] Grünthal, *Välkkyvä virran kalvo*, p. 35.

faithful love is proven through death, or forbidden love causes the demise of the main protagonist(s). In ballads fatal things happen: there are violent crimes, murders, and suicides.[40] The protagonists are stereotypical figures: noble knights and beautiful maidens. The settings are dangerous: the tempting but frightening wood, the edge of a pit, high mountains, the brink of a stream, the storming sea, the edge of a spring, etc.[41] Almost always the figures – usually female but sometimes male – exist in the liminal space between the real and unreal worlds. In this borderline world, there are spirits of water, air, earth, wood, or fire: undines, sylphides, gnomes, nymphs, salamanders, etc.[42] A liminal female spirit both terrifies and enchants man; she becomes the projection of man's fears and hopes, but also a means for man to gain access to the infinite, to tap inspiration and to attain immortality.[43] The nymph is a symbol of the frightening, uncontrollable sexuality of man; additionally, in the nymph, man projects his inner fear of unfaithfulness onto a spirit.[44]

James Parakilas employs the concept of "ballad process" to describe the order of events in a ballad.[45] The process is initiated by an act of the protagonist or agent, which defies "the nature of things"; as Parakilas observes, "the act of defiance carries within itself the seed of its failure."[46] Irrespective of the norm that the principal character defies – authority, truth, the laws of family and social life – the process is immutable, the protagonist cannot redeem himself by repenting.[47] According to Parakilas the ballad process articulates "the structure of a guilty conscience" and "structure of powerlessness."[48] Folklore generally is connected with the fears of an individual or a community "around times of anxiety" in life, and fairy-tales reflect the anxieties "on the transition from childhood to adulthood," whereas ballads are closely linked with "the anxieties of adults coming to realize the limits of their powers as adults."[49] Ballads present young adults, especially their doubts about their worthiness or faithfulness as lovers (as for instance in Bürger's *Lenore* set to music by Joachim Raff, Herder's *The Elf-King's Daughter* by Niels Gade, and *Skogsrået* by Sibelius), fear of being disloyal to one's family (*Edward* by Carl Loewe, etc.), men's doubts about their authority and strength (the folk ballad *Chevy Chase* transformed into an overture by George Alexander Macfarren), feelings

---

[40] Ibid., p. 25.
[41] Ibid., pp. 26, and 35.
[42] Ibid., p. 67.
[43] Ibid., p. 42.
[44] Ibid., p. 86.
[45] James Parakilas, *Ballads without Words. Chopin and the Tradition of the Instrumental*

Ballade (Portland, OR: Amadeus Press, 1992), p. 34.
[46] Ibid., p. 35.
[47] Ibid., pp. 36–37.
[48] Ibid., p. 37.
[49] Ibid., p. 38.

of inadequacy by parents (Goethe's *The Erl-King* by Franz Schubert), powerlessness of youth (Goethe's *The Sorcerer's Apprentice* by Paul Dukas) or that of old age (Mickiewicz's *Czaty* set to music by Pyotr Tchaikovsky in his *Voyevoda*).[50]

Western and Nordic ballads were originally written in stanza form with refrain and rhymes; Eastern ballads were formally free. When composers began setting ballads to music – Johann Rudolf Zumsteeg (c. 1791), Schubert (c. 1815), and Loewe (c. 1818) wrote the first significant balladic songs – they partly retained the stanzaic structure in their music, and partly modified it to create through-composed forms. These ballads often maintain a characteristic figuration in the accompaniment, which is based on one or more reiterating motives. Much more important was the general formal principle inherent in the ballad: it is a structure which resolves at the end. However, the resolution is surprising; it is not a recapitulation or a restoration as in the sonata form model since the end of the piece differs dramatically from its beginning.[51] Thus, the ballad is characterized by a teleological form.[52]

The instrumental ballad appears relatively late in the nineteenth century, i.e., after the vocal ballad. Frederic Chopin and Clara Wieck Schumann composed the first piano ballads in the same year: 1836.[53] While the first orchestral ballads were composed in the 1860s by Carl Tausig and Hans von Bülow, it was not until the 1870s that the ballad became an established genre of orchestral music.[54] As an orchestral work based on a balladic poem with an emphatically narrative character, the orchestral ballad established itself as a subgenre of the symphonic poem.[55] Whereas in the "proper," more philosophical symphonic poem as established by Liszt the audience was often given only a title or a brief written motto as a hint for listening,[56] in the ballad the composer generally provided an elaborate scenario; to

[50] Ibid.

[51] Ibid., p. 87.

[52] James Hepokoski discusses the concept of the "telos" in *Sibelius. Symphony No. 5* (Cambridge: Cambridge University Press, 1993), pp. 26–27. According to him, it is a principle typical of modern composers like Strauss, Mahler, and Sibelius, in whose music the "telos" is identical with the last, climactical "rotation" of the form. Although this is an adequate notion, the "ballad process" generates another and, perhaps, a more genuine type of teleological form already in the musical repertoire of nineteenth-century Romanticism, in which the last "rotation" is a surprising and deviating one, thus being in accord with the sudden turn of the plot towards the end of the ballad. Seen this way, the balladic form principle is a truly "modern" one, as it enabled composers to overcome the rigidities of the traditional textbook sonata form.

[53] These are Chopin's Ballad in G Minor Op. 23 and Ballade Op. 6, No. 4 from Clara Wieck's *Soirées musicales.*

[54] Parakilas, *Ballads without Words*, pp. 203 and 205.

[55] Ibid., p. 204.

[56] For instance, in Liszt's *Hamlet* and *Faust*, Sibelius's *The Oceanides*, *The Dryad*, and *Tapiola.*

understand the progress of the piece, the audience had to be familiar with the plot.[57]

Sibelius's symphonic ballad *Skogsrået* (1894/5) is an excellent representative of its genre. It is based on a ballad by the Swedish writer Viktor Rydberg (1828–95), one of the leading figures in the cultural life of Sweden who, in his writings and many other activities, tried to build bridges between Greek antiquity, Christianity, and ancient Nordic mythology. He fought for liberal ideas, believed in democracy and the victory of freedom against oppression, and supported the left-wing political movement with its aspiration for a better life for workers.[58] No wonder then, that Sibelius set many of Rydberg's poems to music: in addition to *Skogsrået*, *The Song of Athenians*, *Snöfrid*, and several solo songs are based on Rydberg. His poems articulated in "modern" verse the erotic ideas which engaged Sibelius in his personal life; furthermore, his work expressed political ideas which were important for the national life of Finland. Rydberg's mythical poems always contain a strong moral, simultaneously political, imperative. In *Skogsrået*, for instance, the poet's intention was to describe that dangerous power which attracts a man and holds him in a treacherous dream, thus preventing him from fulfilling his task as a hero: the hero is required to devote himself to higher endeavors but is distracted.[59] When Sibelius began composing his orchestral ballad in Bayreuth, the dimension of fulfilling one's duty to society was probably not of central importance; instead, he emphasized the personal level of experience in the composition. However, the implicit message might

[57] The most significant orchestral ballads or symphonic works based on ballads before Sibelius's *Skogsrået* are Joachim Raff's Symphony No. 5 (*Lenore*, 1873), Zdenek Fibich's *Toman and the Wood Nymph* (1875), Vincent d'Indy's *La forêt enchantée* (1878), Cesar Franck's *Le chasseur maudit* (1882), Mily Balakirev's *Tamara* (1884), Pyotr Tchaikovsky's *Voyevoda* (1891), and Sergey Liapunov's *Ballad* (1883/96); after Sibelius's *Skogsrået* come Antonin Dvořák's symphonic poems *The Water Goblin*, *The Noon Witch*, *The Golden Spinning Wheel*, and *The Wild Dove* (all 1896), Paul Dukas's *L'apprenti sorcier* (1897), Alexandr Glazunov's *Ballad* Op. 78 (1903), and Sergey Taneyev's *Ballad* (1907).
[58] *Kansojen kirjallisuus 9. Naturalismi (1860–1890)*, ed. Lauri Viljanen (Porvoo: WSOY, 1978), pp. 286–89; Kinberg, *Jean Sibelius. Sinfoninen*, p. 64. It is interesting to note that, although Sibelius certainly did not share Rydberg's socialist ideas, he could still

compose in 1896 a *Workers' March* (*Työkansan marssi*). Also in Adolf Paul's book Sillén (Sibelius) expresses opinions with a strong democratic tendency, saying, for instance, that "art belongs to everybody . . . everybody should have access to it . . . The life and passions of a lumberjack on the street should be described through art as well as those of a child of luxury and riches. . . . Art functions as the third person who is procuring justice between them." (Den [konsten] är till för alla . . . Alla ha rätt till den [. . .] Hamnbusen på gatan bör få sitt lif, sina passioner lika väl skildrade, som lyxens och rikedomens barn. [. . .] Och konsten som tredje person må vara den som skipar denna rättvisa!), Paul, *En bok om en människa*, pp. 227–228.
[59] Hjalmar Alving and Gudmar Hasselberg, *Svensk Litteratur-historia* (Stockholm: Bonniers, 1957), p. 234; Kinberg, *Jean Sibelius. Sinfoninen*, p. 62.

be that the hero should not neglect his social responsibilities towards his family and relations.

The poem consists of four stanzas.[60] The first stanza presents the protagonist Björn, who is "a strong and handsome lad" and takes himself off towards a "tempting" wood. The second stanza describes his wandering in the forest, where he is waylaid by "dwarves in blackest garb." The third stanza depicts Björn's blissful state "in peace of love in the whispering, numbing wood."[61] The tone of the fourth and final stanza is desperate since Björn "cannot love a wife" but "expects only death and a bier." The four-stanza structure is also reflected in the structure of the composition, which is divided into four main sections (A, B, C, and D). The A section (mm. 1–69) is a march (Alla marcia) in C major; the B section (mm. 70–296) constitutes a "fast movement" or a "scherzo" (Vivace assai–Molto vivace) in A minor;[62] the C section (mm. 376–556) may be designated a "slow movement" (Moderato) in C♯ major, the D section (mm. 556–639) forms a tragic "slow finale" (Molto lento) in C♯ minor perhaps akin in spirit to the Adagio lamentoso conclusion of Tchaikovsky's *Pathétique* Symphony.[63] Thus, the tonal structure of *Skogsrået* is one of the earliest examples, parallel to Mahler's Second Symphony (composed in the same year, 1894), of "progressive tonality" in the symphonic literature.

[60] The text of the poem in the original Swedish language and its English translation by William Jewson can be found in the recording of Sibelius's *Skogsrået* on BIS-CD-815.

[61] In Rydberg's poem the female figure, Skogsrået, is presented as a beautiful and sexually tempting seducer; this is a "modern" interpretation of that figure. In ancient Nordic mythology and in written collections of Swedish fairytales and stories beginning around 1600, the word "rå" (translated in the title *Skogsrået* as "nymph"), is a special Nordic word. The "rå" was a dangerous figure that could be either female (most often), male, or a neutral creature, and very often close to or identical with a beast, half-goblin, ghost, spook, or even a vampire, and furnished sometimes with a cow's tail. According to the stories, these creatures inhabited not only the forest but also the water, the mountains, etc. See Elof Hellqvist, *Svensk etymologisk ordbok*, vol. II (Lund: C. W. K. Gleerups, 1948, [3rd edn]), title word "5. rå," p. 861; and Olof Östergren, *Nusvensk ordbok*, vol. III (Stockholm: Wahlström & Widstrand, 1981), title words "Rå4," pp. 921–22, and "Skogsrå," p. 1677.

[62] My measure numbers refer to the edition

of the score that Peter Revers is preparing for Breitkopf & Härtel. This edition is based on the only existing orchestral score, which is an autograph fair copy made by the composer and preserved in the manuscript collection of the Helsinki University Library (No. 0102 in Kilpeläinen's catalogue); see Kilpeläinen, *Tutkielmia Jean Sibeliuksin käsikirjoituksista*, p. 26.

[63] Since the *Symphonie pathétique* was performed for the first time in Helsinki on 26 October 1894 and Sibelius was active at that time in Helsinki (see Tawaststjerna–Layton, *Sibelius. Vol. I*, p. 162), it is probable that he attended that concert, especially as he felt a deep spiritual affinity with Tchaikovsky at that point in his career. Hearing the *Pathétique* could have decisively influenced Sibelius, since the idea of ending a multi-movement piece in a minor key and with a slow, tragic movement was brand new, only introduced by Tchaikovsky. See also Veijo Murtomäki, "Russian Influences on Sibelius," in *Sibelius Forum. Proceedings from the Second International Sibelius Conference. Helsinki, November 26–29, 1995*, ed. Veijo Murtomäki, Kari Kilpeläinen and Risto Väisänen (Helsinki: Sibelius Academy, 1998), pp. 153–61.

The poem's rigid stanzaic structure is mitigated by Sibelius's musical procedures, for Sibelius has not simply composed *Skogsrået* in four sequential, contrasting sections. It is also possible to consider *Skogsrået* as a "four-movement symphony," unified as a single movement by tonal and formal means, or as a "super-sonata structure," to use a term coined by Timothy Jackson.[64] Several salient features are worthy of note. Firstly, the march texture (A) returns (mm. 297ff.) after the fast "dwarf" section (B), analogous to the refrain structure of the ancient ballad, even if the modern Scandinavian and European art ballad does not usually have it.[65] Secondly, a transitional section bridges the modified restatement of the A section and the C or "love" section (mm. 346–75). The slow C section is in ABA form, and the "fate or funeral rhythm" (a dotted quarter note preceded and followed by a sixteenth note) that pervades the final D section is heard already at the end of the C section (mm. 541ff.), thus preparing the merciless character of the last section.

The *Ursatz* of the ballad is shown in Ex. 6.1. The phrase structure of the first section resembles the poem in the way it is divided into "verses" (Ex. 6.2). Taking into account the cuts made by Sibelius at a very early stage of the compositional process – probably before the first performance of *Skogsrået*[66] – the first A section consists of two "stanzas" each containing six "lines of verse" composed of three distinct melodic phrases (identified as a, b, and c) as shown in Ex. 6.2 (the slash showing the grouping of the "verses" into "stanzas"): a b a b1 c b/a b1 c b c b2. Tonally this section prolongs C major and the primary tone ($\hat{3}$); the music reveals a strong tendency to move to the modal scale degrees ii, iii,

[64] Timothy L. Jackson designates certain multi-movement symphonies in late Romantic repertoire – for instance Tchaikovsky's *Manfred* Symphony and *Symphonie pathétique* – "super-sonata" structures, by which he means that those multi-movement entities find their formal, cyclical resolution only with the last movement's "recapitulatory space," whereas the earlier movements fill the "exposition space" (first movement) and the "development space" (middle movement[s]); this concept is also known as "sonata-in-one," recognized already in Beethoven's last works and Liszt's large-scale works (symphonic poems, B minor Piano Sonata, etc.). See Timothy L. Jackson, *Tchaikovsky. Symphonie pathétique*, Cambridge Music Handbooks (Cambridge: Cambridge University Press, 1999). I am indebted to the author for allowing me to read his monograph prior to publication.

[65] According to the "super-sonata" interpretation, the second, A minor, section would be a massive second group, and the return of the first section would take the place of an abridged recapitulation of the first group only. Then, the third section, the "slow movement," would occupy the "development space," and the last section, the "tragic slow movement," would fill the "recapitulatory space" in the "super-sonata" form.

[66] The whole issue of the cuts in the case of *Skogsrået* is an extremely complicated one because Sibelius used several pens (ordinary pencil, red, blue, and green pencils, and also ink) when revising the piece for further performances in 1899 and 1936; regarding Sibelius's corrections and crossings out see Kilpeläinen, *Tutkielmia Jean Sibeliuksen käsikirjoituksista*, p. 26.

Ex. 6.1   Sibelius, *Skogsrået*, formal and tonal schemes

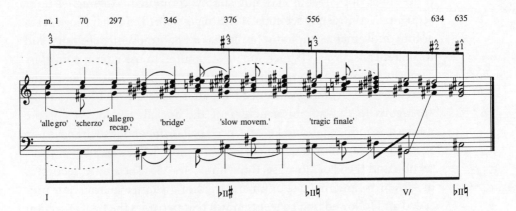

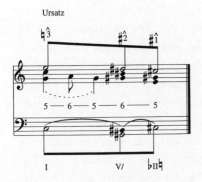

and vi, and it concludes with a turn to A minor (vi). The C major march alludes both to *Die Meistersinger* and Sibelius's own *Karelia* Overture Op. 10, which depicts the pomp and circumstance of the medieval court in Viborg, old Karelia.

The B section is dominated by the fast "dwarf theme" (Ex. 6.3), which is based on a dense superimposition and repetition of short figures with a small ambitus. The form of the B1 or the first sub-section of the B section is as follows: a b a c/a b c′ a′ a′ a″. B1 (mm. 70–79) alternates five times with a modification of the "dwarf theme" (subsection B2; mm. 80–96), which has a strong tendency to emphasize the tone F♯, thus giving the B2 subsection and its repetitions a pronounced Dorian inflection. The B1 section is repeated featuring different canonic combinations, firstly a canon between clarinet and bass clarinet (mm. 97ff.), then between oboe I and II (mm. 122ff.), joined later (mm. 128ff.) by other bass instruments, namely double bass and bassoon. In the fourth statement of B1 (mm. 155ff.) the canon begins in three parts (oboe I, oboe II, with bass clarinet, bassoon, and double bass), whereas the subsequent restatements

Ex. 6.2   Sibelius, *Skogsrået*, mm. 1–69

Ex. 6.3   Sibelius, *Skogsrået*, the theme of the B section, mm. 70ff.

rely on unison reinforced by the orchestration (trumpets mm. 206ff.; later double basses, cellos, and bassoons, mm. 228ff.). The last B1 (mm. 255ff.) was originally based on canon by augmentation in three parts between trombones and trumpets and bass clarinet assigned doubled note values; however, Sibelius later crossed out the trumpet and bass clarinet parts and cut the whole passage with the canon in doubled values (the page following m. 264 in the autograph).

The B section with its close resemblance to Karelian rune singing strongly evokes primitive shamanism; it also brings to mind the hypnotic minimalism of our day. The entire B section lasts about six minutes – and in the original version, with three additional pages (later crossed out) it was calculated to continue even longer. The section recalls Bruckner's orchestration in its majestic reiteration of a single chord;[67] additionally, this prolongation of a single sonority harks back to Wagner's description of the Rhine at the beginning of the *Ring*. The musical material representing the dwarves conforms perfectly to the fundamental aesthetic of the literary ballad since "the rushing dwarves are symbols for the man's

---

[67] Sibelius attended the performance of Bruckner's Third Symphony (the 1888–1889 version) in Vienna on 21 December 1890, after which he wrote Aino: "To my mind he is the greatest of all living composers . . . you cannot imagine the enormous impression it has made on me"; quoted by Tawaststjerna–Layton, *Sibelius. Vol. I*, p. 77. He could have known also Bruckner's Fourth Symphony, the Schalk and Löwe version of which was published in 1889, and his Seventh Symphony (1885 version), which includes a slow movement in C♯ minor with the character of a funeral march analogous to the conclusion of *Skogsrået*; see Peter Revers, "Jean Sibelius and Vienna," in *The Sibelius Companion*, ed. Glenda Dawn Goss (Westport, CT: Greenwood Press, 1996), p. 16.

Ex. 6.4   Sibelius, *Skogsrået*, tonal scheme of the B section

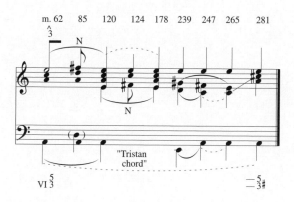

awakening sexuality that frightens him."[68] The B section as a whole con-stitutes a massive prolongation of a single harmony, A minor, flavored by the Dorian added sixth (mm. 124ff.), thus foreshadowing the crucial role of the *Tristan* chord quality later in the piece (Ex. 6.4). The B2 subsec-tions emphasize the subdominant D major harmony, introducing the tone F♯, the upper neighbor tone to the primary tone E (3̂), which antici-pates the central role of the same tone, i.e., F♯, in the last section of the piece as a chord tone of D major (as the ♭II degree of C♯ minor).[69]

The *tempo primo* returns abruptly with brass fanfares, which seem akin to the "Glockenmotiv" in *Parsifal* (possibly reflecting Sibelius's experiences during his Bayreuth pilgrimage of 1894). The abbreviated restatement (mm. 304ff.) of the main A section (Ex. 6.5), preceded by introductory fanfares in C major (mm 297–303), permits no cadences on modal degrees, thus reinforcing the C major tonic and strengthening the role of A1 as a recapitulatory section within the "super-sonata" form.[70] A shift to A minor concludes this section (mm. 342–43).

A transition now takes the music from A minor via C♯ minor to the beginning of the third main section in C♯ major (Ex. 6.6, p. 116). The tran-sition itself is an interesting demonstration of Sibelius's new methods of harmonization based on techniques derived from his knowledge of ancient Finnish and Karelian folk music. Although in crucial places he might still use conventional tonic and dominant harmonies, he derives chords from modal scales – or mixed scales he invented himself – by

[68] Grünthal, *Välkkyvä virran kalvo*, p. 91.
[69] Additionally, the half-diminished seventh harmony F♯–A–C–E is identical with the *Tristan* chord that had for Sibelius a special significance as a symbol of despair and death, as we shall see in analyses of other pieces by Sibelius in this chapter.
[70] Sibelius has abandoned the full recapitulation by removing pages 37–40 from the autograph score.

Ex. 6.5   Sibelius, *Skogsrået*, tonal scheme of the A section's recapitulation

moving in parallel chords through these scales. Excluding a few functional chord progressions, in this transition he generally employs the minor-major scale or Aeolian-Ionian mixed scale, on A, C, [E♭] and C♯.[71]

In his fascinating academic paper "Some reflections on folk music," dating from 1896, Sibelius mentions "the Nordic scale similar to the aeolian scale," although he observes that the "the two last notes [of the scale] were usually sung at higher pitch level."[72] He employs precisely this scale in the first half of the transition. Here, notwithstanding the V–I progressions in A and C minor (mm. 347–52) (Ex. 6.6), the harmonization is primarily derived from chords moving through the minor-major scale, first on A (mm. 347ff.), then on C (mm. 349ff., last quarter note); the harmony is about to continue the minor third sequence on E♭ (m. 353, last quarter note) but turns towards C♯ (m. 355). Once C♯ minor as the new tonic key (mm. 359ff.) is attained, the scalar basis of the harmony changes to the pure Aeolian mode, later with Dorian inflections

[71] On Sibelius's harmonization of the modes, especially that of the minor pentachord, see Jouko Tolonen, "Jean Sibeliuksen koeluento ja mollipentakordin soinnutus, in *Juhlakirja Erik Tawaststjernalle 10. X 1976* (=Acta Musicologica Fennica 9), ed. Erkki Salmenhaara (Keuruu: Otava, 1976), pp. 79–92.

[72] Sibelius means by this that the sixth and seventh degrees of the Aeolian mode are usually sung as sharp notes (♯$\hat{6}$ and ♯$\hat{7}$), which according to the music theory textbooks results in an upward-going melodic minor scale; however, in Sibelius's music the scale remains the same both upwards and downwards, thus resulting in the Aeolian-

Ionian mixed mode, or the minor-major scale. See Jean Sibelius, "Några synpunkter beträffande folkmusiken och dess inflytande på tonkonsten. Joitakin näkökohtia kansanmusiikista ja sen vaikutuksesta säveltaiteeseen," *Musiikki* 10 (1980:2), p. 100; the entire lecture in the original Swedish language and the Finnish translation by Ilkka Oramo comprises pages 86–105. See also Ilkka Oramo, "Vom Einfluß der Volksmusik auf die Musik unserer Zeit. Ein unbekannter Aufsatz von Sibelius aus dem Jahre 1896," in *Bericht über den internationalen musikwissenschaftlichen Kongreß Bayreuth 1981* (Kassel: Bärenreiter, 1984), pp. 440–44.

(mm. 365ff.). The oscillation between the C♯ minor and A minor chords, the latter with the added F♯, reflects the close relationship of the old and new keys and hesitant stabilization of the new key; the A minor chord with added sixth can be interpreted as a minor subdominant chord with lowered fifth in C♯ minor (F♯–A–C–E), thus being a pivot chord between the keys of A and C♯ minor. Because of the modal underpinning of the harmony, the second main section and the transition are the most "Finnish"-sounding passages in the piece.

With the third main section, C, which occupies the space of the development in the "super-sonata" form, we enter the Wagnerian realm. The C section exhibits ABA form (Ex. 6.7, p. 118); the outer subsections of this slow movement linger in the blissful paradise of love, while the central subsection (mm. 432–81) with its accelerating waltz tempo, increasing dynamic level, and wild and surprisingly oriental, even orgiastic, woodwind texture depicts the act of love with its climax (Presto at mm. 467–81). The first subsection C1 (mm. 376–431) of the rounded form is divided into an introductory phrase (mm. 376–85) and two extended phrase groups (mm. 386–403; mm. 404–31) characterized by a chromatically ascending and descending melody played by solo cello supported by solo French horn; the melody assumes the character of the male protagonist's love song. Most notably, in the second phrase group, the sighing half-step motive evokes languishing tenderness. This blissful state is supported by "floating" harmony on tonic and dominant pedals with strong emphasis on the subdominant side.

The middle section, C2 (mm. 432–81; see Ex. 6.7), has as its local key F♯ minor, which can be interpreted either as minor subdominant of the earlier C♯ major or as a temporary resolution of the C♯ major.[73] Excluding the G♯ major chord (mm. 436–39), the entire middle section conforms to the C♯ Aeolian or F♯ Dorian mode. Following four different versions of the syncopated waltz melody (C2), the culmination is reached on the A minor chord with added sixth, i.e., the *Tristan* chord (Presto; mm. 467–72), the same chord that had been so prominent earlier (in the second main B section and in the transition to the C section). After this climax – both musical and sexual – the Moderato tempo with its *amoroso* character returns, as does the violoncello melody (mm. 482–513= mm. 404–31). But this melody's second statement (mm. 514ff.) possesses a decidedly more somber character due to its flattened sixth and seventh degrees of the C♯ major-minor mode (mm. 514–17; mm. 533–37) and its

---

[73] The C♯ major can be heard as dominant of F♯ because a strongly prolonged major chord tends to be heard as a dominant.

Ex. 6.6   Sibelius, *Skogsrået*, bridge section, mm. 347–374

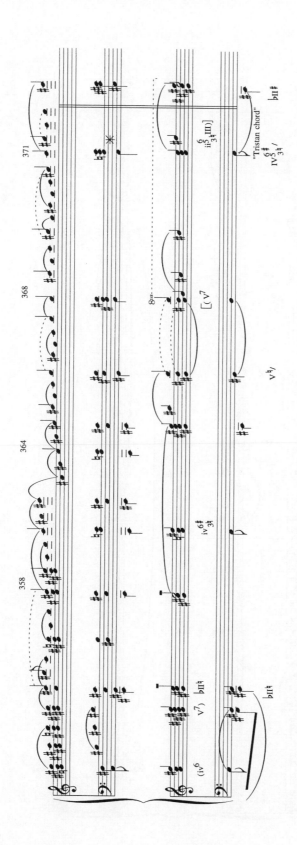

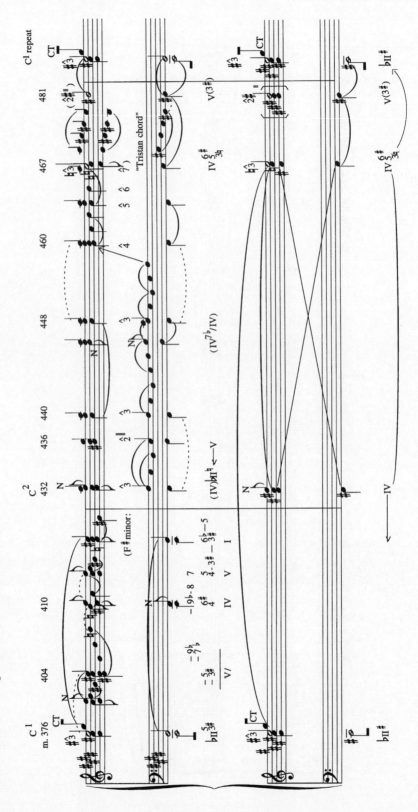

Ex. 6.7   Sibelius, *Skogsrået*, the C section, mm. 376ff.

Ex. 6.8   Wagner, *Lohengrin, Frageverbotmotiv*; Sibelius, *Skogsrået,* motives from the D section

harmonization with the diminished seventh chord (mm. 524–27). Through this "darkening" of the melody and harmony and the gradual appearance of what might be called the "rhythm of destiny" (mm. 541ff.) the music foreshadows its tragic conclusion.

At the beginning of the final section, D, the character of the material changes dramatically, as C♯ major mutates to C♯ minor, and the ethos of a funeral march is evoked by the repetitious rhythmic and harmonic patterns. Tawaststjerna senses in this music "shades of *Lohengrin*"; at least a suggestion of the "motive of the forbidden question" (*Frageverbotmotiv*) from *Lohengrin* can be discerned in two places of the melody (mm. 569–70; mm. 577–78) (Ex. 6.8). Perhaps the final section depicts not only the death of the protagonist Björn, but also (metaphorically) Sibelius's "burial" of his former hero Wagner. The form of the final section consists of three "stanzas" of different lengths (D1 D2 D3) (Ex. 6.9). The chromatic descent at the beginning of the "destiny theme" (mm. 568–69) expresses sorrow and suffering (Ex. 6.8). Perhaps this chromatic line recalls the love music in the C section (especially the violoncello theme, mm. 388–91) (Ex. 6.10, p. 122), while the rhetorical "ascent" from the C♯ minor chord to the E major chord (mm. 568–69) might represent Björn defiantly "rising up" to resist his destiny, a momentary promise of transfiguration (Ex. 6.9). But resistance proves futile as the continuation from

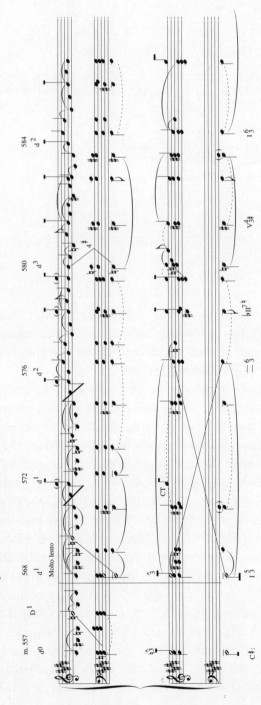

Ex. 6.9   Sibelius, *Skogsrået*, the D section, mm. 568ff.

Ex. 6.10   Sibelius, *Skogsrået*, the theme of the C section, mm. 386ff.

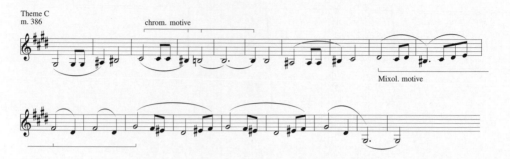

the E major chord to the G♯ dominant in second inversion reaffirms tragic C♯ minor. The most distinct harmonic feature in the final section is the appearance of the Neapolitan seventh harmony on D (D–F♯–A–C). The chord functions on two levels. In the larger C♯ minor context, the seventh chord on D sounds like an augmented sixth chord D–F♯–A–B♯. But in the local context (mm. 588–90) it also resolves as V7 of G minor (mm. 612ff.), into which key it does indeed lead later (mm. 612ff.), also evoking G minor's relative major B♭. Considered in poetical terms, the Neapolitan harmony sounds like an attempt to escape to another world or dimension. The "wild" suspension 4♯–3♯ (G♯–F♯ above D) containing the tritone D–G♯ (for the first time at m. 580) embodies Björn's "inconsolable grief."

In the musical ballad, the narrative provides the central focus: the poem itself or the "ballad process" (as the background context) maintains coherence irrespective of the heterogeneity or homogeneity of the musical material used. In view of this, the issue of thematic unity or organic continuity in the ballad is of secondary importance; but this does not mean that ballads as musical artworks cannot exhibit musical unity and continuity. The highly original sequence of keys in *Skogsrået* has a marked psychological effect: C♯ major is "uplifting" in relation to the initial C major; it represents a state of being that is "apart" from the real world. The "darkening" of C♯ major to C♯ minor has clear semantic significance: that of death as the consequence of forbidden love. Perhaps the effect of the modulation upwards from C major to C♯ major deliberately "inverts" the descending semitonal motion in *Tristan's Liebestod* from C major to B major. Whereas in *Tristan*, the music "sinks down" in eternal love, in *Skogsrået* the "ascent" to C♯ major/minor and the "darkening" of the C♯ major to C♯ minor signifies "eternal despair."[74] Mahler's

[74] Only rarely does a large-scale work in the musical repertoire of Romanticism end in a minor key after having begun in a major key; here the influence of Tchaikovsky's *Pathétique*

Fifth Symphony (1902) offers another parallel: it begins in C♯ minor with a funeral march; its D major conclusion signifies transfiguration within the symphony's *per aspera ad astra* narrative.

As a whole, *Skogsrået* is not a highly unified organism like Sibelius's subsequent large orchestral works: the four *Lemminkäinen* legends and the first two symphonies. Compared with these later pieces, *Skogsrået* appears to be a fantastic improvisation comprising four heterogeneous *Stimmungsbilder* or characters. The characters themselves are well elaborated, original and inventive – even if partially based on Bruckner's and Wagner's typical orchestral techniques and conventional *topoi* of Romanticism. The formal problem is that the links are, for the most part, missing; Sibelius simply juxtaposes different formal sections without connective elements smoothing over the junctures. And when he does try to bridge the gap between sections with a true transition (as when moving from the "Björn theme" to the "Love theme"), the result is only partially satisfying. However, there are points of continuity: the chromaticism of the "Love theme" reappears in the "Funeral theme," thus linking these two final sections; that the final "Funeral theme" is anticipated by the end of the "Love" section must be also noted. In view of his later mastery of the "art of transition," achieved by subtly overlapping different textures and tempos, in *Skogsrået* Sibelius is still at the beginning of his development. However, one of the most fascinating aspects of the tone poem is its unforced freshness of vision and tonal audacity. It is possible, however, that Sibelius tried to compensate for the lack of smooth transitions by embedding common features in the themes, even though the "profound logic" and close thematic interconnectedness characteristic of the symphony was not required of the ballad.

III

Skogsrået's chromatic motif might be modelled on Wagner's "suffering motif" from *Tristan*, but its source probably lies in "German" or Austro-Hungarian, French, and Russian musical representations of orientalism. In addition to this, we must consider the portrayal of "woman" as a

might be crucial. (Mendelssohn's *Italian Symphony* offers another parallel case, although its narrative is a different one.) C♯ has been traditionally associated with suffering and death; a famous instance of this connotation is Bach's fourth fugue with its "cross motive" theme in *The Well-Tempered Clavier* Book I. The wild torment in the finale of Beethoven's *Moonlight* Sonata is also associated with C♯ minor. In Sibelius's String Quartet in D minor ("Voces Intimae"), the slow movement, *Adagio di molto*, contains a striking C♯ minor section with an obvious programmatic idea at the conclusion of the movement (mm. 107–15).

subject in art during the last half of the nineteenth century. During the first half of the nineteenth century, the image of "woman" had been colored by the neo-Platonism of Medieval chivalry, where she was thought to be something unattainable, unreal and distant (*die ferne Geliebte*), in short, an object of idealistic love. But by the end of the Romantic era, sexuality could no longer be encapsulated in artificial and allegorical presentations. Thanks to the rediscovery of the "Orient" and the resulting vogue of orientalism, the "Orient" provided a context in which sexuality and eroticism could be boldly represented. The "Oriental" *topos* facilitated "release from a regimented bureaucratic society and rigid sexual mores that demanded the sacrifice of pleasure for duty"; furthermore, the "Orient" "seemed to serve as the passive landscape upon which the Western artist projected his fantasies."[75]

In this view, "Woman" was "the Other" who with her overwhelming sexuality threatened the "innocent" man: "Woman as vampire, man as victim was a strong current of male feeling in the nineteenth century."[76] "Orientalism" connected with "Otherness" resulted in a cultural situation whereby "Woman" was understood to be essentially different from a normal, decent woman respectable enough to become "wife" and "mother."[77] Thus the role of "Woman" was usurped by oriental seducer, sorceress, Jewess, gypsy, even a working girl (Puccini's Mimi, Charpentier's Louise), or, in the case of Sibelius, by a wood nymph.

To be sure, the French operatic tradition was replete with portraits of "oriental" women and women representing "Otherness."[78] But this issue was also treated in Austro-Germany, Russia and Scandinavia.[79] In this

[75] Susan McClary, *Georges Bizet. Carmen*. Cambridge Opera Handbooks (Cambridge: Cambridge University Press, 1992), pp. 35–36.

[76] Ibid., p. 37.

[77] Some exceptions would be perhaps Micaëla in Bizet's *Carmen* or the "artist's wife" in Strauss's autobiographical symphonic poems. At the time, Strauss was accused of dealing with the too-commonplace episodes of family life.

[78] The list begins with Halévy's *La Juive* (1835), includes Félicien David's *Le Désert* (1844), Gounod's *La reine de Saba* (1862), Meyerbeer's *L'Africaine* (1864), Bizet's *Carmen* (1875), Saint-Saëns's *Samson et Delila* (1877), Delibes' *Lakmé* (1883), Massenet's *Thaïs* (1894), and Charpentier's *Louise* (1896), and ends with Roussel's *Padmâvatî* (1918). See McClary, *Carmen*, p. 33; also Ralph P. Locke, "Constructing the

Oriental 'Other': Saint-Saëns's *Samson et Delila*," *Cambridge Opera Journal* 3/3 (1991), pp. 261–302. Worthwhile reading also is McClary, "Narrative Agendas in 'Absolute, Music.' Identity and Difference in Brahms's Third Symphony," in *Musicology and Difference. Gender and Sexuality in Music Scholarship*, ed. Ruth A. Solie (Berkeley: University of California Press, 1993), pp. 326–44; especially 338–39.

[79] In operas, symphonic works, and programmatic piano pieces such as Schumann's *Das Paradies und die Peri* (1843), Karl Goldmark's symphonic poem *Sakuntala* (1865) and opera *Die Königin von Saba* (1875), Balakirev's famous *Islamey* (1869) for piano and his symphonic poem *Tamara* (1882), Rimsky-Korsakov's Symphony No. 2, *Antar* (1868/1897) and *Sadko* – a symphonic poem (1867/69/92) and an opera (1896), both based on the same story – Rachmaninov's

regard, Sibelius was probably influenced in his early years by his Austro-Hungarian teacher Karl Goldmark in Vienna in 1890–91. Goldmark (1830–1915), although now almost forgotten, was then considered, at least in German-speaking countries, the leading operatic composer after Wagner.[80] Sibelius was proud to be a pupil of this famous composer, as is revealed in his letter to Martin Wegelius (on 19 November 1890): "I say, he has a damned good reputation here in Vienna and as his pupil I enjoy great prestige everywhere. This is the kind of education after my own heart."[81] It is probable that Goldmark influenced Sibelius's first orchestral pieces.[82] Sibelius must have known his most popular orchestral composition, the overture *Sakuntala* (1865), and he had many opportunities to hear his teacher's other works too.[83]

Two of Goldmark's compositions are especially important for *Skogsrået* – *Sakuntala* and *The Queen of Sheba* – since both share with Sibelius's orchestral ballad the *topos* of "Oriental Woman" or mysterious nymph as seducer. In Goldmark's overture, based on *Mahabharata*, the female protagonist is a nymph living in a grove. A male protagonist, Dusjanta, is a king who, during his hunt, encounters Sakuntala, falls in love with her and possibly has intercourse with her. However, Sakuntala is punished by her foster father, a priest, for her disloyalty. She then loses the ring that the king had given her in order to recognise her. Only after the ring has been found does Dusjanta recognize her and feel remorse; he defeats evil demons and is united with Sakuntala in eternal happiness. Although *Sakuntala* – unlike *Skogsrået* – conforms to textbook sonata form, the pieces share significant narrative elements: the nymph, the brave male protagonist, and the love

opera *Aleko* (1893), Grieg's incidental music to *Peer Gynt* (1875), and Sibelius's *Skogsrået* (1894/5). All portray a forbidden exotic, erotic and, in most cases, also destroying love. The issue of fateful love with a liminal figure had served as an inexhaustible source of inspiration for Romantic composers ever since E. T. A. Hoffmann's *Undine* (1813–16) and it still appears as late as in Dvořák's second-last opera *Rusalka* (1900). The Russian late-Romantic musical tradition dealing with themes of sexuality and orientalism is discussed in Albrecht Gaub's "Balakirevs 'Tamara'. Entstehung, Analyse, Programmatik," in *Theorie der Musik. Analyse und Deutung* (=Hamburger Jahrbuch für Musikwissenschaft Band 13), ed. Constantin Floros *et al.* (Laaber: Laaber-Verlag, 1995), pp. 165–99.
[80] Harald Graf, "Carl Goldmark.

Beziehungen zu den Zeitgenossen," *Studia Musicologica* (1997: 38/3–4), pp. 371–407; see especially pp. 371–73 (about Goldmark's position in the musical world), and pp. 402–405 (concerning Sibelius and Goldmark).
[81] Tawaststjerna–Layton, *Sibelius. Vol. I*, p. 73.
[82] Ibid., pp. 88–90. Goldmark justifiably criticized Sibelius's musical themes as lacking character and thus influenced decisively his art of elaborating themes.
[83] Especially the operas *The Queen of Sheba* (1875) and *Merlin* (1882–84/1904), and the *Rustic Wedding Symphony* (1876). See Peter Revers, "Jean Sibelius and Viennese Musical Tradition in the Late Nineteenth Century," in *Proceedings from The First International Jean Sibelius Conference Helsinki, August 1990*, ed. Eero Tarasti (Helsinki: Sibelius Academy, 1995), pp. 169–76.

scene. *Sakuntala* concludes with an apotheosis after sorrowful and repenting stages, whereas *Skogsrået*'s final section is a shocking outburst of repentance.[84] After the first section that depicts Sakuntala in the grove, the nymph is characterised by two themes. The first of them, a slowly rising and then descending melody, is played by cellos and first clarinet (in *Skogsrået* Sibelius analogously employs solo cello and horn); the second is assigned to oboes and first violins in order to depict Sakuntala's oriental origin. Dusjanta is characterised with a brisk fanfare theme based primarily on triplets (analogous to the Björn theme, which uses triplets in a similar way). Unconventional semitonal motion governs the key structure of both pieces: Whereas in *Skogsrået* the love scene takes place in C♯ major, a semitone higher than the beginning of the piece, in Sakuntala it is in E major/C♯ minor-major, a semitone below the primary key of F major;[85] in *Sakuntala*'s recapitulation, before the happy end is attained, the love scene sinks down yet another semitone into the "soft" key of E♭ major/C minor-major.

The opera *The Queen of Sheba* is also concerned with forbidden love for an "oriental" seductress. Assad, the favorite courtier of Solomon, is seduced by the Queen of Sheba when sent by Solomon to invite her to Jerusalem (cf. Tristan, Isolde, and King Marke in Wagner's *Tristan*). Bewitched by the sensual Queen, Assad abandons his intended wife, the virginal Sulamith, at their betrothal and is condemned to death, but the sentence is commuted to banishment in the wilderness. There he rejects the Queen to die in Sulamith's arms. The orientally serpentine theme, evoking sexual desire and Sheba, is a rising melody assigned to the cello, as in *Skogsrået* (although it bears perhaps even stronger resemblance to the cello theme in Sibelius's first *Lemminkäinen* legend). When Assad recalls his encounter with the Queen in Lebanon – "am Fluss des Libanon" (by the river of Lebanon) – and succumbs to her charms – "aus klaren Fluten steigt ein Schwanenleib" (out of the clear stream emerges a swan-like body) – Goldmark's colorful orchestration anticipates Sibelius's imaginative writing for strings in *Skogsrået*'s love scene. Like Björn, Goldmark's male protagonist is enslaved – "und taumelnd sink' ich und verworren hin" (I reel and fall before the demon fair) – as is common in all such "oriental" stories.

---

[84] This was recognized by Sibelius's audience. The critic of the newspaper *Uusi Suometar* wrote after the 1899 performance (27 April 1899) that "hardly ever has music been written, which would more clearly describe remorse. This is 'The Song of Repentance'"; quoted by Kinberg, *Jean Sibelius. Sinfoninen*, p. 118.

[85] E major is the most common key depicting love in Romantic music, beginning with Beethoven's aria "Komm, Hoffnung" in his opera *Fidelio*, and employed by Liszt in *Consolations* Nos. 1, 2, 5, and 6, *Notturno No. 2*, *Sonetto 104 del Petrarca*, and in the second themes of *Les Préludes* and the *Faust Symphony* (first movement), and also by Brahms (in the second movement of his Symphony No. 1).

Goldmark's Austro-German erotic exoticism bears a striking resemblance to the Russian nineteenth-century *topos* that Richard Taruskin has identified as the *nega*, the origin of which lies in Arabic music.[86] The *nega* has been translated as "sweet bliss," "gratified desire," or "tender lassitude." The female seducer of oriental or eastern origins emasculates, enslaves, and renders passive the man, robbing him of his heroic power. In musical terms, the *nega* is realized by a serpentine, descending and ascending chromatic melodic line, "tied or syncopated melodic undulations, and the reversible chromatic pass between the fifth and sixth degrees of the scale," often articulated by the English horn. If Sibelius did not adopt the "oriental" *topos* from Goldmark, he may have been influenced by this Russian *topos*.[87]

Indeed, the *nega* topos is essential to *Skogsrået*'s depiction of Björn sinking into passive "sleep and dream in peace of love," and is in accord with the ballad concept, which dictates that the protagonist become powerless after an act of defiance. *Skogsrået* depicts a forbidden affair, a fatal sexual conjunction, in which the hero (Björn, possibly a self-portait of Sibelius) cannot resist the nymph "so fine and smooth." The strong autobiographical element in *Skogsrået*[88] is unmistakable: in the "opera libretto" (described above) and in the symphonic ballad, Sibelius probably confesses an affair to Aino.[89]

---

[86] Richard Taruskin, "'Entoiling the Falconet': Russian Musical Orientalism in Context," *Cambridge Opera Journal* (1992:4/3), pp. 253–80; this article is included also in his *Defining Russia Musically. Historical and Hermeneutical Essays* (Princeton: Princeton University Press, 1997), pp. 152–85.

[87] See Veijo Murtomäki, *Symphonic Unity. The Development of Formal Thinking in the Symphonies of Sibelius*, trans. Henry Bacon, Studia Musicologica Universitatis Helsingiensis 5 (Helsinki: University of Helsinki, 1993), pp. 38–41; also Murtomäki, "The Problem of Narrativity in the Symphonic Poem En saga by Jean Sibelius," in *Musical Signification. Essays in the Semiotic Theory and Analysis of Music* (=Approaches to Semiotics 121), ed. Eero Tarasti (Berlin and New York: Mouton de Gruyter, 1995), pp. 485–87.

[88] A comical detail concerning Sibelius is the following crisp assessment by Charles Ives that cannot be left unmentioned: Ives described the Finn as "Sibelius, an emasculated cherry." For this notion I am indebted to Leo Treitler's article "Gender and Other Dualities in Music History," in Solie, *Musicology and Difference*, p. 37.

[89] Tawaststjerna had proposed this autobiographical dimension when he hinted that the *Scène de ballet* (1891) might be based on Sibelius's "escapades in Berlin and Vienna"; Sibelius himself confessed that it "springs from a bitter experience or very sad episode . . . I have never wept as profusely as I did while writing this [*Scène*]." See Tawaststjerna–Layton, *Sibelius. Vol. I*, p. 91, and p. 156. Furthermore, the *Scène de ballet* is a waltz, as is the climactic central section of *Skogsrået*. The climax in *Scène de ballet* is achieved on a half-diminished seventh chord (the *Tristan* chord) on B, and just before the end of the piece the strange-sounding woodwind texture in the *Presto* (mm. 455–59) resembles the oriental-sounding "moment of orgasm" (mm. 467–481) in *Skogsrået*. The *Scène de ballet* is based on an *idée fixe* F♯–G♯–B–A, the cross motive in a diatonic version, whereas in the Fourth Symphony it is chromatic: C–D–F♯–E; the *idée fixe* of the *Scène de ballet* is played first by the oboe.

Ex. 6.11   Sibelius, *Kullervo* and *En saga* (1892), comparison of themes

In Sibelius's orchestral music, features connected with the *nega topos* are static chords with pedal points, syncopated rhythms, and shimmering string colors; at the same time the *nega* melody itself is generally assigned to a solo instrument, i.e. solo cello, solo horn, solo oboe, etc. When combined with the *nega topos*, the *Tristan* chord has special significance: it appears on certain pitch levels at crucial, culminating moments in the early works. At the end of the 1902 version of *En saga*, the *Tristan* chord reappears at the "original" transposition of Wagner's *Tristan* Prelude (F–A♭–C♭–E♭, m. 83), whereas it is transposed to F♯–A–C–E in other pieces at points where either fatal love is revealed or forbidden sexual relations are intimated.

The exposition of the first movement of *Kullervo* presents a chromatic descending and ascending theme played by the French horn against a murmuring accompaniment in the low strings (11,2–) (Ex. 6.11).[90] On

---

[90] The marking 11,2– refers to the score page 11 and measures 2 and following.

the basis of its later presentation in the fifth movement (392,1–), where the text refers to Kullervo's unwitting incest with his sister, Eero Tarasti identifies this motive as "the sister's theme in contrast to Kullervo's forceful motive."[91] In the third movement, at the point when Kullervo is about to seduce his sister, a *dolcissimo* oboe melody (219,1–) is related to the "sister's theme." The climax is set against an A minor chord with added sixth (230,2–233,4) – the same *Tristan* chord which had played such a prominent role in *Skogsrået*.[92] Here, as in the symphonic ballad, forbidden incestuous love, defying society's moral norms, results in the deaths of both protagonists in the manner predicted by the "ballad process."

The first, 1892, version of *En saga* (which is very different from the revision of 1902) shares the *nega topos* with *Kullervo* and *Skogsrået*.[93] The original middle section (46,1–) – a pastoral (love) scene – presents a French horn theme with descending and ascending chromatic lines (49,3–6), followed by variants played by high strings and leading to the *fortissimo* culmination (54, 4–7) on the same transposition of the *Tristan* chord (F♯–A–C–E) which had played such a prominent role in *Kullervo* and *Skogsrået*.

IV

The "balladic problem" was common at the end of the nineteenth century. Since men generally got married only at a relatively late age, they usually had their first sexual experiences with prostitutes. In their concealed or "unofficial" sexual life, they experienced a certain type of female sexual adventurousness that their wives could not easily match. For Sibelius, too, this was probably the case. Sibelius's letters to Aino from Bayreuth and Munich disclose that during the night preceding his departure for Germany they had reached a new level of intimacy and Aino had been less reserved than earlier.[94] Against this background, it is plausible to surmise that Sibelius was coping with his unfaithfulness and, through

[91] Eero Tarasti, *Myth and Music. A Semiotic Approach to the Aesthetics of Myth in Music, especially that of Wagner, Sibelius and Stravinsky* (The Hague and Paris: Mouton, 1979), p. 240.

[92] The *forte fortissimo* culmination is, however, on Neapolitan harmony on F, echoing perhaps the climactic moment in the development section of the first movement of Beethoven's "Eroica" Symphony.

[93] The original version of *En saga* (1892) is preserved only as a handwritten copy of the score (not by the composer); it belongs to the collection of The Helsinki Philharmonic Orchestra's Library. Since the score is unpublished, my page and measure numbers refer to this copy.

[94] This can be noticed in the letters written by Jean to Aino, now preserved in the Sibelius collection in the National Archives of Finland; see for instance the letter dated Munich, 24 July 1894.

these early pieces, he was writing himself free from lapses. Considered in this light, *Scène de ballet, Kullervo, En saga, Skogsrået*, the first *Lemminkäinen* legend and *The Maiden in the Tower* become strongly autobiographical, confessional works in which the same sexual issues are confronted through the musical *topoi* of the *Tristan* chord and the *nega*.[95]

Sibelius relives personal experiences through the ballad genre (or balladic procedures) since it was expected that the singer/storyteller/composer should reveal himself ("das Dichter-Ich" or "das lyrische Ich").[96] *En saga*, like *Skogsrået*, can be considered within this context. Many writers have characterized this work as a tone poem concerning an "ancient hero" (Downes), or "a haughty knight" (Frosterus); Niemann and Furuhjelm associate it with *Ossian Songs*, and according to Sibelius it comes "closer to the *Edda* than the *Kalevala*."[97] But if, on one level, *En saga* is situated in Nordic mythological time, on another, deeper level it has profoundly autobiographical significance: Sibelius identified himself with his ancient heroes. Later in the 1940s he confessed to his secretary Santeri Levas:

> *En saga* is one of my most profound works in psychological meaning. I could even say that it contains all my youth. It is the expression of a state of mind. I had undergone a number of painful experiences at the time and in no other work have I revealed myself so completely. It is for this reason that I find all literary explanations quite alien."[98]

If we take it as axiomatic that the ballad genre is closely connected with "the anxieties of adults coming to realize the limits of their powers as adults" (Parakilas), this is exactly the subject of *En saga*.[99] Indeed, like *Skogsrået, En saga* is connected with Sibelius's "balladic problem." The

---

[95] Sometimes in connection with other motives, e.g. the "cross motive" or motives derived from Wagner's operas.

[96] See Carl Dahlhaus, "Zur Problematik der musikalischen Gattungen im 19. Jahrhundert," in *Gattungen der Musik in Einzeldarstellungen*, ed. Wulf Arlt, Ernst Lichtenhahn, and Hans Oesch (Bern: A. Francke, 1973), pp. 850–51; see also Weissert, *Ballade*, pp. 7–8.

[97] Erik Furuhjelm, *Jean Sibelius. Hans tondiktning*, pp. 137–138; Levas, *Muistelma suuresta ihmisestä*, p. 115. When referring to the *Edda*, Sibelius obviously means that in *En saga* the dramatic action has a more significant role in the narrative than it has in his other tone poems, which are based on the *Kalevala*, as in the *Kalevala*, according to Sibelius, the "story is far less important than

the moods and atmosphere conveyed"; see Tawaststjerna-Layton, *Sibelius. Vol. I*, p. 76, and Murtomäki, *The Problem of Narrativity* (1995), pp. 472–75. This is in accord with the literary ballad theory, where two principal categories of the ballad are discerned: the numinous ballads, which are Nordic and nature-magical, and the heroic ballads, which are more southern and historically or ideologically oriented; see Weissert, *Ballade*, pp. 20–45. On the basis of this model Sibelius's *Skogsrået* would be a representative of the former category, whereas *En saga* would belong to the latter one.

[98] Levas, *Muistelma suuresta ihmisestä*, p. 116.

[99] See the discussion of the possible programmatic content of *En saga* in Murtomäki, *The Problem of Narrativity* (1995).

balladic essence of *En saga* is further supported by the "tragic reversed recapitulation,"[100] as the recapitulation section in the final version (1902) begins after a powerful dominant preparation (56,5–58,9); instead of the return of the epic main theme in the tonic C minor, the recapitulation is initiated with the *pianissimo* statement of the second group (58,10–), while the return of the epic theme is heard much later (67,1–), and then only after distant *lamento* phrases separated with long pauses (63,16–). Also the shot-like *fortissimo* interruption on the *Tristan* chord on F (82,7), followed by a *morendo* conclusion, can be interpreted as death and mourning of the fallen hero; furthermore, the conclusion of *En saga* in the unexpected key of E♭ minor conforms to the main principle of the "ballad process," according to which the ending should deviate significantly from the beginning of the piece. The last pages of *En saga* reveal Sibelius's affinity and indebtedness to Tchaikovsky: the E♭ minor *morendo* ending is probably inspired by the end of Tchaikovsky's *Manfred* Symphony, i.e., the representation of Manfred's death.[101]

With the four *Lemminkäinen* Legends Op. 22 (1895/97/1939) we are confronted, again, with Sibelius's own "balladic" problems. In the first legend, *Lemminkäinen and the Maidens of the Island* (cantos 11 and 29 of the *Kalevala*), Lemminkäinen, the "Finnish Don Juan," satisfies his sexual appetite. In the second legend – following the final order of the movements – *The Swan of Tuonela* (canto 14), Tuonela's River, the Hades of Finnish ancient mythology, with its swan is described; Lemminkäinen is

[100] See Timothy L. Jackson, "The Tragic Reversed Recapitulation in the German Classical Tradition," *Journal of Music Theory* (1996: 40/1), pp. 61–111.

[101] It is also similar to the conclusion of Tchaikovsky's *Pathétique Symphony* (still to be written, of course), depicting the final collapse and death of its protagonist (Tchaikovsky himself); see Timothy L. Jackson's more extensive study of Tchaikovsky's *Pathétique Symphony* (*Tchaikovsky, Symphony No. 6 (Pathétique)*, Cambridge Handbook, [Cambridge: Cambridge University Press, 1999]). The conclusion of *En saga* suggests the sudden, violent demise of the hero; similarly, in Tchaikovsky's symphonic ballad *Voyevoda* (1891), the coda represents the hero's mortal wounding. Of course, in the cases of Tchaikovsky's *Pathétique Symphony* and *Voyevoda* the similarity with Sibelius's early orchestral works is based on common romantic *topoi* derived from the operatic tradition and the "spiritual affinity" of both composers that Sibelius admitted, saying that "there is much in that man that I recognize in myself"; quoted in Tawaststjerna–Layton, *Sibelius. Vol. I*, p. 209. See also my "Russian Influences on Sibelius," pp. 156–57.

En saga may also have been influenced by Strauss's *Don Juan* and *Till Eulenspiegel* (Sibelius had heard *Don Juan* in Berlin in 1889). Like *Skogsrået* (*En saga* only to a lesser extent), *Don Juan* is a symphonic poem about a balladic hero who is unable, or more correctly, does not wish to control his sexuality. Strauss's work, like Sibelius's, culminates in dramatic *fortissimo* chords (the diminished seventh chord in mm. 420–22; the dominant seventh chord in mm. 576ff.) followed by shocking *pianissimi* and terrifying minor chords, which describe Don Juan's horrible end. Also in *Till Eulenspiegel* the protagonist's adventures are interrupted by a *fortissimo* diminished seventh chord (m. 573) when the sentence of death is declared.

asked to shoot the swan but instead he is killed and falls into the river. In the third legend, *Lemminkäinen in Tuonela* (canto 15), he is raised from the dead by his mother's healing skills. In the last legend, *Lemminkäinen's Return* (cantos 29 and 30), he returns home purified and full of energy and self-pride. In the first legend, Sibelius employs two motives connoting love. The first is a diatonic descent of two or three notes followed by a downward skip of a third or fourth with upward motion continuing the line (see Ex. 6.12d; *Lemminkäinen and the Maidens of the Island*; rehearsal number 1, fifth measure ff.=1+5–). The source of this motive might be Wagner's *Die Walküre*, where it functions as the *Geschwisterliebemotiv* (motive of sibling love, Ex. 6.12a); interestingly, this motive is employed by Puccini in *Madame Butterfly* in the big love scene at the conclusion of the first act (Ex. 6.12b) and in the beginning of the first act of *La bohème* (Ex. 6.12c).[102]

The other motive is the *nega* in varied form; again it is assigned to the cello, which presents a long, passionate melody (7+18–; Ex. 6.12e). In this case, the melody is only slightly chromatic but proceeds in a wavelike, circling way (8+6–); sometimes the melody skips upward, forming a cross figure (1+16– , 22+1–; Ex. 6.12f–g). A dialogue between the cello melody and by the high woodwind phrases (9+9–) depicts the amorous duet between Lemminkäinen and the maidens.[103]

In *The Maiden in the Tower* (1896),[104] at the end of the first scene, when the bailiff abducts the fainting maiden and imprisons her in his tower, Sibelius employs in passing an A minor chord (mm. 250–53) with chromatic inflections of D♯ and F♯. Instead of an emphatic *Tristan* chord, this time he uses a modification of the *Sehnsuchtsschmerzmotiv* from *Tristan* or *Wundemotiv* from *Parsifal* in C minor (Ex. 6.13a–c) with the text: "Now you are mine." A long passage *Mit Pathos*, depicting the maiden's anguish, is based on a syncopated, chromatic, and oscillating melody, i.e., the *nega*.

The Ferryman's Brides Op. 33 (1897), a ballad for baritone or mezzo-soprano and orchestra, is based on the oldest Finnish literary ballad

---

[102] It is, of course, difficult to determine whether Sibelius was influenced in this case by Wagner or Puccini, whose operas he knew very well, or if these three composers simply share a common symbolic vocabulary of Western music at this juncture.

[103] This duet might reflect Sibelius's study (in September 1894 in Berlin) of Liszt's *Faust* Symphony, where a similar dialogue (between Faust and Gretchen) initiates the first movement ("Faust") transition (mm. 111ff.).

See Tawaststjerna–Layton, *Sibelius. Vol. I*, p. 161.

[104] The story is based on a folk ballad arranged by Rafael Herzberg. A fair copy of the score by the composer exists (see Kilpeläinen, *The Jean Sibelius Musical Manuscripts*, pp. 245–47), but it has never been published. However, my measure numbers have been taken from a copy written by an anonymous copyist and preserved in the Library of the Finnish Music Information Center.

Ex. 6.12   Wagner, *Die Walküre, Geschwisterliebemotiv*; Puccini, *Madame Butterfly* and *La bohème*, motives; Sibelius, *Lemminkäinen* and the *Maidens of Island, nega* and "cross" motives

(1852) by August Ahlquist-Oksanen. This poem presents the Finnish version of the Lorelei theme. In it there are two female protagonists: Anna, who wants to die with the male hero, Vilhelmi, during a moment of ecstatic love, and a water nymph, Vellamo, who wants to live with Vilhelmi. The poem is filled with sexual themes: the story takes place in rapids, symbolizing passion and perhaps even ejaculation; Vilhelmi sinks in the deep water with his bride, which might be interpreted as symbols of intercourse ("He stepped down in his craft / and let his boat go

Ex. 6.13   Wager, *Tristan and Isolde*, *Sehnsuchtsschmerzmotiv*, *Parsifal*,
Wundemotiv; Sibelius, *The Maiden in the Tower* and *The Ferryman's Brides*,
motives

Wagner: *Tristan and Isolde*
"Sehnsuchtsschmerzmotiv"

Wagner: *Parsifal*
"Wundemotiv"

Sibelius: *The Maiden in the Tower*

Sibelius: *The Ferryman's Brides*

freely").[105] At the turning point of the ballad, when Vellamo finds out that
Vilhelmi already has a bride, she bursts out lamenting: "Unhappy maiden
of Vellamo / he loves of human kind." At this point in the ballad (54,4–),
the music turns to A minor and remains there for the rest of the piece.
A modified version of the *Sehnsuchtsschmerzmotiv/ Wundemotiv*
(Ex. 6.13d) is heard, and against the background of the syncopated
rhythm in the countermelody of woodwinds (55,7–58,4) the tone F♯
enters emphatically, producing the *Tristan* chord. It is worth mentioning
that the main motive of the piece is a slightly modified version of the
principal motive of *Lemminkäinen's Return* (Ex. 6.14).

[105] Grünthal, *Valkkyvä virran kalvo*, p. 72. The
English translation is taken from the booklet
of the Ondine record ODE 823-2.

Ex. 6.14   Sibelius, *The Ferryman's Brides* and *Lemminkäinen's Return*, motives

V

Sibelius's role as a national hero participating in the struggle against Czarist oppression became an increasingly important aspect of his ideology in 1899, when Nicolai Ivanovich Bobrikoff became the new Governor General and representative of the Czar in Finland. The February Manifesto proclaimed by Czar Nicolai II threatened the autonomy of the Grand Duchy of Finland, which had been granted by Alexander I in 1809. In some works dating from the 1890s Sibelius had expressed patriotic feelings,[106] but specially by the turn of the twentieth century (along with other leading figures of Finnish cultural life) he encouraged the Finnish nation with a succession of compositions. Besides writing openly patriotic pieces (cantatas, etc.), where the political content was easily understood, he also began writing symphonies in this period of national crisis, and sought to win wider acceptance by participating in the European, i.e., Austro-German, tradition. On the one hand, he wished to show European audiences that Finland was a country culturally advanced enough to be accepted among the old Middle-European community and that it had earned the independence for which it was striving. On the other hand, when composing "absolute" music – which is "absolute," however, only for those who follow rigidly a Hanslickian dogma – he could more readily conceal both his personal thoughts and patriotic/political

---

[106]   These pieces include, for instance, the choir song *Aamusumussa* (*Morning Mist*, 1896) and the cantata *Sandels* (1898) for male choir and orchestra.

messages;[107] perhaps he took this position because it was becoming too awkward for him (as a figure on the national stage) to express his personal anxieties explicitly.[108]

Sibelius found his vocation as a composer whose role it was to address not only a Finnish but a worldwide audience and, at the same time, participate in the effort by Finnish intellectuals to support national liberation. This new vocation distracted him and, to a certain extent, made it possible for him to overcome – or perhaps more accurately – to put aside for a moment his own personal "balladic" problems. Sibelius the Bohemian did not disappear, but as the "son of the nation" he was partially rescued from his Don Juanian inclinations. He continued composing in the romantic balladic tradition, but instead of lingering in his own imaginary sensual world infused with the anxieties of maturing, he now directed his creative energies towards new artistic goals guided by his passionate desire to serve his country. In the period of the turn of the century, he matured as both an individual and an artist.

But not completely. The episode at Rapallo in 1901 is symptomatic of Sibelius's behavior and bespeaks his difficulties in becoming a responsible husband and father. When his daughter Ruth became seriously ill with typhoid fever, and with money running short and the situation becoming too stressful, Sibelius simply abandoned his family and traveled to Rome "to gain some remarkable ideas about the essence of the music."[109] In Helsinki, on more than one occasion, Aino had to search for her husband, who could be "lost" for days, and bring him home. Nor was she always successful in retrieving him or able to pry him away from his jolly comrades. Once Sibelius sent his wife a visiting card with words (dating probably from winter 1902/03): "Dear A. I'm at the Kämp [tavern] just now. Forgive me for not receiving you. Your own J."[110] When Aino was still in a weak condition after the birth of their fourth daughter, Sibelius used to linger all too often at the Kämp or the König; on one occasion he sent a message to Aino (spring 1903): "Dear Aino,/How are you? Nipsu (the baby) and the others. Send a line in reply. I am at the

[107] Recall that Beethoven in his middle and late periods communicated with his closest friends and patrons mostly through instrumental music in order to avoid censorship, since hidden messages could be transmitted via untexted instrumental music. See Maynard Solomon, *Beethoven* (London: Granada, 1980 [1977]), pp. 362–65.
[108] It is symptomatic that as early as 1890, when two movements of Sibelius's Piano Quintet in G minor were played for the first

time in public in Helsinki, his former teacher Martin Wegelius and Hanna, Wegelius's wife, blamed Sibelius for being too autobiographical in his music. Martin wrote to Sibelius: "that sort of autobiography has no appeal for me: a composer ought to keep his gropings to himself"; quoted in Tawaststjerna–Layton, *Sibelius. Vol. I*, p. 64.
[109] Ibid., p. 239.
[110] Ibid., p. 273.

moment engrossed in a most absorbing discussion./your own Janne/I shall come presently."[111] Family life, as immortalized in Strauss's *Sinfonia domestica*, on the one hand was something Sibelius needed, on the other hand distracted his creative work. When returning from his long trip to London, Paris, and Berlin in 1909, he noted in his diary (12 June 1909): "Strange to live again in family."[112] In order to get the Fourth Symphony ready, he made two further foreign trips and periodically went off to Helsinki and shut himself away in a hotel room. When one thinks of his adventures with Busoni in London in 1921 and his uncontrolled drinking still during the 1920s and 1930s,[113] which not only hindered him from composing but almost ended his marriage, it is little wonder that Aino after the death of Jean told the Finnish composer Olavi Pesonen that "she never in her life had had any pleasure with her husband."[114]

In relatively short time Sibelius composed several pieces imbued with deep patriotic feeling.[115] *The Song of Athenians*, *Impromptu*, and *Snöfrid* are all settings of poems by Viktor Rydberg. In *Snöfrid*, which is not explicitly identified as a ballad (but the story was inspired by the ancient balladic stories of Scandinavia), the female protagonist is a maiden who belongs to the past of the *Edda*, the epic poem recalling the ancient Nordic heroes and their deeds. She appeals to her compatriots in order to stimulate them to fight for freedom. Gunnar, the hero in the poem, is sorely tempted by the gold of dwarves, earthly fame, and, especially, the sweet dream of resting in the embrace of a tempting nymph for the rest of his life, but Snöfrid's injunctions compel him not to abandon his responsibility and duty:

> better the noble poverty of the warrior, than the dragon's wily repose and
> gold, better derided death for what is good than peace of mind, won in
> selfish striving, better the embrace of danger than that of peace. If you

---

[111] Ibid., p. 272.

[112] Ibid., p. 140.

[113] See Tawaststjerna–Layton, *Sibelius, Volume III, 1914–1957* (1997 [1978 and 1988]), p. 200. Sibelius's excessive drinking is painstakingly documented in his numerous diary entries, for instance: "If I could only stop these drinking bouts. But it will always remain a forlorn hope" (18 December 1920), p. 195; "Alcohol, which I gave up, is now my most faithful companion. And the most understanding!" (11 November 1923), p. 214.

[114] Olavi Pesonen reported this in his eightieth birthday interview (*Helsingin Sanomat*, 8 April 1989).

[115] These pieces include *The Song of*

Athenians Op. 31, No. 3 for boys' and men's voices, brass septet, and percussion (1899); *The Breaking of the Ice on the Oulu River* Op. 30 (1899), improvisation for recitation, or a melodrama for male choir, speaker, and orchestra; *Press Celebrations Music* (1899), including the tableau *Finland Awakes*, later *Finlandia* Op. 26, No. 7 (1899/1900); *Snöfrid* Op. 29 (1900), improvisation for recitation, or a melodrama for mixed choir, speaker, and orchestra; *Ukko the Firemaker* Op. 32 (1902/10) for baritone solo, male choir, and orchestra; *Impromptu* Op. 19 (1902/10) for a female-voice chorus and orchestra; and *The Captive Queen* Op. 48 (1906), ballad for mixed or male choir and orchestra.

choose me, then you choose the storm ... fight the hopeless fight, and die unnamed. That is life's true heroic story. Do not seek the isle of fortune.[116]

In *Snöfrid* the bay or shore nymph is the counterpart of the wood nymph in *Skogsrået*, as the bay nymph says to Gunnar with a tempting voice: "A cottage awaits you ... there may you sweetly dream among the rushes on the shore! The fairest arm that ever made embrace, Gunnar, will fondle the fabric of your life."[117] But the message contained in Snöfrid's words is clear: the hero must abandon the nymph and fight for his country.

In another major work from this period, *The Captive Queen*, based on a ballad by Paavo Cajander about a cruel tyrant who keeps the queen in captivity, the political-allegorical content is obvious: Finland is succumbing as a prisoner of Russia. The first half of the ballad begins in D minor with the "rhythm of destiny," a triplet played by the timpani and the strings, somewhat in the manner of a funeral march. When the hero approaches at the beginning of the second half of the piece in order to liberate the Queen, a victory march in C major is heard. At this moment the text does not even attempt to conceal its patriotic message: "Take heart! The hero cometh, Lo, o'er the distant field, See, the clear dawnlight, uprising, Gleams on his helmet and shield! The battle cry rings free! 'For our glorious queen and for freedom! Who dares to follow me?'"[118]

Imbued with patriotism, both *Snöfrid* and *The Captive Queen* reveal Sibelius's new course: he has outgrown his early adventurism and Freudian *Angst*. And even if Sibelius later contested patriotic interpretations of his First (1899) and Second Symphonies (1902), the defiant and combative character of these works (and Sibelius's other compositions dating from this period) clearly reflects Finland's yearning for political independence. His Fourth Symphony reveals that by 1911 at the latest Sibelius wished to be something more than a national hero; this remarkable achievement opens a new chapter in his development as a composer.

[116] The English translation is by John Skinner and is included in the booklet of the Ondine record ODE 754-2.
[117] Ibid.
[118] The English translation is by Rosa Newmarch and is included in both the vocal and the orchestral scores of the piece, published by Schlesinger'sche Buch- and Musikalienhandlung (Rob. Liebau), Berlin (1907, 1935).

7 *Pohjola's Daughter* – "L'aventure d'un héros"

Timo Virtanen

Introduction

From February to April 1901, Jean Sibelius spent almost two months in Italy with his wife, Aino, and his six-year-old daughter, Ruth. He rented an apartment for them in a pension at Rapallo, and a working-room for himself near the town. At this time he was composing his Second Symphony. In March Aino and Jean were deeply shaken when Ruth was taken seriously ill with typhoid fever. The composer, after being assured of his daughter's recovery, left Aino and Ruth and fled to Rome to collect his thoughts and surround himself with beauty and artistic visions.

For Jean Sibelius the husband and father, this period in Italy must have been a great trial; but the composer Sibelius seems to have regarded this *purgatorio* as a part of his artistic-heroic struggle. In April 1901 he wrote to Axel Carpelan in Rome: "Rather this great tragic destiny than the every-day cycle of life. After all I believe that a man does not suffer in vain."[1] With these words, Sibelius describes his artistic vocation or, at least, how at that particular juncture he perceived himself as a creative artist. The confession reveals that he had deliberately chosen his "great tragic destiny" – whatever it might have been – instead of "the every-day cycle of life." In this letter, Sibelius seems to identify himself with what we might call a romantic hero, a martyred artist who has to sacrifice his hope for a balanced life on the altar of his art.

In the following pages, I shall discuss Sibelius's ideas regarding "the heroic" and their ramifications for one of his most important orchestral works, the symphonic fantasy *Pohjola's Daughter*. Interestingly, Sibelius set down the first sketches during his two-week stay in Rome in April 1901, and, when the symphonic fantasy was finally completed over five years later, he planned to give it the title *L'aventure d'un héros*. Through an examination of the sketches, I shall trace the work's remarkable genesis; my study of the sources and analysis will illuminate the relationship between the music and its program.

---

[1] Erik Tawaststjerna, *Jean Sibelius. Åren 1893–1904* (Keuruu: Söderström, 1994), p. 157.

I Sketch studies

The manuscripts of *Pohjola's Daughter* in the Helsinki University Library and the genesis of *Pohjola's Daughter* in light of the sketches

The compositional process of *Pohjola's Daughter* was much longer and more intricate than scholars have generally believed. In his Sibelius biography, Salmenhaara claims that Sibelius put aside an orchestral work, "*Luonnotar*,"[2] which he had been composing during the spring of 1906 and had reached the fair copy stage. Salmenhaara believes that Sibelius then "composed the new Symphonic Fantasy [i.e. *Pohjola's Daughter*] in a short period of time during the summer of 1906."[3] The rapid completion of the new symphonic fantasy is, according to Salmenhaara, a "mystery."

There are three possible explanations for this "mystery." Firstly, as Salmenhaara suggests, Sibelius composed an entirely new work in a very short period of time in the summer of 1906. Secondly, the composer reworked earlier material when composing *Pohjola's Daughter*. The third solution is that the orchestral poem "*Luonnotar*" evolved into *Pohjola's Daughter* and that these two pieces are essentially one and the same piece. This third solution is supported by evidence to be gleaned from the manuscripts. The source material for *Pohjola's Daughter* in the manuscript archive of the Helsinki University Library is exceptionally abundant. Only for the Violin Concerto in its two versions and for the Seventh Symphony are there even more pages of sketches than for *Pohjola's Daughter*. Since Sibelius planned several works simultaneously with *Pohjola's Daughter* (for instance, the Third Symphony), the manuscript sources for the Symphonic Fantasy contain many fragments of material for other pieces. Sometimes the manuscript pages are tightly filled with musical notes, other pages may contain only a fragment of a few measures, and part of the sketch material is fragmentary and written in unclear handwriting, so identifying the sketches can be problematic. For this reason, the list of the manuscript material for *Pohjola's Daughter* remains inevitably speculative.[4] As an overview, the pages can be divided into four types:

[2] In order to distinguish between the incomplete early composition based on the Luonnotar legend dating from the years 1905–06 and *Luonnotar* Op. 70 for soprano and orchestra, the former is placed in quotation marks ("*Luonnotar*").
[3] Erkki Salmenhaara, *Jean Sibelius* (Helsinki: Tammi, 1984), p. 221.
[4] According to Rainer Fanselau, the total number of manuscript pages for *Pohjola's Daughter* is 201. Giving such an exact number seems to me, however, too optimistic, and the number given by Fanselau is probably too small. See Rainer Fanselau, "Jean Sibelius. Pohjolas Tochter," in *Programmusik*, ed. by Albrecht Goebel (Mainz: B. Schott's Söhne, 1992), p. 219.

1   pages of full score with complete or almost complete markings of orchestration,
2   score sketches with incomplete references to orchestration,
3   sketches on 2–10 staves without any or with occasional references to instrumentation,
4   sketches on one stave.

In addition to the sketches in the Helsinki University Library there is the fair copy of the final score of *Pohjola's Daughter*, which Sibelius sent to his German publisher Lienau in the summer 1906, as well as the programme text written by the composer and worked up into poetic form by the publisher.[5]

Although *Pohjola's Daughter* assumed its final shape in the summer of 1906, Sibelius's sketchbooks reveal that he entered the first sketches for the work later published as *Pohjola's Daughter* as early as in 1901, during his sojourn in Italy, as mentioned above. The manuscript page 1548/1[6] (Pl. 7.1) contains possibly the earliest fragment – at least the earliest found to date – of the material that Sibelius used five years later in *Pohjola's Daughter*. This sketch, outlining the melody which appears in m. 28 (letter B) in the printed score of *Pohjola's Daughter*, is dated 20 March 1901 in Rome. From the journey to Italy there are two other sketches for the same oboe theme, in manuscripts 1551b and c. Manuscript page 1551b contains the following date: "*Accademia di S. Cecilia / Lunedi 25 Marzo* [1901]." The fragment on manuscript page 1555/1 (Pl. 7.2, staff 7 from top), which occurs later in the work, in the theme associated with Pohjola's daughter (m. 60, 12:1), obviously dates from the same period. [7]

The sketchbooks reveal that Sibelius planned a work based on the Luonnotar legend (the *Kalevala's* first poem) as early as the first years of this century. Among the sketches intended primarily for the Second Symphony there is an annotation in Swedish on manuscript page 1542/1: "*eller till Luonno / tar / temat om bön föregår / det ledes ingenom*" (or for Luonno / tar / the theme if the prayer precedes / it is led through). The meaning of this reference to Luonnotar has remained unclear. The sketch does not contain any hint of the Second Symphony, *Pohjola's Daughter* or *Luonnotar* Op. 70 for soprano and orchestra (1913), and neither does another sketch, marked "*Luonnotar motiv*" in manuscript 1066.

---

[5] The autograph score differs slightly from the printed score in its details. It seems obvious that Sibelius, even after having sent the score to the publisher, made further changes.
[6] The first number (before the line) marks the code of the manuscript in the Helsinki University Library, the second number marks the page number in the manuscript.
[7] In my text and examples, the page number and the measure number on the page in the Lienau score are given. The annotation 12:1 means the first measure on page 12.

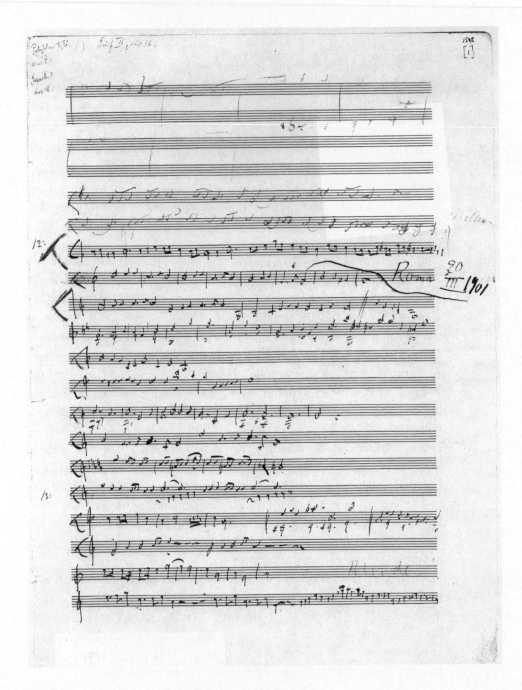

Plate 7.1   HUL 1548, p. 1 (sketches for *Pohjola's Daughter*)

Plate 7.2   HUL 1555, p. 1 (sketches for *Pohjola's Daughter*)

Plate 7.3　HUL 0225, p. 1 (sketches for *Pohjola's Daughter*)

　　Sibelius's sketchbooks show how fragmentary ideas gradually began to coalesce into the final work "*Luonnotar*"/*Pohjola's Daughter*, and the characteristic features – for example melodic formulae – of the Fantasy crystallized. Sibelius did not begin composing the Fantasy with the first measures of the introduction, but rather assembled the work using fragments conceived over a period of several years. Probably the first draft for the opening of the work is the elegiac melody in C minor found on manuscript page 0225/1 (Pl. 7.3).[8] On manuscript page 0194/1, there is another version of this melody: as a continuation for the initial measures Sibelius has written two alternatives, the second with downward stems (Pl. 7.4; see staff 11 from top). After these earliest sketches, the opening material is transposed to various keys – E, F♯ and B♭ minor consecutively – before being fixed in the key of G minor. The order of the transpositions can be inferred from the different stages of the material on manuscript pages 0225/8, 0217/1 and 2, 0220/1 and 3, and 0222/1. The versions in E minor and F♯ minor on manuscripts 0225 and 0222, the "Marjatta" sketches, are especially interesting

[8] The sketch under discussion is written in black ink and the numbers, clearly entered after the sketch, in pencil. Markku Hartikainen has discovered that the numbers refer to building costs of Sibelius's home *Ainola*. Thus, the sketch predates the end of October 1904.

Plate 7.4   HUL 0194, p. 1 (sketches for *Pohjola's Daughter*)

because of Sibelius's accompanying remarks. These references, which have provided fascinating new information concerning the genesis of *Pohjola's Daughter*, will be discussed below.

The opening music of the Fantasy was still experiencing profound development even after the beginning had been anchored in G minor. In the light of sketches, the right word to characterize the compositional process would perhaps be condensation or crystallization. Without letting the material sprawl in too many directions, Sibelius carefully explored the thematic substance, and possible chains of metamorphoses. As the work evolved, he lopped off branches and eliminated repetitions. For example, the early versions of the slow introduction create a discontinuous and static impression because of many rests and clear-cut phrases which frequently conclude with a long note. Sibelius accelerated the musical flow by eliminating rests and fermatas and by placing the formal units elliptically so that one unit overlaps another.

The features mentioned above can be observed by comparing the final printed score of *Pohjola's Daughter* with manuscript 0163 – a comparison which sheds light on many aspects of the compositional genesis. The exact date of this untitled manuscript comprising twenty pages of fair-copied score written in ink is unknown; but it is evident that Sibelius intended the score to be a close-to-final version of a work, and this work was probably "*Luonnotar,*" which Sibelius left incomplete and reworked into *Pohjola's Daughter* in June of 1906. However, the manuscript may have been written even earlier, in the autumn of 1905. During that time, Sibelius was hastily composing an orchestral work, which he had been asked to conduct in Heidelberg at the end of November. The work was never completed, however, and Sibelius had to cancel the performance at the last moment. Preparing the score for the Heidelberg concert could explain the copyist's measure numberings in manuscript 0163 (Pl. 7.5b): in order to take the orchestral parts with him to Heidelberg, Sibelius gave part of the score to the copyist before the work was completed.[9]

This early version of the beginning of the work is in total 208 measures, the 4/4 measures of the final version being notated in 2/4 meter. Towards the end of the draft Sibelius's handwriting changes dramatically to become much rougher; the last pages are sketches. The initial pages of the manuscript, corresponding to mm. 1–49 (9:4) in the final score, are in their broad outline the same as in the final version. Most of the differences consist in details of orchestration,[10] dynamics, and phrase mark-

---

[9] The rehearsal numbers in the manuscript suggest that it was intended to be the final version of the work.

[10] In the early version there are, in addition to timpani, parts for glockenspiel, cymbals, bass drum, and triangle.

ings, but additionally there are more profound and revealing differences between the introductions to the two versions. The final version's condensation of the thematic material and its organic growth of ideas and phrases becomes evident when we compare the version with the manuscript draft (Ex. 7.1, p. 150). The dialogue between English horn and clarinet – in the manuscript English Horn and bassoon – beginning at m. 15 (letter A) in the printed score is twenty-two measures of 2/4, that is, eleven measures of 4/4. In the final version, this passage is only the half of that duration, i.e. six measures. Additionally, in the manuscript, the passage concludes with a long G, which is sustained through two measures and concludes with a sixteenth-note rest extended through a fermata. This halt is followed directly, and rather awkwardly, by the *Poco a poco più con moto al Allegro molto moderato*, corresponding to the passage which begins in m. 21 in the printed score.

The most remarkable differences between the two versions are to be found in the section beginning at m. 50 (10:1) in the final score. Instead of the B♭ major statement in the brass, which occurs in mm. 53–56 (10:4–11:3) in the final version, in the manuscript draft there is, similarly orchestrated for the brass instruments, a chorale-like passage which ends with an F major triad, the dominant of B♭, at rehearsal number 5 (Ex. 7.2, pp. 152–54).[9] In the manuscript, the chorale is followed by a D♭ major six-three chord at rehearsal 5, and a passage which is placed at the end of the coda (mm. 240–52, 46:1–13) in the final version. In the earlier draft, this passage leads to a G♭ major statement of a *cantabile* theme in the high register which is repeated in E♭, after a six-measure passage (beginning at rehearsal 6) formed out of the thematic material from the introduction. The statement in E♭, like the G♭ major before, coalesces on a half-diminished seventh chord, and the whole section ends with a prolonged dominant of E♭ minor. The four pizzicato measures before rehearsal 7 are located in mm. 111–13 (18:11–13) in the printed score.

The music corresponding to mm. 57–66 (11:4–13:1) in the final version is presented twice, in E♭ minor and C♯ minor in the earlier version. The registral and orchestral expression and the character of the following section are very different in the two versions: the light and airy theme associated with Pohjola's daughter herself becomes in the manuscript version gloomy and threatening.

Even if Sibelius did not use all of this material in the final version of *Pohjola's Daughter*, he did employ fragments in two other works, namely the Third Symphony (1907) and the Second Orchestral Suite, *Scènes historiques* (1912). In the Third Symphony, second movement, beginning six measures before rehearsal 7, the woodwinds present a short reminiscence of the chorale-like theme in the brass in the manuscript version (compare

Plate 7.5a   HUL 0191 (sketches for "*Luonnotar*"/*Pohjola's Daughter*)

Plate 7.5b   HUL 0163, p. 11a (draft of "*Luonnotar*"/*Pohjola's Daughter*)

Ex. 7.1   HUL 0163, passage corresponding to mm. 15–22 in the printed score of *Pohjola's Daughter*

Ex. 7.1 (*cont.*)

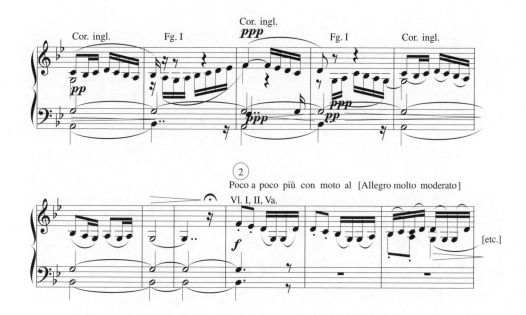

with mm. 7 and 8 in Ex. 7.2). According to manuscript 0238/1, Sibelius also planned to place a statement of the G♭/E♭ major theme, transposed to C major, at the opening of the symphony's finale (see Pl. 7.6, HUL 0238, p. 1, p. 155).[11] Finally, this theme found its way into the second movement, "Minnelied," of the *Scènes historiques II*, in its original G♭ major.[12]

The sketches reveal that, although "*Luonnotar*" and *Pohjola's Daughter* shared a great deal of musical material, the evolution from the earlier work to the later was not merely a change of titles. Sibelius made many far-reaching changes before the composition assumed its final shape. Once he had decided to connect the work with the eighth poem of the *Kalevala* (i.e. with the episode concerning Pohjola's daughter), he had to recompose the nearly complete composition, change the order of its elements, rearrange the formal and tonal design, and omit material which he seems to have regarded as intrinsically valuable.

[11] These observations do not, of course, imply structural connections between the final score of *Pohjola's Daughter* and the Third Symphony, but I think Tawaststjerna's assertion that "it is difficult to draw any developmental lines between *Pohjola's Daughter* and the Third Symphony" needs to be explored further. See Tawaststjerna, *Jean Sibelius. Åren 1904–1914* (Keuruu: Söderström, 1991), p. 67.

[12] This is why Sibelius's son-in-law, the conductor Jussi Jalas, has marked this statement "Minnelied" on many of the manuscript pages of *Pohjola's Daughter*.

Ex. 7.2   HUL 0163, passage corresponding to mm. 50ff. in the printed score of *Pohjola's Daughter*

Ex. 7.2 (*cont.*)

Ex. 7.2 (*cont.*)

Marjatta, Luonnotar and *Pohjola's Daughter* – manuscripts and programmatic sources

During the autumn of 1905 and spring of 1906 Sibelius was composing a symphonic poem – at times he even planned a symphony – based on the *Luonnotar* legend, the first poem of the *Kalevala*. As already mentioned, he had envisaged a work based on the *Kalevala* legend earlier, perhaps as early as the 1890s and certainly in the early 1900s, when he made the first sketches for the piece that finally was published as *Pohjola's Daughter*. Thus the plans for a Luonnotar composition seem to have been gestating for many years. But the composer was distracted by other projects. One of these was an oratorio based on the *Kalevala*'s fiftieth poem, the Marjatta legend. Like the early "*Luonnotar*," this oratorio was never completed.

Plate 7.6 HUL 0238, p. 1 (canceled draft of the Third Symphony showing the "Aino" theme from the draft of "*Luonnotar*"/*Pohjola's Daughter*)

Until recently, the *Marjatta* oratorio project remained an unknown episode in Sibelius's biography. The oratorio was mentioned in Sibelius's correspondence primarily during the summer and autumn of 1905. As early as 1902 the writer Jalmari Finne had proposed that Sibelius compose an oratorio based on the Marjatta legend. This idea evolved further in 1904 and, in June of 1905, Finne sent a part of the oratorio text to Sibelius.[13] At the beginning this collaboration between Finne and Sibelius seemed very promising, and the composer was eager to get the large work ready for a performance the following year, but his enthusiasm waned during the autumn of 1905, and the oratorio was left unfinished.[14]

The Marjatta legend is a Finnish-national paraphrase of the legend of Christ's birth. "Marjatta" (a Finnish female name corresponding to "Maria," the English "Mary"), "the lowly maiden" – a shepherdess – enters the woods and, after eating a lingonberry, becomes pregnant. Bearing a fatherless child, she is rejected by her parents and has to seek a place where she can give birth to her child. Finally a boy is born in a shelter built for cattle. The boy turns out to be even wiser than the old hero Väinämöinen, and is soon crowned king of Karelia. In Finne's libretto, which, like the *Kalevala* legend, is based on other old Finnish poems, the young king called Kiesus or Jeesus (Jesus) dies and is buried but, after Marjatta's lamentations and prayers, is brought back to life by an eagle which, carried by sunbeams, descends to his grave.

According to the composer's letters, he had written a lot of music for the oratorio, but unfortunately only two fragments of this material have been found or identified, in manuscripts 0222 and 0225 mentioned above. Page 1 of manuscript 0222 (Pl. 7.7) contains a sketch for music that was destined to become the slow introduction to *Pohjola's Daughter*. The fragment is written in F♯ minor instead of G minor (as in the final version).[15] After the opening measures, played by the solo cello in *Pohjola's Daughter*, there is an E in the bass supporting a major triad. At this point, on the upper stave a new melodic line unfolds, which is extended in the continuation sketches. In the first measure of this new line Sibelius writes the name "Marjatta," and after seven measures there is the word "kaiken" ("kaiken" means "all" or "all [of] the").

---

[13] Sketches and versions for the entire oratorio libretto have been preserved in the Finne archives of the Finnish Literature Society. I am most grateful to Mr. Markku Hartikainen for the many interesting facts concerning *Marjatta*.

[14] There are perhaps many reasons for this quite sudden change of mind, but the main one seems to be the oratorio text, which Sibelius did not find suitable for his artistic aims. Finne was still hopefully asking Sibelius to compose his text as late as in 1908.

[15] Although the fragment is without key signature, the key can be deduced from temporary sharps altering Ds to D sharps (see, for instance, staffs 9 and 13).

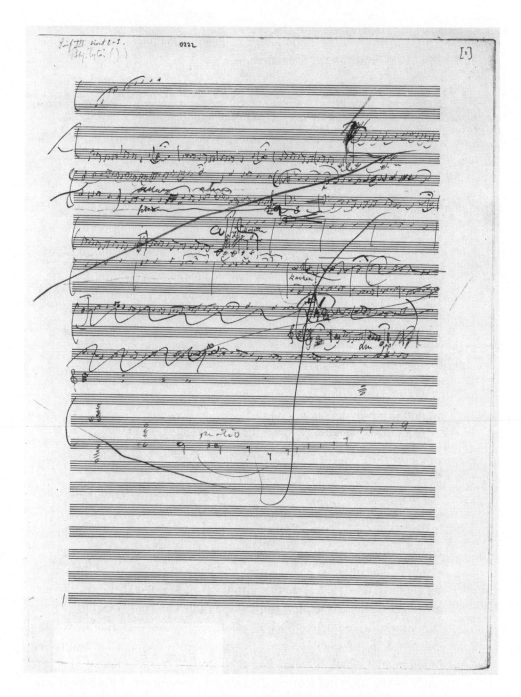

Plate 7.7   HUL 0222, p. 1 (sketches for *Marjatta oratorio/Pohjola's Daughter*)

Ex. 7.3   Melodic line of HUL 0222/1 with *Marjatta* poem

Ex. 7.3: Melodic line of HUL 0222/1 with Marjatta poem

Mar-jat - ta, ko- re -a kuo-pus, tuo on pii - ka pik - ka - rai-nen, viik - ko

py - hyyt - tä su - o - si, a - jan kai - ken (kai - no - ut

These words occur both in the last, fiftieth, poem of the *Kalevala* (lines 17 and 20) and in the first lines of Finne's libretto (see the words in italics).[16]

Finne's libretto	*Translation*[17]
Marjatta, korea kuopus,	*Marjatta*, the fine youngest child,
tuo on piika pikkarainen,	she is the tiny little maiden,
viikkoista pyhyyttä suosi,	week after week savored she holiness
ajan *kaiken* kainoutta.	*all the* time remaining bashful.

In view of the concordance with Finne's poem, it is possible to connect the other words with the melodic line (see Ex. 7.3).

On manuscript pages 0225/8 and 9 (Pl. 7.8) there is another, probably earlier, sketch for the beginning of the oratorio. It is written on two staves with a texture alternating between two and three parts, most likely for the choir. In this sketch, also, two words refer to the Marjatta text, "Tuo on" ("that is," meaning "she is"), which are the first two words of the second line in the poem (Pl. 7.8; see the sixth stave on page 8). These verbal references reveal that, at least at some stage in the compositional process of the *Marjatta* oratorio, Sibelius planned to use material eventually employed in *Pohjola's Daughter*. If we take into account the unfinished "*Luonnotar*," which Sibelius began to compose immediately after the work on the *Marjatta* oratorio foundered, the sources of the Symphonic Fantasy begin to appear multidimensional.

[16] As a matter of fact, the lines of the fiftieth poem of the *Kalevala* contain clear reminiscences of the first poem. The two maidens are even characterized in similar words in the two poems.

[17] My translation is freely based on Keith Bosley's translation of the *Kalevala*. Keith Bosley, *The Kalevala. An Epic Poem after Oral Tradition by Elias Lönnrot* (Oxford: Oxford University Press, 1989), p. 649.

Plate 7.8   HUL 0225, pp. 8 and 9 (sketches for *Marjatta*)

Of course, it is the *Kalevala* that unites the two incomplete works with Pohjola's Daughter. But there are also many features which the three *Kalevala* legends – Marjatta of the last poem, Luonnotar of the first and Pohjola's Daughter of the eighth poem – hold in common. They all are creation legends. Marjatta is a legend of Christ's birth modified to become a Finnish-national myth. Luonnotar describes the creation of the world (like the Marjatta episode a paraphrase of a Biblical legend) and the birth of Väinämöinen. And the eighth poem of the *Kalevala*, the legend of Väinämöinen and Pohjola's daughter, presents the creation of the boat – the legend on which Sibelius planned to compose an opera as early as 1894.

The creation process as described in all of these legends is difficult and painful; but all of them are also optimistic *per aspera ad astra* narratives. After suffering lonely birth pangs (Marjatta, Luonnotar) or a frustrating striving to solve an impossible task (the legend of Väinämöinen and Pohjola's daughter), these legends project far-reaching visions of the future, the beginning of new life or transfiguration. Rainer Fanselau has called attention to the correspondences between the stories of Luonnotar and Pohjola's Daughter:

> How the composer, without time for thorough changes, could change the programmes [i.e. from Luonnotar to Pohjola's Daughter], can be explained only in this way, that the musically inspiring fantasies of both programmes are similar: the monotonous beginning, the drifting in the sea / the sledge journey, the floating of the bird / sitting on the arch in the sky etc. Väinämöinen, whose name Sibelius planned to use as the title, is a character held in common by both stories, he is the son of Luonnotar and the suitor of Pohjola's daughter. In the history of the Epos there could also be a correspondence between Väinämöinen and vein emonen = the mother of water (Luonnotar).[18]

In addition to Fanselau, Tawaststjerna and Salmenhaara have discussed the possible connections between *Pohjola's Daughter* and the early "*Luonnotar.*" According to Tawaststjerna, "it cannot be determined to what extent the new Symphonic Fantasy on Väinämöinen and Pohjola's daugh-

---

[18] Wie der Komponist, ohne Zeit zu durchgreifender Veränderung zu haben, das Programm wechseln konnte, ist nur so zu erklären, daß musikalisch inspirierende Vorstellungen beider Programme ähnlich sind: monotoner Beginn; Treiben auf dem Meer/Gleiten im Schlitten; Schweben der Taucherente/Sitzen auf dem Himmelsbogen usw. Väinämöinen, dessen namen Sibelius als Titel wünschte, verbindet beide Inhalte, ist Sohn Luonnotars und Freier um die Nordlandtochter. In der Überlieferungsgeschichte des Epos könnte es sogar eine Gleichsetzung von Väinämöinen und vein emonen = Wassermutter (Luonnotar) gegeben haben. Fanselau, "Jean Sibelius. Pohjolas Tochter," p. 219.

Ex. 7.4   *Pohjola's Daughter*, the "tritone motive" in m. 66

ter derives from the tone-poem *Luonnotar*."[19] Salmenhaara writes that "the Symphonic Poem *Luonnotar*, the new Symphonic Fantasy [*Pohjola's Daughter*] and the Third Symphony are works which may share something in common" and that "it is possible that during the work on the early *Luonnotar* there was born material which he [Sibelius] removed to the new Symphonic Fantasy and perhaps to the Third Symphony."[20] As we have seen, both musical and programmatic connections between "*Luonnotar*" and *Pohjola's Daughter* are evident.

L'aventure d'un héros?

On the manuscript pages there are verbal references which suggest further programmatic connections. In numerous manuscripts containing music that found its way into *Pohjola's Daughter*, Sibelius wrote "Aino," the name of his wife; his daughter's name, Ruth, also appears on two pages. References to Aino in particular, but sometimes also to Ruth, are not rare in manuscripts of other works, but the way in which they are associated with the music in "*Luonnotar*"/*Pohjola's daughter* is of special interest.

At first glance, the marking "Aino" is not clearly and consistently associated with any particular thematic material. On page 0204/1 (Pl. 7.9), there is a marking in Swedish, "accomp till Aino," (accomp[animent] to Aino) in connection with a figure which is formed out of the idea called "tritone motive" by Tawaststjerna (Ex. 7.4). The accompanimental figure can be found in manuscript 0191 (Pl. 7.5a) in connection with the *cantabile* Gb major theme, which is still present in manuscript 0163 (Pl. 7.5b).

In his letters to Aino from May–June 1906 Sibelius still called his symphonic fantasy *Luonnotar*. However, when he sent the score to Lienau at the end of June, he employed the more general title *Eine sinfonische Fantasie. Frei nach dem Finnischen National-Epos Kalevala*. The idea for composing a work based on the Luonnotar legend may have originated with Aino, and Sibelius obviously wanted to save the title *Luonnotar* as long as possible. In fact, *Luonnotar* seems to have had

---

[19] Tawaststjerna, *Jean Sibelius. Åren 1904–1914*, p. 58.

[20] Salmenhaara, *Jean Sibelius*, p. 221.

Plate 7.9   HUL 0204, p. 1 (sketches for *"Luonnotar"/Pohjola's Daughter*)

intimate associations for Aino and Jean Sibelius. In his letters to his wife, Sibelius refers to the Fantasy as "our work in common"[21] in a manner that clearly underlines the special meaning of the piece for their relationship.

The fact that Sibelius, at least at this stage of the compositional process, associated his wife with the G♭ major theme recalls another tone poem in which the composer presents an autobiographical-heroic program and refers to his wife: Richard Strauss's *Ein Heldenleben*. In 1905, only a year before completing his Symphonic Fantasy, Sibelius had heard Strauss conducting *Ein Heldenleben* in Berlin, and, as he himself remarked, the music made a deep impression on him. It is also interesting that in the correspondence between Sibelius and Lienau during the late summer of 1906 Sibelius's proposals for the name of the Fantasy changed from "Luonnotar" to "Väinämöinen" and "L'aventure d'un héros," respectively, the latter clearly reflecting the title of Strauss's symphonic poem. The feminine creator of the Luonnotar legend had been turned into a masculine hero. In fact, it was the publisher who had the last word concerning the name of the Fantasy; the correspondence reveals that he managed to get Sibelius to return to a feminine character for the title of the Fantasy, namely *Pohjola's Daughter*.

Indeed, the programmatic idea of *Ein Heldenleben* can be regarded as a counterpart to the *Kalevala* legend of *Pohjola's Daughter*. The heroes of both works are creative men who have to struggle against their critics (the mockery of Pohjola's daughter and *des Helden Widersacher*). This struggle compels them to achieve a new kind of self-understanding, they experience spiritual "rebirth" and begin a new life: Väinämöinen's resignation and new hope (as described in the program text written by Sibelius and published with the score of *Pohjola's Daughter*) and *des Helden Weltflucht und Vollendung* (in the coda of Strauss's tone poem).

It is possible that Sibelius identified himself with the hero of the *Kalevala* legend, Väinämöinen. Already in 1892, after the legendary first performance of *Kullervo*, Sibelius, the messianic "inventor of the Finnish tone," was compared to Väinämöinen. Also Sibelius's conception of Väinämöinen as a *young* hero in his libretto sketch for the opera *Veneen luominen* (*The Building of the Boat*, 1894), which was freely based on the eighth (cf. *Pohjola's Daughter*) and sixteenth poems of the *Kalevala*, may identify Sibelius with the Kalevalaic hero, although Väinämöinen was described as elderly in the epic and in paintings and graphic art illustrating

---

[21] Tawaststjerna, *Jean Sibelius. Åren 1904–1914*, p. 41.

the *Kalevala* legends. And, as mentioned above, Sibelius's view of his artistic vocation seems altogether to have been strongly influenced by heroic images.

Pohjola's Daughter was the last part in the series depicting true Kalevalaic heroes in Sibelius's output, the other parts being the *Kullervo* and *Lemminkäinen* legends, both of these composed in the 1890s and, interestingly enough, rejected by the composer himself for decades. Although Sibelius composed works based on or referring to *Kalevala* poems after *Pohjola's Daughter*, he did not return to his heroic ideas – the legend of *Luonnotar* Op. 70 is not at all comparable with the heroic legends. In spite of its name, the focus of *Pohjola's Daughter*'s program text – and the musical treatment of it – is not the feminine character but the "Finnish Orpheus," the creative man.

II Analytical view

The sonata form and programmatic aspects of *Pohjola's Daughter*

Many scholars have regarded the form of *Pohjola's Daughter* as – "free" or "strict" – sonata form, or at least have considered the sonata principle as a background for the formal design of the symphonic fantasy. In addition to the surface thematic features noticed by Tanzberger, Tawaststjerna, and others, there is also a deep-level correspondence between the sonata-based formal design and the narrative structure of the program text in *Pohjola's Daughter*.

The program text written originally by Sibelius himself retells the story of the Kalevalaic hero Väinämöinen on his homeward journey from the gloomy land of Pohjola. He sees a young and beautiful maiden, the daughter of Pohjola, sitting and spinning on "heaven's arch." Väinämöinen falls in love with her, and asks her to join him. The maiden promises to follow him only after he has managed to accomplish an impossible task (in the original *Kalevala* poem there are several of them). After a difficult and unsuccessful struggle, Väinämöinen has to abandon Pohjola's daughter and continue his journey disappointed and humiliated (in the *Kalevala* legend, Väinämöinen wounds himself accidentally with an axe and has to leave Pohjola's daughter in order to find a healer). Väinämöinen accepts his bitter failure, but rediscovers his pride and attains new, even greater heroism after his vain struggle and admission of his own weakness and limitations. The program text printed in the score is given here as a whole (the translation taken from the Dover edition of *Pohjola's Daughter*):[22]

Pohjola's Daughter

Väinämöinen, old and truthful,
Rides his sleigh and travels homeward
From the dark realm of Pohjola,
From the land of gloomy chanting.

Hark! What sounds? He glances upward:
Up above there on the rainbow
Sits and spins Pohjola's Daughter,
In the airy blue, so radiant.

Thrilled and drunken with her beauty,
"Come down here to me, O fair one,"
Thus he pleads, Coy, she refuses,
At his new plea, her demand is:

"You must conjure from my distaff
What I have long desired: a vessel.
Show to me your wondrous powers
Then most gladly will I follow."

Väinämöinen, old and truthful,
Toils and shapes and seeks . . . but vainly.
Ah, the proper incantation,
Never will it be discovered!

Full of anger, sorely wounded.
Since the fair one has renounced him,
To his sleigh he springs . . . and onward!
But once more his head he raises.

---

[22] *Pohjolas Tochter*

Wainämoinen, alt und wahrhaft,
Fährt auf seinem Schlitten heimwärts
Aus dem finstern Reich Pohjolas,
Aus dem Heimat dunkler Lieder.

Horch! Was rauscht? Er schaut zur Höhe:
Droben auf dem Himmelsbogen
Sitzt und spinnt Pohjolas Tochter,
Strahlend, hoch im luftigen Blau.

Ihre Schönheit packt, berauscht ihn.
"Steig' herab zu mir, o Holde,"
Fleht er. Doch sie weigert's neckisch.
Wieder fleht er . . . und sie fordert:

"Sollst ein Boot aus meiner Spindel
Zaubern, was ich lang' ersehnte.

Zeig' mir deine Wunderkräfte,
– Und ich will Dir gerne folgen."

Wainämoinen, alt und wahrhaft,
Müht sich, schafft und sucht . . . vergeblich.
Ach, die rechte Zauberformel
Will sich nimmer finden lassen!

Voller Unmut, schwer verwundet,
Da die Holde ihm verloren,
Springt er in den Schlitten . . . Weiter! . . .
Und schon hebt sein Haupt er wieder.

Nimmer kann der Held verzagen,
Alles Leid wird überwunden.
Der Erinn'rung sanfte Klänge
Lindern Schmerz und bringen Hoffnung.

Never can the hero falter,
All his grief is put behind him.
Gentle tones from his remembrance
Bring him hope and lighten sorrow.

The three-part sonata framework corresponds to three large sections in the programmatic text: the exposition represents the verses describing Väinämöinen's journey, his falling in love with Pohjola's daughter and receiving the assignment of the impossible task. The development section depicts his effort to build the boat, and his failure. The recapitulation corresponds to the continuation of his journey and his rebirth as a hero. My view of the correspondence between the overall sonata-form design and the program text is as follows:

Formal design	*Program text*
EXPOSITION (mm. 1–113)	Strophes 1–4 of the program text
Introduction (mm. 1–27)	"Väinämöinen, old and truthful, Rides his sleigh and travels homeward
Transitional passage (mm. 28–52)	From the dark realm of Pohjola, From the land of gloomy chanting."
Heroic theme (mm. 53–56)	
The theme associated with Pohjola's daughter and the bridge to the development (mm. 57–113)	Strophes 2–4 of the program text
DEVELOPMENT (mm. 114–158)	Fifth strophe of the program text
RECAPITULATION (mm. 159–259)	Sixth strophe of the program text
Recapitulation of the latter part of the introduction and transitional passage (mm. 159–212)	"To his sleigh he springs … and onward!"
Recapitulation of the heroic theme (mm. 213–220) and the coda (mm. 221–259)	"But once more his head he raises," the last strophe of the program text

In fact, some scholars have come quite near this interpretation in their writings. It is, after all, not very difficult to hear the G minor opening of the Symphonic Fantasy as a musical image of the land of Pohjola and to recognize the heroic theme and the theme depicting Pohjola's daughter in the sky, as well as to connect the stirring middle section (development) with the fury in which Väinämöinen tries hopelessly to build a boat of splints. But the outline of the sonata form presented above exhibits a number of peculiarities; perhaps the most important difference between my analysis and most others concerns the way in which the musical structures are understood.

First of all, the introduction to *Pohjola's Daughter* is considered an integral part of the exposition, not as a separate slow-tempo section in a traditional sense. It is noteworthy that the introduction leads seamlessly – for instance, without modulating to the dominant of the main key, as in the traditional sonata movement introduction – to the new tempo, *Moderato*, at m. 27 (5:8). Furthermore, the opening is remarkable because of its thematic features: it is a starting point of the thematic process that continues throughout the first part of the exposition. The thematic material presented in the introduction is repeated in the recapitulation; in my opinion, this recapitulation confirms the role of the introduction as an integral component of the exposition.

Secondly, in my analysis – in contradistinction to most other interpretations – the section following the opening G minor introduction, mm. 28–52, is not the main or first theme, but rather a transitional passage. This reconfiguration of the sonata principle may appear radical. But what can we call a section without a stable tonal center, a section that is a bridge from the opening G minor to the main tonality of the piece as a whole, namely B♭ major, established by the "heroic theme" at mm. 53–56 (10:4–11:3)? This idea of transition from G minor to B♭ major can be accepted, providing the B♭ major at mm. 53–56 is viewed as a firm and stable key.

In terms of its tonal structure, the sonata principle in *Pohjola's Daughter* deviates even further from the traditional procedures. The Symphonic Fantasy seems not to begin in its tonic key B♭ major, but in G minor (vi). How one explains the arrival on B♭ major in m. 53 (without cadential preparation) is crucial for the interpretation of the tonal design and voice-leading structure of the whole piece. Is this B♭ the "real" tonic or is it, on a deeper level, still connected with the G minor chord? What is the key of the theme associated with Pohjola's daughter? Is it really cast in E major, as usually claimed? Obviously, the exposition does not end with a dominant chord, so where does the development actually begin and what is its harmonic function? How does the recapitulation recall the tonic key and where is the final tonic reached? These questions will be discussed with reference to harmony and structure.

Harmonic and voice-leading structure

One possible overview of the voice-leading structure of *Pohjola's Daughter* is displayed in Ex. 7.5. The graph shows the G minor chord of the introduction as deriving from an upper-neighbor sixth to the fifth of

Ex. 7.5a–b   *Pohjola's Daughter*, overview of the harmony and voice-leading structure (Middleground)

a)

Page:measure	10:4	11:4	18:7	25:5	28:1	29:2	30:1	39:4	40:1
Measure	53	57	107	146	156	161	165	209	213

	Exposition				Development	Recapitulation		+Coda
	Intr. Tr. H. th. P. d. th.					"Tr."		H. th.

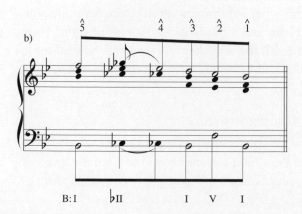

Intr.	=	Introduction
Tr.	=	Transitional passage
H. th.	=	"Heroic theme"
P. d. th.	=	Theme associated with Pohjola's daughter

b)

B:I   ♭II   I   V   I

the tonic B♭ major chord.[23] B♭ as a bass note is implied here rather than explicit. The B♭ major chord is not yet stable in the introduction or the transition; however, the tendency of B♭ to serve as a bass note, temporarily in the introduction and reinforced later in the transitional passage, is reflected in this reading. Thus the opening G minor chord is understood only in connection with the B♭ major that follows. In this context, the transition in mm. 28–52 (5:9–10:3) signifies a passage where the center of gravity is shifted almost imperceptibly from the G minor to the B♭ major chord, and without traditional modulatory procedures. But even if there is no cadential V–I progression in B♭ major, the tonic is nevertheless achieved at m. 53 (10:4), where the "heroic theme" emerges forcefully.

Tim Howell has observed that, in the introduction and in the transition, "the flattened leading tone [in g minor], F, becomes the main pivot in this initial definition of B♭ major."[24] The neighbor-note figure F–G is the central motivic feature in the Symphonic Fantasy and it figures prominently in mm. 5–8 in the bass,[25] producing the first change of sonority in the opening measures. The motive permeates the musical surface during the first half of the exposition (mm. 1–56), culminating in the "heroic theme." When the interval frame G–D of the opening G minor chord is transposed to B♭ major, F – often reinforced by its own

[23] According to another reading, the G minor chord of the introduction is interpreted as a structural chord and the B♭ major chord at mm. 53–56 is not regarded as a real, structural tonic. In this case, the G minor chord is prolonged throughout the exposition, development, and recapitulation until the dominant chord arrives at m. 210, and the harmonic and voice-leading structure of the whole Symphonic Fantasy is built on a huge auxiliary cadence, whereby the G minor chord (vi) is prolonged over two hundred measures and the structural descent (here $\hat{3}$–$\hat{2}$–$\hat{1}$) in the upper voice takes place in a few measures. Because D is clearly the most prominent upper-voice note connected with the G minor chord during the introduction, the structural descent is understood to begin from $\hat{3}$.

The attenuated G minor prolongation could reflect the underlying idea of the program text: Väinämöinen is released from the spell – or should I say the obsession – of the gloomy land of Pohjola, represented by the G minor chord, only after he has gone through his purgatory. And, to put it another way: Väinämöinen's heroic character is real or fully established for the first time only after he has won his struggle – also the repetition of

the "heroic theme" in the recapitulation could reinforce this. I am grateful to Lauri Suurpää for discussing this reading – as well as many other points – with me. Timothy Jackson's analysis of *Pohjola's Daughter*, with which I became acquainted later, is closely related to this alternative interpretation of the auxiliary cadence (Timothy L. Jackson, "'The Maiden with a Heart of Ice:' Crystallization and Compositional Genesis in Sibelius's *Pohjola's Daughter* and Other Works," in *Sibelius Forum. Proceedings From the Second International Jean Sibelius Conference. Helsinki November 25–29, 1995*, ed. Veijo Murtomäki, Kari Kilpeläinen and Risto Väisänen (Helsinki: Sibelius Academy, 1998), pp. 260–65.

[24] Tim Howell, *Jean Sibelius. Progressive Techniques in the Symphonies and Tone Poems.* (London: Garland, 1989), p. 230.

[25] Interestingly, in manuscript 0222 discussed above, Sibelius has marked a small letter "a" in the corresponding place, i.e. where the neighbor note is heard in the bass (see Pl. 7.7, p. 157, between staffs 7 and 8). Could this marking indicate the importance of the neighbor-note sonority in the composer's mind?

leading tone, E♮ in the introduction and in the transition – functions as the top voice in m. 53.[26] F is also understood here as *Kopfton* of the structural line in *Pohjola's Daughter*.

The "second theme" or the theme associated with Pohjola's daughter herself is, in my view, not cast in E major; instead, F♯ minor (enharmonically G♭, the lowered sixth degree) is the basis of the sonority at mm. 57–60 (11:4–12:1). The opening phrases of oboe and English horn are clearly in F♯ minor, and the D♯ adds the Dorian sixth to the pitch collection. In fact, this passage is not in any stable key, but the F♯ sonority derives from a chromatic alteration of the fifth of the B♭ major chord, or a 5–8–5 voice leading which eliminates the parallel fifths between B♭–F of the tonic chord reached at m. 53 and B♮–F♯ (C♭–G♭) at the end of the exposition, m. 106.

An explanation of E major as the key of the second theme is obviously based on the new four-sharp key signature, and the E major seventh chord heard at mm. 61 and 62 (12:2–3). But neither the key signature nor the single – dissonant – sonority based on E decisively defines the tonality. The E major seventh chord is actually situated as a neighboring sonority between the two F♯ based sonorities at mm. 57–60 (11:4–12:1) and 63 (12:4). It may be significant that Sibelius employed a three-sharp key signature in the equivalent places in manuscripts 0174 and 0183, writing the D♯s with accidentals.[27] Thus, he may have conceived the passage as F♯ minor with the Dorian sixth and added the D♯ into the key signature to simplify the notation.

B♭ and G♭ are juxtaposed in the recapitulation, at mm. 213–220 (40:1–42:2): the "heroic theme" is heard twice, first in B♭, then in the context of the neighboring G♭ major sonority, B♭ sustained in the bass through this passage. Already in the sketches the lowered submediant key is assigned an important role in the tonal design of the work. The "heroic theme" was originally sketched in G♭ major and marked *Gesthema* (theme in G♭ [major]) by the composer in the manuscripts. The "Aino theme" in manuscript 0163 is associated with the G♭ major sonority, and at the corresponding place in the final version, the theme representing Pohjola's daughter is heard within a Dorian F♯ (G♭) minor sonority. But, as already observed, the theme associated with Pohjola's daughter is tonally unstable, and, in my view, the idea of leaving the theme tonally ambiguous mirrors the poetic image of the program text: she hovers in the air, weightless, without firm ground (i.e., firm tonality) under her feet.

---

[26] E♮ has not merely a role of modal (Dorian or Lydian) coloring here, but it takes part in the tonal process of shifting between G minor and B♭ major.

[27] In manuscript 0163 discussed above (see Plate 7.5), the passage is to be heard (from rehearsal number 7 onward) in E♭ minor prepared by its dominant. The corresponding tonality of the final version would be F♯ (or G♭) minor – if the key were established.

Analysts are divided regarding the end of the exposition and the beginning of the development. Howell[28] proposes the "tonally diverse passage" to begin as early as at page 13 of the score (most probably at m. 66 or 70, 13:1 or 13:5); Jackson[29] interprets the first part of the development at m. 68 (13:3), followed by a recapitulation of the second group at mm. 86–113 (15:3–18:13) and the second part of the development from m. 116 (19:3). Tawaststjerna mentions m. 76 (14:3), the beginning of the pizzicato passage, as a borderline.[30] I share the opinion of Collins, Fanselau, and Tanzberger,[31] who suggest m. 114 (19:1) as the starting point of the development. The halt at m. 113 on the tremolo unison B with a fermata and the marking *Lunga*, and the fresh tempo, *Allegro*, at m. 114 all speak in favor of drawing the borderline here. From a harmonic point of view, the most remarkable element is the bass note, B♮. At mm. 106–111 (18:6–13) the chord based on B♮ is a major chord, and there is a suggestion of the minor seventh, A, in the oboe and the clarinet parts; thus the sonority as a whole can be heard as a dominant of E minor. Unlike the traditional major-mode sonata, the development does not prolong the dominant (of the B♭ major tonic) reached and established at the end of the exposition.

Against the programmatic background, the strange arrival on B♮ can be interpreted as the task which Väinämöinen has to solve: since the dominant F has not yet been reached, in the development Väinämöinen must discover the right way, or "the proper incantation," in order to reach it. The dominant (seventh) chord based on B♮ points to E minor, not to F major. The real goal remains elusive; it is as distant as possible, the interval between B♮ and F being a tritone.

The many whole-tone passages in the development may express the hero's efforts to find a way to fill in this tritonal gap between B♮ and F. The goal seems to be the nearest at mm. 145–151 (25:4–26:4), where a ninth chord based on C, the dominant of the dominant, is articulated with overwhelming force. Väinämöinen utters his most powerful incantation – in vain. The dominant remains lost, and the development returns to its point of departure: the culmination at mm. 156–158 (28:1–3) re-establishes B♮ in the bass. What is more, the violent roar before the fermata at m. 158 ends with a tritone leap F–B♮, thus compressing Väinämöinen's

[28] Howell, *Progressive Techniques*, p. 231.

[29] Jackson, "'The Maiden with a Heart of Ice,'" pp. 262–64.

[30] Tawaststjerna, *Jean Sibelius. Åren 1904–1914*, p. 65.

[31] M. Stuart Collins, "The Orchestral Music of Sibelius" (Ph.D. diss., University of Leeds,

1973), p. 162; Fanselau, "*Jean Sibelius. Pohjolas Tochter,*" p. 228; Ernst Tanzberger, *Die symphonischen Dichtungen von Jean Sibelius (Eine inhalts- und formanalytische Studie)* (Würzburg: Konrad Triltsch, 1943), p. 42.

frustration into two notes: F, the dominant never reached, and B♮, the unsolved problem.

If F ($\hat{5}$) functions as the primary tone of the structural line, then a question arises as to the continuation of this line via E♭ ($\hat{4}$). As shown in the graph, $\hat{4}$ of the structural line (E♭) is not supported by a diatonic degree of B♭ major in the bass, but by B♮, the sharp I or, enharmonically, flat II.[32] At m. 161 (29:2) E♭ is reinterpreted as D♯, the leading tone of E minor. Thus the development both opens and ends with a sonority based on B♮, which in both cases points towards E minor.

The recapitulation does not commence in the tonic key, but the music begins to find its way back to B♭ major: after bitter failure, Väinämöinen's homeward journey continues. The way home is as long as the path from B♮ (at the end of the exposition and beginning of the development) to F (implied but not reached in the development). Measures 159–161 lead the music temporarily to the E minor chord, and the recapitulation of the material heard in the transitional passage of the exposition; m. 161 (29:2) initiates a passage in which mm. 161–164 are sequentially repeated a minor third higher in mm. 165–168 (30:1–4). Again, in this passage as a whole, progression through a tritone is important: now the music moves from the E minor chord to the "home key," B♭ major. B♭ is secured in the bass at m. 165 (30:1); but the sonority above it is a G minor $^6_3$ chord, and the B♭ major sonority at mm. 188–204 (34:4–38:4) – partly because it contains the dissonant major seventh, A – does not yet resolve the tension created through the entirety of the development and beginning of the recapitulation. However, the D ($\hat{3}$) reached in the upper voice at m. 165 participates in the structural line descent from E♭ ($\hat{4}$).

Measures 205–212 (38:5–39:7) represent *the* crucial juncture for the harmonic and voice-leading structures: here, the dominant ninth chord on F – the only dominant in the entire piece – is finally articulated (at mm. 209–210). Now, after the expression of frustration in the development and the desperate escape at the beginning of the recapitulation, Väinämöinen rediscovers his heroic identity. The $\hat{2}$ (C), supported by the

---

[32] In the deep middleground graph in Ex. 7.5b, the B♮s are written enharmonically (as C♭s) in order to clarify the voice-leading structure. Here the consonant support for $\hat{4}$ is achieved by a non-diatonic bass note, C♭, the upper neighbor of B♭. Edward Laufer, in his analysis of the first movement of Sibelius's Fourth Symphony, "On the first movement of Sibelius's Fourth Symphony. A Schenkerian view," in *Schenker Studies 2*, ed. Carl Schachter and Hedi Siegel (Cambridge: Cambridge University Press, 1999), pp. 127–59, presents another example of supporting a structural line note by a non-diatonic degree. In Laufer's analysis the structural note in the upper voice, C♯ (3), is also non-diatonic. In Timothy Jackson's analysis of *Pohjola's Daughter* ("'The Maiden with a Heart of Ice'") almost every bass and upper-voice note in the fundamental structure is non-diatonic.

structural dominant, is not heard directly in the uppermost voice, but the line resolves to B♭ (1̂) within the tonic chord at m. 213 (40:1).

The "heroic theme" is – significantly enough – recapitulated simultaneously with the arrival on the final tonic and restated within the neighboring G♭ major sonority in mm. 217–220 (41:2–42:2), while B♭ is sustained in the bass throughout. This G♭ to B♭ progression recapitulates the juxtaposition of F♯ minor (of the "theme associated with Pohjola's daughter") with B♭ major (of the "heroic theme") in the exposition. Programmatically, this recomposition could signify that Väinämöinen has finally overcome his humiliation. Now the lowered submediant sonority is related to the final tonic chord – bound to it as a neighboring sonority: the bitter failure has became a part of Väinämöinen's self-consciousness, reinforcing his self-conception as a true hero. He has won his inner struggle. He has not suffered in vain.

Epilogue

"The hero's adventure" is not entirely over with the arrival on the structural tonic at m. 213. In the coda, from m. 221 (42:3), there is still the powerful outburst of the material heard in the *con passione* episode of the solo clarinet (mm. 205–210, 38:5–39:5) and the theme associated with Pohjola's daughter, as well as the sudden change to the almost resigned mood of the last page of the score. Indeed, the concluding measures crystallize many of the features that have been so important in the course of the work. Firstly, there is the high note F juxtaposed with the low G – i.e. the primary tone of the fundamental structure reached in the glorious "heroic theme." Secondly, the concluding ascent G–A–B♭ recalls the hero's overall path from the gloomy land of Pohjola to his apotheosis. However, the vague last note imparts an interrogative quality to the ending, and it is interesting that in one of his sketches (0172) – not even one of the earliest ones – Sibelius planned to end the Symphonic Fantasy on an unstable G minor six-three chord.

The last strophe of the program text, written as a whole by the publisher, did not satisfy the composer. According to him, it was "slightly over-dreamy."[33] In the last page of the score, Sibelius himself paints a picture which is quite different from the pathetic redemption or transfiguration described in the last strophe of the program text. His conception of the hero – and of himself as a creative man – is darker in tone, more contradictory, almost ironic – and deeper, more human, at the same time. It is as if Sibelius in these last tones had created a musical counterpart to

---

[33] Tawaststjerna, *Jean Sibelius. Åren 1904–1914* (1991), p. 63.

the hesitant words which he, already an appreciated master all over the world, wrote to his diary in April 1915, when composing his Fifth Symphony: "It is as if Father God had thrown down pieces of mosaic from heaven's floor and asked me to determine what kind of picture it was. Maybe a good definition of 'composing.' Maybe not. How would I know?"[34]

[34] Tawaststjerna, *Jean Sibelius. Åren 1914–1919* (Keuruu: Söderström, 1996), p. 55.

8 Observations on crystallization and entropy in the music of Sibelius and other composers[1]

Timothy L. Jackson

> Formula virtutis maris astrum porta salvis
> Prole Maria levat quos conivge subdidit Eva
>
> (Model of virtue, star of the seas, portal of healing;
> Through her Child Maria frees those whom Eve with her husband betrayed)
>
> *Twelfth-century inscription*[2]

Preliminary aphorisms

"Nebular spirals solidify and become stars. Music, born from the original irrational state as if from a nebular spiral, and made ever more dense with diminution, grew into a star in the heavens of the spirit."[3] With these words – unfortunately banished to an appendix in the English translation of *Free Composition* – Heinrich Schenker compared the formation of music with the creation of stars out of cosmic gases. Schenker's "crystallization" metaphor aptly delineates the essential compositional idea in many of the symphonies and tone poems of Jean Sibelius and other composers. While the concept of "crystallization" naturally informs those tone poems by Sibelius which depict creation, such as *Luonnotar*, it also may be discovered in many of the composer's other works, including the symphonies. The composer himself appears to have been fully conscious of this aspect of his musical thought, once describing the Finale of his Third Symphony as "the *crystallization* [my emphasis] of ideas from chaos."[4]

Sibelius was equally fascinated by the concept of entropy as the "failure" of crystallization – the devolution of order into chaos. I have

---

[1] An earlier version of this essay was read at the Second International Sibelius Conference at Helsinki University in November 1995. I would like to thank Veijo Murtomäki for many helpful comments and suggestions.

[2] Quoted from Ernst Guldan, *Eva und Maria. Eine Antithese als Bildmotiv* (Graz–Köln: Hermann Böhlaus, 1966), p. 41. Guldan traces the theology of the "Eve–Mary" duality through Western iconography.

[3] Heinrich Schenker, *Free Composition*, trans. Ernst Oster (New York: Longman, 1979), p. 158.

[4] Quoted from Erik Tawaststjerna, *Sibelius, Vol. II, 1904–14*, trans. Robert Layton (London: Faber, 1986), p. 66.

proposed that, in his 1903–04 setting of Viktor Rydberg's *På verandan*, Sibelius discovers a metaphor for both crystallization and entropy in ascending 5–6 sequences that, through an auxiliary cadence, "crystallize" on the putative tonic C, and then "devolve" beyond it in implied continuing sequences:

> the inferred links in the sequential chain potentially extend backwards and forwards in cycles of entropy and rebirth around cataclysmic instances of cosmic *Nullpunkt* at the implied cadence on C. [Sibelius] interprets the [poem's] conclusion ironically; in the "crystallizing" moment of revelation, both God and the essential existential questions remain inscrutable and unanswered![5]

I hypothesized that *På verandan* is related to the Fourth Symphony, which also unites metaphors for "crystallization" – the creation of life in the first movement – with its dissolution in the last; furthermore, in the Finale, "entropy triumphs and the hero's life inexorably ebbs and dissipates back into chaos and nothingness."[6] My "observations" will suggest that these intertwined narratives of "crystallization" and "devolution" or "entropy" inform a Sibelian "*meta*-narrative" culminating in the Seventh Symphony. Unlike those commentators who interpret the Seventh as a triumphant work, I understand it, like the Fourth, as dualistic, simultaneously embodying crystallization and its failure. For Sibelius, crystallization and entropy also possess sexual connotations related to his concept of Woman.

Over the past fifty years, much has been written on "the profound logic" (in Sibelius's famous words to Mahler) "that creates an inner connection between all of the motives." Certainly, the "compelling vein that goes through the whole" (as Sibelius described his symphonic technique to Karl Ekman) depends on the transformation of "germ" motives investigated by earlier students of Sibelius's compositional technique.[7] However, the distinctly Sibelian effect of "symphonic unity" – to use Veijo Murtomäki's

---

[5] Jackson, "'The Maiden with a Heart of Ice': 'Crystallization' and Compositional Genesis in Sibelius's *Pohjola's Daughter* and Other Works," in *Sibelius Forum. Proceedings from the Second International Jean Sibelius Conference. Helsinki November 25–29, 1995*, eds. Veijo Murtomäki, Kari Kilpeläinen, and Risto Väisänen (Helsinki: Sibelius Academy, 1998), pp. 254–58.

[6] Jackson, "The Finale of Bruckner's Seventh Symphony and the Tragic Reversed Sonata Form," in *Bruckner Studies*, ed. Paul Hawkshaw and Timothy L. Jackson

(Cambridge: Cambridge University Press, 1999), pp. 201–203.

[7] For an account of the meeting between Sibelius and Mahler, see Tawaststjerna, *Sibelius, Vol. II*, p. 77, and Paavo Helistö, "Mahler's Helsinki Concert in 1907," *Finnish Music Quarterly* 4 (1995), pp. 17–21. Writings on Sibelius's "profound logic" include David Cherniavsky, "The Use of Germ Motives by Sibelius," *Music and Letters* 23 (1942), 1–9, and Lionel Pike, *Beethoven, Sibelius and "the Profound Logic"* (London: The Athlone Press, 1976).

term – may be created by large-scale linear and/or harmonic progression towards a distant goal, which "crystallizes" only very late in the work.[8] As Donald Francis Tovey observes, "the essence of the whole is just this, that nothing takes shape until the end. Then comes the one and all-sufficing climax."[9]

Central to the idea of "crystallization" – and to "symphonic process" – is the concept of the "definitive tonic arrival," which I designate "DTA." In a symphonic context, the "crystallization" effect may be created by "anticipating" DTA with "weak" or "initially strong" but subsequently "devalued" tonics. As I shall attempt to show, the process of "tonic devaluation" may be connected with the "tonic auxiliary cadence," whereby an apparently "strong" initial tonic is "weakened" so that it can resolve to the definitive tonic (DTA). For Sibelius, as for other nineteenth- and twentieth-century composers, this process of tonic "crystallization" may become a metaphor for the inner struggle to attain the heroic. Additionally, when the "goal" is a beloved woman (Clara Schumann, Aino Sibelius), this "crystallization" process may have psycho-sexual connotations of "yearning" or "longing" for the beloved.

Ave Maria, mutans evae nomen!

Since the second century, Christian theology has posited the Virgin Mary as "the second Eve" who, through the Immaculate Conception, helps to redeem mankind from Original Sin. This concept of Woman as *simultaneously* Temptress and Redemptress, derived from Christian theology, permeates Western art and music. In Medieval and Renaissance iconographies, the Virgin and Eve are frequently depicted together. Sometimes Eve is shown accepting the Apple from the Serpent, while the Virgin crushes him beneath her feet; on other occasions, the Virgin tramples Eve instead, crushing her like the Serpent. Later nineteenth-century artists gave this theme a personal twist. For example, with regard to Gauguin's painting *Nave, Nave, Moe* (*Delightful Mystery*, 1894) Ziva Amishai-Maisels observes:

> [Gauguin] represented Mary as the second Eve, the complement and
> redeemer of the first Eve. He first used Eve and Mary together to state his

[8] Veijo Murtomäki, *Symphonic Unity. The Development of Formal Thinking in the Symphonies of Sibelius*, trans. Henry Bacon, Studia Musicologica Universitatis Helsingiensis 5 (Helsinki: University of Helsinki, 1993).

[9] From the essay on Sibelius's Third Symphony in Donald Francis Tovey, *Symphonies and Other Orchestral Works* (Oxford: Oxford University Press, repr. 1989), p. 496.

understanding of these opposite but complementary aspects of his women in *Nave, Nave, Moe*... Through it [i.e. through this juxtaposition] Gauguin stressed the dual personality of his Tahitian women, who combine the purity of Mary with Eve's desire to yield to Temptation.[10]

The next step, the synthesis of "Eve-Mary" in a single woman, discovers an especially powerful Northern advocate in Munch's *Madonna* (1895), where the bare-chested Temptress, who beckons with an alluring gesture of sexual abandon, is nevertheless depicted with the Virgin's halo. A similar conception of Woman – i.e., as both Temptress precipitating the Fall and Redemptress, the "healer" and "portal" to resurrection and immortality – underlies Brahms's and Schumann's representations of Clara, and Sibelius's portrayal of Aino. This projection of the "Eve-Mary" synthesis onto Woman implies as its corollary that the male protagonist – the narrative persona – must assume the complementary synthetic identity of "Adam-Christ." Through Eve's Temptation, Adam falls, succumbing to Original Sin, which Christ expiates, through his suffering on the Cross. Thus, Schumann's, Brahms's, and Sibelius's symphonic self-projections must experience Adam's fall and Christ's agony: as "*Men* of Sorrows," they must be crucified before they can be resurrected.[11] But Sibelius is a modernist because he doubts the possibility of resurrection, while Schumann and Brahms, as men of the optimistic nineteenth century, do not.

Sibelius's mythic language is saturated with this *dichotomy* of Woman: the wood nymph and Pohjola's daughter are Temptresses, while the "wife-mother" Mary (Marjatta)/Aino – the "Mother of God" and "Bride of Christ" – simultaneously affords redemptive rebirth: perhaps in the "pure" Virgin womb, "fallen" Adam may be "resurrected" Christ-like.[12] In his essay in this book, Murtomäki posits that Temptation is *the* major obstacle facing the young Sibelius's narrative persona. Extending his argument, I argue that the problematic duality of Woman remains a central concern *throughout* Sibelius's oeuvre. Surely it is significant that Sibelius named his house "Ainola" after his wife, thereby associating her with the redemptive roles of *both* "mother" and "wife," the home being analogous to the "womb" as the source of the hero's life and inspiration,

[10] Ziva Amishai-Maisels, *Gauguin's Religious Themes* (New York: Garland, 1985), pp. 317–18.

[11] For a discussion of composers' and artists' self-representations as Christ, see my book *Tchaikovsky. Symphony No. 6 (Pathétique)* (Cambridge: Cambridge University Press, 1999), pp. 50–56.

[12] See Timo Virtanen's essay in the present volume, especially the section "*Marjatta, Luonnotar* and *Pohjola's Daughter* – Manuscripts and Programmatic Sources," for information on Sibelius's work on the Marjatta legend from the *Kalevala* in 1905–1906. For discussion of Woman as "Temptress" in Sibelius and other nineteenth- and early twentieth-century composers, see Murtomäki's chapter, pp. 123–34.

and the matrix of his connection to nature. Since the "wife-mother" Aino is "home" – "Ainola" – and "mother earth" is Finland, the "crystallization" metaphor as struggle to "attain" the "wife-mother" becomes associated with Finnish nationalistic aspirations. In this way, matrimonial and nationalist issues intertwine in Sibelius's music from *Kullervo* to the Seventh Symphony and *Tapiola*.

The hero's libidinal struggle is manifested not only in the early works (as Murtomäki has so compellingly argued), but also in the very last pieces. I interpret the Seventh within a genre of "domestic" symphonies, initiated by Schumann's Second, Third, and Fourth Symphonies, continuing through Brahms's First Symphony, and further developed by Richard Strauss's *Sinfonia domestica* and Sibelius's Seventh Symphony. Through musical *topoi* evoking the "Adam-Eve" and "Christ-Virgin" dichotomy, Schumann, Brahms, and Sibelius "theologize" – and thereby universalize – their domestic dramas. This assertion of a theologized domestic drama in the Seventh Symphony may come as a shock to those readers who imagined the later symphonies to be paradigms of "absolute" music – abstract exercises in "symphonic logic." To be sure, the logic never fails; but Sibelius's working sketches and manuscripts, the structure of his music, and indeed the compositional ideology informing that structure, provide compelling evidence of a "meta-symphonic" narrativity spanning the oeuvre.[13]

Arnold Schoenberg asserted that great music is still to be written in the key of C major. Late in life (1949), reaffirming his admiration for both Sibelius and Shostakovich, he wrote that "[earlier in my career] I said something which did not require the knowledge of an expert. Every amateur, every music lover could have said: 'I feel they have the breath of symphonists.'"[14] Perhaps, through this combination of remarks, Schoenberg admits that it is *more difficult* to achieve new, artistically valid statements using old means – i.e., tonality as epitomized by C major – than with the new post-tonal language he himself had invented, and that Sibelius in his Third and Seventh Symphonies (both in C major) had accomplished this feat. If we may ask why Sibelius's music, like Schoenberg's, is "so difficult to understand," I argue that this is because Sibelius has mastered the full complexity

---

[13] The foreword to my *Tchaikovsky. Symphony No. 6*, p. ix, posits that "there is no structure without ideology," denying the purity of "pure" structure. The present study supports this theorem by explicating the connection between Sibelius's psycho-sexual/nationalistic ideology and the technical aspects of his musical language.

[14] "Criteria for the Evaluation of Music" (1949), in Arnold Schoenberg, *Style and Idea. Selected Writings of Arnold Schoenberg*, ed. Leonard Stein, trans. Leo Black (London: Faber, 1975), p. 136.

of design-structure correlation in the post-Beethovenian line of development, and yet managed to give it an innovative twist. Therefore,
Schenkerian models cannot be applied to Sibelius's music in a logically
positivistic way; rather, they must respond to nuances both in the historical design-structure discourse (within which Sibelius's music operates and
achieves creative efficacy) and the ideological impulses propelling structure. For this reason, to explain Sibelius's *modus operandi*, we must contex-
tualize it against the practice of Beethoven, Chopin, Schumann, Brahms,
Tchaikovsky, and especially Bruckner, whom the young Sibelius lionized as
"the greatest living composer."

If many of Sibelius's formal *designs* are sonata forms or variants
thereof, his *structures* tend to be undivided.[15] This is to say that the distinctly Sibelian concept of "crystallization" depends upon the unfolding
of a mono-directional, goal-oriented undivided structure, which evolves
progressively towards its goal, either reaches or fails to achieve it, and
then dissipates. Thus, there is a *non-congruence* between the repetitive or
"rotational" aspect of the sonata design and continuous evolution in the
undivided structure, which relate to each other *contrapuntally*.[16] My
subject, then, is this design-structure counterpoint in relation to the
"crystallization" narrative.

In a number of places, I have posited a "meta-symphonic narrative"
whereby a series of symphonies – or large-scale works, e.g. tone poems –
within an oeuvre participate in an over-arching, on-going narrative.[17]
Sibelius's manner of composing – specifically of allowing ideas to germi-
nate and migrate from one composition to another – supports the
hypothesis that his works are programmatically interrelated. Of special
concern is the role played by his wife Aino and daughter Ruth in this
meta-symphonic discourse. In early sketches for *Pohjola's Daughter*, Aino

---

[15] In this context, the term "undivided"
signifies that the fundamental line or *Urlinie*
is not "divided" through the technique of
interruption. As I have observed in my studies
of the reversed recapitulation, interruption is
not an essential feature of sonata form (see
my "Tragic Reversed Sonata Form," especially
pp. 150–51). Indeed, sonatas with reversed
recapitulations, for example, tend to be
supported by undivided backgrounds. As I
shall attempt to show, in his fantasia-like
sonata forms, Sibelius discovers ways to
bridge over or eliminate interruptions so that
the structure remains undivided.

[16] Building upon the formal theory of James
Hepokoski, Warren Darcy defines "rotational
form" in "Bruckner's Sonata Deformations"

in *Bruckner Studies*, ed. Timothy L. Jackson
and Paul Hawkshaw (Cambridge: Cambridge
University Press, 1997), pp. 264–71. Notice
that I employ the term "non-congruent" in a
different sense than Darcy. While he focuses
on "non-congruence" between rotations in
the design and the three spaces of sonata form
(exposition, development, and
recapitulation), my primary concern is "non-
congruence" between design and *tonal
structure*.

[17] For a discussion of the "meta-symphonic
narrative" concept and its application to the
nineteenth- and twentieth-century
symphonic literature, see my *Tchaikovsky.
Symphony No. 6*, pp. 11–12, and 67–68.

Ex. 8.1a–e   "Aino" and "Clara" themes in Sibelius and Brahms

and Ruth are already associated with specific themes and motives. In the early draft for *Pohjola's Daughter* (Ex. 8.1a), Aino's theme is explicitly a lyrical rising sixth (see Pl. 7.5b on page 149 above: HUL 0163, p. 11a).[18]

At this point in the genesis of *Pohjola's Daughter* (c. 1905), Woman appears as "Eve-Mary" – i.e., as *both* Aino and the Other. Thus, Aino's

[18] The association of motives with "Aino" and "Ruth" is discussed briefly by Timo Virtanen in "*Pohjola's Daughter* in the Light of Sketch Studies," in *Proceedings*, pp. 318–19; see also his essay in this volume. The hypothesis that "Aino" and "Ruth" participate in a "meta-

theme in the violins is projected against figuration associated with Pohjola's daughter in the harps (Pl. 7.5b on p. 149, HUL 0163, p. 11a). Sibelius decided to remove Aino from the composition; she could not be portrayed if the focus were to be placed on the Temptress (Pohjola's daughter). But Aino (Mary/Marjatta, the redeeming "Mother" and "Bride of Christ"), represented by her theme transposed to C major, was destined to "break through" triumphantly at the beginning of the Finale of the Third Symphony, i.e., at the outset of the Introduction (Ex. 8.1b, and Pl. 7.6 on page 155 above: HUL 0238, p. 1). For reasons still unknown, Sibelius excised Aino's apotheosis. But her theme resurfaced as the main theme of the fifth *Scène historique*, appropriately entitled *Amor* (Ex. 8.1c). Even more significantly, Aino's *symphonic* apotheosis was destined to be realized in the second C major symphony, the Seventh, where the great C major trombone theme (Ex. 8.1d) is explicitly associated with Aino in the later sketches (Pl. 8.1a–b, HUL 0359, p. 20, left and central panels, cf., for example, to the annotation "Ai[no]" in the left margin). Notice the emphasis on the rising sixth G–E in the trombone melody (compare the brackets in Exx. 8.1b and d). Indeed, the Third and Seventh Symphonies, and *Maan virsi* – all in C major – participate in a "meta-narrative" concerning "Aino" as the potentially redemptive aspect of Woman.

Sibelius's concept of "crystallization" – realized through large-scale auxiliary cadences into the definitive tonic – is intimately connected with psycho-sexual programmatic elements in this on-going meta-narrative. The youthful hero is seduced by a series of Eve-like temptresses – the *Wood Nymph*, *Pohjola's Daughter*, the *Maidens of Saari* – with catastrophic results: they either unman him or, to control his libido, compel his self-castration (like Alberich in *Das Rheingold* or Klingsor in *Parsifal*). As Timo Virtanen observes, for example, in the *Kalevala* version of *Pohjola's Daughter*, Väinämöinen "accidentally" wounds himself with an axe and has to leave the girl to seek a healer. But the moment of "crystallization" on DTA in the over-arching auxiliary cadence – the instance of "arrival," of "home-coming," and/or of the hero's self-realization – ultimately is the "return to the wife-mother." Only through Aino, i.e., only through "return" to the "pure," virginal, nurturing womb of the wife-

Footnote 18 (*cont.*)
symphonic narrative" beginning with the early version of *Pohjola's Daughter* and continuing through to the Seventh Symphony is my own. It is surprising that, in the first systematic survey of the extensive manuscripts for the Seventh Symphony, Kari Kilpeläinen makes no mention of Sibelius's association of the trombone theme with "Aino" (see his "Sibelius's Seventh Symphony. An Introduction to the Manuscript and Printed Sources," in *The Sibelius Companion*, ed. Glenda Dawn Goss (Westport, CT: Greenwood Press, 1996), pp. 239–72).

mother (Mary/Marjatta), can the hero be reborn and "re-sexed," his virility and vitality restored. The *legitimate* child, Ruth, as "proof" of both "potence regained" and the physical incarnation of melded spiritual-sexual love for the wife-mother, symbolizes heroic regeneration with intimations of immortality. Sibelius's explicit identification of Aino with the "redemptive" trombone theme – with its eschatological-ecclesiastical connotations – intimates that he "lived" – and "died" – this personal drama in his music.

Diachronic transformation of macro-symphonic and super-sonata forms

My focus is large-scale tonal-formal organization in conjunction with tonal structure, and specifically those factors that create the impression of Tovey's "one and all-sufficing climax." Central to this discussion is Sibelius's coordination of different types of auxiliary cadences with "macro-symphonic," sonata, and super-sonata forms. In recent writings, I have posited that

> "normative" formal categories operate on three levels: (1) on the "global" level of a group of interrelated symphonies, i.e. the "meta-symphony" comprising interrelated symphonies ... (2) the "macro"-level of the individual symphony as a whole, and (3) on the "micro"-level of the individual symphonic movement.[19]

In terms of tonal structure, I have proposed that, within a multi-movement symphony, the effect of "macro-symphonic unity" may be produced by a "meta-*Ursatz*" – that is, a single *Ursatz* embracing the individual background structures or *Ursätze* of each of the component movements, welding them into a unified structure.[20] In a symphony unified by the meta-*Ursatz*, the super-sonata principle may be realized by recomposing, in the Finale, the tonal structure of the first movement. This super-sonata principle already informs the later Beethoven symphonies (beginning with the Fifth Symphony, if not earlier), and is further developed throughout the nineteenth century.

[19] Jackson, *Tchaikovsky. Symphony No.6*, p. 23.
[20] See, for example, my analysis of Sibelius's Fourth Symphony, where I read an *Anstieg* to the *Kopfton* $\hat{5}$ (e^2) in the first movement, which is completed by a structural descent in the finale. Thus, I argue that the *Ursätze* of the individual movements are integrated within a single meta-*Ursatz* spanning the whole symphony (see Jackson, "'The Maiden with a Heart of Ice,'" Ex. 3, p. 253). For another example of the meta-*Ursatz*, see my reading of Tchaikovsky's *Pathétique* in *Tchaikovsky. Symphony No. 6*, Appendix A, pp. 116–17.

Plate 8.1   HUL 0359, Sketchbook, p. 20, left and central panels (drafts of the conclusion of the Seventh Symphony showing the "Ai[no]" theme of the trombone at the "catastrophe")

Drawing upon the theory of diachronic transformation posited in my study of Tchaikovsky's Sixth Symphony, I have argued that this type of transformation can be applied to normative macro-symphonic form:

> Saussure's distinction between synchronic and diachronic "facts of a different order" can illuminate the entelechy of musical structure . . . A musical work may embody in its endstate a conceptually prior state, which has become the endstate through a diachronic transformation. From a synchronic perspective, the endstate is a "distortion" of the previous state and vice-versa . . . Diachronic transformation ruptures a steady state to create a duality of previous state and endstate and, from a single synchronic perspective, distortion and paradox.[21]

If normative macro-symphonic form defines the four-movement disposition of the symphony as standardized in the later symphonies of Haydn and Mozart, and especially the earlier Beethoven symphonies, then the macro-symphonic paradigm can be subjected to diachronic transformation. In his Third Symphony, for example, Sibelius employs diachronic transformation at the macro-symphonic level. A hypothetical "previous state" of the Third Symphony conforms to the normative paradigm. Then, through a diachronic transformation, the third movement, the scherzo, is elided with the introduction to the finale (Ex. 8.19, p. 232 below). As a result of this transformation, the space assigned to the scherzo and the space allocated to the finale's introduction overlap, spatial elision reinforcing the super-sonata effect. The tonal consequences of this overlap will be explored.

I have observed that in "super-sonata" form (sometimes called a "sonata-in-one"),

> the three spatial divisions of sonata form – exposition, development, and recapitulation – are superimposed upon the design of a unified – usually (but not always) continuous – four movement macro-symphonic form. In this superposition, the first movement generally fills the exposition space containing the first and second groups of a normative sonata form, and the Finale is assigned to recapitulation space and encompasses the recapitulation of the first and second groups. The spatial envelope of either "development space" or "recapitulatory space" is then extended by interpolating spatial envelopes for the other movements, usually a slow movement and Scherzo, into the spatial envelope of the development or recapitulation.[22]

[21] Ibid., p. 28, which quotes my article, "Diachronic Transformation in a Schenkerian Context. Brahms's Haydn Variations," in *Schenker Studies 2*, ed. Hedi Siegel and Carl Schachter (Cambridge: Cambridge University Press, 1999), p. 239.

[22] *Tchaikovsky. Symphony No. 6*, pp. 26–27.

Sibelius's most notable, explicit super-sonata forms are *Skogsrået*, *Tapiola*, and the Seventh Symphony, while the super-sonata *principle* informs much of his symphonic writing. Sibelius's model probably was Richard Strauss's *Don Juan* (1888–89), which pioneered insertion of the scherzo into the development space within super-sonata form. (Sibelius had heard Strauss conduct *Don Juan* in 1890 in Berlin.)

The super-sonata principle may be applied to normative four-movement macro-symphonic form so that the first movement occupies exposition space and the finale recapitulation space, with the inner movements functioning as episodes filling development space.[23] Within sonata form, an episode-like development may occupy development space (as in the *Im Legendenton* in the first movement of Schumann's *Fantasy*, or the development in Brahms's *Tragic Overture*); at the macro-symphonic level, the inner movements may function analogously as episodes within development space (as in Brahms's Third Symphony, where the inner movements prolong the dominant).[24] The critical factor creating the super-sonata effect is structural parallelism between the outer movements, whereby the finale recomposes the deep middleground of the opening movement.[25] Additionally, the super-sonata effect is reinforced when the inner movements together with the finale participate in a large-scale auxiliary cadence into the concluding tonic.[26] Thus, the effect of "crystallization" may extend across the inner movements into the finale.

Types of auxiliary cadences

Auxiliary cadences may be defined as "initial," "over-arching," or "internal." Additionally, when two or more auxiliary cadences are combined, I distinguish two different procedures: "nested" and "linked" auxiliary cadences. In itself, the auxiliary cadence comprises at least two terms or functions, and generally three. The essential function is the dominant ("d"). This dominant resolves, usually – although not always – to its tonic

[23] This idea already informs the later Beethoven symphonies, the super-sonata effect being especially strongly marked in the Ninth.

[24] For an analysis of the Brahms *Tragic Overture*, see my "Tragic Reversed Sonata Form," pp. 172–77.

[25] Again, the notion that the finale can recompose – and even "correct" – the middleground of the first movement can be traced back to the later Beethoven symphonies. The super-sonata effect is evident in Bruckner's symphonies, where the finale tends to recompose the middleground of the first movement (see my remarks concerning Exx. 8.9a–b, 8.11a–b, and 8.12a–b below).

[26] Brahms's Third Symphony and Sibelius's First Symphony (discussed below) provide clear examples of the inner movements and the finale all contributing toward an extended V–I auxiliary cadence.

resolution ("r"). Frequently the auxiliary cadence involves a preparation, some kind of pre-cadential chord or chords ("p"). Auxiliary cadences are "linked" if the "r" of one auxiliary cadence is revalued as the "p" of the subsequent auxiliary cadence. Auxiliary cadences are "nested" if the "p," "d," or "r" of one auxiliary cadence becomes the "r" of one or more auxiliary cadences.

The "initial" auxiliary cadence frequently occurs in introduction or "secondary" space, and serves to introduce the "primary" space, which is assigned to the form proper (sonata, rondo, binary, ternary form, etc.).[27] Typically, the "initial" auxiliary cadence supports an introduction, the envelope of introduction space being defined by the auxiliary cadence. The tonic as the resolution of the initial auxiliary cadence concludes the introduction space and marks the beginning of the form proper.

Over-arching and internal auxiliary cadences occur within primary space. The "over-arching" auxiliary cadence spans an entire movement or several movements whereby the composition as a whole is supported by the auxiliary cadence, and DTA is postponed until late in the form. The "internal" auxiliary cadence is an auxiliary cadence which unfolds once the form is under way. Within a sonata form, it may support one or more formal components.[28] One may posit a "structural caesura" separating the beginning of the internal auxiliary cadence from the preceding harmony.

The "tonic" auxiliary cadence introduced

In his masterly study of the first movement of Sibelius's Fourth Symphony, Edward Laufer contrasts "complete cadential progressions," i.e., progressions which begin on the tonic, with "auxiliary cadences":

> the harmonic progression cuts off a firm opening tonic, beginning *in medias res*. It is important to note that the crossed-out initial tonic is not to be understood as being conceptually present. As a result, the psychological effect is altogether different ... the moment of arrival is now decisively directed to the tonic at the end of the progression, and only there. The sense is that of starting at some less definite place and moving toward the point of

---

[27] My use of the word "space" in discussing sonata form derives primarily from the work and teaching of Saul Novack; I am also indebted to discussions of "space" in the writings of James Hepokoski, Warren Darcy, and Carl Schachter.

[28] Typically, in more elaborate sonata forms, the second subject is placed above an auxiliary cadence; it then falls to the third, closing, group to reinforce the new tonic secured at the *end* of the second group.

tonic arrival ... The compositional intent is all important, namely the notion of reaching for the eventual point of arrival.[29]

In this chapter, I shall explore the use of a special type of auxiliary cadence, which I describe as the "tonic" auxiliary cadence (identified here for the first time). To be sure, the tonic auxiliary cadence appears to be a contradiction in terms because – as defined by Laufer and others – the auxiliary cadence "cuts off a firm opening tonic." I shall attempt to show that, in certain circumstances, although a piece, or a formal section, may begin with a "firm opening," root-position tonic, this initial tonic chord may be devalued and subsumed – in light of subsequent events – within the "p" of an auxiliary cadence; the result, then, is a postponement of DTA until late in the work, sometimes until the final chord.[30] But before considering this possibility, it will be helpful to further distinguish the various types of auxiliary cadences employed by Sibelius and his predecessors.

I identify two broad categories of auxiliary cadences: "monotonic" and "bitonic." "Monotonic" auxiliary cadences evoke the key of the concluding tonic chord while simultaneously delaying DTA; "bitonic" auxiliary cadences, on the other hand, create the impression of two competing tonics whereby the first tonic ultimately gives way to the second. Only retrospectively – i.e. as the composition reaches its conclusion – is the listener able to perceive the first tonic as subsidiary to the second, i.e. as "p" rather than "r."

The auxiliary cadence as "crystallization" metaphor

The effect of "crystallization" is connected with the use of large-scale auxiliary cadences, since DTA is also the instance of "crystallization." Sibelius's technique of structuring an entire movement, sequence of movements, or super-sonata (the Seventh Symphony, for example) above an over-arching auxiliary cadence builds upon precedent in the literature; his models include Beethoven, Chopin, Schumann, Brahms, Tchaikovsky, and especially Bruckner; I shall focus on examples that illuminate particular techniques.

From the outset, Sibelius appears to have been drawn to the genre of the "fantasy." The finale of his First Symphony (1898) is designated "Quasi una Fantasia," and he seriously considered the title "Fantasia

---

[29] Edward Laufer, "On the First Movement of Sibelius's Fourth Symphony: a Schenkerian View," in *Schenker Studies 2*, pp. 135–37.
[30] As far as I have been able to ascertain, this technique is first employed by Beethoven and Schubert in their later works, and then becomes part of the vocabulary of tonal composition.

Ex. 8.2a   Schumann, *Fantasie*, first movement, overview

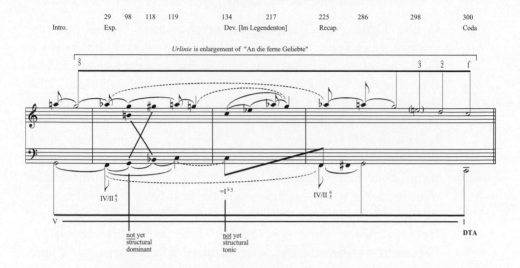

Sinfonica No. 1" for his Seventh Symphony (1924).[31] One way of evoking the fantasy genre is to let the music evolve in a quasi-improvisatory manner towards its goal; formulated in more technical terms, tonal "crystallization" may be realized through a large-scale auxiliary cadence or a series of linked or nested auxiliary cadences leading to DTA.

The auxiliary cadence sonata and super-sonata forms

The first movement of Schumann's *Fantasie* (Ex. 8.2) provides a compelling example, within the fantasy genre, of an "over-arching" V–I auxiliary cadence spanning an entire sonata design. The crux of Schumann's "fantasy" concept in the first movement is that "crystallization" – the definitive resolution of V to I – be withheld until the concluding measures. Since the first movement coordinates sonata form with a large-scale "over-arching" auxiliary cadence, I shall designate this type of sonata "auxiliary cadence sonata form." Auxiliary cadence *super*-sonata form projects the auxiliary cadence beneath a super-sonata (see the discussion of Sibelius's *Skogsrået*, *Tapiola*, and Seventh Symphony below). Additionally, the auxiliary cadence super-sonata effect can be created in multi-movement symphonies when the outer movements are structurally

[31] Veijo Murtomäki ("'Symphonic Fantasy.' A Synthesis of Symphonic Thinking in Sibelius's Seventh Symphony and *Tapiola*," in *The Sibelius Companion*, pp. 147–63) discusses Sibelius's fascination with the fantasy genre.

Ex. 8.2b Schumann, *Fantasie*, exposition

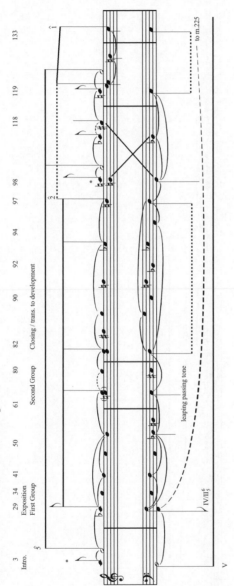

Ex. 8.2c Schumann, *Fantasie, Im Legendenton* (development)

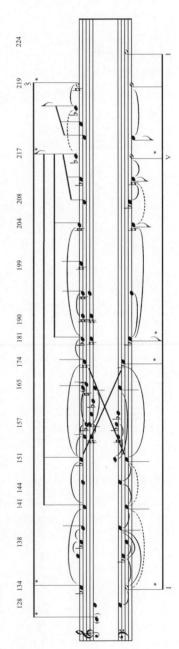

Ex. 8.2d   Schumann, *Fantasie*, recapitulation

related and the inner movements and the Finale participate in an over-arching auxiliary cadence.[32]

The sonata design of the first movement of Schumann's *Fantasie* may be outlined as follows:

Introduction, mm. 1–28

Exposition (Ex. 8.2b), mm. 29–127
  First group, mm. 29–52
    Cadenza/Bridge, mm. 53–60
  Second group, mm. 61–81
  Closing group, mm. 82–118
    Transition to Development (based on Introduction), mm. 119–27

Development (*Im Legendenton*, Ex. 8.2c), mm. 128–224

Recapitulation (Ex. 8.2d), mm. 225–301
  First group, mm. 225–44
    Cadenza/Bridge, mm. 245–52
  Second group, mm. 253–73
  Closing group, mm. 274–301

Coda, mm. 301–end

In the exposition, Schumann's strategies for deferring DTA are especially noteworthy. For example, although the second subject (mm. 61ff.) is placed above an implied C chord, this sonority does not represent the tonic resolution of the prolonged dominant. More precisely, this putative tonic is passing, built on a "leaping passing tone," C, in the bass as F (m. 29) descends a third to D (m. 81, Ex. 8.2b).[33] Schumann extends the effect of the "non-tonic" C chord considerably further in the *Im Legendenton*, an episode-like development which, within the sonata form, occupies the development space (mm. 134–224, Ex. 8.2c). Here, the tonic minor chord, prolonged through the entire development, is revalued as "the upper fifth" of the subdominant rather than a definitive tonal arrival.[34] Its C minor – as opposed to C major – mode is a clue that this harmony is not yet the goal tonic. Another, even more compelling, indication is the initiation of the

[32] See, for example, Brahms's Third Symphony (discussed below).
[33] For a detailed explanation of Schenker's concept of the "leaping passing tone," see my book *"The New Teaching." Heinrich Schenker, Reinhard Oppel, Hans Weisse, and Wilhelm Furtwängler 1928–1935* (forthcoming), especially Chapter 5, "Reinhard Oppel's and Heinrich Schenker's *Freie Satz*: the *Kleine Klavierstück* No. 3 and Bach's *Sinfonia* in E minor."

[34] For a sensitive – and informed – view of the *Fantasie*, see Nicholas Marston, *Schumann. Fantasie, Op. 17* (Cambridge: Cambridge University Press, 1992). Clearly, a central point of disagreement between Marston and myself concerns the role of the "tonic" in the development. For him, the *Im Legendenton* is "the most tonally stable of the three sections" (p. 47), while in my reading this putative minor tonic is rendered unstable as the "upper fifth" of the subdominant.

recapitulation on the same II 6/5/♭3 or IV♭3 with added sixth (m. 225) as in the exposition (m. 29), suggesting that *this* chord, as a neighbor to the prolonged V rather than the intervening C minor chord, acquires fundamental significance (Exx. 8.2a, b, and d). "Crystallization" occurs only at the final cadence (mm. 297ff.), which is achieved through the definitive resolution of the prolonged V to I. It is noteworthy that this moment of harmonic resolution coincides with the most explicit reference to Beethoven's *An die ferne Geliebte*, which functions as a *telos*, or goal of thematic evolution – a concept developed by James Hepokoski and Warren Darcy.[35] In other words, Beethoven's theme, evoked earlier in the work, achieves its definitive C major form only at the end.

In context, "crystallization" of DTA acquires psycho-sexual connotations. As Nicholas Marston observes,

> Schumann described the first movement of the *Fantasie* as a "deep lament" for Clara; it was composed at a time when the lovers were completely separated, unable to take comfort even from an occasional exchange of letters. The whole subject of Beethoven's cycle is of course the "distant beloved," and in the last song the poet suggests that by singing the songs which he has sung, his beloved will lessen the distance between them.[36]

Coincidence of DTA with the most explicit quotation at the end associates *Clara* with the definitive C major tonic: as "pure" and "virginal" C major Redemptress, *she* becomes the harmonic goal towards which the piece journeys; in the final instance, as DTA is achieved, the "distance" separating the lovers is overcome and Clara as Virgin triumphantly "heals" Schumann as "Man of Sorrows" of his melancholy "longing." This technical and programmatic-metaphorical dimension of Schumann's *Fantasie* profoundly influences Brahms and Sibelius.

Schumann's concept of placing a large-scale sonata design over a V–I cadence is further developed by Sibelius in fantasy-like works such as *Skogsrået* and the finales of the First and Seventh Symphonies. Especially noteworthy is Schumann's "weakening" of the putatively "strong" C minor "tonic" of the *Im Legendenton*, demonstrating that even a prolonged tonic – in this case, the minor tonic – can be "devalued" (here, it functions as "the upper fifth" of another chord, Ex. 8.2a). Schumann's practice confirms a fundamental principle of sonata and super-sonata forms, namely that development space be assigned *unstable* harmony. As we shall see, this technique of "weakening" the tonic in development space is fundamental to Sibelius's compositional practice in his super-sonatas.

[35] For a sustained discussion of "teleological" form, see Warren Darcy, "Bruckner's Sonata Deformations," in *Bruckner Studies*, especially "teleological genesis," pp. 259–62.

[36] Marston, *Schumann. Fantasie*, p. 36.

Beethoven, Brahms, and Bruckner employ auxiliary cadence sonata form in finales as a means of creating the super-sonata effect across multi-movement symphonic forms – a technique that Sibelius further develops in his own symphonies. Within the meta-*Ursatz* of a multi-movement work, i.e., within the macro-symphonic structure, the finale is composed so that the moment of "crystallization" – i.e., the decisive achievement of the tonic (DTA) – resolves all of the tensions, not just of the finale, but of the work as a whole. The finale of Brahms's Third Symphony (Ex. 8.3) provides an eloquent example of auxiliary cadence sonata form. The design may be schematized as follows:

Exposition (mm. 1–103)

Introductory Exposition (mm. 1–35)
  First group proper (mm. 36–51)
  Second group (mm. 52–74)
  Third group (mm. 74–103)

Transition to Development (mm. 104–48)

Development (mm. 149–71)

Recapitulation (mm. 172–233)
  First group (mm. 172–93)
  Second group (mm. 194–216)
  Third group (mm. 217–32)

Coda (mm. 233–end)

Brahms's over-arching auxiliary cadence is "monotonic" in F minor; that is to say, although C is prolonged through the first 216 measures (i.e. the main body of the sonata form), the listener is provided with many clues that F minor is the key center with C major-minor functioning as dominant rather than goal tonic. As the graph (Ex. 8.3) suggests, the turn to C minor, i.e., to the minor dominant (F minor: $V^{\flat 3}$), in the third group of the exposition (mm. 74ff.) is revalued in the recapitulation (mm. 217ff.) as a cadence in F minor. But this putative tonic minor does not represent DTA – not yet. Instead, the moment of "crystallization" – the resolution of the prolonged V–I auxiliary cadence – is deferred until tonic *major* in the coda (m. 280). The upper voice composes out the rising sixth from C to A *natural*, which reaches its goal, a^2 ($\hat{3}$), at the same time as the auxiliary cadence achieves the definitive tonic. The extended coda then becomes responsible for asserting the primacy of F *major* over F minor, and bringing the fundamental line down to $\hat{1}$.

Noteworthy is the role of the finale's auxiliary cadence sonata form in reinforcing the super-sonata effect across the symphony. In the first movement, Brahms avoids the dominant (C) within the sonata space proper, shifting it into the coda (m. 183). "Devalued" within the first

Ex. 8.3   Brahms, Third Symphony, finale

Ex. 8.4   Bruckner, Quintet, finale

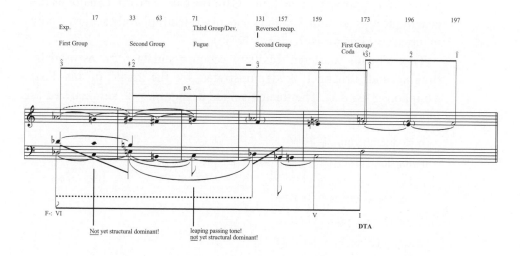

movement's exposition space (i.e., exposition space within the super-sonata form), the dominant is featured in development space occupied by the symphony's inner movements; through the second and third movements, C major – and then minor – is prolonged, preparing this same modal shift in the finale's exposition. Thus, within the meta-*Ursatz* of the symphony conceived as a super-sonata, the finale's tonic resolution represents a "crystallization" of the tonal forces, not simply within the finale itself, but across the symphony's unified tonal-formal structure. As we shall see shortly, Sibelius employs this same technique in his First Symphony, where a massive auxiliary cadence embodying the harmonic tension of the symphony as a whole resolves in the coda.

The finale of Bruckner's Quintet, which Sibelius may have heard in Vienna, is in auxiliary cadence sonata form with the further complexity that its recapitulation is reversed (Ex. 8.4). As suggested by the graph, the movement as a whole is placed over a VI–V–I auxiliary cadence. Again, the compositional idea is to delay "crystallization" – the arrival on the definitive, structural dominant (C) – until the reprise of the first group (mm. 159ff.). To achieve this postponement, the earlier arrivals on C (mm. 12–32 and mm. 71–130), although strongly emphasized, must be revalued. The initial C chord (mm. 17ff.) is devalued, "caught" within the unfolding from the initial D♭ nine-seven chord to its "upper third" F♭ (mm. 1–33). Enharmonically reinterpreted as E major, F♭ major becomes the key of the second group. The role of the fugal third group, which doubles as a development, is to regain the initial D♭ for the reprise of the second group (mm. 131ff.). In the third group/development, the upper voice fills in the descending third from Ab/G♯ to F with a passing G supported by a "leaping passing tone," C, in the bass. The tonic major as the goal of the over-arching auxiliary cadence is triumphantly achieved only in the concluding measures (mm. 173ff.).

That Sibelius mastered auxiliary cadence sonata form as used by Brahms and Bruckner is demonstrated by the finale of his First Symphony (Ex. 8.5). The finale's sonata design may be summarized as follows:

Introduction, mm. 1–49

Exposition, mm. 50–196
    First group, mm. 50–162
    Second group, mm. 163–96

Development, mm. 197–267

Recapitulation, mm. 268–404
    First group, mm. 268–353
    Second group, mm. 354–404

Coda/ "catastrophe," mm. 405–end

Example 8.5 suggests that the sonata design is supported by an over-arching V–I auxiliary cadence, whereby DTA is deferred until the end of the coda (m. 422). If other analysts have interpreted the E minor chord in m. 77 as the tonic arrival, *against* this common-sense reading speaks the fact that the sonata form proper – the first group – is initiated in m. 50 on the *dominant*.[37] The motion to the putative tonic (m. 77) is deferred until *after* the primary motivic material has been introduced, so as to "devalue" this tonic as the "upper third" of the VI chord in m. 106.[38] Furthermore, the structural outer voices subsume the "tonic" recapitulation (m. 268) within a colossal passing motion as the bass ascends chromatically from B to D♯ (mm. 1–354). In other words, DTA (m. 422) is deferred well past the putative tonic recapitulation of m. 268; revalued as a subdominant four-two chord of B (m. 338), this chord resolves irregularly to a submediant six-four (m. 354). Surely, this bold use of a chromatically ascending bass

[37] Joseph Kraus, for example ("The 'Russian' Influence in the First Symphony of Jean Sibelius," in *Proceedings*, p. 150), offers a reading which takes the tonic at the beginning of the finale. In my view, this interpretation derails Kraus's analysis of the larger tonal progression. Sibelius's meta-*Ursatz* prolongs V (B), moving from Eb/D♯ (second movement) – as "upper third" of B – to C (third movement) to B in the finale, which only resolves to E at the very end.

[38] Considered from a diachronic perspective, the emphasis on the E minor tonic in m. 77 may be the "residue" of a previous state in which the finale's introduction prolonging V resolved to a strong tonic at the beginning of the sonata form proper; but in the endstate, this resolution is avoided by the temporal displacement of the beginning of the sonata design from tonic to dominant harmony.

Ex. 8.5 Sibelius, First Symphony, finale

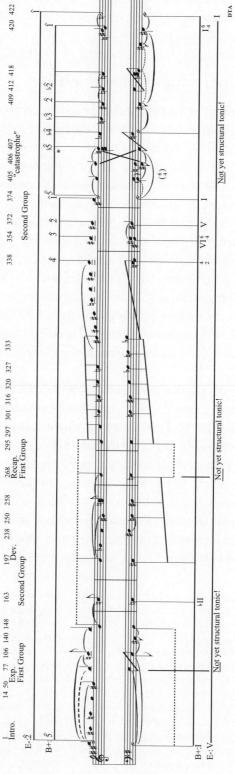

to unify a large-scale dominant prolongation throughout the sonata design bestows upon this movement its fantasia-like dimension.[39]

The initial tonic auxiliary cadence

If the concept of the tonic auxiliary cadence is problematic because of the apparent contradiction between "the firm opening tonic" and "the auxiliary cadence" (as defined by Laufer and others), nevertheless this apparent paradox is essential to the post-Beethovenian line of symphonic thought.[40] At the beginning of a piece, an opening root-position tonic chord can be easily mistaken for *the* tonic. The distinction between a cadence prolonging the tonic with a dividing dominant and a tonic auxiliary cadence depends entirely upon context, especially the interaction between form and design. Essential to the concept of the tonic auxiliary cadence is that even a "firm opening tonic" may be subordinated to DTA by devaluing it as the "p" of an auxiliary cadence into DTA. An important clue that even a firm opening tonic is *not* DTA may be provided by the design if its main thematic material is deferred. Another clue may be that the putative DTA occurs in the wrong mode, minor instead of major or vice versa.

The tonic auxiliary cadence may be defined as a true auxiliary cadence in which the root-position tonic becomes subordinated to "d"–"t" as a component of "p." This concept is related to the bitonic auxiliary cadence insofar as the listener is compelled – retrospectively – to re-interpret the harmony: the overall tonality is never in doubt but rather the role and function of the initial tonic. Examples of the tonic auxiliary cadence in Beethoven, Chopin, Schumann, Brahms, Bruckner, and Sibelius are associated with the idea of "growth towards a goal" (DTA) – a notion that quickly becomes highly significant for Sibelius's compositional technique and ideology. More specifically, the technique of beginning with a

[39] Notice the *binary* organization of the tonal structure whereby two descents from $\hat{5}$ in B are supported by bass arpeggiations within dominant prolongation.

[40] In a recent presentation entitled "Quasi-Auxiliary Cadences" (at the Third International Schenker Conference in New York in March 1999), Roger Kamien called attention to I–V–I cadences where a root-position tonic occurs before the "definitive" arrival on I. In Kamien's examples, all of which are internal "quasi-auxiliary" cadences, it is the upper voice descent to $\hat{1}$ that determines the definitive tonic arrival. The tonic auxiliary cadence as postulated in this study differs from Kamien's quasi-auxiliary cadence. The "initial tonic auxiliary cadence" occurs at the beginning of a composition; Kamien, on the other hand, restricted his examples to internal cadences. Kamien's "quasi-" auxiliary cadence is a I–V–I perfect cadence that functions *as if it were* an auxiliary cadence; my tonic auxiliary cadence, by contrast, is a true auxiliary cadence in which the initial tonic is subsidiary to some other preparatory chord ("p").

"false" or "weakened" tonic is a fundamental aspect of Sibelius's thinking early in his career.

Beethoven – a seminal influence – in the finale of his Seventh Symphony, places tremendous weight on the dominant at the beginning of the primary theme (mm. 1–12), while the tonic resolution in m. 12 is relatively "weakened," almost perfunctory (Ex. 8.6). The return of the opening theme at the beginning of the reprise (m. 220) emphatically reasserts this "strong" dominant. In the coda, the music spends considerable time and effort "finding its way back" to this dominant (mm. 349–89), which, once re-attained, is re-articulated with overwhelming force (mm. 389–450). In the instance of "crystallization," this dominant resolves to the definitive tonic (m. 451); thus, DTA is postponed until late in the movement, almost to the final chord.[41]

In the finale, Beethoven achieves this remarkable effect of an overarching V–I auxiliary cadence not only through the tremendous emphasis placed on the dominant. Example 8.6 proposes that the tonic resolution of the emphasized dominant in mm. 12ff., 231ff., and 332ff. is "weakened" by its conversion into the "p" of an internal auxiliary cadence. In other words, the tonic in these measures is reinterpreted as the "upper third" of F, more specifically as the mediant in a $III^{\sharp 3}$–V–I (A–C–F) auxiliary cadence in the key of the flat submediant, F major. The graph suggests that, in the exposition and development, the guiding idea is first to modulate to the key of the diatonic mediant (C♯ minor) for the second group (m. 74). But this diatonic progression is violently undermined in the transition to the development (mm. 121–45) as C♯ minor is enharmonically reinterpreted as D♭ minor, i.e., as upper neighbor to C major (m. 153), the dominant of F major (m. 198). Especially striking is the manner in which Beethoven "draws out" the resolution of C to F major in the retransition (m. 198) by moving through D minor (m. 173) and E major, the putative dominant (m. 190), as passing harmonies between C and F. This remarkable effect is created by "sliding" a half-step beyond the expected dominant (m. 194) to the lowered submediant (m. 198). If the main body of the recapitulation is "regular" in its preservation of the tonic through the second subject in A major (m. 285), this "regularity" is contradicted by the closing group (m. 319), which again postulates a V–I cadence in F major. Thus the recapitulation summarizes the F major $III^{\sharp 3}$–V–I auxiliary cadence spanning the exposition and development. The coda tritonally "deforms" this internal auxiliary cadence on F as

[41] Beethoven's idea is to create the supersonata effect by prolonging a I (first movement) – I^3 (second movement) – ♭VI (third movement)–V–I (finale) cadential progression across the whole symphony.

Ex. 8.6 Beethoven, Seventh Symphony, finale

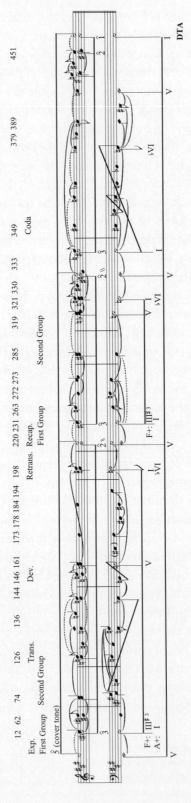

III$^{\sharp 3}$–$\sharp$IV–I (A–B–F); only the final peroration (m. 405) triumphantly asserts A major diatonicism.[42]

Beethoven's "macro-symphonic" thinking – more precisely, his techniques for attenuating the definitive resolution through over-arching and tonic auxiliary cadences – decisively influenced his successors. Since the tonic auxiliary cadence technique lends itself to the improvisatory character of the fantasy, our next examples are fantasies. Chopin's *Polonaise-fantasie* and the last movement of Schumann's *Fantasie* prefigure the effect of gradual "crystallization" in Sibelius's fantasy-like works.

The A♭ minor chord with which the *Polonaise-fantasie* opens might be interpreted as the tonic minor in root position, and this is precisely how it has been described in the literature.[43] However, Ex. 8.7 suggests that this initial A♭ minor chord functions not as the tonic but the "upper fifth" of the subdominant D♭ in m. 3. As indicated in the graph, this subdominant in m. 3 leads to the dominant in m. 5, which resolves to the tonic only in m. 27.

Various considerations involving the interaction between design and structure support this reading. The first twenty-three measures serve as a quasi-improvisatory introduction, creating the impression that the piece is not yet underway. In other words, the music begins in secondary, introduction space with primary, expositional space yet to be activated. The opening is a *process* of "searching" for the tonic and "finding" it only *after* the first theme begins to unfold (m. 27, thus blurring the boundary between secondary and primary spaces). The fact that the initial chord is in the "wrong" (minor) mode is also a clue that it is not the definitive tonic, although the listener must confirm this perception retrospectively. The main body of the *Polonaise-fantasie* recomposes the substance of mm. 11–27, this

---

[42] Especially noteworthy is the manner in which the finale's A–C–F auxiliary cadence is prepared earlier in the symphony. Indeed, in the introduction to the first movement, Beethoven posits an auxiliary cadence A (m. 1)–C (m. 23)–F (m. 42). However, this implied cadence – this "thesis" in Kantian dialectics – finds its "antithesis" in the more background voice leading, whereby the bass descends chromatically through the tetrachord, A–G♯–F–E, I (m. 1)–V^6 (m. 34)–♭VI (m. 42)–V (m. 53). In the first movement's development, C (m. 185) again attempts to resolve as dominant to F (m. 221), but is prevented from doing so by an antithetical, more background chromatic bass: C–C♯–D–D♯–E, ♭III (m. 185)–IV (m. 254)–V (m. 271). Only once the symphony progresses to the F major scherzo

can F as goal be "synthesized" within the meta-*Ursatz*. And, as we have shown (Ex. 8.6), the finale realizes the A–C–F thesis in its background voice leading.

[43] See, for example, Harald Krebs's graph ("Third Relation and Dominant in Late 18th- and Early 19th-Century Music" [Ph.D. dissertation, Yale University, 1980], fig. II.4), where he reads the initial A♭ minor chord as the tonic. While Anthony Newcomb calls attention to the quasi-improvisatory nature of the introduction (speaking evocatively of "bardic fingers wandering across the strings of harp or lyre"), he does not discuss the "devaluation" of the putative tonic at the beginning (see "The *Polonaise-Fantasy* and Issues of Musical Narrative," in *Chopin Studies 2* [Cambridge: Cambridge University Press, 1994], p. 89).

Ex. 8.7 Chopin, *Polonaise-fantasie*

recomposition, being realized as B in the contrasting middle section (mm. 148–213), ascends stepwise through D♭ (m. 226) to E♭ (V, m. 254). Thus, the bass B–C♯–D♯=E♭ of the opening improvisation foreshadows the structure of the *Fantasie* proper (see the brackets labeled "x" in Ex. 8.7).

The third, final movement of Schumann's *Fantasie* presents an especially subtle example of "teleological" form supported by a tonic auxiliary cadence (Ex. 8.8). The listener is inclined to construe the initial chord as a structural tonic; however, the graph suggests that, as the piece unfolds, this tonic is devalued within a large-scale over-arching auxiliary cadence into DTA at the end (m. 119).[44]

As in the Chopin *Polonaise-fantasie*, the opening gesture constitutes a tentative, improvisatory beginning – a form of strumming the instrument to "warm up" before getting underway. The finale of Schumann's *Fantasie* "tries out" *several* beginnings: when the opening figuration returns in m. 30, the music makes a "second attempt" to find its "true" point of departure. This time (m. 34), at least the theme is "discovered," reaching a powerful culmination in m. 68. Then, beginning on F (m. 68), the music "re-lives" the introductory "search" of the first thirty measures transposed down a fifth so that the next goal becomes D♭ (m. 87). It would seem, then, that Schumann's compositional idea is to represent a process of "searching" whereby the "correct" thematic material is first "tried out" in the "wrong" keys of A♭, F, and D♭ before finally being "achieved" in the "true" key of C major at the end (m. 119). The form may be understood as a "strophic search" for the *telos* comprising two stanzas:

> "Initial search," mm. 1–29
> *Telos I*, in the "wrong" keys of A♭ major and F major, mm. 30–71

> "Renewed search," mm. 72–86 (mm. 72ff. = mm. 15ff.)
> *Telos* II, initially in the "wrong key" of D♭ major, finally "corrected" to C major, mm. 87–end

Coordinating this teleological form with the tonal structure, Ex. 8.8 shows the design supported by an over-arching ♭VI (m. 30)–♭II (m. 87)–V (m. 97)–I (m. 132) auxiliary cadence, with nested III–(♯V–) I auxiliary progressions. Notice that the pivotal ♭VI and ♭II harmonies serve as the resolution chords of nested auxiliary cadences whereby the initial chord of each nested progression functions as the "upper third" of the goal chord. Thus, in the first "nested" auxiliary progression, the initial "tonic" C is reconstrued as the "upper third" of A♭. The effect of the deceptive cadence as C moves to A♭ (m. 30) is created by the 5–6 (G–A♭) exchange above C.

---

[44] Marston (*Schumann. Fantasie*, pp. 80–81) does not doubt that the third movement begins with a structural tonic, although he does propose that the opening might be "introductory" in nature.

Ex. 8.8   Schumann, *Fantasie*, finale

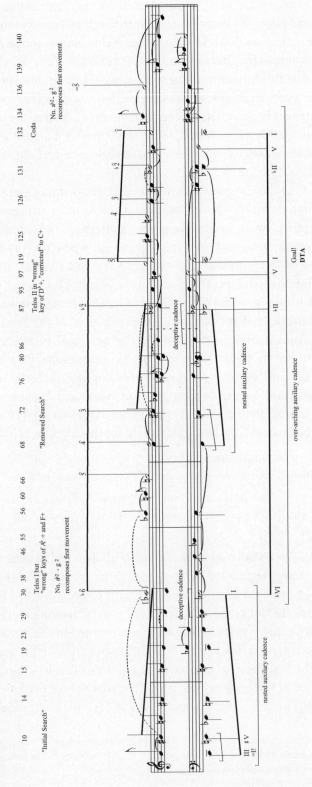

Considering the *Fantasie* as a whole, the over-arching auxiliary cadences in the outer movements parallel and counterbalance each other. These over-arching auxiliary cadences also possess programmatic significance: in both the first and last movements, the search for DTA supporting the primary theme represents – metaphorically – Schumann's "quest" for Clara as wife (hence the allusion to *An die ferne Geliebte* at the end of the last movement, as well as the first).[45]

Brucknerian models: sonata form and linked internal auxiliary cadences

When Sibelius arrived in Vienna in October 1890 hoping to become Bruckner's pupil, he had already composed a substantial number of chamber works testifying to his assimilation of Beethoven and the early Romantics. If Sibelius's compositional language, even in his last works, remains profoundly indebted to these earlier masters, Bruckner was to become a seminal influence (although private study was precluded by Bruckner's declining health). It is probable that, by the time of his departure in June 1891, Sibelius had studied Bruckner's recently published Third, Fourth, and Seventh Symphonies. Although the First was published in 1893 and the Eighth in 1892, shortly after Sibelius had left Vienna, given his admiration for Bruckner, he probably familiarized himself with these symphonies as well.

The concept of gradual "crystallization" toward DTA realized through large-scale auxiliary cadences is a central aspect of Brucknerian symphonic thought, especially in the finales.[46] Many commentators have drawn attention to Sibelius's incorporation of particular "surface"

---

[45] A further striking example of the tonic auxiliary cadence, which Sibelius may have known, is provided by the third, "march" movement from Tchaikovsky's Sixth Symphony (*Pathétique*). This movement in G major begins with a G major chord; however, this putative tonic does not function as such but rather as the initial term ('p') in a III–V–I auxiliary cadence in E minor. Thus Tchaikovsky reserves DTA for the final apotheosis of the March theme (mm. 229ff.). For a detailed account of the March's structure and programmatic aspects, see *Tchaikovsky. Symphony No. 6*, pp. 33, 45–50, and Appendix A, Ex. c, p. 117.

[46] The complex auxiliary cadence is already an important procedure in Bruckner's

technical arsenal by his First Symphony, if not earlier. This aspect of Bruckner's tonal thinking was first identified in my article "Schubert as 'John the Baptist to Wagner-Jesus.' Large-scale Enharmonicism in Bruckner and His Models," in *Bruckner Jahrbuch* 1991/1992/1993 (Linz, 1995), p. 77, where I discussed the elaborate auxiliary cadence underlying the second group of the Second Symphony's finale. Edward Laufer elucidates the auxiliary cadence in the second group of the Fourth Symphony's first movement in his article "Continuity in the Fourth Symphony (First Movement)" in *Perspectives on Anton Bruckner*, ed. Paul Hawkshaw, Timothy L. Jackson, and Crawford Howie (London: Ashgate Press, forthcoming).

elements of Bruckner's style; while this may be the case, I would argue that Bruckner's influence is most strongly felt at deeper levels, especially in the coordination of auxiliary cadences with sonata form, the gradual "crystallization" of DTA, and the super-sonata effect. I would suggest that Sibelius assimilates these Brucknerian *strategies*, while the specific parallels identified by Philip Coad and Peter Revers may be superficial, possibly coincidental, in nature.[47] Additionally, Bruckner's application of the super-sonata principle to the four-movement symphony reverberates through Sibelius's super-sonata influenced structures.[48] In the finales of the published versions of Bruckner's Third (1890), Fourth (1889), and Seventh Symphonies (1885), "deformed" sonata forms are coordinated with internal auxiliary cadences to deliver the concluding tonic with maximum punch. In other words, the symphony is composed – and revised – to insure that the moment of "crystallization" be postponed until the definitive tonic resolution in the finale's coda (DTA). As we have seen, Sibelius has mastered the technique of deferred DTA in the finale of his First Symphony (1899) – which suggests careful study of Bruckner.

An important technique for increasing the weight of the final cadence in a sonata form is to avoid the structural tonic at the beginning of the recapitulation. In the revisions of the finales of his Third and Fourth Symphonies – the versions that Sibelius knew and studied – Bruckner cuts both the thematic return of the first group and the associated structural tonic. If Sibelius could not condone this kind of formal truncation (he condemned the form of Bruckner's Third Symphony as "ridiculous"), nevertheless his own practice suggests that he found the underlying principle appealing.[49] From a Schenkerian perspective, Bruckner's truncated reprises eliminate the two-part background structure (created by interruption) in favor of a single, undivided background (i.e. a one-part structure). Additionally, Bruckner may anticipate the goal tonic before its realization, thereby increasing the desire for definitive attainment – a technique also absorbed and mastered by Sibelius.

[47] Philip Coad's pioneering study of Bruckner's influence on Sibelius ("Bruckner and Sibelius," Ph.D. dissertation, Cambridge University, 1985) and Peter Revers's article "Jean Sibelius and Vienna," in *The Sibelius Companion*, pp. 13–34, provide important information on Bruckner's influence on Sibelius.

[48] My article "Schubert as 'John the Baptist'" also calls attention to deep-structural parallelism between the outer movements of Bruckner's Second Symphony (see p. 76),

foreshadowing my present concept of the "super-sonata" principle.

[49] In a letter to his fiancée Aino, Sibelius wrote, "you cannot imagine the enormous impression it [Bruckner's Third Symphony] has made on me. It has its shortcomings like everything else but above all it has a youthful quality even though its composer is an old man. From the point of view of form it is ridiculous." Quoted from Coad, "Bruckner and Sibelius," p. 67.

Ex. 8.9   Bruckner, Third Symphony (1890), first and fourth movements

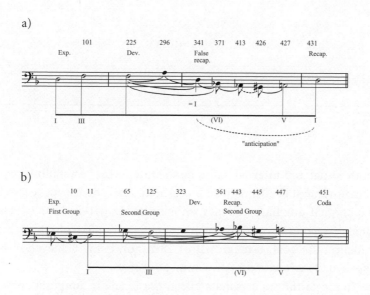

The first movement of Bruckner's Third Symphony, the Bruckner symphony which Sibelius heard as a student in Vienna, provides an eloquent example of the Sibelian technique of "anticipating" the goal tonic. While the overall harmonic plan leads from the tonic (m. 1) through the mediant at the beginning of the second group (m. 101) to the dominant at the end of the development (m. 427), the putative tonic (m. 341) – caught in the middle of on-going development – "anticipates" the tonic of m. 431. Example 8.9a proposes that the strong V–I cadence embedded within the development (mm. 296–341) "anticipates" rather than realizes the definitive V–I cadence, which "crystallizes" only at the end of the development (mm. 427–31). In the larger context, the D minor chord of m. 341 does not function as the tonic but rather is "caught" within a descending bass arpeggiation F–*D*–B♭ (–G♯)–A. If the F of the second and third groups in the exposition is reinterpreted as the "upper fifth" of the augmented sixth that ushers in the dominant at the end of the development, then the second and third groups in the exposition and the development as a whole can be understood as an extended auxiliary cadence VI (German sixth)–V–I.

In the finale (Ex. 8.9b), the "crystallizing" effect of the final cadence is heightened by Bruckner's omission of the tonic at the beginning of the recapitulation, which is initiated by the *second group* in the lowered dominant A♭ (m. 361). Indeed, in the final version, Bruckner eliminates the first group's recapitulation in its entirety to achieve the effect of an undivided structure "crystallizing" in the final cadence. Auxiliary cadences –

Ex. 8.10   Bruckner, Fourth Symphony (1889), finale

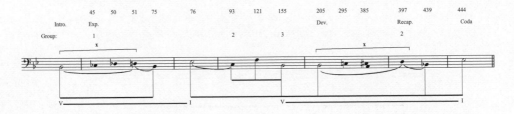

both initial and internal – also contribute to the "crystallization" effect: the movement begins with an initial auxiliary cadence, more specifically, a phrygian auxiliary cadence, moving E♭–D (♭II–I, mm. 1–11).[50] The finale's second group also plays out an extended phrygian auxiliary cadence, the goal, F major, III of D minor, being achieved only as G♭ (spelled F♯) resolves to F (♭II–I, mm. 65–125).

To create the super-sonata effect, the Finale recomposes the internal auxiliary cadence VI (German sixth)–V–I from the first movement. F as "upper fifth" of B♭ is inverted to become a rising fourth, which is filled in with ascending passing tones. From the second group (m. 125), F gradually but inexorably works its way up to B♭ (m. 443). It is noteworthy that, with the excision of the tonic reprise of the first group, the recapitulation of the second group in A♭ is revalued as a passing event within this internal auxiliary cadence. The structural dominant A (m. 447) definitively – and triumphantly – resolves to the major tonic at the beginning of the coda (m. 451). *This* is the culminating instance of DTA, when all of the forces unleashed at the beginning of the symphony "crystallize" in the final cadence.

The finale of Bruckner's Fourth Symphony provides a compelling example of a large-scale internal V–I auxiliary cadence recomposing the introductory V–I auxiliary cadence (Ex. 8.10). The first group, placed over a V–I initial auxiliary cadence, is synthesized with the introduction as the bass line fills in the ascending third B♭–D chromatically: B♭–C♭ (m.45)–D♭/C♯ (m. 50) –D (m. 51, labeled "x"). In the course of the development, Bruckner recomposes this chromatically ascending third. In the revised version (the version which Sibelius knew), Bruckner again cuts the recapitulation of the first group to avoid a premature tonic resolution. Instead, the recapitulation is initiated by the second group poised on D as the termination of "x." Thus the moment of "crystallization" is

---

50 Within the larger context of the meta-*Ursatz*, this ♭II–I cadence resolves the ♭II of the slow movement to I, this resolution being "anticipated" in the scherzo.

Ex. 8.11   Bruckner, Seventh Symphony (1884), first and fourth movements

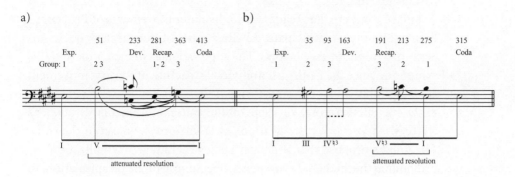

reserved for the final, definitive cadence into the tonic at the beginning of the coda.

In spite of the different ways in which the outer movements of Bruckner's Seventh Symphony are composed (normative sonata form in the first movement, the reversed recapitulation in the finale), Bruckner nevertheless creates the super-sonata effect. From a tonal perspective, the background structures of the outer movements are both undivided, each realizing the final, definitive "crystallization" of the tonic in its own way. The first movement provides a compelling example of both "undivided background" and "anticipation" techniques. In this sonata-form movement, Bruckner creates an "undivided" structure *not* by eliminating the tonic reprise of the first group (as in the finales of the Third and Fourth Symphonies); rather, his strategy is to devalue the tonic associated with the reprise. As suggested by Ex. 8.11a, the putative tonic E (m. 281) is reinterpreted as the middle term of an ascending arpeggiation from C (m. 233) to G (m. 363). Extending this E through the recapitulation of the first and second groups "anticipates" DTA, which is "saved" for its "crystallization" at the beginning of the coda proper (m. 413). The harmonic motion C–G–E (E major: ♭VI–♭III–I) can be regarded as an unusual auxiliary "progression" interpolated within the background V–I cadence in order to delay the "crystallization" of I.

Structural parallelism between the first and last movements is created by the attenuated resolution of the structural dominant. As in the first movement, in the Finale (Ex. 8.11b) the resolution of V to I is "stretched out" through the main body of the reprise, the structural V at the beginning of the reprise (m. 191) resolving to I at the recapitulation of the first group (m. 275). In the Finale, then, Bruckner analogously "saves" the tonic for its definitive "crystallization" both by reversing the recapitulation and by delaying the tonic arrival until the reprise of the first group (m. 275).[51]

Linked tonic auxiliary cadences in the outer movements of Bruckner's Eighth Symphony anticipate Sibelius's use of this technique in his Seventh Symphony (see below). The super-sonata concept underlies this symphony since the I–III–V–I undivided structure of the first movement is recapitulated, albeit transformed, in the Finale (compare Exx. 8.12a–b). Furthermore, in each of the outer movements, Bruckner's strategy is to delay "crystallization" of DTA until the onset of the coda. The graphs propose that Bruckner achieves gradual "crystallization" by prolonging the mediant E♭ *through* the beginning of the recapitulation. In the first movement (Ex. 8.12a), the second group (mm. 51ff.) – the *Gesangsperiode* – is placed above G as dominant of C, which is then revalued as "p" in a III–V–I auxiliary cadence into the E♭ major of the third, closing, group (m. 97).[52] The development passes from E♭ (m. 153) through D♭ (the Neapolitan, m. 227) to the putative tonic C at the beginning of the recapitulation (m. 229). In this way, the return to C at the outset of the reprise recomposes the D♭–C (♭II–I) auxiliary cadence of the opening (mm. 1–4).[53] There are, however, compelling reasons *not* to interpret this C (major) at the beginning of the recapitulation as DTA. Generally, the dominant introduces structural tonic in the reprise; but neither the exposition nor the development presents a structural dominant that could assume this function. Furthermore, the recapitulation occurs in the "wrong" mode: C *major,* not C minor. For these reasons, the graph proposes that the recapitulation features an internal tonic auxiliary cadence whereby the C major "tonic" is reinterpreted as the submediant of E♭ in a VI♯3–V–I auxiliary progression. Thus, the E♭ of the recapitulated *Gesangsperiode* (m. 311) continues the mediant prolongation initiated by the third, closing, group in the exposition (m. 97). The

[51] In light of my recent work, I have slightly revised my reading of the finale as presented in *Bruckner Studies* (pp. 187–90). Whereas I considered the V (B) at the beginning of the reprise (m. 191) to be passing, caught between IV (A, m. 93) and ♭VI (C, m. 213), I now read it as the structural dominant. The VI chord (C major), which supports the recapitulation of the second group, then serves to delay the resolution to I, which is being held in abeyance for the return of the first group (m. 275). In other words, C occurs as a ♭6–5 exchange over E. Not only does my newer interpretation better explain the finale, it calls attention to the structural parallelism

between the outer movements: in both undivided backgrounds, the DTA resolution of the structural V is "delayed" until late in the movement.
[52] Notice that while the third group initially is in E♭ *minor*, it mutates to E♭ *major* (m. 125).
[53] In other words, Bruckner's daring compositional idea is to reproduce the opening ♭II–I auxiliary cadence in its traditional place in sonata form, i.e. at the beginning of the recapitulation, but to revalue this tonic as the initial term ("p") of a VI–V–I auxiliary cadence in the key of the mediant.

Ex. 8.12a   Bruckner, Eighth Symphony (1890), first movement

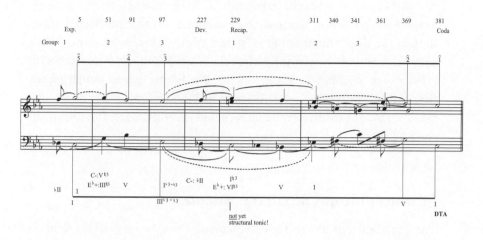

Ex. 8.12b   Bruckner, Eighth Symphony, finale

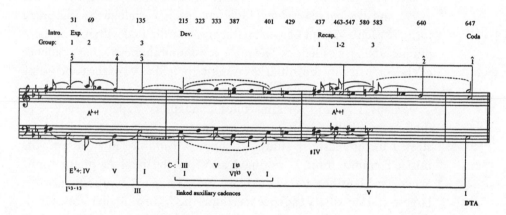

result: the structural dominant is attained only at the beginning of the coda (m. 369), where it is elided with DTA.

In the Finale (Ex. 8.12b), Bruckner recomposes the internal tonic auxiliary cadence of the first movement by again revaluing I as VI of III: as in the first movement, the compositional idea is to by-pass the tonic reprise. The arrival on C major in the fourth (final) part of the development (m. 387), although de-emphasized through dynamics and other compositional parameters, serves as the goal "tonic" of a clearly delineated and emphatic III (m. 301)–IV (m. 323)–V (m. 333) auxiliary cadence in C. But this putative C major tonic does not represent DTA: rather, the initial III–(IV–)V–I auxiliary cadence (mm. 301–87) is linked to a second auxiliary cadence in E♭, whereby the "tonic" C major becomes "p" in a VI (m. 387)–V (m. 400)–I (m. 401) auxiliary cadence in the mediant.

It is noteworthy that the Finale places the *Gesangsperiode* in the same key (A♭ major) in both the exposition and the recapitulation (compare mm. 69 and 547). But A♭ is revalued by context: in the exposition, it functions as the subdominant of E♭ as "p" in a IV–V–I auxiliary cadence, while in the recapitulation it assumes the role of VI in C minor – more specifically, upper neighbor to V (Ex. 8.12b). Furthermore, recapitulating the first and second groups over A♭ (mm. 463–567) in place of the exposition's C (m. 31) facilitates the larger strategy of delaying DTA until the coda (m. 647).

Sibelius's bitonic auxiliary cadences

The "crystallization" strategies discussed thus far are all present in Sibelius's early large-scale orchestral works. While *En saga* (1892, revised 1902), *Skogsrået* (1894), *Lemminkäinen's Return* (1896, revised 1897 and 1899), and *Pohjola's Daughter* (1906) engage in a "dialogue" with sonata form, in each a variant of sonata design is coordinated with one or more bitonic auxiliary cadences. The most common bitonic auxiliary cadence is VI–V–I, whereby the initial key is reinterpreted as VI of the concluding key.

Perhaps Chopin's striking bitonic auxiliary cadences served as models for Sibelius's own bitonic essays. As Carl Schachter has demonstrated in his masterly study of Chopin's *Fantasie* "in F minor," the initial F minor tonic is revalued as VI of the final A♭ major tonic. Schachter identifies nested auxiliary cadences, each component of the largest-scale auxiliary cadence serving as the "r" of a smaller-scale auxiliary progression.[54] Another striking example from Chopin is the Second Ballade (Ex. 8.13), a work featuring sustained struggle between the keys of F major and A minor. Through the first return of the A section (mm. 83ff.), F asserts its hegemony, compelling the first A minor section (mm. 47–82) to assume the identity of the "upper third" of F. In the development section (mm. 94–140), the bass gradually works its way up chromatically from F to A as A vehemently tries to re-establish itself. Finally, from m. 140, the key of A minor prevails; when the bass regains F in m. 156, it is heard now as VI of A (F becomes the bass of an implied augmented sixth chord F–A–C–D♯), which resolves to V and I (mm. 157–69). The initial oscillation between the two keys is created by

[54] Carl Schachter, "Chopin's Fantasy, Op. 49. The Two-Key Scheme," in *Chopin Studies*, ed. Jim Samson (Cambridge: Cambridge University Press, 1988), pp. 221–53, repr. in Schachter, *Unfoldings. Essays in Schenkerian Theory and Analysis* (New York: Oxford University Press, 1999), pp. 260–88.

an upper voice $\hat{8}$–$\hat{7}$–$\hat{8}$ in F major as the bass ascends from F to A and returns to F.[55]

Sibelius's *Skogsrået* provides a remarkable example of super-sonata form superimposed upon a bitonic ♯VII–♭II–V–I auxiliary cadence in C♯ minor (Exx. 8.14a–b). In accord with our definition of the bitonic auxiliary cadence, the background harmonic progression is *goal-oriented* with the first tonic revalued as a non-tonic scale step in the concluding key. Thus the initial tonic C major is reinterpreted enharmonically to become the leading tone B♯ (♯VII) of the final, definitive C♯ minor tonic. Within the "super-sonata" form, the scherzo (mm. 70–296) and the slow movement (mm. 376–556) – the "love scene" – may be understood as "inserted" into development space, while the tragic finale (mm. 568–639) is assigned to recapitulation space (it is a tragic, freely recapitulatory "deformation" of the opening triumphant march).[56] In its synthesis of four movements within a super-sonata form supported by an auxiliary cadence, *Skogsrået* is remarkably prescient of later developments in Sibelius's music; indeed, as I shall attempt to show, it prefigures *Tapiola* and the Seventh Symphony in a number of significant ways.

An essential attribute of development space in both sonata and super-sonata forms is the *instability* of the projected harmony – even if it seems to be a tonic – DTA generally being postponed until the recapitulation. In super-sonata forms, this principle of tonal instability in development space dictates that the movements inserted into development space be tonally unstable. In *Skogsrået*, as in *Tapiola* and the Seventh Symphony, Sibelius holds fast to this fundamental principle: in *Skogsrået*, the putative tonic reprise (in C major) of the opening march (mm. 297ff.) is caught within development space, "entrapped" within the prolonged *Tristan* chord of the Scherzo spanning mm. 70–374 (Ex. 8.14b).[57]

[55] For a sensitive and insightful reading of the Second Ballade, see Kevin Korsyn, "Directional Tonality and Intertextuality: Brahms's Quintet Op. 88 and Chopin's Ballade Op. 38," in *The Second Practice of Nineteenth-Century Tonality*, ed. William Kinderman and Harald Krebs (Lincoln: University of Nebraska Press, 1996), pp. 45–86. In contrast to Korsyn, I read the top line of the F major music from F ($\hat{8}$) – not C ($\hat{5}$) – which then, in the greater A minor scheme, is revalued as a neighbor note to E (6–5). To suggest the programmatic idea of "unfulfilment," Chopin suppresses the putative dominants of F in mm. 82 and 129; only E (m. 157) as dominant of the "tragic" key of A minor manages to function as a structural dominant.

[56] Here I adopt Murtomäki's measure

numbering of the presumably final version. The manuscript reveals that the piece in its original form (in 1894) contained over 700 measures. Compared with the almost 900 measures of the first (1892) version of *En saga*, the initial draft of *Skogsrået* already represents a trend toward greater concentration and concision in the later works. *Pohjola's Daughter*, for example, is only 260 measures long.

[57] This greatly expanded *Tristan* chord in *Skogsrået* foreshadows *Tapiola* (see Ex. 8.23). In the Seventh Symphony the root-position tonic supporting the scherzo (inserted into development space) is analogously unstable, "trapped" within the over-arching dominant prolongation (see the discussion of Ex. 8.30b below).

Ex. 8.13   Chopin, Second Ballade

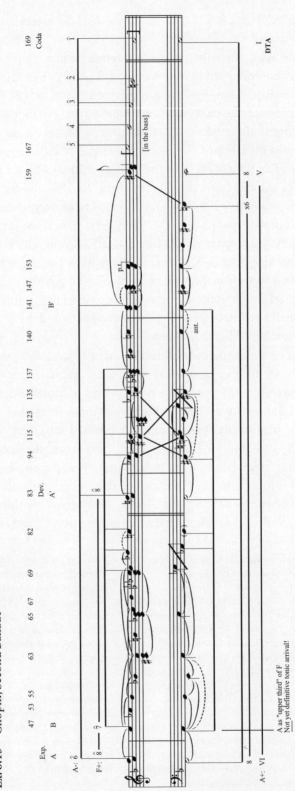

Ex. 8.14a–b   Sibelius, *Skogsrået*

a)

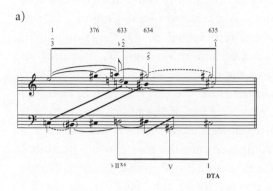

b)

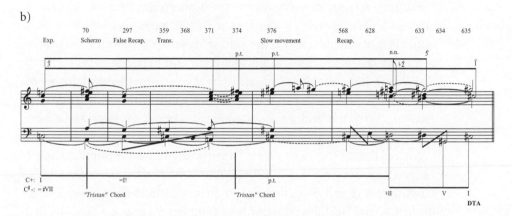

Analogously, the C♯ major-minor of the slow movement/development does not fully establish the new tonic – not yet; rather, this C♯ functions as an unstable passing harmony leading to D as the Neapolitan augmented sixth chord (or ♭II^{x6}) of C♯ minor. After five anticipatory moves to the Neapolitan augmented sixth (mm. 580, 588, 604, 610, 620), the definitive achievement of this chord in m. 628 leads to the structural dominant (m. 633), which resolves to the tonic (DTA, m. 635). As suggested by Exx. 8.14a–b, over the main body of the composition, the bass composes out a diminished third C=B♯ (m.1)–C♯ (m. 376)–D (m. 628).[58]

[58] The linear diminished third is then verticalized in the Neapolitan augmented sixth D–B♯. In contrast to Murtomäki's analysis (in this volume), I consider the harmonic process to be *goal-oriented*, with the concluding C♯ (m. 635) serving as the final *tonic* (rather than the Neapolitan of the initial C). In my view, Sibelius's "crystallization" metaphor dictates postponing DTA until the end. Thus the C♯ of the love scene (mm. 376ff.) does not represent an arrival (of the C♯ either as tonic or as the Neapolitan of C) but a passing chord on its way to D, which, in my reading, is part of the background harmonic progression.

Sibelius's remarkable way of composing – creating a "false" reprise of the opening and transforming the apparently stable tonic of the love scene into a passing harmony – is motivated by the program. Björn's confident self-pride and hubris, represented by the C major march, already intimates the hero's destruction through its tendency to devolve to A minor, the key of the dwarves' scherzo. Certainly, Björn believes himself to have escaped from the dwarves' trap, hence the apparent triumph of the C major reprise of the march (mm. 297ff.). But this self-confidence proves unwarranted: Björn's inability to free himself from their spell is composed into the music as his truncated reprise collapses and C major is overwhelmed by the dwarves' *Tristan* chord (m. 374).[59] Through this device of the "false" reprise in the orchestral version of *Skogsrået* – the undermined heroic fanfare – Sibelius adds a *moralistic* dimension to the narrative, which is only implicit in Rydberg's poem: the "failed" reprise of Björn's march suggests that self-pride leads to self-delusion and hence to catastrophe.[60] The hero falsely imagines himself to have overcome the dark forces of nature and of his own sexuality. This idea will be further developed in *Pohjola's Daughter* and *En saga*, where the hero's fanfares are analogously undercut and "chastened."

My reading of the "false reprise" interpolated into development space receives support from Sibelius's melodrama version of *Skogsrået*, which, omitting this return altogether, moves directly from the dwarves' music to the love scene. Sibelius could not have countenanced such a cut if he had deemed the reprise of the march essential to the form and structure. Sexual passion is ultimately revealed to be a "transient" emotion ("passing" like the passing C♯), which "sucks out" the hero's life force; the "pain" of "emasculation" is poignantly represented by the goal of the passing motion, the Neapolitan augmented sixth chord on D. "Crystallization" of the Neapolitan augmented sixth chord (m. 628) becomes the instance of castration: divested of his manhood, the hero is – in the words of the poem's final stanza – incapable of taking a wife and producing children.[61]

[59] Sibelius was concerned that the C major return of the march should *not* possess sufficient weight to re-establish C major as a tonic; therefore, he trimmed its dimensions.

[60] This moral is less explicit in the melodrama version of *Skogsrået* since it simply omits the "false" reprise. Following the poem, the melodrama's music leaps directly from the dwarves' scherzo to the nymph's slow movement.

[61] *Skogsrået*'s VII–♭II–V–I bitonic auxiliary cadence is not unique in Sibelius's output. In *Scene with Cranes* (1906), based on the incidental music for *Kuolema* (1903), Sibelius begins on E, which is analogously revalued as the "upper third" of V of F. The overall progression is F major: VII–II–V–I. The upper voice is especially bold: instead of supporting G♯ ($\hat{3}$ of E major, ♭$\hat{3}$ of F major), Sibelius projects A as an "eleventh" above E, which is ultimately revalued as $\hat{3}$ of the goal tonic F major.

Ex. 8.15a–b   Sibelius, *Lemminkäinen's Return*

a)

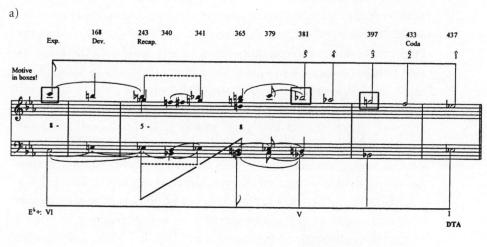

b)

In *Lemminkäinen's Return*, a variant of sonata form is placed over a VI–V–I bitonic auxiliary cadence (Ex. 8.15a), which leads from C minor to "crystallize" in the E♭ major DTA only at the end (mm. 437ff.). The primary motive (bassoons, mm. 5–11) is recomposed in enlargement in the upper voice across the piece as a whole; thus C–B♭–G, $\hat{8}$–$\hat{7}$–$\hat{5}$ in C minor, is reinterpreted as $\hat{6}$–$\hat{5}$–$\hat{3}$ in E♭ major (compare Exx. 8.15a–b). As in *Skogsrået*, the development space (mm. 168–242) supports an "unstable" chromatic passing tone; here, the passing tone is B♮ filling in C–B♭. As indicated in the graph, the E♭ minor chord prolonged at the beginning of the recapitulation (mm. 243ff.) does not represent DTA; rather, the underlying compositional intent is to move from the initial C to B♭ (the dominant of E♭, m. 381), DTA being achieved only at the coda (m. 437).[62] Thus, the E♭ minor of the recapitulation is "anticipatory" in nature; in context, the bass participates in an unfolding E♭–B.

In *Pohjola's Daughter*, the undermining of Väinämöinen's B♭ major "tonic" fanfares programmatically represents this hero's ultimately false

---

[62] As I had suggested in my 1995 analysis (Ex. 6 in "'The Maiden with a Heart of Ice'" in *Proceedings*, p. 261), the E♭ "tonic" in m. 243 does not represent DTA. However, I have revised my interpretation of the top voice; reading it from C (rather than G) reveals the upper enlargement of the motive C–B♭–G across the movement.

conception of his own invincibility and the precariousness of his puffed-up self-pride and sexual hubris. The work is structured over a bitonic auxiliary cadence leading from G minor at the outset to DTA on B♭ major, which "crystallizes" only at the very end (m. 242, Ex. 8.16); thus the extended G minor prolongation (mm. 1–241) undercuts the hero's B♭ major fanfares (mm. 38 and 210). The apparently strong B♭ major chord in m. 38 "anticipates" the ultimate goal; however, this B♭, although emphasized by the fanfare and extensively prolonged, does not represent DTA but rather the middle term of an arpeggiated tritone: G (m. 1)–B♭ (m. 38)–D♭ (m. 205). And when Väinämöinen's fanfare is recapitulated even more emphatically in m. 210, B♭ remains "trapped" within the same ascending tritone as part of an even larger arpeggiation: G (m. 1)–B♭ (m. 210)–D♭ (m. 240). Thus, *G – not* B♭ – is prolonged through the main body of the work. In m. 241, G *minor* mutates to G *major*, sounding as if it might resolve definitively to C as its dominant, but at the last moment (m. 242) the C chord swerves through F to achieve DTA on B♭. The overall progression, then, is VI–V–I, with the I delayed until the coda.[63]

The *essential* point for the correlation of structure with program is this: Väinämöinen's pompous B♭ major fanfares do *not* establish DTA on B♭. Rather, these B♭ "arrivals," like the hero himself, are devalued – "unmanned" – by the hegemony of the G minor-major prolongation. Only in the final measures (mm. 242ff.) is a "chastened," modally uncertain B♭ released: perhaps, like Alberich before him, Väinämöinen has stilled lust through self-castration, the "hollow," "empty," modally indeterminate B♭ of the concluding bars evoking "the hero unmanned."

A significant observation to arise from the interpretation presented in Ex. 8.16 is the role of "tritonality" in *Pohjola's Daughter* as a metaphor for sexual abandon and possibly perversion.[64] As already noted, G–D♭ plays a

---

[63] In my 1995 graph (Ex. 7 in "'The Maiden with a Heart of Ice,'" in *Proceedings*, pp. 262–63), I interpreted the *second* B♭ major appearance of Väinämöinen's heroic brass fanfare in mm. 210ff. as DTA. Since then I have become convinced that this is premature; rather, I believe that G is prolonged until m. 241, i.e., *through* the hero's *second* attempt to assert B♭ major as tonic. In accord with the massive G minor-major prolongation over the main body of the piece, I read the top line from D (5̂ of G) rather than F (5̂ of B♭). By postponing DTA on B♭ so late (mm. 242ff.), my reading essentially inverts that of Timo Virtanen in this volume.

[64] For a discussion of "tritonality" and its connotation of "sexual perversion," see

Jackson, "Aspects of Sexuality and Structure in the Later Symphonies of Tchaikovsky," *Music Analysis* 14 (1995), pp. 3–25, and *Tchaikovsky. Symphony No. 6*, especially my discussion of "The Unsuccessful Attempt to 'Cure' Homosexual Tritonality," pp. 64–68. In *Pohjola's Daughter*, background tritonality is associated with Väinämöinen's sexual appetite exaggerated to the point of sexual deviance – and the extreme measure he must take to control it. As I have suggested, Sibelius already connects sexual deviance – in this case incest – with chromatic displacement of the structural dominant in *Kullervo and His Sister* (see Jackson, "'The Maiden with a Heart of Ice,'" p. 265).

primary structural role, with Väinämöinen's B♭ "caught" within its grip. The E of Pohjola's daughter, which is prolonged through the development (mm. 57–161), also stands in a tritonal relationship to the extended prolongation of Väinämöinen's B♭ (spanning mm. 38–165). As I observed in my 1995 essay: "The chromatic 'diversion' of F to F♭/E corresponds to Väinämöinen's 'distraction' by Pohjola's daughter. The 'irrational' . . . F♭ also represents the 'impossibility' of the tasks she will set Väinämöinen. . . The chromatically lowered dominant (F♭) may be understood to displace the diatonic dominant (F major)."[65]

In *En saga*, the hero is *never* "validated" by support from the ultimate tonic (E♭ minor): instead, he is born, lives, makes love, and collapses in non-tonic space. Here, again, the hero is undercut as the recapitulation of his primary theme (i.e., the first group) is placed over a highly *unstable* G chord (mm. 597ff.) leading from the first key, C minor, to the concluding key, E♭ minor (Ex. 8.17, p. 224). This destabilization results from the coordination of the "tragic reversed recapitulation" with linked auxiliary cadences.[66] In principle, *En saga* conforms to my definition of the genre, the recapitulation of the second group (mm. 457ff.) being "tragically" displaced to precede the first group (mm. 597ff.). However, Sibelius departs from the practice of earlier masters in one crucial respect. While they almost invariably allow the reprise of the first group to coincide with resolution to DTA (where it frequently does double duty as the coda), Sibelius places the first group's recapitulation above the *dominant* of the initial key (i.e., above G as V of C minor); it is then revalued as the preparation ("p") for the second auxiliary cadence in the concluding key (i.e., G as V of C becomes ♯III⁴³ of E♭ minor). Thus, the recapitulation of the first group occurs over G, tonal resolution on E♭ being postponed until the retrospective coda.

The introduction (mm. 1–114) presents an initial auxiliary cadence, C major: I^6 (m. 1)–v^4_3 (m. 96)–$I^{\flat3}$ (m. 114).[67] The initial A minor six-four chord (mm. 1ff.) substitutes for the paradigmatic I^6; the six-four is created by eliding G with A to create a fourth instead of a third above the bass E. This initial auxiliary cadence represents the amorphous "Rausch" (intoxication) of the still-forming proto-world, as Sibelius described it in

---

[65] Jackson, "'The Maiden with a Heart of Ice,'" pp. 260–61.

[66] The genre of the tragic reversed recapitulation comprises "a small number of reversed sonata forms in the German tradition post ca. 1770 [in which] the reversed recapitulation combined with the displaced tonic has programmatic significance, representing tragic *peripety* wrought by capricious and unkind fate . . .

This formal and tonal *hyperbaton* bespeaks a deep-structural compositional rhetoric, which supports and, in certain cases, even peripheralizes the tragic gestures of the foreground" (Jackson, "Tragic Reversed Sonata Form," pp. 142–3 and 208).

[67] If the V four-three is understood to substitute for a root-position dominant, then the auxiliary progression is C major: I^6–V–$I^{\flat3}$.

Ex. 8.16a–b *Sibelius, Pohjola's Daughter*

a)

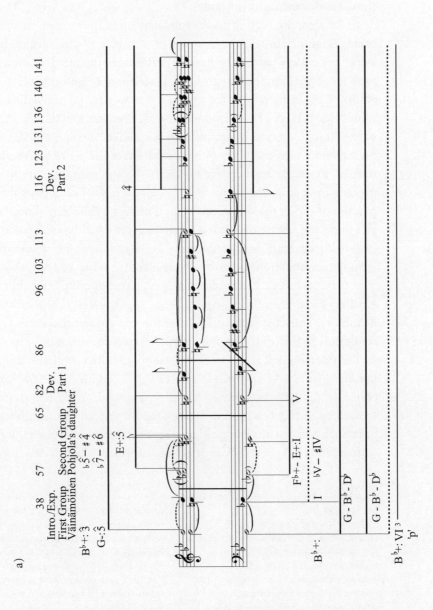

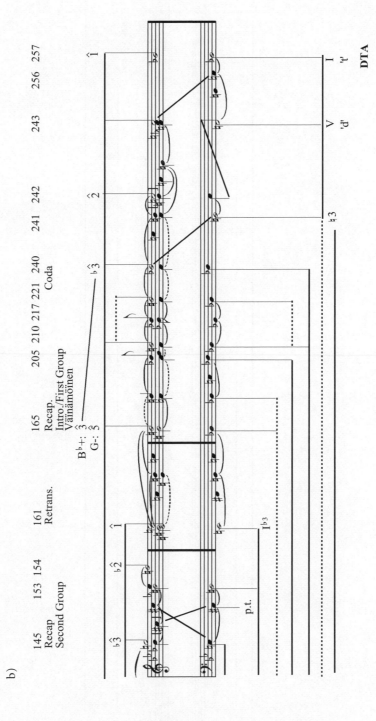

Ex. 8.17 Sibelius, *En saga*

a letter to Adolf Paul.[68] Perhaps the hero's birth pangs are articulated by the striking D♯–E dissonance of mm. 9ff. By the recapitulation, his strength has been sapped: his tonic recapitulation of the second theme (mm. 457ff.) is "exhausted"; worse still, in spite of a vigorous attempt, he is unable to secure a firm tonic for the recapitulation of his first theme (mm. 597ff.). Indeed, tragic *peripety* is realized in the instant that the G chord, the putative dominant of C, is reinterpreted as the initial term (i.e., "p") of the linked auxiliary progression into E♭ minor.[69] The implication that the over-sexed hero has been "unmanned" is confirmed by his subsequent demise to the sustained *Tristan* chord, the half-diminished seventh chord on F (mm. 707ff.).[70]

In *Skogsrået, Pohjola's Daughter, En saga,* and *Lemminkäinen in Tuonela,* the "crystallization" metaphor expresses a psycho-sexual drama in which the hero is destroyed as a consequence of sexual hubris and libidinal urges. This Sibelian meta-narrative inverts the Brucknerian "crystallization" metaphor: for Bruckner, crystallization represents the hero's triumphant self-realization, but for Sibelius it "suffers" tragic inversion as sexual excess is punished by death or castration. Ironically, the very *process* of "crystallization" (realized through the auxiliary cadence) becomes that of the hero's undoing: Sibelius's *Lemminkäinen in Tuonela,* for example, intimates that the hero is "unmanned" or "cut to pieces" as punishment for his sexual abandon. If liminal figures divert – and pervert – the hero, castrated he is able to resume his journey "home" to the "wife-mother" (Aino, Virgin, mother earth, Finland), whose "healing," i.e. restoration of life and sexual power, is sought.[71] An optimistic outcome is projected in works like *Lemminkäinen's Return,* the Third Symphony, and *Maan virsi,* where the "wife-mother" lovingly "restores" the hero by "sewing" him back together; but ultimately, in the Seventh Symphony, "resurrection" becomes ambiguous if not tragically precluded.

[68] See Veijo Murtomäki, "The Problem of Narrativity in the Symphonic Poem *En saga* by Jean Sibelius," in *Musical Signification. Essays in the Semiotic Theory and Analysis of Music,* ed. Eero Tarasti (Berlin: Mouton de Gruyter, 1995), p. 489.

[69] If DTA on E♭ is postponed until the beginning of the coda (m. 779), earlier emphasized E♭s in the bass (mm. 185–310 and 480–570) "anticipate" rather than realize the final goal tonic – a feature not present in the first version (see Murtomäki, "The Problem of Narrativity," pp. 86–87). Notice that these "anticipatory" E♭s are all

"trapped" within the prolongation of C, which spans most of the work. As we have seen, the same "anticipatory" technique is employed in *Pohjola's Daughter,* where "anticipatory" Bs are "caught" within the prolongation of G.

[70] In his essay in this volume, Murtomäki explores the significance of the *Tristan* chord in Sibelius's early music. Sibelius's later music also contains significant references to *Tristan,* especially the Seventh Symphony (see below).

[71] Notice the synthesis of sexual and national metaphors.

Sibelius's tonic auxiliary cadences

The concept of the initially "strong" but subsequently "weakened" tonic is central to Sibelius's compositional technique. Attenuating this procedure in Chopin, Schumann, Brahms, and Bruckner, Sibelius elevates it to a stylistic-ideological principle. It is astonishing how early in his career, in addition to absorbing and even extending the technique of the bitonic auxiliary cadence, Sibelius masters the tonic auxiliary cadence. The opening of the *Kullervo* Symphony's finale already reveals command of this technique. Although the movement begins with a tonic E minor chord embellished by D♯ and F♯ neighbors, this chord does not initiate tonic prolongation. Instead, this "weak" tonic functions as a neighbor chord embellishing a "strong" F♯–A♯–C♯–E chord, i.e., a V_5^6 of V, which resolves to the dominant at rehearsal E. Thus the main body of the Finale is placed above the prolonged dominant, with DTA achieved only at rehearsal S, i.e., at the orchestral peroration and the return of the primary theme from the first movement.

Sibelius employs linked tonic auxiliary cadences in another relatively early work, *Lemminkäinen in Tuonela* (1895–96, revised 1899) from his *Lemminkäinen* Suite (Ex. 8.18a). As in the finale of Schumann's *Fantasie*, the compositional idea here is to begin with a "weak" tonic, which evolves "teleologically" towards a different harmonic goal: in a manner strongly reminiscent of Schumann, *Lemminkäinen in Tuonela* combines "strophic searching" for the *telos* supported by over-arching and nested auxiliary cadences.

This teleological effect is the result of the 1899 revision. Sibelius's initial conception was fundamentally different. The first version opened conventionally with a thirty-five-measure slow introduction in the low brass reinforcing the initial F♯ minor tonic.[72] But to make the movement commence with "wispy" figuration in a tentative, furtive manner – a bolder and more original way of beginning – Sibelius deleted this brass fanfare. In its final version, the opening is characterized by thematically

---

[72] The final measures of the introduction are crossed out in the first extant page of the manuscript full score (the deleted opening pages are missing). I have been able to reconstruct the original introduction from the orchestral parts for the first performance, which are preserved in the Sibelius Academy Archives (I am grateful to Veijo Murtomäki for making these parts available to me). Andrew Barnett, in the program notes to the recently released recording of the original first and fourth movements of the *Lemminkäinen Suite* (Osmo Vänska conducting the Lahti Symphony, BIS CD-1015, 1999), incorrectly states that "the only substantial change in *Lemminkäinen in Tuonela* concerns the return to the opening material"; surely, the omission of the extended introduction and numerous other revisions warrant reconstruction, performance, and recording of the original version of this movement as well.

indeterminate figuration growing out of the "depths" (i.e. "darkness") of the Finnish Hell. Although a theme enters above the putative F♯ minor tonic in m. 37, it dissipates inconclusively in m. 71 as the entire growth process "slides" down a semitone. The definitive point of tonal departure is attained only with the arrival on the D♯ major chord with minor seventh and ninth (D♯–F𝄪–A♯–C♯–E) in m. 92. This "howling" dissonant chord – representing the "pain" of Lemminkäinen's private Hell (his castration?) – marks the movement's "true" beginning.

The movement as a whole replicates this growth process in three evolutions toward the "howling" chord as *telos*:

A section, mm. 1–185, Lemminkäinen "dismembered" (Ex. 8.18a)

>   Introduction (mm. 1–91)
Telos I: "howling" chord (mm. 92–97)

>   Recomposed Introduction (mm. 98–147)
Telos II: "howling" chord (mm. 148–85)

B section, mm. 186–276, the "wife-mother" as "healer" (Ex. 8.18b)[73]

A' section, mm. 277–342

>   Recomposed Introduction (mm. 277–92)
Telos III: "howling" chord (mm. 293–end)

The tonic auxiliary cadence principle operates in two keys simultaneously: firstly, in F♯ minor, the key of the *movement*, and secondly, in E♭ major, the key of the *suite*. By adding a seventh, D♭, to the tonic E♭ major in the *first* movement, which ultimately rises as C♯ (m. 90 of the first movement), Sibelius's *Lemminkäinen* Suite becomes a Finnish "Eroica": as in the Beethovenian model, the D♭/C♯ seventh added to the tonic functions as *the* irritant – the destabilizing "tragic flaw" embedded in the "Eroica chord" propelling the hero's tragic fate. Therefore, in the *Tuonela* movement, the "howling" chord as goal functions on two levels. In terms of the symphony as a whole (i.e., in terms of its macro-symphonic meta-*Ursatz*), it represents a recurrence of the tonic "Eroica-chord," now with a further destabilizing factor: the "painful" Neapolitan ninth added to the seventh (i.e. E=F♭ added to C♯=D♭, Ex. 8.18d, p. 230). Thus, at the macro-symphonic level, this chord represents a *tonic* ninth. Notice that, in the B section, the "wife-mother" "heals" Lemminkäinen by converting *his* "painful," dissonant *ninth* (F♭=E) into the consonant *fifth* and *third* of *her* A minor and C♯ minor chords respectively.

[73] Sibelius labeled the sketches for this passage "Tuonen tytti" ("The Maiden of Tuoni [Death]"), a reference to the *Kalevala*'s description of a maiden rowing *Väinämöinen* across the river to Tuonela. Thus the material originally intended for the abandoned opera *The Building of the Boat* was reused in *Lemminkäinen in Tuonela*, the maiden's music being reinterpreted to represent Lemminkäinen's mother.

Ex. 8.18a–b   Sibelius, *Lemminkäinen in Tuonela*

a)

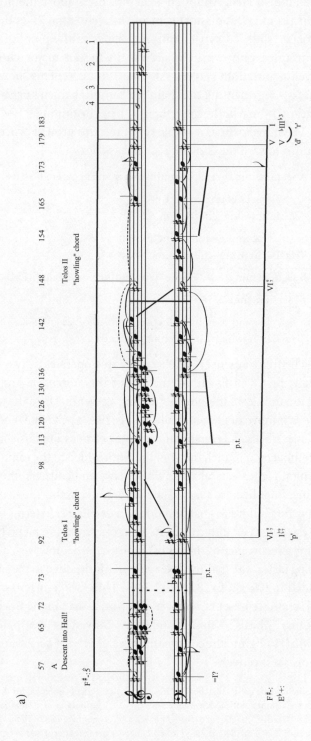

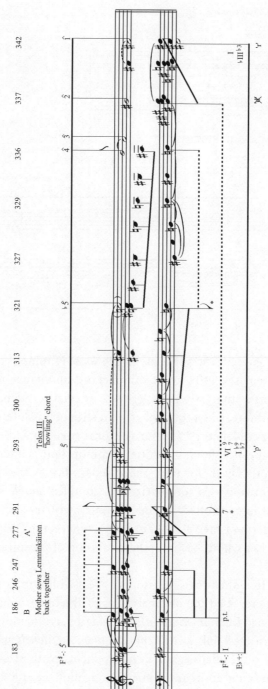

Ex. 8.18c –d   Sibelius, *Lemminkäinen in Tuonela* and *Lemminkäinen's Return*

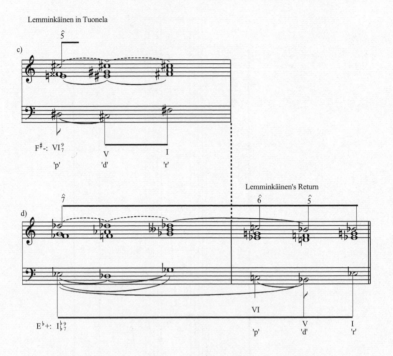

But as Ex. 8.18c suggests, in the *local F♯* minor context of the third movement, the D♯/E♭ "tonic" ninth chord simultaneously functions as the first term, the "p" of a VI–V–I auxiliary cadence in F♯ minor.[74] Furthermore, when the background structure is interpreted as a VI–V–I auxiliary cadence in F♯ minor, the tonic auxiliary cadence principle operates at the local level: the initial F♯ minor tonic is interpreted not as DTA (which is "saved" for mm. 183 and 342) but as the "upper third" of D♯ (Exx. 8.18a–b). To summarize this complex *double entendre*: the background is controlled by linked tonic auxiliary cadences whereby the initial term of the VI–V–I auxiliary cadence, the D♯/E♭ tonic of the symphony as a whole, becomes the resolution of the initial F♯ tonic auxiliary cadence.

To strengthen the super-sonata effect within the *Lemminkäinen* Suite, Sibelius reversed the original order of the inner movements, which had positioned *Lemminkäinen in Tuonela* as the second movement. As Ex. 8.18d demonstrates, linkage of *Lemminkäinen in Tuonela* with *Lemminkäinen's Return* in the final sequence of movements synthesizes auxiliary cadences to create an over-arching tonic prolongation, i.e., the succession of move-

---

[74] Compare with Bruckner's Eighth Symphony, outer movements, where the tonic C is revalued as the submediant of the mediant E♭ (Exx. 8.12a–b).

ments joins parallel auxiliary cadences beginning and ending on D♯/E♭ (E♭ major: $I = $ F♯–: ♯VI–V–I, E♭ major: VI–V–I, i.e. $D♯$–C♯–F♯, C–B♭–E♭).

In the finale of Sibelius's Third Symphony, the putative C major tonic prolonged in mm. 4–108 is *not* DTA, which is being "saved" for the beginning of the finale proper (mm. 246–end, Ex. 8.19).[75] In other words, the introduction/scherzo overlap is organized as a V (m.1)=III[♯3] (m. 210)–I (m. 246) initial auxiliary cadence into DTA, achieved with the activation of finale space proper (supporting the triumphant chorale as *telos* – another Brucknerian concept).[76] Into this initial auxiliary cadence, Sibelius inserts a tonic auxiliary cadence whereby the tonic of the scherzo (mm. 4–104) is reinterpreted as III[♯3] of A♭ major, i.e., as "p" in a III[♯3]–IV–II[6]–I auxiliary cadence in A♭ (mm. 108–18). The putative tonic of mm. 4–108 may be understood as "residue" of a tonic initiating the scherzo in a previous state of the macro-symphonic form, i.e., *before* the scherzo was superimposed upon the introduction to the finale.

Especially subtle examples of the tonic auxiliary cadence can be found in Sibelius's late works, most notably *Maan virsi* (1920) – which in certain respects serves as a preliminary study for the Seventh Symphony – and *Tapiola* (1926). The apparent simplicity of the tonal language in *Maan virsi*, a setting for choir and orchestra of Eino Leino's *Song to the Earth*, belies the work's structural complexity. Example 8.20 proposes that a I[6]–V–I auxiliary cadence underlies this piece, with the "strong" initial I gradually "weakened" to become the "upper sixth" of I[6]. As we shall see, this process also underpins the Seventh Symphony (compare Exx. 8.20b–c with 8.21c–d). In other words, Sibelius's compositional strategy is a tonic auxiliary cadence whereby the initial root-position tonic C – ostensibly a "firm opening tonic" – is progressively devalued as "the upper sixth" of E. The form of *Maan virsi* is bipartite, subdividing into two large sections (Ex. 8.22): Part I (mm. 1–77, stanzas 1–6) is separated from Part II (mm. 98–end, stanzas 7–8) by an orchestral interlude

---

[75] In Ex. 2b in "'The Maiden with a Heart of Ice'," p. 252, I interpreted the tonic arrival in m. 4; according to my present view, this is premature, DTA being postponed until m. 246. Furthermore, I now believe it preferable to read the upper voice from $\hat{5}$ rather than $\hat{3}$.

[76] Although the chord in m. 216 is a C♯ minor six-three, it functions is if it were an E major chord dividing the progression from dominant (m. 1) to tonic (m. 246). Thus Ex. 8.19 suggests that the middleground voice leading conforms to the V–III[♯3]–I paradigm. For examples of this progression in the classical repertoire, see Edward Laufer, "Voice-leading Procedures in Development Sections," *Studies in Music* 13 (1991), pp. 69–120; David Beach, "A Recurring Pattern in Mozart's Music," *Journal of Music Theory* 27 (1983), pp. 1–27; "The Initial Movement of Mozart's Piano Sonatas K. 280 and K. 332: Some Striking Similarities," *Intégrale* 8 (1994), pp. 125–46; "Schubert's Experiments with Sonata Form. Formal–Tonal Design versus Underlying Structure," *Music Theory Spectrum* 15 (1993), pp. 1–18; and Channan Willner, "Chromaticism and the Mediant in Four Late Haydn Works," *Theory and Practice* 13 (1998), pp. 79–114.

Ex. 8.19   Sibelius, Third Symphony, finale

Ex. 8.20   Sibelius, *Maan virsi*, backgrounds

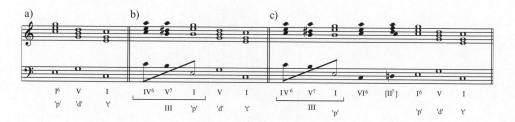

(mm. 78–97). The two parts convert the initial tonic into the "p" of auxiliary cadences so that the tonic's definitive "crystallization" (DTA) can be reserved for the climactic conclusion (m. 177).

The setting of the first two stanzas in C minor (mm. 1–25) is conventional; the initial tonic sounds firm. However, stanza 3 begins a slow but inexorable process of shifting the center of tonal gravity from C to E as the fundamental tone in the bass. By valorizing A over G (notice the emphasis on the A minor chord in mm. 32 and 37), the upper voices begin to destabilize C as a root-position tonic triad.[77] Through stanzas 4–6 (mm. 45–77), this process of devaluing C by converting it into A (through a 5–6 exchange, A displacing G) gathers momentum; ultimately, C metamorphoses into A as the subdominant of E, confirmed by the powerful cadence on E in mm. 74–75.

If the bass "reaches under" a sixth from C to E in Part I, this process is recomposed in Part II (Ex. 8.22). The ground bass, evoked in the first part, is realized in the second: the orchestral interlude and stanzas 7–8, unfold above seven iterations of an eight-measure pattern. The ground's arpeggiation of the tonic C contradicts the upper voices which, through their insistence on A, delineate a prolongation of the submediant A. The climax is reached (m. 157) as the bass "reaches under" from C to E, shifted down an octave through mm. 157–72. Only when the bass is firmly anchored on E in m. 172 is the C major tonic triad – now unequivocally celebrated as a six-three chord – able to participate in an auxiliary progression I⁶–V–I (mm. 172–77).

As in *Maan virsi*, in *Tapiola* (Ex. 8.23, p. 236) the opening measures suggest a "firm opening tonic," but this impression is undermined by subsequent events. The work begins with a timpani roll on B, which serves as a pedal point throughout the first six measures. The listener is strongly tempted to interpret this B as a tonic pedal, if not *the* tonic.

[77] At this point (mm. 32ff.), A still functions as an appoggiatura to G; however, by mm. 45ff. A has displaced G as the harmonic tone.

Ex. 8.21 Sibelius, Seventh Symphony, backgrounds

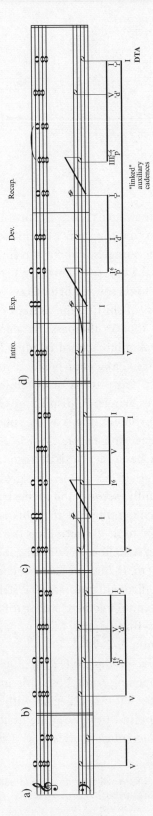

Ex. 8.22   Sibelius, *Maan virsi*

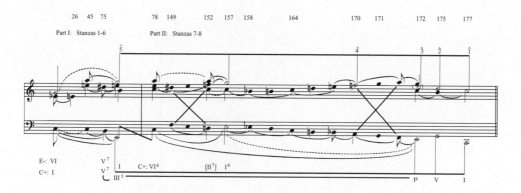

However Ex. 8.23 takes a different position, proposing that all of the initial tonic pedals are subsumed within a submediant seventh chord, i.e. the half-diminished seventh chord G♯–B–D–F♯ built on G♯.[78] At the opening, then, it is the G♯ sustained in the horns through mm. 1–20 – not the B in the timpani – that functions as the "true" bass, G♯ having been "placed above" the pedal B. Thus, this initial low B "anticipates" rather than realizes DTA. Considered from this perspective, the background progression projected through the work as a whole is a modified VI[7]–V[6]–I auxiliary cadence into DTA whereby the bass ascends through the third G♯–A♯–B. Again, as in *Maan virsi*, the fundamental compositional idea is to *postpone* DTA until the very end of the work (m. 607).

Tapiola's super-sonata form amalgamates two formal principles: the super-sonata (cf. *Skogsrået* and the Seventh Symphony) and the reversed recapitulation (*En saga*). The super-sonata inserts the scherzo (m. 208) into the development space (as in *Skogsrået* and the Seventh Symphony). The reversed recapitulation is clearly demarcated, recapitulation space being initiated by material from the *second* group in the exposition (m. 470), while the reprise of first-group material (m. 588) participates in the climax (prepared by an extended dramatic cadenza, m. 513). Supporting this super-sonata design is a two-part tonal structure delineated by the parallelism between mm. 356–58 and mm. 588–607. In other words, the endpoints of the parallel tonal structures delineate a bi-partite tonal framework, the emphatic 3̂–2̂–1̂ *Urlinie* descent over A♯–D in the bass in mm. 356–58 anticipating the definitive descent over A♯–B in mm. 588–607 (Ex. 8.23).

[78] Perhaps it is significant that this chord is equivalent – *untransposed* – to the "dysfunctional" seventh chord in the *Adagio lamentoso* of Tchaikovsky's *Pathétique*. Thus, it may allude to the *Pathétique* rather than *Tristan*. For a valuable discussion of the role of G♯–B–D–F♯ collection in *Tapiola*, see Tim Howell, "Sibelius's *Tapiola*. Issues of Tonality and Timescale," in *Sibelius Forum*, pp. 240–41, and also his essay in this book.

Ex. 8.23 Sibelius, *Tapiola*

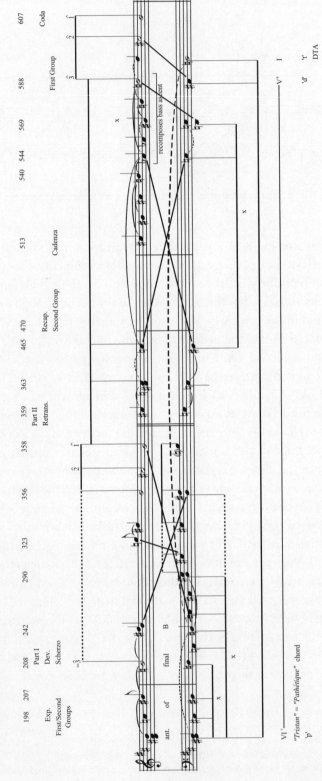

The two tonal parts (mm. 1–358 and mm. 359–607) create an antecedent-consequent effect whereby Part I encompasses a motion from the initial G♯ seventh chord to a cadence on the unstable tonic six-three chord in mm. 356–58, while Part II resolves this cadence to a stable tonic five-three chord in mm. 588–607. The second part initiates an extended developmental retransition to the (reversed) recapitulation. The supersonata form relates to the binary tonal structure as follows:

Part I (mm. 1–358)

Exposition, mm. 1–207
First group, mm. 1–105
Second group, mm. 106–207

Development, mm. 208–358
Scherzo, mm. 208–241
Developmental transformation of first group, mm. 242–358

Part II (mm. 359–606)

Developmental retransition, mm. 359–470

Recapitulation (reversed), mm. 470–606
Second group, mm. 470–512
Cadenza, mm. 513–87
First group (varied), mm. 588–606

Coda, mm. 606–end

Central to our deliberations is the delayed "crystallization" of DTA whereby the moment of "crystallization" is deferred until the coda (m. 606–end). Each time the bass seems to "secure" B (as at the outset), this putative tonic is subsumed within an ascending progression. Let us consider mm. 51–99 in the exposition. Here, the contrabasses "sit" on B for no less than forty-eight measures, yet this B pedal is revealed to be the middle term of an ascending bass arpeggiation through the tritone G♯–D, leading from the first to the second group, G♯ (m. 1)–B (m. 51)–D (m. 106). Arpeggiating the lower triadic component of the opening VI^7 chord, G♯–B–D becomes a fundamental motive in the work as a whole, labeled "x" in Ex. 8.23. In mm. 242–325, through the development of first group material, the bass is again "anchored" on the tonic B, this time in an even more extended passage of eighty-three measures. Yet again, this "tonic" pedal is subsumed within an even larger arpeggiation of "x," G♯ (m. 1)–B (m. 242)–D (m. 357), which overarches the earlier statement of "x" spanning the exposition (mm. 1–208).[79] The guiding idea through the developmental retransition, the reprise of the second group, and the

[79] Compare with the role of B♭ in the
arpeggiation G–B♭–D in *Pohjola's Daughter*.

cadenza is to re-secure G♯ in the bass (m. 465), which then ascends through C (m. 544) to D (m. 569) in yet a further recomposition of the tritone G♯–D. Through the cadenza, from m. 544 to the climax in m. 588, "x" is shifted from the bass into the upper voice to lead to the primary tone (d⁴: $\hat{3}$) in its highest register.

In spite of the extensive use of pedal tones, *Tapiola*'s middleground voice leading is highly active, its dynamism concentrated in large-scale ascending motions (especially in the bass) through "x" and huge registral shifts involving voice exchange (Ex. 8.23). These sweeping "ascents" through "x" beneath the extensive "foliage" of tonic pedals – anticipating rather than realizing DTA – intimate the gradual epiphany of the god Tapio from the canopy of the primeval Finnish forest.

Clara as DTA: synthesis of initial, internal tonic, and over-arching auxiliary cadences in Schumann's Second and Brahms's First Symphony

If "crystallization" of DTA represents "the quest" for the beloved Woman as Redemptress in Schumann's Second Symphony, Brahms's First Symphony, and Sibelius's Seventh Symphony, this theological dimension both exalts and universalizes the domestic drama.[80] In Schumann's Second, the "motto" trumpet calls interpret the "search" for Clara in eschatological terms: in the finale's apotheosis (as in Michelangelo's *Last Judgement* in the Sistine Chapel), Clara-Mary appears triumphantly at the side of the resurrected Schumann-Christ. Brahms's First Symphony begins "*in höchster Not*" with Clara-Eve: the first movement plays out the Temptation, the Fall, and the expulsion from Eden. Only through Faith – represented by the chorale in the finale – can the paradigmatic dichotomy shift from "Adam-Eve" to "Christ-Virgin."

In all three symphonies, intertextual references provide further seman-tic keys to the domestic drama. In the First Symphony's opening move-ment, Brahms represents himself as Schumann's Manfred who, having been "tempted" by his beloved "sister" (Clara/Astarte/Eve), is wracked with

---

[80] I am probably the first to posit a close parallelism between Sibelius's Seventh Symphony and Brahms's First. Although I can draw upon no incontrovertible historical evidence to support my hypothesis, I observe that, as a student in Vienna, Sibelius had wanted to study with Brahms (as well as Bruckner) and met him on at least two occasions. Furthermore, we may take it for granted that Sibelius was familiar with the Brahms symphonies; later in life he remarked cryptically that "Brahms's symphonies have had enormous moral significance for the history of music."

guilty longing.[81] Thus Brahms associates himself with Manfred's "yearning" chromatic motive (F–F♯–G, C–C♯–D and its inversions, see
Exx. 8.24–25). As David Brodbeck has shown, the second subject is clearly
derived from Astarte's music in *Manfred*, especially No. 11 ("Manfred
addresses Astarte"), where Brahms/Manfred poses the fateful question,
"Du liebst mich noch?," to which Clara/Astarte replies with the ambivalent
exclamation "Manfred!"[82] Extending Brodbeck's observation, Ex. 8.25a
suggests that the bridge to the second subject (mm. 97–128), as well as the
second subject itself (mm. 129–57), are preoccupied with the chromatic
descending tetrachord B♭–A–A♭–G–F evoking Adam/Manfred/Brahms's
"Original Sin" with Astarte/Clara's motive "x." The finale transposes this
descending tetrachord to C; but as Clara metamorphoses from Temptress
(Astarte/Eve) into Redemptress, C–B♭–A♭–G, "purged" of its chromaticism, becomes C–B–A–G in both the first (mm. 61ff.) and second subjects
(mm. 118ff., where it rejoices as an ostinato). Clearly, the "Alp horn"
theme, and the first and second themes (with their allusions to the "rejoic-
ing" finales of Beethoven's Ninth and Schumann's Second), are associated
with this transformation.[83]

Sibelius's Seventh Symphony also begins "*in höchster Not.*" Sibelius as
narrator/protagonist associates himself with the initial "yearning" rising
chromatic theme, which is designated "rt" throughout the discussion.
Again, an intertextual reference helps to clarify this semantic: the
opening presentation of "rt," with its rising minor sixth G–E♭, filled in
stepwise, evokes Tristan's opening interval, his fatal "longing" – his
"*Sehnsucht*" (Ex. 8.30, p. 262).[84] In m. 4, the E♭ in the horns slowly and
deliberately attempts to move upward, ascending "painfully" through E
to F; accompanying this chromatic rise, the horns and bassoons present
transpositions of the *Tristan* chord (E–G–B♭–D and G–B♭–D♭–F).

[81] David Brodbeck, *Brahms. Symphony No. 1*
(Cambridge: Cambridge University Press,
1997), p. 40: "We need not settle the question
of dating in order to profit from Kalbeck's
notion that the roots of the music [of the First
Symphony] somehow lay in the young
composer's troubled personal life." Robert
Fink ("Desire, Repression and Brahms's First
Symphony," *repercussions* 2 (1993), pp. 79–81)
has suggested that Brahms derived the rising
chromatic motive from *Tristan*; in my view,
the source was probably the introduction to
Schumann's *Manfred*.
[82] Brodbeck, *Brahms. Symphony No. 1*,
pp. 46–49.
[83] The hymn-like "Clara" theme extolling her
as "healer" introduced as *telos* in the finale of

Schumann's Second Symphony (mm. 280ff.)
metamorphoses into the "hymnic" second
group in the finale of Brahms's First
Symphony, mm. 118–47 and mm. 302–32 (see
below).
[84] Cf. Eero Tarasti, "Sibelius and Wagner," in
The Sibelius Companion, pp. 61–75. Notice
the parallel with the *Adagio lamentoso* of
Tchaikovsky's Sixth Symphony where, in a
"'diseased' *Tristan* deformation," Tchaikovsky
dresses up his beloved nephew "Bob" Davidov
as Isolde and plays Tristan's role himself (see
Tchaikovsky. Symphony No. 6, pp. 56–64). I
am grateful to my graduate student, William
Pavlak, for drawing my attention to the
Tristan allusion at the beginning of Sibelius's
Seventh Symphony.

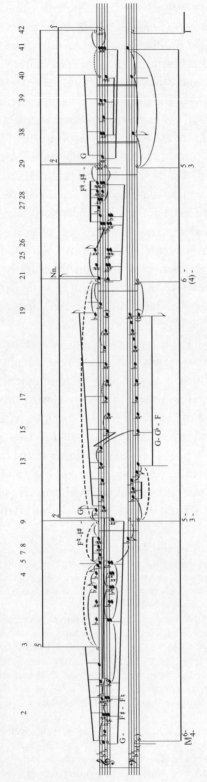

Ex. 8.24 Brahms, First Symphony, first movement, introduction

Ex. 8.25a Brahms, First Symphony, first movement, second group

Ex. 8.25b–c   Brahms, First Symphony, first movement, exposition and development

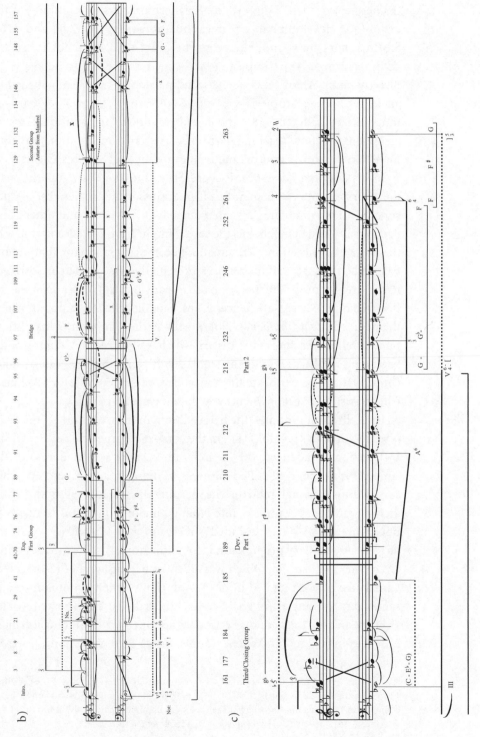

Aino, like Clara a potential agent of redemption and transfiguration, is represented by her "Alp-horn-like" main theme articulated by the solo trombone (compare Exx. 8.1d–e). Furthermore, at the beginning of the exposition, development, and recapitulation (mm. 60, 208, and 476), Sibelius pairs the "Aino" theme in the brass with his own "rt" in the accompaniment, superimposing "rt," stated as the rising octave C–C, directly upon "Aino." Since each ascending step of "rt" is embellished by an upper appoggiatura (f^2–e^2, mm. 64–65; $a\flat^1$–g^1, mm. 71–72; $b\flat^1$–a^1, mm. 75–76; c^2–b^1, m. 78), these sequentially rising semitonal *sospiri* create the effect of "reaching over," of voice "crossing", and thereby intimate "Crucifixion" as the distinguishing attribute of Sibelius/Christ.[85]

In his *Sinfonia domestica*, Richard Strauss analogously superimposes the Man's and Wife's themes. But if in Strauss – the "materialist" – such superposition simply implies intercourse (which Mahler and others condemned as vulgar), in Sibelius the sexual implication is "redeemed" by the theological connotation: "Crucifixion" becomes expiation for Temptation, Fall, and Original Sin. If the *sospiri* represent Sibelius as "Man of Sorrows," it is entirely appropriate that Aino accompany him as "*Mater dolorosa.*" So it will be on the Last Day (hence, the eschatological connotation of Aino's theme in the *solo trombone*). Noteworthy is the symphony's inability to purge itself of the chromatic *sospiri*, which, reinforced in C minor at the beginning of the development (mm. 208ff.), provoke the "catastrophe" (mm. 503ff.), and permeate the final collapse (mm. 510ff.): for Sibelius as Christ/Tristan, *Erlösung* will prove to be equivocal at best.

In all three symphonies, the beloved woman (Clara/Aino) as "the goal" is represented by C major DTA. In the context of large-scale over-arching V–I auxiliary cadences, the "search" for C major DTA connotes the "quest" for the beloved as Redemptress: as the agent of the hero's psychosexual and spiritual rebirth, she becomes associated with the over-arching auxiliary cadence into the C major tonic: to "return" to unchromaticized – i.e. "unsullied" – C major as the "goal" (DTA) of the large-scale auxiliary progression is to "come home" to the pure, diatonic "Mary-*not* Eve" so that which was "dismembered" can be "resurrected" Christ-like ("*re*-erected"?) in her womb. Thus, when Schumann represents Clara as "longed-for goal," he structures the outer movements of his *Fantasie* and the finale of his Second Symphony as over-arching auxiliary cadences into C major. When Brahms, in his First Symphony, portrays

[85] Cf. Laufer's Exx. 12.2.4, 12.15.4, and 12.25.2. For further discussion of this connotation, cf. the section "*Ecce homo!* The Crucified Artist," in *Tchaikovsky. Symphony No. 6*, pp. 50–56. The "Crucifixion" connotation of "reaching-over" is especially striking in the C minor presentation of the superimposed themes at the beginning of the development (mm. 208ff.).

"reconciliation" with Clara as *his* Redemptress – and relives the joyful agony of "displacing" his mentor – he recomposes Robert's over-arching auxiliary cadences into C major. And when Sibelius portrays Aino as *his* Redemptress, she too becomes the C major DTA of his Seventh Symphony.[86] But while Aino is indeed attained in the harmonic dimension – i.e. in the final C major DTA – reconciliation and healing fail in other, crucial structural dimensions.

Techniques employed by Schumann, Brahms, and Sibelius to "weaken" the "strong" tonic and thereby postpone DTA ("crystallization") include reinterpreting I in root position as the "upper sixth" of I in first inversion in a I^6–V–I auxiliary cadence, I in root position as the "upper third" of VI in root position in a VI–V–I auxiliary cadence, and I in root position as VI of III in a VI–V–I auxiliary cadence. The connection between Sibelius's Seventh Symphony and the finale of Brahms's First Symphony seems especially close: in both, DTA is strategically postponed by "devaluing" the root position I as the "upper sixth" of I^6 in tonic auxiliary cadences.

To attenuate the effect of "crystallization," over-arching, initial, and internal tonic auxiliary cadences may be deployed simultaneously within the same piece, as is demonstrated by the finale of Schumann's Second Symphony (Ex. 8.26). Paradoxically, the opening destabilizes the initial tonic C by suggesting an extended prolongation of the dominant G (Ex. 8.26a). Although the emphatic flourish (mm. 1–4) comprising an ascending C major scale seems to assert a "firm, root-position opening tonic," the music quickly contradicts this impression by emphatically cadencing on G in m. 4 for the first subject proper. This reinterpretation of the initial C as the *subdominant* of G is confirmed by the opening theme (mm. 9–22), which supports a descending *Urlinie* from $\hat{3}$ in G. However, the music contradicts this G prolongation with a strong cadence on C at the beginning of the bridge (m. 46), paradoxically suggesting that tonic prolongation spans mm. 1–46; on the other hand, the C of m. 46 may continue to function as the subdominant of G, which is reaffirmed by the second group (m. 96). The graph (Ex. 8.26a) indicates this paradoxical dualism of tonic–dominant prolongation spanning mm. 1–96 with overlapping dotted beams and question marks. By preventing the unequivocal assertion of the tonic at the outset, this harmonic-structural paradox "postpones" DTA.

[86] Similarly, when Berg portrays Helene as his redemptive "wife-mother" in the first of his *Schliesse mir die Augen beide* settings, he employs a C major resolution; and when Hanna Fuchs is to be lauded in the later, twelve-tone setting, she is celebrated with the analogous all-interval "mother chord."

Ex. 8.26a–e   Schumann, Second Symphony, finale

a)

b)

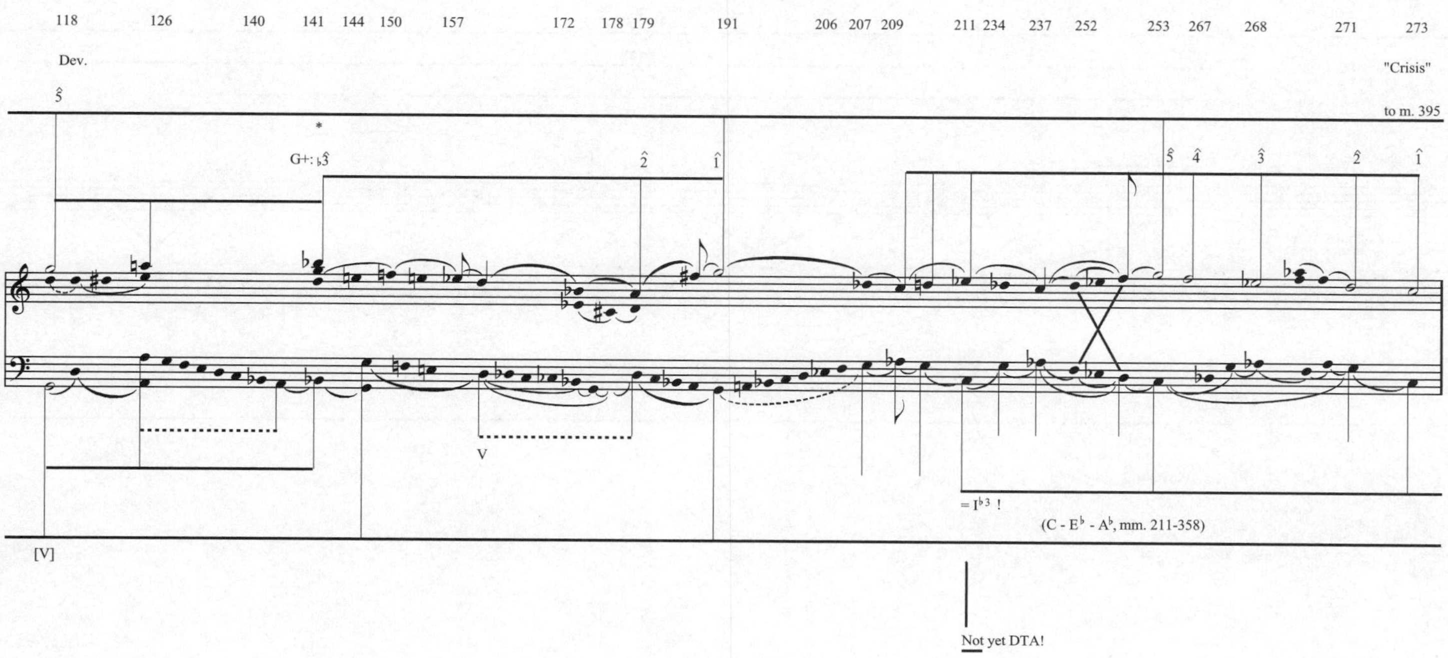

118
126
140
141
144
150
157
172
178
179
191
206
207
209
211
234
237
252
253
267
268
271
273
Dev.
"Crisis"
to m. 395
G+: ♭3̂
2̂
1̂
5̂
4̂
3̂
V
[V]
= I♭3 !
(C - E♭ - A♭, mm. 211-358)
Not yet DTA!

Ex. 8.26 (cont.)

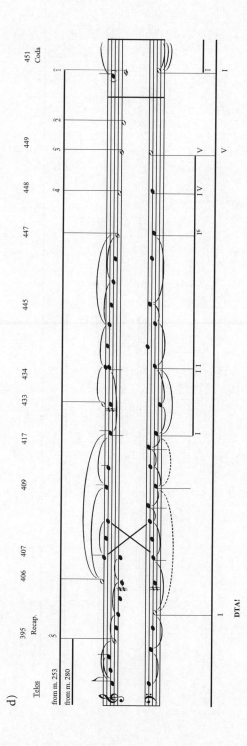

Ex. 8.26 (cont.)

e)

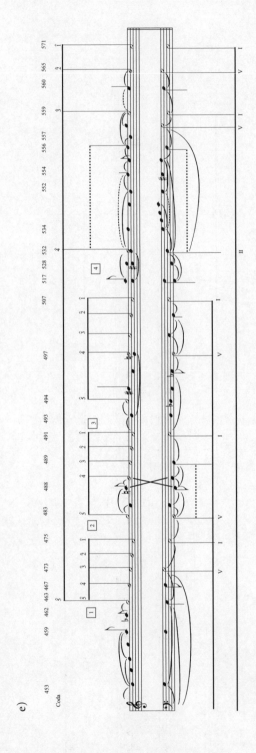

Anthony Newcomb, in his justly celebrated analysis of this symphony, links the teleological process with healing and redemption:

> Schumann's often-quoted letter to D. G. Otten of April 1849 offers another specific and personal exemplification of the same plot archetype, as he talks of his struggle through to mental and physical health during his actual work on the [Second] Symphony. Thus, although the plot archetype of a particular work may have no connection with the life of the composer, that of op. 61 had an autobiographical dimension. The struggle in the symphony from suffering to healing and redemption seems also to have been Schumann's own.[87]

Towards the end of his article, Newcomb calls attention to the connection between the final theme of the Second Symphony's finale and the *Fantasie*, with its allusion to Beethoven's *An die ferne Geliebte*.[88] We may extend his argument by proposing that, in the Second Symphony (as in the *Fantasie*), the *telos* supported by DTA represents "Clara" as "healer." Through the teleological process, then, the music must overcome tonal and thematic "distance" to attain "Clara." In Schumann's teleological strategy, both the design and structure must "evolve" toward the "Clara" *telos* supported by DTA, this design-structural process being superimposed upon the spatial categories of sonata form:

Introductory flourish, mm. 1–4 (Ex. 8.26a)

Exposition space, mm. 5–117
    First group, mm. 5–45
      Bridge, mm. 46–62
    Second group, mm. 63–92
    Closing group, mm. 93–117

Development space, mm. 118–358
    Contrapuntal fantasia on exposition material, mm. 118–272 (Ex. 8.26b)
    "Crisis" on C minor "tonic," mm. 273–79
    Telos (hymn-like "Clara" theme extolling her as "healer") is introduced, but
      not yet in its definitive form, mm. 280–358 (Ex. 8.26c)

Retransition, mm. 359–93

---

[87] Anthony Newcomb, "Once More 'Between Absolute and Program Music': Schumann's Second Symphony," *19th-Century Music* 7 (1984), p. 237.

[88] Ibid., p. 246: "The final theme is, of course, another of Schumann's allusions, this time with a double reference. The primary reference in point of chronology is to the last song of Beethoven's song cycle *An die ferne Geliebte*. The secondary one is to Schumann's previous reference to Beethoven's cycle in his *Phantasie*, op. 17 – like the C-Major Symphony a product of 'dark days,' in which Schumann worked his way in music from suffering and despair to rough affirmation and finally serene confidence."

Recapitulation space within the macro-symphonic structure (super-sonata effect), *Telos* evolves to definitive form supported by DTA and combined "motto" from first movement, mm. 394–450 (Ex. 8.26d)

Coda, mm. 451–end (Ex. 8.26e)

The teleological evolutions of sonata design and tonal structure are coordinated so that DTA supports the "Clara" *telos*'s achievement of its definitive form at the beginning of the recapitulation (m. 394). Example 8.26 displays the finale as a whole placed above an over-arching V–I auxiliary cadence with DTA and the recapitulation coinciding in m. 394. As suggested by Ex. 8.26e, in the coda no less than four emphatic *Urlinie* descents are required to anchor the colossal V–I cadence on the tonic. It is noteworthy that DTA also reinforces the *super-sonata* effect created by the return of the fateful "horn fifths" motto (from the first movement) at the beginning of the finale's recapitulation space.

How then does one explain the clearly articulated arrival on the minor tonic at the "crisis" in m. 211? Commentators have analyzed this chord as the tonic – which, from the common sense perspective, it is. However, as in the *Im Legendenton* of the *Fantasie* and in the Chopin *Polonaise-fantasie*, the "incorrect" mode of this putative "tonic" warns against interpreting DTA at this juncture (it would be premature). Indeed, subsequent events reveal this C minor chord to be the "upper third" of an augmented sixth leading to the dominant (mm. 358–59), which then resolves to the *major* tonic (mm. 394ff., Exx. 8.26b–d). The underlying progression, then, is a tonic auxiliary cadence, $I^{\flat 3}$–$\flat$VI (A6)–V–I, nested within the over-arching V–I.

This interpretation clarifies the finale's tonal structure and, by implication, its program. If the ultimate goal is DTA at the triumphant presentation of the hymn-like "Clara" theme as *telos* (mm. 394ff.) – accompanied by the now-triumphant "motto" in the brass – then earlier "strong" tonics (like the opening C major chord and the "crisis" C minor chord) cannot represent it. Thus, the finale evolves through a series of "weakened" tonics towards DTA in m. 394. In the course of achieving it, the minor tonic is overcome as its minor third, E♭, reinterpreted as D♯, "ascends" – redemptively – to E (mm. 281–359, Ex. 8.26c). This outcome is foreshadowed in the symphony's very first measure since the chromatically "rising" D–E♭=D♯–E–F is present *in nuce*. Metaphorically, if the C minor "low point" suggests "the Temptation" and "the Fall," the "crystallization" of the C major DTA may be understood to embody the "healing process" facilitated by Clara as Redemptress. To be sure, the C minor "crisis" casts uncertainty on the outcome, but through Clara-Mary all obstacles are surmounted.

Analogous "questing" for DTA informs the outer movements of Brahms's First Symphony. While a common sense analysis would explain the first movement's introduction as beginning firmly on the tonic, Ex. 8.24 (p. 240) prefers to interpret the opening eight measures as a tonic auxiliary cadence.[89] Here, the initial eight-measure phrase prolonging the tonic is understood as the upper component of a cadential dominant six-four over an implied G in the bass. This interpretation accounts for the great emphasis on the initial "tonic" as an *unprepared dissonance* above the *implied* bass.[90] Thus, the comparatively brief initial tonic followed by sustained dominant prolongation subordinates tonic to dominant (to read it the other way around is to get things "upside down"). According to this logic, the background harmony of the *entire* introduction is *dominant* prolongation. Brahms's astonishingly bold idea, then, is to *assume* that the initial eight-measure root-position tonic occurs *above* a dominant pedal.

As if to reconfirm this paradoxical notion of the unstable root-position tonic, the development recomposes the bold tonic auxiliary cadence of the introduction (Exx. 8.25a–b). The development's first part (mm. 189–212) moves from E♭ minor to an augmented sixth chord on A♭ (m. 212), which resolves to a C minor chord above G (m. 215, Ex. 8.25b). In the second part (mm. 215–72), Brahms converts this C minor six-four chord into a major root-position triad (mm. 223 and 252ff.). To be sure, this putative tonic does not represent DTA; rather, as in the introduction, it is destabilized above an assumed G (in mm. 215ff.).

By recompo***sing** the first movement's tonic auxiliary cadences – both initial and internal – in the finale, Brahms reinforces the super-sonata effect across the symphony. In the introduction (mm. 1–61), the minor tonic – both in root position (m. 1) and first inversion (m. 27) – is reprojected above a dominant pedal; in other words, the tonic is recomposed above an assumed pedal G (Ex. 8.27a). More precisely, subsumed

[89] In the first movement of his Fifth Symphony, Beethoven "passes through" the tonic (m. 253), thereby postponing tonic arrival until *after* the design recapitulation (m. 277). Brahms seems to have been fascinated by this effect of the "tragic" undermining of the tonic, since in the first movement of his Piano Quartet in C minor, op. 60, a work intimately connected – like the First Symphony – with his tragic love affair with Clara, he takes Beethoven's technique a step further. In this movement, the harmony tragically "undermines" the tonic associated with the recapitulation (m. 201) so that the large-scale progression is from III in the exposition (m. 70) to V in the recapitulation (m. 236). The introduction to the First Symphony represents a further attenuation of this technique since the tonic, which is "passed through," occurs precisely at the point where it is usually asserted, i.e. at the outset!

[90] In the substantial literature on Brahms's First Symphony, the status of the opening tonic has remained a non-issue. However, as is clear from my remarks, I believe the instability of the initial "root-position tonic" to be *the* central "problem" in the symphony as a whole. For information on the late addition of the introduction, see Brodbeck, *Brahms. Symphony No. 1*, p. 31.

Ex. 8.27a–c Brahms, First Symphony, finale, introduction

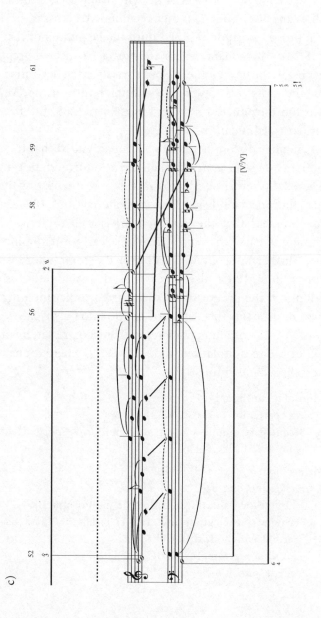

within the introductory V–I auxiliary cadence (mm. 1–61), the initial root-position I (m. 1) is "weakened" as the "upper sixth" of its six-three position (m. 27), the I^6 being superimposed upon the V. Destined to be replicated later in the movement (mm. 186–284 and mm. 360–69, Exx. 8.28 and 29b–c), the bass's descending sixth C–E♭ (mm. 1–27) is motivically related to the descending sixth E–G of the "Alp horn" motto (Exx. 8.1e, p. 181, and 8.27b).

The teleological process of delaying tonic arrival until the beginning of the exposition (m. 62) is then recomposed across the rest of the sonata form proper, postponing DTA until the beginning of the coda (m. 391, Ex. 8.28). The sonata design features a "truncated" reprise: since the opening of the development closely parallels the beginning of the exposition, the recapitulation begins with the return of the "Alp horn" theme from the introduction's second part in m. 285, the first group being omitted as redundant.

A number of commentators have maintained that the recapitulation begins in m. 186 because the main theme returns in the tonic. In my view, however, this return alludes to the tradition of repeating the exposition.[91] But as the music subtly modifies the material (mm. 186–231), it gradually becomes clear that the development is well underway, the extended contrapuntal fantasia (mm. 232–78) clearly functioning as its second part. Furthermore, as we shall see, the tonic chord supporting the "return" in m. 186 is "devalued"; thus, this tonal return is revealed to be an illusion, the progressively destabilized tonic initiating development space. By inserting the "Alp horn" motto into the bridge in the exposition (mm. 114–17), Brahms prepares its climactic restatement at the beginning of the recapitulation (mm. 285–301), where it analogously introduces the second group:

Introduction, mm. 1–61
  First part, mm. 1–29 (Ex. 8.27a)
  Second part, mm. 30–61, "Alp horn" motto, interpolated "chorale,"
    mm. 47–51 (Exx. 8.27b–c)

Exposition, mm. 61–185 (Ex. 8.29a)
  First group, mm. 61–105
    Bridge incorporating the "Alp horn" motto, mm. 106–17
    "Hymnic" second group, mm. 118–47, recalls the "Clara" *telos* of Schumann
    Second Symphony, finale
    Closing group, mm. 148–75
    Codetta, mm. 176–85

[91] See also the first movement of Brahms's Fourth Symphony, which I have described as a "partially reversed recapitulation" ("Tragic Reversed Sonata Form," pp. 178–87).

Ex. 8.28   Brahms, First Symphony, finale

Ex. 8.29a–c Brahms, First Symphony, finale

a)

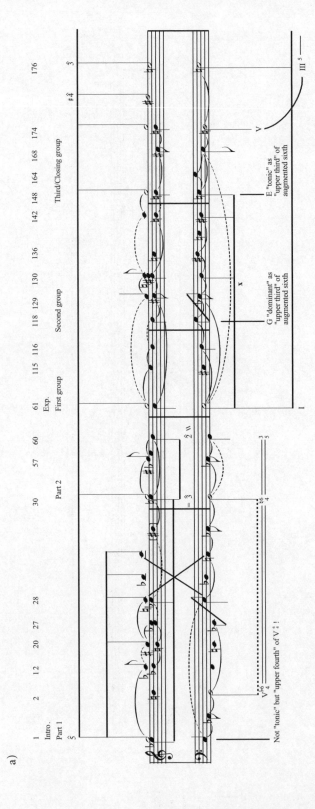

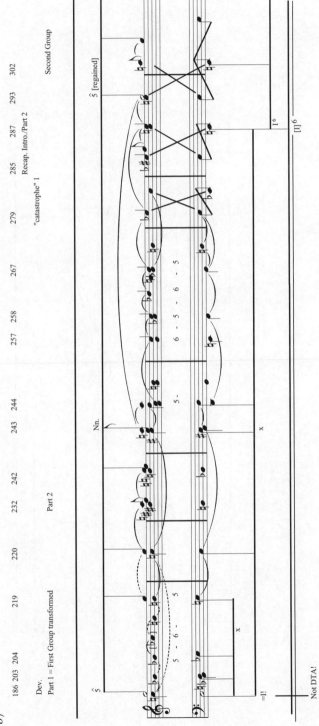

Ex. 8.29 (*cont.*)

c)

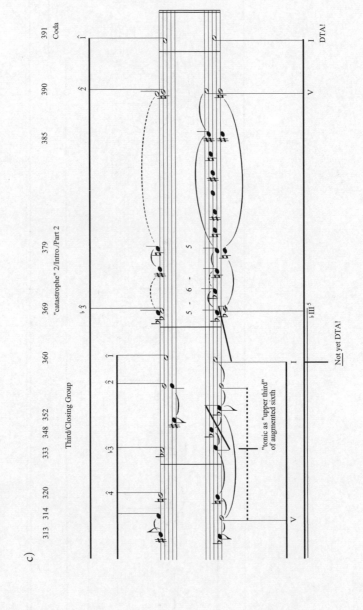

Development, mm. 186–284 (Ex. 8.29b)
  First part, return of main theme, mm. 186–231
  Second part, contrapuntal fantasia on the bridge, mm. 232–78
First "catastrophe," chromatic deformation of "Alp horn" theme (C–E♭), mm. 279–84

"Truncated" Recapitulation, mm. 285–367
  "Alp horn" theme from introduction, second part, mm. 285–301
  "Hymnic" second group, mm. 302–32 (Ex. 8.29c)
  Closing group, mm. 333–59
  Codetta, mm. 360–67

Second "catastrophe," chromatic deformation of "Alp horn" theme (C–E♭), and introduction, mm. 368–90

Coda, mm. 391–end, interpolated "chorale," mm. 407–13

As indicated in the graph (Ex. 8.29a), the exposition moves emphatically from C major to E minor, i.e. from I to III, without asserting a structural dominant.[92] Although the development begins with the opening theme over a root-position tonic (as at the outset, Ex. 8.29b), this tonal-thematic return is *revalued* in context. Brahms's point is that – in spite of the *appearance* of return – the tonic of m. 186 does *not* represent DTA, which is being strategically "saved" for the coda. Over the course of the development, the putatively "strong" tonic (m. 186) is progressively "weakened" as the bass composes out an enlargement of the descending sixth of the "Alp horn" theme, reinterpreting the tonic C (m. 186) as the "upper sixth" of the *lowered* mediant E♭ (m. 284). This pessimistic C minor "deformation" of the "Alp horn" theme is then summarized by the first "catastrophe" (mm. 279–84). Thus the C major version of the "Alp horn" theme ("Clara as redemptress"/"beacon in the darkness") is almost subverted by its C minor deformation; but Schumann's work indicates the "right path", as Brahms's recapitulation essentially recomposes the "healing" process of Schumann's Second Symphony.[93] The "restored" diatonic "Alp horn" motto (C–E in the bass, mm. 285–87 and 293–302) leads to the reprise of the "hymnic" second theme – a transformation of Schumann's "Clara" *telos* – extolling her as "healer."[94] Although the recapitulation cadences firmly on the tonic C minor (m. 367, Ex. 8.29c), this

---

[92] Exx. 8.29a–b show that the bass's ascending third C–E, filled in chromatically in the exposition (mm. 61–148, motive "x"), is recomposed over the course of the development (mm. 186–287). As indicated in Ex. 8.29a, the dominant G of the second group (mm. 118ff.) functions as "the upper third" of the augmented sixth built on E♭ (m. 129) – *not* as a structural dominant.

[93] The "right path" also has religious connotations, hence the chorale interpolated into the introduction and coda.
[94] Brodbeck, *Brahms. Symphony No. 1*, pp. 72–73, also calls attention to this connection with Schumann's Finale.

tonic is again revalued as the "upper sixth" of Eb by the second "catastrophe" (m. 368). In other words, notwithstanding the emphatic cadence
(m. 367), the music fails to achieve expected closure, the DTA promised
by the tonic being undermined by the lowered mediant.[95] Only in m. 390
is the structural dominant definitively attained, completing the I–III–V
arpeggiation initiated by the exposition. The coda triumphantly, if somewhat grimly, asserts DTA: a *modus vivendi* with Clara has been found.

Aino as DTA: linked tonic auxiliary cadences in the Seventh Symphony

In his Seventh Symphony, Sibelius combines and synthesizes all of the
compositional techniques identified in the course of this study.[96] This
symphony is organized as an auxiliary cadence super-sonata form – i.e.
an over-arching V–I auxiliary cadence controls the entire structure
(Ex. 8.21, p. 234).[97] This basic V–I auxiliary cadence (Ex. 8.21a) is elaborated by an internal auxiliary cadence with a tonic preparation ("p") so
that the over-arching progression becomes V[–I⁶–V]–I (Ex. 8.21b). As in
Maan virsi and the finale of Brahms's First Symphony, a root-position
tonic prepares the tonic first inversion as its "upper sixth" yielding
V[I–I⁶–V]–I (compare Exx. 8.20b, 8.21c, and 8.28).

Example 8.21d coordinates linked tonic auxiliary cadences with
super-sonata form. The I⁶–V–I tonic auxiliary cadence becomes paradigmatic for the harmonic plan of the entire symphony, which is composed

---

[95] This extension of the mediant *beneath* the tonic as a means of shifting DTA into the coda is reproduced by Sibelius's Seventh Symphony; in the Sibelius, the putative DTA at the beginning of the recapitulation (m. 476) is devalued as the upper sixth of E (m. 495), true DTA being achieved only in the final chord.

[96] I have benefited from the masterly analyses of the Seventh Symphony by Murtomäki (*Symphonic Unity*, especially chapter 8, pp. 242–78) and Laufer's analysis presented in this volume, as well as Kilpeläinen's previously cited introduction to the sketches. To be sure, there are many points of contact between my interpretation and theirs; nevertheless, the divergences are significant enough to warrant presentation of my own analysis. Murtomäki's dissertation surveys the analytical literature on the Seventh up to 1993.

[97] Compare with Schumann, *Fantasie*, first movement (Ex. 8.2); Brahms, Third Symphony (Ex. 8.3); Sibelius, Symphony No. 1, finale (Ex. 8.5); Beethoven, Seventh Symphony, finale (Ex. 8.6); and Schumann, Second Symphony, finale (Ex. 8.26). The symphony as a whole constitutes an auxiliary cadence form in which the super-sonata design is supported by linked tonic auxiliary cadences into DTA (Ex. 8.21d). The commentary on Murtomäki's Ex. 124 (*Symphonic Unity*, p. 279) suggests a similar view, whereby the initial V resolves to the final I. A significant difference, however, is that Murtomäki organizes the bass as a series of "anticipatory" cadences into the root-position tonic (C), where I read auxiliary cadences into the mediant (E), as will be clarified in the course of my analysis.

of "linked" I^6–V–I cadences whereby the resolution I becomes the "upper sixth" of I^6 – the "p" – in the next cadence. As Ex. 8.21d suggests, the E minor chord in root position (III) may replace the first inversion tonic, III substituting for I^6 in the auxiliary cadence. Thus, the powerful E minor chords in mm. 243 and 495 may assume the role of "p" in the auxiliary progression. According to this interpretation, DTA is achieved only in the final measures (m. 522); only at this point is the long-promised closure of the "Aino" theme finally achieved. Metaphorically, "crystallization" of DTA at the end is associated with a "return" to Aino. But the symphony is Janus-faced: while the sense of "arrival" in the final cadence is greatly attenuated precisely because the apparently "strong" tonics of mm. 60, 226, 285, and 476 have been devalued, nevertheless the effect of "home-coming" in m. 522 is undermined by the failure of "crystallization" in the upper voice (to be explained).

The symphony's design is a super-sonata form, preceded by an extended introduction (mm. 1–59); indeed, given the impressive dimensions of the super-sonata space, a two-part introduction of generous proportions is entirely appropriate (Ex. 8.30a). As far as I have been able to ascertain, Sibelius does not name the initial stepwise "rising theme" of mm. 1–2 in the sketches; however, as I have suggested, "rt" evokes Tristanesque "yearning" (*Sehnsucht*) – the "seeking" of a goal. That "rt" is halted on E♭ (♭$\hat{3}$) in m. 3 further intimates that "the search" encounters a "crisis" at the very outset – "blockage" by some kind of obstacle or immobile object. This, *in nuce*, is the tragedy of the upper voice: for Schumann, the path to Clara is "opened up"; Brahms, too, somehow finds a way forward – a *modus vivendi* – but Sibelius's "rt" ultimately fails.

Almost immediately, E♭ becomes associated with its enharmonic equivalent D♯ (m. 6), which is left unresolved (m. 7) as a C major chord supporting contrasting material is tentatively "tried out" (mm. 7–10). Sketches identified as "Ruth" suggest that Sibelius associated this thematic idea with his daughter Ruth.[98] In mm. 12–13, the music again focuses on the E♭/D♯ transformation (which had been "left hanging" in m. 7), now resolving D♯ as leading tone to E. With this resolution, the path upwards is re-opened and the middleground line continues to ascend through F (m. 18) to G (m. 21). Thus, in the first part of the introduction, the upper voice succeeds in composing out an enlargement of the G–G octave ascent embedded in "rt" in the first two measures.

[98] Ruth appears to have had special significance for Sibelius; as the only daughter to appear in his sketchbooks, it is clear that she played a role in his inner compositional world. Born in 1894 and artistically inclined, she became a professional actress and performed in plays for which her father had composed the incidental music (see Eija Kurki's essay in this book).

Ex. 8.30a–b   Sibelius, Seventh Symphony

a)

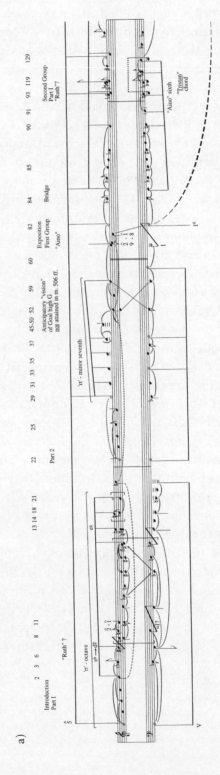

b)

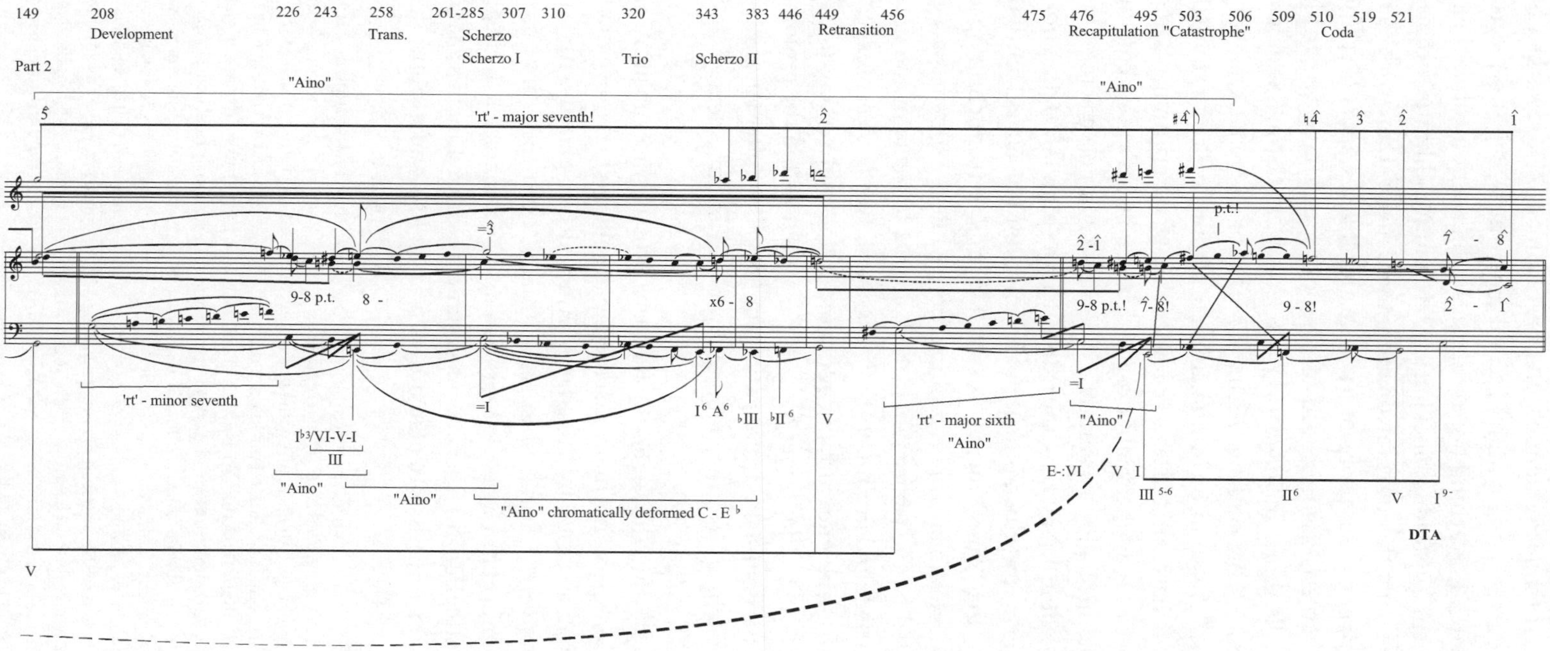

149 208 226 243 258 261-285 307 310 320 343 383 446 449 456 475 476 495 503 506 509 510 519 521

Part 2 Development Trans. Scherzo Scherzo I Trio Scherzo II Retransition Recapitulation "Catastrophe" Coda

"Aino" 'rt' - major seventh!

"Aino"

$\hat{5}$ $\hat{2}$ $\hat{2}$ - $\hat{1}$ $\hat{2}$ $\natural\hat{4}$ $\sharp\hat{4}$ $\hat{7}$-($\hat{8}$) $\hat{3}$ $\hat{2}$ $\hat{1}$ $\hat{7}$ - $\hat{8}$ $\hat{2}$ - $\hat{1}$

9-8 p.t. p.t. 9 - 8!

9-8 p.t. 8 - 8 -

'rt' - minor seventh

"Aino" "Aino" "Aino" 'rt' - major sixth

"Aino" chromatically deformed C - E♭ "Aino"

$I^{♭3}$/VI-V-I III I⁶ A⁶ ♭III ♭II⁶ V III⁵⁻⁶ V I II⁶ V I⁹⁻

x⁶ - 8 E-:VI V DTA

V

If the introduction's first part (mm. 1–21) is marked by conflict and hesitancy, its "hymnic" second part (mm. 22–59) projects a contrasting state of "yearning hopefulness." In this section, all of the chromatic elements, instead of blocking forward motion (like the "problematic" Eb/D#), are smoothly integrated within the C major framework. Nevertheless, the upper voice's "problem" (i.e. the unfulfilled search of "rt" for its goal) now manifests itself: instead of composing out the *octave* (as in Part I), "rt" "falls short" of its goal on the *seventh*, as G (m. 22) ascends through D (m. 37) only as far as F (m. 59, see the brackets in Ex. 8.30a). This "failure" is a "premonition" of the ultimate inability of "rt" to attain the goal G.

I have offered this "blow-by-blow" description of the introduction because, as one might expect – given Sibelius's preoccupation with "symphonic logic" – its motivic ideas are recomposed across the symphony as a whole. In my view, the introduction (mm. 1–59) does not support tonic harmony, which is held in abeyance until m. 60, i.e., until the "epiphany" of the "Aino" theme. In other words, introduction space is assigned entirely to *dominant* prolongation, while the sonata space proper is initiated by the tonic. What, then, are we to make of the C chord which is "tried out" in mm. 9–14?[99] Lasting only five measures in the midst of a fifty-nine-measure introduction, it does not represent DTA; rather, it is passing – the "upper fifth" of F – caught within the prolonged dominant. This dominant prolongation supports the upper voice statements of "rt," which are counterpointed by a descending octave G–G in the bass (Ex. 8.30a).

Within the super-sonata space proper, the exposition and recapitulation spaces normally assigned to the allegro first movement and finale are here assumed by the adagio "Aino" theme paired with "rt" as described above.[100] "Aino" plus "rt" initiates exposition/first movement space (mm. 60ff.), while its reprise in m. 476 demarcates the beginning of recapitulation/finale space. As is standard procedure in sonata form, exposition space is articulated into first and second groups, distinguished by

[99] This is an issue of great significance. For Laufer the arrival on C in m. 6 represents a tonic arrival; in his reading, the C achieved at this point is prolonged throughout the symphony (cf. Laufer's Ex. 12.27.1). As will become clear from my remarks, I dispute the structural value of this "tonic," interpreting it as "caught" within the introduction's dominant prolongation; as will become evident in the course of my remarks, I also consider the much "stronger" Cs at the "Aino" theme in mm. 61 and 476 to be "devalued" as the "upper sixth" of E.

[100] As is clear from my remarks, I interpret the Seventh Symphony's form as a super-sonata rather than a rondo. This view is supported not only by the final version's formal-tonal organization but its compositional genesis whereby originally individuated movements were synthesized within the super-sonata configuration. It is significant that Sibelius never referred to the entire symphony as a "hellenic rondo," but only to the original third movement within his 1918 multi-movement conception.

contrasting thematic material linked by a bridge. Here "Aino" assumes the role of first group (mm. 60–83), while the second group (mm. 93–207), which has a contrasting *scherzando* character associated with "Ruth," is connected to the first group by a bridge (mm. 84–92).[101]

The symphony conforms to the sonata paradigm by initiating development space with a *transformation* (rather than a literal restatement) of first group material, i.e., "Aino" plus "rt" (mm. 208–42). The conclusion of development space is heralded by the retransition (mm. 449–75), which leads into the recapitulation of "Aino" plus "rt" in its original guise. Within development space, Sibelius inserts the scherzo movement (mm. 261–448), as is standard procedure in super-sonata form (see above). A transition (mm. 243–60) leads from the beginning of the development to the scherzo, which is subdivided into Scherzo I (mm. 261–315), Trio (mm. 316–42), and Scherzo II (mm. 343–408). An episode based on scherzo material (mm. 409–48) links the end of Scherzo II to the retransition.

In the recapitulation (mm. 476ff.), the "Aino" theme returns more or less literally, albeit ornamented by embellishing counterpoint. However, the *scherzando* "Ruth" material from the introduction and the second group is considerably transformed (mm. 487–96). I identify a "catastrophe" in mm. 500–10, precipitating the final structural "devolution" realized through the *Urlinie* descent from $\hat{5}$. The coda (mm. 510–end) composes the retrospective "collapse" of motives associated with both Aino and Ruth.

The super-sonata design may be summarized as follows:

Introduction, mm. 1–59 (Ex. 8.30a)
   "Crisis," mm. 1–3
   Redemptive "Ruth" material, mm. 3–21
   Hymnic "Aino" material, mm. 22–59

Exposition, mm. 60–207
   First group, mm. 60–83 "Aino"
      Bridge, mm. 84–92
   Second group, mm. 93–207 "Ruth"

---

[101] The section encompassing mm. 93–207 exhibits all of the characteristic features of a second group. Both thematically and harmonically, this music contrasts with the first group. From a design perspective, it presents new thematic material. Harmonically, too, it is distinct from the tonic-rooted harmony of the first group. In m. 149, it settles firmly on the dominant, which is then prolonged through the beginning of the development (mm. 208ff.) – as is standard practice in the second group of a major-mode sonata. Nor is it unusual for the initial section of the second group (mm. 93–207) to be harmonically unstable; indeed, in this instability, we may detect the influence of Beethoven, Schumann, Bruckner, and Brahms, who frequently place the opening of the second group over an auxiliary cadence (see, for example, my discussion of the second group in the finale of Bruckner's Third Symphony, Ex. 8.9b).

Development, mm. 208–448 (Ex. 8.30b)

  Transformation of "Aino," mm. 208–42

    Transition to scherzo, mm. 243–60

  Introduction to scherzo, mm. 261–84

  Scherzo I, mm. 285–319

  Quasi-Trio, mm. 320–42

  Scherzo II, mm. 343–408

    Episode linking scherzo to retransition, mm. 409–48

Retransition, mm. 449–75

Recapitulation, mm. 476–99

"Catastrophe," mm. 500–10

Coda, mm. 511–end

Let us now consider the interaction between this super-sonata design and the tonal structure. The general principle in tonal music is to reserve melodic closure and tonal stability for the *end* of a theme or formal section. But the "Aino" music embodies a strong melodic *close* $\hat{2}$–$\hat{1}$ (d–c, m. 60) at its *beginning* – a truly remarkable thematic opening – while "rt," spun-out, migrates upwards through the orchestral fabric, extending stepwise through the ascending octave ($\hat{1}$–$\hat{8}$, mm. 60–80). Harmonically, $\hat{2}$–$\hat{1}$ is supported as a 9–8 suspension above the root-position tonic, while the definitive achievement of the primary tone $\hat{5}$ (g^1) in the first group is delayed until just before the beginning of the bridge (m. 82), where it occurs above a tonic six-three chord. If the crucial move is to the first-inversion tonic supporting the primary tone $\hat{5}$ in m. 82 (Ex. 8.30a), then the root-position tonic supporting the extended "rt" 1–8 becomes subordinate to it; to be sure, subordinating the "stable" initial root-position tonic to the "unstable" tonic six-three is an odd way of composing, "placing the cart before the horse." The oblique line (Ex. 8.30a, mm. 60–82) suggests that, in a deeper sense, D–C is also supported by the first-inversion rather than the root-position tonic; thus, the impression of closure at the beginning of the "Aino" theme is an illusion. (In this, we see a different manifestation of the same principle of devaluing the putative tonic as realized in *Skogsrået*, *Pohjola's Daughter*, and other works; in each case, the strong – "heroic" – tonic is "weakened" by the larger context.[102]) In the course of the symphony, the apparently stable $\hat{2}$–$\hat{1}$ close at the beginning of the "Aino" theme is further destabilized as the extended C (1–8) is reinterpreted as a *passing tone* within the third D–C–B (Ex. 8.30b, mm. 149–243 and 449–98), the emphatic cadences on E forcing this

---

[102] Cf. the "false" C major recapitulation in *Skogsrået* and the B♭ major fanfares in *Pohjola's Daughter*.

devaluation; only in the final cadence (m. 523) does $\hat{2}$–$\hat{1}$ receive the unconditional support of DTA.

Towards the catastrophe

Example 8.30 coordinates the middleground voice leading with the super-sonata design, suggesting ways in which the issues raised in the introduction – especially "rt" – are worked out across the symphony. The role of I^6 and III as "p" in the auxiliary cadence helps to explain the organization of the bass, which places tremendous emphasis on "contrabass" E. Indeed, E seems firmly "anchored" throughout much of the symphony, E – the mediant, rather than the tonic – functioning as the primary bass note at important formal junctures. Bass enlargements of "Aino's" motivic sixth, E–C (Ex. 8.1d), contribute to this effect. In the exposition, the low E of m. 82 – which "picks up" the trombone's E in m. 67 – becomes the point of departure for the bridge to the second group, centered on G (m. 149). The bass reaffirms the "Aino"-inspired idea that C is the "upper sixth" of E as E (m. 82) ascends stepwise to C (m. 130, see the beam in Ex. 8.30a). This ascending sixth, realized in a complex way, synthesizes the end of the "Aino" theme with the bridge and second group: the bass line rises from E (m. 82) through F (m. 90) to an implied G. But, instead of permitting a tonic resolution at this juncture, the bass articulates a deceptive cadence to a half-diminished (*Tristan*) chord on A (m. 93), "bridging over" the beginning of the second group. As this music is sequenced up a semitone, the bass continues to ascend through A#=B♭ (m. 119) to C (m. 130).

The "contrabass" E of mm. 76 and 82 is regained through forceful cadences on E in the development (m. 243) and in the recapitulation (m. 495, Ex. 8.30b). As a corollary to this emphasis on E, whenever DTA on C threatens, Sibelius invariably converts C into the "upper sixth" of E. For example, when the "Aino" theme returns at the beginning of the development (now transformed in C minor), it lands on a strong root-position tonic (m. 226). However, this putative tonal return supporting the thematic reprise quickly proves illusory, the tonic return being revalued as "p" of an internal VI–V–I auxiliary cadence in the key of the mediant (E major). In other words, the putative C minor tonic of m. 226 is revalued as the flat submediant of E, reinterpreting C as the "upper sixth" of E (m. 243). This strategy is strikingly reminiscent of the outer movements of Bruckner's Eighth Symphony (compare Exx. 8.12a–b and 8.30b).

Example 8.30b suggests that, through Scherzo I (m. 285), the "Quasi-Trio" (m. 320), and Scherzo II (m. 345), the bass composes "Aino's"

descending sixth C–E (filled in stepwise), C functioning as the "upper
sixth" of E. But in a chromatic "deformation" of the "Aino" motive, C–E
becomes C–E♭ as the bass transforms E into F♭ (an augmented sixth chord
built on F♭ leads to E♭ for the final repetition of the scherzo, mm.
374–75).[103] In the recapitulation, the tonic is again reinterpreted as the
submediant of the mediant: after the drawn-out retransition over the
dominant (mm. 449–75), the tonic return of the "Aino" theme in m. 476
receives tremendous – one would think, decisive – emphasis. But it too
"devolves" (analogously to the tonics of mm. 60 and 226), the overwhelming force of the *ff* cadence on E in m. 495 subsuming it within
another VI–V–I auxiliary cadence in the key of the mediant (with C again
compelled to function as the "upper sixth" of E). It is clear that, in the
Seventh Symphony, harmonic stasis is an illusion; rather than "sitting" on
the root-position tonic C throughout, the bass is highly active, articulating colossal ascending and descending motions through "Aino's" motivic
sixth C–E.

Much of the second subject in the exposition (mm. 149–207), the
entire development (mm. 208–448), and the retransition (mm. 449–75)
are contained within the aegis of the *dominant* (Ex. 8.30b). Thus, if the
development functions analogously to the introduction, its massive
dominant prolongation analogously prepares the epiphany of the "Aino"
theme. And if the bass is preoccupied with sweeps through "Aino's" sixth,
the upper voice is animated by "rt": in both the introduction and development, this dominant prolongation supports colossal upper voice
enlargements of "rt" filling in the octave G to G.[104] The enharmonic
motive D♯/E♭ – *the* impediment "blocking" "rt's" further ascent (mm. 3ff.)
– is worked into the cadence on E in m. 226 at the beginning of the development (paralleling the cadence in m. 12). As the development unfolds,
this apparent "victory" of D♯ suffers a reverse as E♭ prevails in the final
repetition of the Scherzo (m. 375); but with the strong cadence on E in
the recapitulation (m. 495), E♭ is definitively reconverted back into D♯.
Example 8.30b's upper stave proposes that, over the course of the development, the top voice reworks the first leg of "rt" (the rising fifth G–D),
which definitively "breaks through" E♭/D♯ to E in the recapitulation's
cadence on E (m. 495). Especially noteworthy is the manner in which the
retransition (mm. 456–75) foreshadows the upper voice's "progress"
through "rt" as far as E: (F♯) G–A–B–C–D–E.

[103] Brahms employs precisely the same
chromatic deformation in the finale of the
First Symphony (see my discussion of the
"crises," Exx. 8.28 and 8.29b–c).

[104] Thus, I identify "rt" at *two* tonal levels:
filling in the tonic octave C–C (1̂–8̂) as shown
by Laufer, and the dominant octave G–G
(5̂–5̂), as shown in Ex. 8.30a–b.

The "deliberate" catastrophe

In the catastrophe (m. 503, Exx. 8.30b–8.31), "rt" desperately "yearns" to ascend to the octave G (as it had done at the very outset and through the introduction's Part I), but instead – at what should be the moment of climactic "crystallization" (m. 504) – reaches only as far as F♯ (m. 504) before collapsing, "exhausted," on F (m. 510). Whereas Schumann and Brahms are able to overcome their "catastrophes," Sibelius/Tristan "collapses," impotent, as "rt" – the "yearning" motive – gets as close as possible to its "longed-for" goal – G ("Aino") – *without attaining it*. The upper voice composes out the major seventh G–F♯, only to "sink down" – impotent – onto the minor seventh G–F (paralleling the second part of the introduction; see the bracket spanning mm. 149–510 in Ex. 8.30b).

Underlying the insignia of collapse in mm. 500–10 is the "anguish" of the diminished third f♯³–a♭³ in the upper voice (mm. 502–506), supported by a chromatic voice exchange involving the root and third of the IV⁷ chord: F, F♯, and A♭ (Ex. 8.31). The a♭³ in the upper voice (m. 500) is shifted into the bass (m. 501) and then back into the upper voice (m. 506), while the chromatically displaced root F♯ (m. 503) migrates to the bass F (m. 510). In the context of this chromaticized voice exchange, the C major chord supporting the "Aino" theme in mm. 508–509 cannot function as DTA but rather is "devalued" as the dominant of the subdominant, which is "trapped" within the aegis of the prolonged IV.[105] Concomitantly, the upper voice g³ (mm. 509–10), preparing the g³–f³ (9–8) suspension over F, is "reduced" to a passing tone "caught" between a♭³ (m. 506) and f (m. 510). Thus, the "catastrophe" intimates not only the "failure" of "rt" to attain its definitive goal (G=5̂), but the "entrapment" of the "Aino" theme itself.

After this disaster, as in the Fourth Symphony's finale, the *Urlinie* descends; "entropy triumphs and the hero's life inexorably ebbs and dissipates back into chaos and nothingness."[106] It is precisely at this point that Sibelius alludes to *Valse triste* from the incidental music to Arvid Järnefeldt's play *Kuolema* (*Death*).[107] In the play, the *Valse* is a Dance of

---

[105] Murtomäki and Laufer, by contrast, interpret the C chord (m. 508) as participating in tonic prolongation. In my view, this C is analogous to that of m. 6, which is caught within subdominant prolongation as the "upper fifth" of IV. This postponement of tonic resolution may be compared to the finales of Brahms's First and Third Symphonies (m. 232 in the Third, m. 360 in the First, Exx. 8.3, 8.28, and 8.29c), where the

tonic at the end of the recapitulation does not represent DTA; rather, the background tonal processes continue *past the recapitulation* to DTA in the *coda*.

[106] Cf. my discussion of the Fourth Symphony's finale in *Bruckner Studies*, pp. 199–203.

[107] Cf. Eija Kurki's discussion of *Kuolema* in this volume.

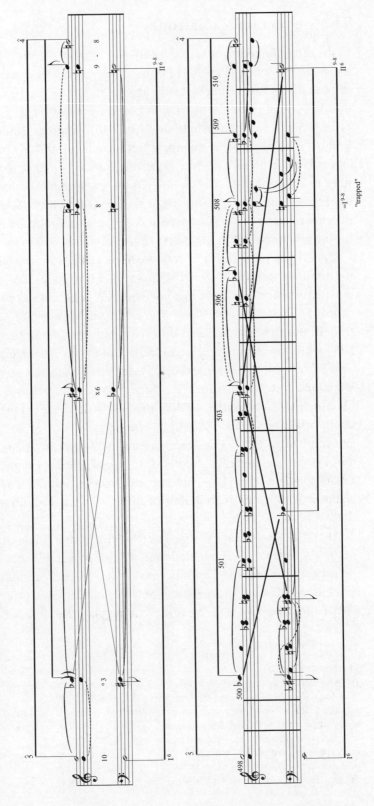

Ex. 8.31   Sibelius, Seventh Symphony, "catastrophe"

Death performed by the Mother in response to the summons of Death, who appears in the guise of the Father. Ultimately, the orphaned Child commits suicide in the burning house. The "failure" of "rt," the "entrapment" of the "Aino" theme, and the *Kuolema* allusion all cast a long shadow over the final achievement of C major DTA with its connotation of transfiguration. The goal – Aino – is indeed attained at long last, but the embrace proves mortal: as in *Kuolema*, even "the child" Ruth – the promise of immortality – fades away.

The sources reveal that the "catastrophic" collapse of "rt," the "entrapment" of "Aino," and the *Kuolema* allusion were not present in the earlier drafts of the Symphony's conclusion; thus, the presence of these elements in the final version is deliberately calculated. In the first version of the "catastrophic" passage sketched on p. 97 of the pencil draft of the complete symphony (HUL 0358, p. 1), and carried over on pp. 98–99 of the ink draft (HUL 0354, pp. 1–2), the "Aino" theme never appears, nor does "rt" "get stuck" on the high F♯; instead, "anxiety" is projected in a more overt ("surface") way: "agitated" syncopated and chromatic figuration in the strings surrounds embellishments of the $\hat{2}$–$\hat{1}$ (9–8) suspension in the brass over the final tonic (cf. HUL 0354, pp. 2–5, i.e. pp. 99–102 of the ink draft, which were subsequently removed). Dissatisfied, Sibelius returned to the Seventh Symphony Sketchbook (HUL 0359) for further sketching, and on p. 20 drafted alternative realizations of the "catastrophe" and conclusion (Pl. 8.1, HUL 0359, p. 20).

That a central concern was to work the "Aino" theme into the final peroration is indicated by the annotation "Ai[no]" at the beginning of the first solution. The first sketch of the "catastrophe" as it appears in its final form is to be found on the middle of p. 20, staves 5–10. Here, the upper voice clearly circles through the diminished third between F♯ and A♭ before collapsing on F (marked with a fermata). Still missing, however, is the final statement of the "Aino" theme. Sketches for its "trapped" presentation are found on HUL 0353, p. 103; originally, as indicated on this page, "Aino" was to be assigned to the bassoon, horns, violas, cellos, and basses. It is here that the allusion to *Valse triste* first appears. A further orchestral draft of this passage realizing this sketch's instrumentation was removed in favor of the final version.[108]

As a result of all of these calculations and modifications, the paradoxical intimation of death and suicide – of impotence yet transfiguration – is not simply a "surface" effect but occurs at the "deepest" structural levels. If *this* can be thought of as the *dénouement* of a "meta-symphonic" narrative

---

[108] HUL 0353 provides another reading of pp. 98–102 of the ink draft.

spanning Symphonies Nos. 1–7 and many of the tone poems, and an equivocal "deformation" of Schumann's and Brahms's triumphant "Clara" symphonies, it is difficult to see a way forward. Was an "Eighth" possible?

Recapitulation

If Brahms evokes Manfred's query, "Du liebst mich noch?," Schumann's Second, Brahms's First, and Sibelius's Seventh Symphonies all conceive the symphonic process as "crystallization" of DTA in answer to this question. The "pure," virginal Wife, as agent of the hero's psycho-sexual and spiritual rebirth, becomes associated with colossal over-arching auxiliary cadences into the C major tonic, i.e. C major as the goal DTA of the large-scale auxiliary progression. Throughout Sibelius's meta-narrative, the hero had been "healed" by the "wife-mother." In *Lemminkäinen in Tuonela*, for example, the mother "sewed" (the self-castrated?) Lemminkäinen/Väinämöinen back together. In the chorale of the Finale of the Third Symphony, through the reference to the euphony of "Aino's" motivic sixths, the hero "reconstituted" Björn's jaunty C major march-chorale from *Skogsrået*. In *Maan virsi*, Aino as "wife-mother" – now explicitly identified with Mother Earth – successfully "regenerated" the hero in her C major womb. But in the Seventh Symphony, the healing process lapses. As the "trapped" Aino theme "echoes" into silence (mm. 506–510), Sibelius/Christ/Tristan summons Aino/Mary/Isolde in the guise of Death, and the Child's (Ruth's) subject appears only in a "shadow" recapitulation (mm. 512–518). The *child* – the incarnation of binding love and intimation of immortality – is reduced to a shade.[109] Does the "silence" of *Ainola* grow organically out of this living death?

---

[109] How different this is from Strauss's *Sinfonia domestica*, where the Child's theme (as the synthesis of the parents' "conflicting" thematic material) concludes the work triumphantly.

PART III

Analytical studies of the symphonies

9 Meter in the opening of the Second Symphony

Tapio Kallio

In the score of Sibelius's Second Symphony, are the barlines at the opening of the first movement located correctly (Ex. 9.1a)? To my ear, the music suggests a different kind of barring, displayed in Ex. 9.1b.

This conflict between the perceived and the notated meters has not passed without comment; M. Stuart Collins describes it as a "rhythmic equivalent of a mis-writing."[1] Most writers, however, appear to have accepted the composer's metrical notation as a correct description of the metrical organization of the music, since they do not question it. However, I believe the problem to be both significant and deserving of careful consideration; so, it seems, did the composer. In fact, the alternative notation of Ex. 9.1b was employed by Sibelius himself in the original composing score.

Metrical notation in Sibelius's compositional process

Sibelius was accustomed to putting down his musical ideas – "themes," as he referred to them – as they came to him "from above" in order to develop them further whenever necessary. Indeed, his sketches show them often to possess a definite melodic identity when they first appear in notation. Whether or not the ideas also have a rhythmic or metric identity is not always obvious, as Sibelius sometimes notates them as mere combinations of pitches, with no durations or meter indicated. Often the sketches consist of many staves of melody without a time signature or barlines.

There are two possible motivations for such a procedure: either the metrical identity of an idea was already clear and self-evident to the extent that it was unnecessary to bother notating it, or it was left open on

---

[1] M. Stuart Collins, "The Orchestral Music of Sibelius" (Ph.D. diss., University of Leeds, 1973), pp. 114–15.

Ex. 9.1a   Second Symphony, first movement, mm. 1–3

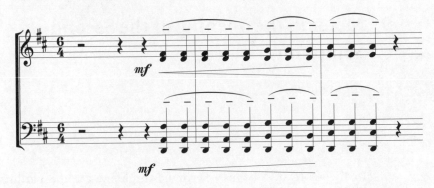

Ex. 9.1b   Second Symphony, first movement, mm. 1–3, hypothetical rebarring

purpose, so that it could be decided upon later. The latter explanation
would imply that these melodic ideas did not always have a clear metrical
profile at the beginning of the compositional process. Since Sibelius was
liable to change either the ideas themselves or their notation when necessary, his compositional process could be described, in this respect, as dis-
covering an optimal metrical structure.

Notating the music for performance is a part of the final phase of the
compositional process. The composer has to notate the music as accurately, clearly, and economically as possible, without at the same time sac-
rificing its originality. Notational compromises are necessary when, for
example, two musical ideas with different metrical identities have to be
presented in combination, either simultaneously or successively. Such
compromises do not represent a loss of artistic value: a successful performance is indispensable for the realization of a musical work, and the
composer's skill in solving the difficulties of the notation is the ultimate
test of his ability.

The different versions

There is regrettably little sketch material that would allow us to reconstruct the compositional process of the Second Symphony. However, the existence of the composing score of the symphony, which was originally used for the first performances, does shed considerable light on the metrical conflict at the beginning of the first movement. The first performance took place in Helsinki on 8 March 1902, but it is obvious that the compositional process had not yet been concluded. This can be demonstrated by comparing the printed score with the original autograph score preserved in the Sibelius Museum in Turku, Finland.[2] The score has been partly damaged by fire – as is visible in reproductions – and is therefore very fragile. It appears to have been used for the first performances, and also for copying the parts, as can be seen from the measure numbers added to the score in the hand of copyist Ernst Röllig.[3] There is also a second manuscript source, a fragment that consists of two removed pages of a fair copy of the score in Röllig's hand, currently in the University of Helsinki collection. This fragment consists of two initial pages, and the rest of the score is missing. It is essentially a copy of the autograph, but there is an interesting detail: there are engraver's numbers added to the score in pencil, which suggests that the copy in question was used for engraving the score.[4]

Regrettably, no documents – for example an exchange of letters – connected with the revisions have survived. A proof copy that probably existed is also lost. Nevertheless, the differences between the printed score and the two earlier manuscript sources indicate corrections; although it is impossible to determine the exact date for the changes, they must have been made some time between the first performance and the printing of the final score in the fall of 1903. For the present purposes, I will confine myself to the changes made to the first movement's initial twenty-four measures. The discrepancy between the notated and perceived meters ends after m. 24 at rehearsal letter A.

Example 9.2 compares reductions of the original manuscript with the final version. Since the autograph score is slightly damaged by fire and parts of the music remain invisible, the reduction is a reconstruction. The corresponding places in the fair copy fragment are practically identical to the original, which suggests that the copy faithfully preserves the reading

[2] The Sibelius Museum does not have a *signum* for the manuscript score.
[3] Kari Kilpeläinen, "Symphony No. 2," *Jean Sibelius Complete Works* (Wiesbaden: Breitkopf & Härtel, 2000).

[4] Kari Kilpeläinen, *The Jean Sibelius Musical Manuscripts at Helsinki University Library. A Complete Catalogue* (Wiesbaden: Helsinki University Library and Breitkopf & Härtel, 1991), p. 33. Manuscript number 1788.

Ex. 9.2   Second Symphony, first movement, mm. 1–32
a (original version) and b (final version)

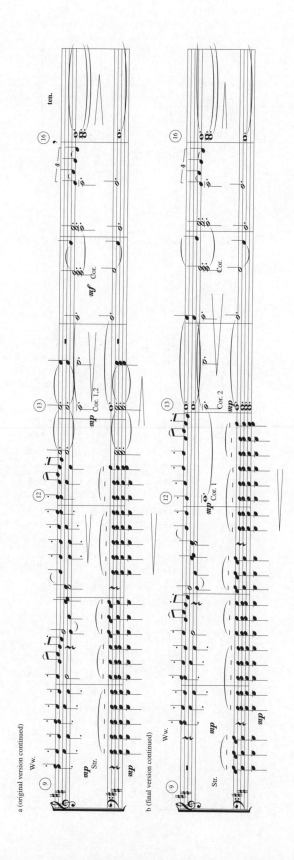

a (original version continued)

b (final version continued)

Ex. 9.2 (*cont.*)

a (original version continued)

b (final version continued)

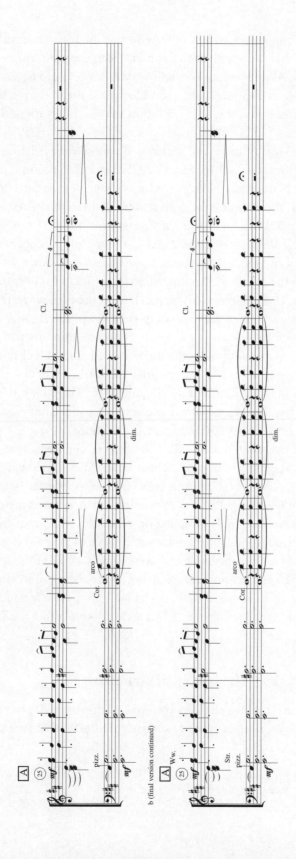

b (final version continued)

in the autograph, unless otherwise specified. As an initial observation, notice that the tempo indication has been changed from *Allegretto moderato* to *Allegretto*. I do not believe that this revision necessarily indicates a change in tempo; rather, I would say that the preferred tempo remains unchanged, and it is the indication that becomes more direct and economical.

Noteworthy also is the omission of the commas included in the original version after mm. 6, 15 and 23. The use of the commas to signify rhetorical pauses may have proved unsatisfactory, because three pauses in such a short time could have threatened continuity and cohesion. Perhaps Sibelius, in the case of the last two commas (mm. 15 and 23), also recognized that their appearance in the middle of a phrase might be disastrously misunderstood by an insensitive conductor.

Like the commas, also the *tenuto* markings (*ten.*) over the horn chords in mm. 16 and 24 have disappeared from the final score. In fact, it is only the *tenuto* in m. 24 that has completely disappeared, since the first *tenuto* sign in m. 16 appears to have been composed into the score by extending the chord in question by the duration of a dotted half note. In this way, the responsibility for determining the duration of the chord has been taken out of the hands of the conductor by writing it into the score; with much less risk of problems in performance, the composer now explicitly controls the correct performance of the chord.

But the most remarkable and striking change is that all string and woodwind parts in mm. 1–22 have been moved half a measure later, with the exception of the hairpin crescendo signs in mm. 1–4, which are left where they originally were in relation to the notated meter. As the horn parts have essentially remained in place, the relation of the horns to the strings and woodwinds has dramatically changed. In the final version, the very first note of the first horn part begins a whole measure earlier in mm. 12 and 20: in the original version both horns begin simultaneously in mm. 13 and 21. In addition to these changes, there are a few minor alterations that concern the placement of staccato dots and other similar details.[5]

Analysis of the metrical structure

The conflict between the perceived and the notated meter in the opening of the symphony is present exclusively in the final version: the notation of

[5] A reader interested in these matters is referred to *Jean Sibelius Complete Works*, see note 3.

the original version conforms to the perceived meter as presented in Ex. 9.1b. The relation of the two meters in the final version can be described as, if not awkward or problematical, at least exceptional. It would be incorrect to claim, though, that the location of the barlines has been changed from normal to abnormal, for the barlines remain in place; it is the music that has been moved, and not even all of the music, for certain elements are left in their original location. The first twenty-four measures of both versions can be shown to consist of three different main elements, each with its own identity: the string introduction, the theme played by the woodwinds, and the horn phrase. The woodwind theme is accompanied by a texture that is derived from the introduction. My analysis will focus on the metrical identity of the different elements; I intend to show that the most important consequence of the alterations concerns the relation of the woodwind theme and the horn phrase.

The woodwind theme

In both the final and the original versions the woodwind theme is notated in 6/4 meter, which is the time signature for the whole movement. Within the final version itself, the theme appears in two different relations to the notated meter. As can be seen from Ex. 9.2, in mm. 9–14 and mm. 17–22 it is in apparent conflict with the notated meter while, by contrast, after rehearsal letter A, in mm. 25–28, it is in agreement. The same conflict is replicated in the recapitulation, where the woodwind theme again appears first in conflict (p. 28, m. 5 to p. 29, m. 2), then in agreement (p. 29, mm. 5ff.). In the original version, on the other hand, the conflict appears only in the recapitulation, not at the opening. I shall argue that the opening of the original version conforms to the true metrical identity of the theme, while the exceptional notation of the final version and the recapitulation results from a compromise in metrical notation and should have no effect on either interpretation or performance of the work.

Example 9.3 shows how the two pulse levels necessary for a metrical interpretation in the form of a time signature, the basic (beat) level and the grouping (measure) level, can be established on the basis of the sound events specified in the score: the notated quarter-note level is the basic level, and the first grouping level is the dotted-half-note level, which corresponds to 3/4 meter. The second grouping level is the notated 6/4 meter. It is a compound meter, an explicit notation of a duple hypermeter in which each hypermeasure consists of two 3/4 measures. Thus the metrical identity of the theme consists of eight 3/4 measures; the extension of

Ex. 9.3   Second Symphony, first movement, mm. 9–13, the hypermetric organization of the woodwind theme

the last chord can be interpreted as a written-out fermata on the final 3/4 bar, as shown in the example.

The metrical identity of the woodwind theme is supported by the sketches: in the Sibelius Collection, the theme appears among sketches made for an uncompleted collection of children's pieces, dated 1897–98.[6] The fragment is in C major; there is no time signature, but the barlines suggest a 3/4 meter. In the fragment, too, there is a fermata placed above the dotted half note of m. 8.

For performance purposes, the metrical conflict in the final notation is not overtly disturbing. The conflict takes place at a slower grouping level, that of the hypermeter, which is more abstract than the measure level, the primary grouping level. On the measure level, a conflict would be harder to "tolerate," as an upbeat would have to be taken as a downbeat and vice versa. The apparent conflict is not an end in itself, but a by-product of another, more important, change that concerns the relation of the woodwind theme and the horn phrase.

The horn phrase

The notated 6/4 meter cannot be considered a compound meter in connection with the horn phrase. Example 9.4 shows how the horn phrase, separated from its notational context, could just as easily be notated in non-compound 2/2 meter; the re-notation describes the metrical identity of the phrase equally well – perhaps even better, since there is no danger of interpreting it as a compound meter. The basic level based on the actual sounding material is the dotted-half-note level (notated meter), and the first grouping level, the measure level, is the dotted whole-note level. The basic level is subdivided in two different ways: a triple subdivision in the second bar, and a quadruple subdivision that is duple in organization in the third bar. Both subdivisions can be held to be ornamental in nature; neither triple nor duple subdivision level can be established, as there is no continuous series of sound events below the basic level present in the passage. It is important to notice that, because the 6/4 meter of the horn phrase is an uncompound duple meter with no definable subdivision of the basic level, it would not tolerate a different barring. The performance of the horn phrase would certainly be problematic if the barlines appeared in the middle of the notated measures.

---

[6] Kilpeläinen, *The Jean Sibelius Musical Manuscripts*, 1991, ms no. 0818.

Ex. 9.4   Second Symphony, first movement, mm. 13–17

a Original notation: a non-compound 6/4 meter

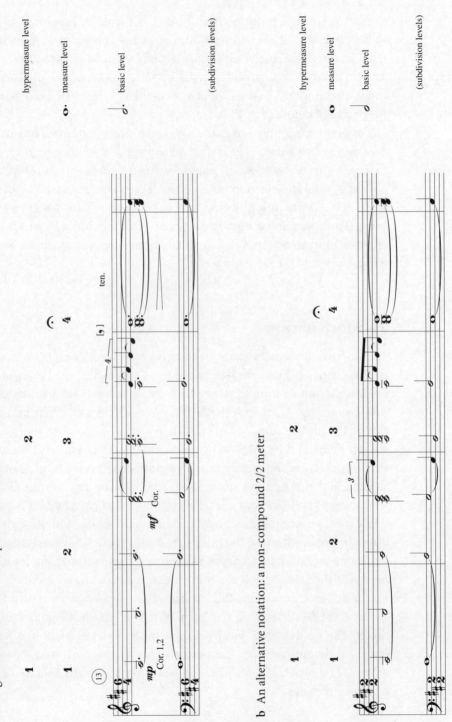

b An alternative notation: a non-compound 2/2 meter

The combination of the woodwind and horn themes

The revision of the passage leaves unchanged the actual metrical identity of both the woodwind and the horn themes. The most important alteration concerns the hypermetric organization of the two different themes with their distinct metrical profiles. In the original version, the horn phrase can be experienced as continuing the hypermeter of the woodwind theme, although it is distinguishable from that theme by its different melodic and metrical identity and sound color.[7] Example 9.5a shows the hypermetrical structure of the passage as it appears in the original version (mm. 9–16); the two different meters neatly follow each other, and one continuous slow grouping level can be established to metrically unify the whole passage.

Example 9.5b displays the same passage in the final version. Since the horn theme now begins before the woodwind theme has concluded, there is an overlap of two separate hypermeters. Thus, no continuous hypermeter governs the entire passage (as was the case in the original version); instead of a slow, continuous grouping pulse common to both phrases there is a collision between the two hypermeters. This collision is unexpected; in terms of perception, it is difficult to pinpoint its exact location, but it can be reconstructed retrospectively.

The linking of the two subjects is an example of Sibelius's tendency to conceal musical events. In the final version (mm. 12 and 20), the first horn enters a full measure earlier than in the original version and, in relation to the woodwind theme, the onset is one and a half measures earlier. The early entrance of the first horn provides a compelling example of a typical feature of Sibelius's style that Sir Donald Francis Tovey described as "the emergence of a long-drawn melody from a sustained note that began no one can say exactly when."[8] Although the horn phrase is hardly an example of a long-drawn melody, the other part of the description fits exactly: the key expression is "begun no one can say exactly when." The onset of the first horn in m. 12 of the final version is hardly noticeable since the listener's attention is focused on the woodwind theme. The second horn's entrance is also concealed by the simultaneous arrival on the final chord of the woodwind theme. In the original version both horns entered together after the final note of the woodwind theme had already been reached and on a hypermetrically relevant point; the alteration effectively minimizes the listener's ability to ascertain the exact beginning point of the horn phrase.

---

[7] There is a motivic connection between the two, though, as has often been pointed out.

[8] Donald Francis Tovey, *Symphonies and Other Orchestral Works. Essays in Musical Analysis* (Oxford: Oxford University Press, 1990 [first published 1935–9]), p. 494.

Ex. 9.5   Second Symphony, first movement, mm. 9–16
a) Hypermetrical interpretation of the original version

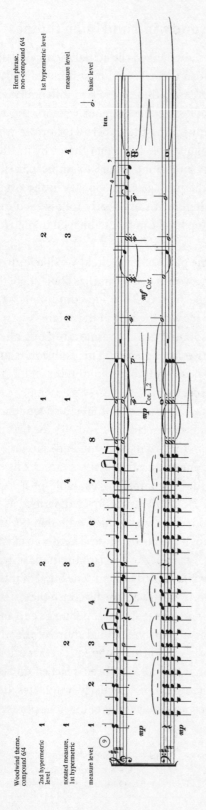

b) Hypermetrical interpretation of the final version

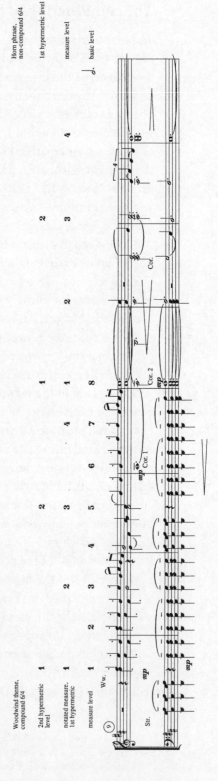

Paradoxically, the effect of the alterations is to make the two subjects stand apart by moving them closer together. Changing the metrical relationship of the two primary thematic elements goes right to the heart of the music: it radically alters the sound material the listener has at his disposal as he attempts to interpret the music metrically as the piece unfolds.

The conflict of notated and perceived meter of the woodwind theme in the final version and the recapitulation of both versions is a result of a notational compromise caused by the linking of two different metrical identities. In the opening of the exposition the notated meter corresponds with the meter of the horn phrase, and the notation of the woodwind theme accommodates to it. In the recapitulation, the notated meter is dictated by the horn, bassoon, and tuba parts (p. 28, m. 3 to p. 29, m. 4).

The string introduction

The conflict caused by the metrical re-notation in the opening is tolerable because of the compound meter of the woodwind theme, but it does cause problems for the performance of the introduction. An attempt to convey the notated meter in the initial measures of the final version may ruin the carefully planned dramatic effect of the opening.

I have observed that the notated meter does not always accurately represent the metrical identity of a passage, nor is this necessarily its primary function. The notation in the original version does describe the introduction's meter more accurately than the final one, but it still does not entirely exhaust the subject. The metrical identity of the introduction is open to various interpretations.

In the introduction (Ex. 9.6), there are four levels of pulse: a quarter-note level established by the attacks of quarter notes; a dotted-half-note level established in the second measure (of the original notation) by the pitch changes and supported by the articulation curves; a dotted-whole-note level established by the D major chord of m. 1 and the sum of the two dotted-half-note chord pulsations in m. 2; and finally the level of two notated measures, confirmed by the repetition of the phrase (not indicated in the example). Which of the four pulse levels established by the sound events would correspond to a time signature that would describe a perceived meter?

Example 9.6a suggests that the notated meter in the original version signifies a compound 6/4 meter comprising two 3/4 measures; then the metrical conflict in the final version could be tolerated. I do not believe this to be the case, due to the insufficiency of sound events that would substantiate an interpretation of 3/4 meter. Instead of the quarter-note

Ex. 9.6   Second Symphony, first movement, mm. 1–2

a) A compound 6/4 meter

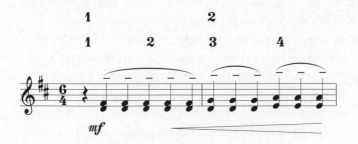

b) A non-compound 2/2 meter

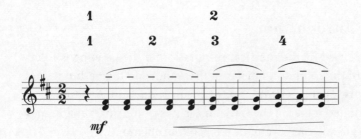

level, the basic level is represented by the dotted-half-note level established by the pitch changes in m. 2. In my view, it is possible to perceive the meter of the passage as a non-compound 6/4 meter, i.e., a duple meter with triple subdivision of the basic level. In another notation, this could be expressed as a 2/2 meter as shown in Ex. 9.6b. According to this interpretation, the pace of the beat and grouping levels of the introduction would be twice as slow as in the following woodwind theme; the doubling of the tempo of the grouping measure-level in the woodwind theme would thus be experienced as a remarkable increase of metrical activity. This is, I believe, in accordance with the subjective listening experience.

With reference to the original notation (Ex. 9.2a), the longest sound event of the introduction is the two-measure phrase. The phrase has an upbeat character, the first measure of the phrase forming an upbeat to the second measure, which is experienced as an expected downbeat in relation to the preceding measure. Furthermore, the two-measure phrase in its entirety may be considered an upbeat for a downbeat located on the onset of a pulsation of the next metrical level, which should be confirmed by a sound event on the first quarter of the third measure. Although the expected downbeat does not arrive (as there is no sound event present), it can be understood to be present but suppressed.

Instead of progressing forward, the phrase is repeated (mm. 3–4), and again the expected downbeat is suppressed in m. 5. The upbeat accumulates momentum: as the two-measure phrase is cut in half in m. 5, the energy reservoir is also halved, which is reflected by the decline in intensity, first to *mp*, then to *p*. The comma after m. 6 in the original version further underscores this loss of energy. It is only after a renewed effort in mm. 7–8 that the upbeat phrase finally achieves continuation with the entrance of the woodwind theme, which establishes slower hypermetric levels.

In my view, the introduction presents a dramatic process, a series of events that could be characterized as "trial and error" embodying a repeated attempt, a decline of energy, a new gathering of resources and final success. Music does not have to be programmatic to incorporate a narrative. The metrical drama presented in the introduction depends on a listener's reaction to the music and is thus purely musical, rather than extra-musical, in nature.

The notation of the final version (Exx. 9.1a and 9.2b) creates a problem for performance: the barline is now located in the middle of the first phrase, tempting a performer to stress the note that follows it. This would destroy the upbeat character of the D major chord, as the third quarter note of the phrase could be interpreted as a downbeat. But the notation makes it very clear that Sibelius does not want a strong accent on the third note in an attempt to convey the notated meter: all of the quarter notes for the duration of the D major chord are placed under a single articulation curve and all of the attacks are to be played in a similar way. To stress the third note would violate the explicit direction to play without differentiating one attack from the others. In the final version, a performance should not attempt to convey the notated meter; it is not "the" meter that governs the music until after rehearsal letter A in m. 25. The primary meter is the perceived, apparently conflicting, meter that is established at the outset by the introduction and continued by the woodwind theme; the meter of the horn phrase is the conflicting one.

It is noteworthy that in the final version the hairpin signs used as crescendo markings remain in exactly the same place where they were in the original version. Their invariant placement contrasts with the other markings, which were moved together with the rest of the string parts. I believe that the location of the hairpins in the final version is simply a mistake, and that they should have been moved together with all of the other signs. For lack of documentary evidence, I cannot prove this assessment, but I think it probable. The first page is the only page on which the hairpins are "misplaced." As presented in Ex. 9.1b, they are originally located where they are for good reason, namely to suggest a growth of intensity directed at the non-existing downbeats of mm. 3 and 5.

Other possible revisions considered

As I have demonstrated, the final version may be problematic to perform. Therefore, we may consider whether there could have been some other way of revising the music that would have guaranteed a completely unambiguous notation for exactly the same music as in the final version. One way to evade the problem would have been to notate the whole movement in simple 3/4 meter. This is a solution Sibelius did not choose and probably did not even consider, since the danger of inviting a performance with the character of a waltz would have been obvious. Other possibilities would necessarily include changes of meter, a procedure that Sibelius sometimes used in later works. For example, the exposition of the first movement of the Third Symphony changes from common time (c) to 3/2 for just one measure, only to return immediately back to common time (Third Symphony; page 9, mm. 4–5).

To test the idea of changing the meter I present two possible solutions. In the first one (Ex. 9.7), I re-notate the music with only two changes of meter, from 6/4 to 9/4 in m. 23 and back, by moving the horn parts instead of the string and woodwind parts. The problem with this re-notation is that moving the horn parts creates another problem. I have already mentioned that the metrical identity of the horn phrase would not tolerate the resulting metrical conflict, because, unlike the woodwind theme, it is not in compound time. Therefore, in addition to the changes of meter, the re-notation of Ex. 9.7 would most certainly cause difficulties for the performance of the horn phrase. The other possible re-notation conforms to the principle of changing the meter freely to adapt to the metrical structure of a given passage. From Ex. 9.8, it is obvious that although the performance of the horn phrase would be unproblematic, the sheer number of changes of meter (six changes within twelve measures) would be intolerable.

On the basis of these various re-notations it is evident that the re-notation finally selected by Sibelius is probably the optimal solution, although its performance is not entirely unproblematic. The apparent metrical conflict bestows upon the opening an element of mystery that Sibelius may have liked; it is like a crack in the smooth surface of the notated work, a beauty spot imperceptible in performance, unless accorded undue attention by the performers. The metrical re-notation

Ex. 9.7   Second Symphony, first movement, mm. 9–(24), re-notated with two changes of meter

Ex. 9.8   Second Symphony, first movement, mm. 9–24, re-notated with six changes of meter results from deliberate and conscious manipulation of disparate themes. There is no rhythmic "mis-notation"; however, while the artistic success of countless performances shows that various conductors and musicians have fully understood the composer's intention, it is understandable that many of us have been perplexed by the notation. But when the object of perception is music, it is wiser to put more trust in one's ears than in one's eyes.

10 The musical language of the Fourth Symphony

Elliott Antokoletz

Sibelius's Fourth Symphony (1911) marks a critical moment in the composer's stylistic evolution, in which principles of the classical tradition and the essence of the Finnish spirit are infused into a highly personal contemporary musical language.[1] During a period of extensive international travels between 1900 (beginning with Paris, the next year Italy) and 1914, Sibelius's symphonic idiom began to undergo significant changes as he turned away from the romantic moods of his earlier nationalistic works towards a more concise and objective conception.[2] Sibelius's turn towards classicism actually began in the first years of the century,[3] but the influence of Beethoven was now manifested in a greater economy of means, more classical handling of orchestration, and increasing concern especially for the pervasive development of thematically derived motifs within classically balanced formal structures. While this is exemplified in the tighter three-movement plan of the Third Symphony (1904–07), it was actually the Fourth Symphony that Sibelius singled out as a reaction against "modern trends."[4] However, the com-

[1] This study expands the discussion of Sibelius's Fourth Symphony presented in Elliott Antokoletz, *Twentieth-Century Music* (Englewood Cliffs, NJ: Prentice Hall, 1992), pp. 153–59.

[2] Although Sibelius produced works in various media – songs and choral music, piano pieces, solo string literature, and chamber music – his "style evolution" is represented most characteristically by his symphonic music. As outlined in David Cherniavsky, "Special Characteristics of Sibelius' Style," in *The Music of Sibelius*, ed. Gerald Abraham (New York: W. W. Norton, 1947), pp. 147–52, the evolution of Sibelius's symphonic idiom can be traced through four periods: Finnish (1892–1902); classical (1903–1909); complex and subjective (1911–1915); mature and synthetic

(1924–1957). See also Preston Stedman, *The Symphony* (Englewood Cliffs, NJ: Prentice Hall, 1979), p. 252.

[3] This change is apparent at least with the Second Symphony (1901/2), after Sibelius's journey to Italy (Rapallo, Rome), and it is obvious already in the revision of *En saga* (1902), as well as the two versions of the Violin Concerto (1903–05).

[4] In accord with Robert Layton, in *Sibelius* (London: J.M. Dent and Sons, 1965), p. 42, it is plausible to assume that the composer was alluding to the grandiose structural designs and indulgent orchestrations of Mahler and Strauss. Cecil Gray, in his monograph, *Sibelius* (London: Oxford University Press, 1931; repr.; Henry Milford, 1938), p. 157, states that Sibelius's "symphonic style is adverse to the picturesque, the opulent, the

poser's more traditional perspective would seem mainly to apply to structural and thematic issues rather than the musical language *per se*, since the tonal relations and harmonic progressions of the Fourth Symphony reveal a significant move beyond the bounds of nineteenth-century assumptions. While the linear voice-leading principles of traditional tonality in Sibelius's music have been addressed by several scholars, the present study, which focuses on the interactions and transformations between functional tonal elements and non-traditional pitch collections (modal, whole-tone, and octatonic), is new in its exploration of the principles underlying the unique sonic essence of Sibelius's musical language. In terms of the musical language itself, we may acknowledge what Howell refers to as the more "problematic," "experimental" (as opposed to "reactionary") position of Sibelius's composition.[5] Sibelius's general use of semi-functional diatonic folk modes and their cyclic-interval (whole-tone and, as we shall also see, octatonic) transformations reveals an affinity more with the melodic/harmonic palette of his folk-inspired contemporaries (e.g., Bartók and Stravinsky) than with the ultrachromaticism of nineteenth-century Romantic composers.[6] The intention in the present chapter is to demonstrate how Sibelius's approach to the relation between a new kind of tonal/harmonic content and the traditional structural framework in this landmark symphony reflects one of the basic tendencies in early twentieth-century music, and how the new musical language contributes to the more intense personal mood of the work. As Layton points out,

> the very opening bars emphasize the immense distance Sibelius had travelled in terms of self-discovery. The firm line, regular phrase structure and unambiguous tonality of the first bars of the Third Symphony contrast markedly with the dark brooding intensity of the Fourth. The confident, optimistic temper of No. 3 is laid aside: here the mood is despondent, the rhythm hesitant and the tonality obscure.[7]

highly coloured, preferring rather a certain austerity, dryness, asceticism even." In view of the Fifth and Seventh Symphonies, however, one doubts that Sibelius would have accepted Gray's ideas.

[5] See Tim Howell, *Jean Sibelius. Progressive Techniques in the Symphonies and Tone Poems* (New York: Garland, 1989), p. 128.

[6] See Erik Tawaststjerna, in "Sibelius und Bartók. Einige Parallelen," *International Musicological Conference in Commemoration of Béla Bartók 1971*, ed. József Ujfalussy and János Breuer (Budapest: Editio Musica; New York: Belwin Mills, 1972), pp. 121–35, who

discusses the question of Sibelius's national style on the basis of the three categories of folk-music influence defined by Bartók. He mentions the status of Sibelius's interest in folk music as compared with Bartók's and his main contributions in this area. Accordingly, Glenda Dawn Goss brings to our attention, in *Jean Sibelius. A Guide to Research* (New York: Garland, 1998), p. 182, that the "comparisons are made particularly tantalizing by the connections believed to exist between Finnish and Hungarian folk music as well as by the affinities between the languages."

[7] Layton, *Sibelius*, pp. 42–43.

Between 1911 and 1915, the outbreak of war and Finland's subsequent loss of autonomy to Russia, as well as illness, may have contributed to the more subjective, personal expression of Sibelius's feelings in a still more concentrated, austere approach to form. Tonal direction was often obscured within a more continuous developmental process, as exemplified in the Fifth Symphony (1915, rev. 1916 and 1919) as well as the Fourth; such continuity of development is permitted by smooth, highly integrated organic transformations between contrasting modal and symmetrical, cyclic-interval pitch constructions.[8] Tawaststjerna points out that Sibelius, in his move away from the national romanticism of his first two symphonies, developed a musical language in accord with the principles of the *junge Klassizität*. While this language came to full fruition in the Third Symphony, the full integration of his individual musical style was not yet entirely evident.[9] It was in the Fourth Symphony that the synthesis of contrasting musical elements was to become complete, even more important than the representation of their individual pictorial qualities. While the musical language of the Third Symphony is often vague and evanescent, that of the Fourth Symphony moves to the extreme limits of these aesthetics "with the utmost severity and austerity."[10]

The four movements of the Fourth Symphony are each set within a classical formal mold, but the highly integrated hybrid musical language of the work could only have developed in the twentieth century.[11] This language suggests, perhaps, some traditional coloring because of the predominating triadic sonorities, but the harmonic progression in the work has a limited relation with the traditional harmonic functions of the major-minor scale system. While triads move within the static framework of the diatonic folk modes, which together with ostinato-like thematic patterns and sustained chords contribute significantly to the national flavor of the work, these modes often acquire an exotic coloring through their local transformations

[8] The basic principles of transformation between modal/diatonic and symmetrical/cyclic-interval formations are discussed extensively in Elliott Antokoletz, *The Music of Béla Bartók. A Study of Tonality and Progression in Twentieth-Century Music* (Berkeley and Los Angeles: University of California Press, 1984), especially chaps. 3 ("Symmetrical Transformations of the Folk Modes") and 7 ("Interaction of Diatonic, Octatonic, and Whole-tone Formations").

[9] See Erik Tawaststjerna, in *Sibelius. Vol. II. 1904–1914*, trans. Robert Layton (London: Faber, 1986), p. 128; originally published in Finnish as *Jean Sibelius 3* (Helsinki: Otava, 1972).

[10] Burnett James, *The Music of Jean Sibelius* (London: Associated University Presses, 1983), p. 69.

[11] Evert Katila, in his review in the Finnish-language publication *Uusi Suometar*, expressed the opinion that the Fourth Symphony was "the most modern of the modern, and in terms of both counterpoint and harmony, the boldest work that has yet been written," whereas the musicologist Otto Andersson wrote, in *Tidning för musik*, that it represented a "synthesis of classicism, romanticism and modernism, which might well serve as the ideal for the music of the future"; see these review citations in Tawaststjerna, *Sibelius*, p. 172.

into octatonic and whole-tone formations. These semi-functional pitch-set interactions, as well as common motivic/rhythmic patterns, are basic to the interrelationships among the various thematic ideas that form the sonata allegro plan of the opening movement:[12]

Exposition	mm. 1–53
Theme 1	mm. 1–31
a	mm. 1ff. (bassoon, lower strings)
b	mm. 6ff. (solo cello)
Transition	mm. 24ff.
c	mm. 29ff. (brass)
Theme 2	mm. 31–40 (opens with combined Theme 1c and Theme 2d to produce contour of Theme 1a)
d	mm. 31ff. (upper strings)
c	mm. 33ff. (brass)
d	mm. 35ff. (violins)
e	mm. 37ff. (horns)
f	mm. 40ff. (trumpet)
Closing	mm. 41–53
b	mm. 41ff. (lower strings)
a	mm. 48ff. (oboes, clarinet)
Development	mm. 54–88
b	mm. 55ff. (lower strings)
b' and d	mm. 66ff. (violins 2 and 1 respectively)

[12] This formal scheme corresponds with that given by Stedman, in *The Symphony*, p. 261. A different formal conception is suggested by Veijo Murtomäki, who convincingly points out, in *Symphonic Unity. The Development of Formal Thinking in the Symphonies of Sibelius*, trans. Henry Bacon (Helsinki: Studia Musicologica Universitatis Helsingiensis 5, 1993), p. 97, that "even if sonata form is accepted as a point of departure it is possible to understand the form in a new way, as a revitalization of ancient form. The principle of implication produces a beautiful two-part solution in which the development corresponds to the beginning of the exposition and the development and recapitulation together to the entire exposition." In this regard, Murtomäki's formal perspective accords with that presented by Howell, in *Jean Sibelius*, p. 132, Ex. 38, who outlines this movement in perfect binary form: *Statement* (Exposition) – First Subject, A (mm. 1–6, 6–31), Transition, B (mm. 31–41), Second Subject, C (mm. 41–57); *Counterstatement* (Development) of First Subject, A1 (mm. 57–86/7) + (Recapitulation) – Transition, B1 (mm. 86/7–97), Second Subject, C1 (mm. 97–114). While Howell's local thematic designations differ from Stedman's, e.g., Howell places the Transition and Second Subject where Stedman indicates Theme 2 and Closing, arguments can be made for both schematic interpretations. Except for the finale, my own formal analyses of the remaining movements (as given below), adhere primarily to those of Stedman. Other guides to the formal schemes of the movements in the Fourth Symphony are also provided by Otto Andersson, "Sibelius' symfoni IV, op. 63," *Tidning för musik* 2 (1911–12): pp. 201–07; William G. Hill, "Some Aspects of Form in the Symphonies of Sibelius," *Music Review* 10 (1949), pp. 165–182; Leo Normet, "Vielä Sibeliuksen neljännestä" [Still More About Sibelius's Fourth], in *Suomen musiikin vuosikirja 1968–1969* (Helsinki: Otava, 1969), pp. 28–45; and, among others, Tawaststjerna, in *Sibelius*, pp. 180ff.

a′	mm. 72ff. (strings)
b″	mm. 80ff. (clarinet)
Recapitulation	mm. 87–114
a/d	mm. 87ff. (oboe/cello/upper strings); m. 88 (strings)
c	mm. 89ff. (brass)
e	mm. 93ff. (horns)
f	mm. 96ff. (trumpet)
Closing	mm. 97–114
b	mm. 97ff. (violins)
a	mm. 104ff. (oboe/clarinet)

Within this traditional formal framework, however, the thematic contours and harmonic unfolding are "cryptic and enigmatic beyond anything even Sibelius himself had achieved before; symphonic form is pared to the bone; and even where extended melody is suggested expectation is not only unfulfilled, but hardly predicted . . . nuclei of melody, harmony, and rhythm interweave and interlock as he contemplates the elements of organic life, in and out of nature."[13] The essential role of the motives in determining the larger formal shape is elucidated by Tawaststjerna:

> [The river] is composed of innumerable tributaries, brooks and streams, and eventually broadens majestically before flowing into the sea. It is the movement of the water that determines the shape of the river bed, and it is this image that entrenches [Sibelius's] view of symphonic thought: the movement of the river water is the flow of the musical ideas and the river bed that they form is the symphonic structure. Yet, if the first movement is formed by the flow of the musical ideas, the basic shape of the "river bed" is a readily discernible sonata form. It is not in its form that this movement is in any way revolutionary but in its syntax, the way in which the actual movement of the music is built up by means of a continuous process of thematic metamorphosis.[14]

This Wagnerian principle of thematic coalescence in Sibelius's music, in which the material is "built up by means of a continuous process of thematic metamorphosis," was originally addressed by Cecil Gray;[15] however, Gray's theory that Sibelius used the technique based on evolving themes from fragments is, according to Murtomäki, only partially true, since Sibelius used many methods of thematic work.[16] Sibelius

[13] James, *The Music of Jean Sibelius*, p. 70.
[14] According to Tawaststjerna, *Sibelius*, pp. 179–180, this analogy of symphonic thought to nature is made by Sibelius in his diary entry of August 1, 1912.
[15] Cecil Gray, *Sibelius: The Symphonies* (London: Oxford University Press, 1935).
[16] In his discussion of "kernel motives," Murtomäki, in *Symphonic Unity*, p. 29, opposes Gray's notion that "the device of linking together the several movements of a

himself denied Gray's theory decisively by saying "I'm not composing my symphonies out of fragments."[17] Furthermore, Tawaststjerna's description (as translated by Layton)[18] of "a continuous process of thematic metamorphosis" cannot automatically be connected with Gray's hypothesis of "fragments"; Sibelius's idea as expressed by Tawaststjerna/Layton meant for Sibelius something else, i.e., a more profound analogy between nature and art.[19]

Sibelius's interest in developing an organic musical fabric, especially from the time of the Fourth Symphony, is also manifested in his meticulous concern for continuity in orchestration: "Don't change the colouring before it is necessary. . . keep a flexible balance that can be adjusted depending on circumstances. A satisfactory sonority still depends to a large extent on the purely musical substance, its polyphony and so on."[20] While our exploration of the interrelations among the various parameters (melodic, harmonic, timbral, etc.) is essential in understanding Sibelius's general style and musical message, our present concern lies primarily with the means by which smooth interconnections between contrasting traditional and non-traditional modal/scalar constructions provide a new kind of structural fluidity and expressive development in the Fourth Symphony.

symphony into one vast whole . . . constitutes a betrayal of the innermost spirit of symphonic style." Murtomäki asserts that "the history of the symphony – and not least Sibelius' late works – shows that Gray is at least partly wrong. Increasing unity is the undying *cantus firmus* of the one and a half centuries of development of the classical-romantic symphony."

[17] See Santeri Levas, *Jean Sibelius. Muistelma suuresta ihmisestä* (Porvoo, Helsinki, and Juva: WSOY, 1986 [1957/60]; Eng. trans. Percy M. Young, entitled *Jean Sibelius. A Personal Portrait* (London: J.M. Dent and Sons, [2nd edn, 1972]), p. 88.

[18] See Tawaststjerna, *Sibelius*, pp. 179–180.

[19] The notion of "a continuous process" was further developed by such scholars as Wilfred Mellers, in "Sibelius and the Modern Mind," *Music Survey* 1 (1949), and "Delius, Sibelius, and Nature," *Romanticism and the 20th Century (from 1800)* (London: Rockliff, 1957), pp. 123–34; and Julian Herbage, "Jean Sibelius," in *The Symphony*, ed. Ralph Hill (Harmondsworth: Penguin, 1958), pp. 326–58. However, Harold Truscott, in "A Sibelian Fallacy," *Chesterian* 32 (1957), pp. 34–43, categorically opposes the idea that

Sibelius composed according to the "coalescing fragment" approach by emphasizing the primary role of tonal development instead. While the thematic and tonal principles are interconnected within the highly fluid unfolding of Sibelius's symphonic structure, the organic generation of material from the distinctive intervallic surface that characterizes the opening line, which has an otherwise amorphous thematic contour, seems to support Truscott's position regarding the primacy of the tonal dimension. See also Robert Simpson, *Sibelius and Nielsen. A Centenary Essay* (London: BBC, 1965), who addresses the Wagnerian conception in conjunction with the developmental strength of the sonata principle.

[20] Tawaststjerna, in *Sibelius*, documents Sibelius's concern for "continuity of musical sonority" in connection with the Fourth Symphony. He quotes the composer's statement regarding the means by which the individual instruments can produce a "more seamless" scoring. This continuity in the instrumental fabric is emblematic of the unity within diversity so characteristic of the melodic, harmonic, and other musical dimensions.

Idea a, which initiates the first-theme group of the first movement, unfolds as an ambiguous modal (C Lydian) or whole-tone segment, C–D–F♯–E, the ambiguity of which establishes the basic tension for subsequent development and fulfilment of the dual (diatonic and whole-tone) pitch-set potentialities inherent in the segment.[21] At the same time, the tonality of A minor is obscured initially by the held C, then E–F♯, the tritone C–F♯ serving as the melodic and harmonic boundary of this thematic segment. As observed by Edward Laufer, this tritone-bounded motive is projected into the overall bass line of the exposition and further extended in the recapitulation, where it also linearly outlines the return of theme 2d (mm. 87–88).[22] These architectonic projections and transformations of the motive are essential to the organic integration of the overall formal scheme of the movement. Tawaststjerna observes the following regarding this introductory motive of the symphony:

> its opening bars give the same impression of entering Tuonela. The basic tritone figure, C–D–F♯–E, resonates *fortissimo* in the bassoons' and muted cellos' and double basses' lowest register. After the *junge Klassizität* Third, the whole approach of the Fourth Symphony represents a thoroughgoing evolution. The modal colouring of the major-minor tonality that distinguishes *Kullervo* is enriched and the treatment of tonality, freer and more masterly than ever before, approaches the very borders of atonality. We even encounter a scale of the type [often referred to as "octatonic"[23]] that Messiaen was to call "modes à transpositions limitées." One can speak of the Fourth Symphony indeed as "the culmination of his inner search" of his Faust-like quest for the transcendental. In a way this is symbolized by the interval of the tritone around whose tensions the whole symphony revolves.[24]

---

[21] The opening motif may have been inspired by Wagner's *Siegfried*: the beginning of Act II by the "Fafner" motif; the end of Act II, Scene 2 (where Fafner is dying), the "Fluch" motif with the C major triad against the F♯ in the bass, which is almost like the beginning of Sibelius's Fourth Symphony (after Fafner's "beräth jetzt des blühenden Tod!" and at the same time with Fafner's words, "Mark' wie's endet!"). This would be in accord with Tawaststjerna's comment (supposedly stemming from Sibelius himself) about the opening measures sounding "as harsh as fate" or the alleged fear of death by Sibelius around that time; see Tawaststjerna, *Sibelius*, p. 180. In any case, the notion of the relations between Sibelius and Wagner is most prominently expressed by Murtomäki, in *Symphonic Unity*, pp. 34, 45, and especially 212.

[22] See Edward Laufer, "On the First Movement of Sibelius's Fourth Symphony. A Schenkerian View," in *Schenker Studies 2*, ed. Carl Schachter and Hedi Siegel (Cambridge: Cambridge University Press, 1999), p. 134, and corresponding Schenkerian graph, Ex. 11d, p. 140.

[23] The interpolation of this "octatonic" reference within the larger quotation from Tawaststjerna is mine.

[24] Tawaststjerna, in *Sibelius*, p. 175, further observes that the tritone is already prominent in the five-movement choral symphony, *Kullervo* (1892). He states that the horn figure in the second-theme group of movement I "seems to symbolize mysticism and the power of fate and this impression is confirmed in the finale when the same theme is intoned by the choir to a Kalevala text. At the same time, this

Idea b of the first-theme group (mm. 6. ff., solo cello) is initiated by an anacrusic G♯, which momentarily extends the pitch content of idea a to five notes of a whole-tone collection (C–D–E–F♯–G♯). However, the downbeat of the solo (m. 7) immediately draws this collection into A melodic minor, so in retrospect the original segment is apparently no more than a whole-tone coloring of this A mode. Howell considers the whole-tone partition (C–D–E–F♯–G♯) within the opening A melodic minor collection (A–B–C–D–E–F♯–G♯) of primary significance because of its paradoxical role in simultaneously disrupting and defining the key center.[25] On the one hand, its symmetrical structure and noncontainment of the tonic note (A) produce conflict with the diatonic hierarchy and, on the other, its symmetrically positioned augmented triad, C–E–G♯, is "in theory the one and *only* triad uniquely to identify a particular minor key." This conflicting, yet pivotal, interaction between modal tonality and the more ambiguous whole-tone sphere was emerging prominently in the early twentieth century, at which time it began to form a new kind of harmonic palette that contributed to the dissolution of the traditional major-minor scale system.[26]

'fate' theme serves to broaden the tonal horizon. Later in the *cor anglais* line in *The Swan of Tuonela* and the whole-tone figures in *Lemminkäinen in Tuonela*, the tritone is identified with the concept of death." The role of the tritone in the organic growth of the Fourth Symphony is also basic to the analysis by Joonas Kokkonen, ["Sibelius's Fourth Symphony"], in *Ihminen ja musiikki. Valittuja kirjoituksia, esitelmiä, puheita ja arvosteluja* [*Man and Music. Selected Writings, Lectures, Speeches, and Criticisms*], ed. Kalevi Aho (Helsinki: Gaudeamus, 1992), pp. 52–60; James, *The Music of Jean Sibelius*, p. 70, who refers to tritone domination of each movement "with the most ominous implication, undermining tonality and spiritual equilibrium alike"; and others.

[25] See Howell, *Jean Sibelius*, p. 134, for his more in-depth discussion regarding the interpretations of the "*Tristan*" chordal partitions (A–C–E–F♯ and B–D–F♯–G♯), their tritones, and the whole-tone partition of the larger A melodic minor referent in cumulatively "affect[ing] the tonal structure of the movement." Howell also presents a detailed outline of the non-traditional tonal schemes of the movements.

[26] Tawaststjerna, in *Sibelius*, p. 176, points to the new integrative aspect of tonality and the

whole-tone scale in Sibelius's music as part of the more global breakdown of classical tonality in the twentieth century, and states that Sibelius and Debussy, who otherwise differ from each other in musical thought, are linked in this process. He identifies the whole-tone theme that opens the third movement of Debussy's *La Mer* with the "germ cell" of the Fourth Symphony, and describes how it "is built up to a tremendous climax whose chords oscillate chromatically between the two opposing poles a tritone apart, only to be resolved by a passage securely in D flat." While Sibelius's first native biographer, Erik Furuhjelm, in *Jean Sibelius. Hans tondiktning och drag ur hans liv* (Borgå: Holger Schildts förlag, 1916), associated the style of the Fourth Symphony with the expressionistic lines of Schoenberg, it seems more appropriate to connect it, as Walter Niemann does in his monograph, *Jean Sibelius* (Leipzig: Breitkopf & Härtel, 1917), with Debussy's impressionism, despite its great originality. According to the Swedish composer-critic Moses Pergament, in *Svenska Dagbladet* (27 March 1924), "Every informed musician realizes in his innermost self that in the Sibelian symphonic voyage the Fourth charts the change of course towards impressionism." On the other hand, Tawaststjerna, in *Sibelius*,

The E–F# ostinato of idea a, now as fifth and sixth degrees of A melodic minor, continues as an accompaniment to idea b, the latter containing linear fluctuations of the seventh degree (G# and G) to produce the A Dorian mode (A–B–C–D–E–F#–G) in bimodal juxtaposition with A melodic minor. While this thematic idea represents the first unambiguous emergence of the A tonic, the main tonic arrival may actually be considered to occur much later in the movement, with the return of theme 2d (mm. 88ff.) at the beginning of the recapitulation. Laufer demonstrates that the asserted tonic pedal, A, at this point is the culmination of an "auxiliary cadence" that is spread out over the entire movement.[27] In his overview of this movement, Laufer shows (in his Example 11a) that the A arrival is the convergent point of the background-level descent (E–D–C#–B–A: i.e., exposition, E–D; theme 2, C#; development, B; recapitulation of theme 2, A) and the bass outline (C–E–F#–E–A, i.e., exposition, C–E; theme 2, F#; development, E; recapitulation of theme 2, A). This scheme reveals one of the essential principles by which large-scale organic coherence is achieved. By means of Sibelius's own statement that all his symphonies "were pure, absolute music . . . [t]hey had no programme element at all – although many people say that they have,"[28] some light may be shed indirectly on this principle of organic coherence. The implications of Sibelius's statement are elucidated by Laufer:

> If one interprets the first movement of the Fourth Symphony as symbolizing a struggle to victory, from darkness to light, from nothingness to life, or from turmoil to serenity (somehow all the same poetic idea), then this idea is not really an *extra*-musical symbol: it is intrinsically part of the compositional idea, an idea which is technically set forth by the vast auxiliary cadence spanning the entire movement – starting as if from nowhere, to attain its goal only at the recapitulation.[29]

Footnote 26 (*cont.*)
p. 177, feels that "perhaps it is more sensible and accurate to think of the work as expressionist. Unlike the impressionist movement, the expressionist was strongly bound up with the human condition, with the tormented psyche and the inner state of being," though Sibelius "never went that far along the road, not even in the darkest moments of the Fourth Symphony."
[27] See Laufer, "On the First Movement of Sibelius's Fourth Symphony," pp. 131–32. This concept, which may be characterized as "emergent tonality," is also essential to works of Bartók, as discussed by David Gow, in "Tonality and Structure in Bartók's First Two

String Quartets," *The Music Review* 34 (August–November 1973), p. 259. Gow contrasts this principle with that of "progressive" or shifting tonalities.
[28] As quoted by Santeri Levas, in *Sibelius. A Personal Portrait*, p. 84; see Laufer, "On the First Movement of Sibelius's Fourth Symphony," p. 132.
[29] See Laufer, "On the First Movement of Sibelius's Fourth Symphony," pp. 132–33. Laufer also addresses other features that together help to emphasize that goal. For instance, the tonal vagueness of the development section contributes to the focus on the tonic arrival in the recapitulation.

The relatively simple bimodality in the combined ostinati (mm. 7ff.), based on ideas a and b, is absorbed (at mm. 17ff.) into a more complex and ambiguous mixture of linearly stated diatonic-modal segments (Ex. 10.1), which together imply the presence of a larger octatonic coloring, E–F♯/G♭–G–[ ]–B♭–C–D♭–E♭[30] (m. 17, beat 3, through m. 19, third eighth note). At the upbeat to m. 17 and the first half note of m. 17, the B in cello I and the E–F♯ ostinato produce C Lydian (C–D–E–F♯–G–[ ]–B, the D being supplied by the first cello II). In the upbeat to m. 18, the viola and celli II shift the pitch-class collection to G♭–Lydian (G♭–A♭–B♭–C D♭–E♭–F), the F♯ of the ostinato supporting G♭ as the modal tonic. (These two Lydian modes, on C and G♭, are separated by the basic tritone, in enharmonic spelling, C–F♯.) The late appearance of the Lydian seventh degree, F (m. 19, fourth eighth note), permits the entire preceding collection (m. 17, beat 3, through m. 19, third eighth note) to have a prominent octatonic orientation: through the intrusion of the non-modal bass note E, the entire pitch content forms seven notes of the octatonic collection E–F♯/G♭–G–[ ]–B♭–C–D♭–E♭, the modal neighbor note A♭ of the viola (circled in the example) being the only note foreign to this octatonic collection. Through further modal shifts (mm. 19–21), new modal mixtures and nondiatonic colorings occur. Cello I, for instance, extends the G♭-Lydian segment linearly (G♭–B♭–C) to five notes of the whole-tone scale, G♭–[ ]–B♭–C–D–E. In the following measures (mm. 21ff.), the first theme group is brought to a close by motion back to the C Lydian mode.[31]

The octatonic and whole-tone implications within the basic diatonic modality of this section are realized fully in the development section.[32]

---

[30] Where a note is missing from a given pitch formation, brackets [ ] will be used.

[31] The interaction of diatonic, octatonic, and whole-tone formations throughout much of this and other works of Sibelius is emblematic of a more general development of these pitch-set interactions in a larger body of twentieth-century music. See Pieter C. van den Toorn, *The Music of Igor Stravinsky* (New Haven: Yale University Press, 1983), and Antokoletz, *The Music of Béla Bartók*, especially chaps. 7 and 9.

[32] While Simon Parmet, in *The Symphonies of Sibelius*, trans. Kingsley A. Hart (London: Cassell, 1959), p. 53, has considered this development section too obscure for analysis, Laufer, in "On the First Movement of Sibelius's Fourth Symphony," pp. 148–49, finds it "neither atonal nor unanalyzable; its logic is formidable, if obscure. And the 'obscurity' is indeed deliberate, having to do with the same poetic idea of complexity

moving toward clarity." While Laufer's graphic analyses focus primarily on motivic manifestations and harmonic/intervallic constructions and progressions partially belonging to traditional harmonic conceptions, the present study explores the integrative role of both semi-functional and non-functional (diatonic, whole-tone, and octatonic) pitch collections. Already before Laufer, Murtomäki's analysis shows, in *Symphonic Unity*, p. 90, that the development section (mm. 54–88) goes from the degree of V (E minor) to the degree of I (A major tonic), and in this sense the development is clearly constructed. Murtomäki observes that "the difficulty of analyzing the development arises from the use of 'vagrant harmonies' (Schoenberg) and whole-tone scales, which eschew unambiguous tonal centres. Yet despite the undeniable novelties also traditional polarity can be found."

Ex. 10.1   Fourth Symphony, first movement, mm. 17–21

A stretto, based on a descending form of idea b (mm. 55ff.) outlines the augmented triad B–G–D♯ (Ex. 10.2). This whole-tone-related segment is extended by the addition of C♯–D♯ of idea a (flute and clarinet) to four notes (B–G–D♯–C♯). Cello I (mm. 58–59) then interlocks the augmented triad with an ascending seven-note octatonic segment (D♯–E–F♯–G–A–B♭–[ ]–D♭), the latter in turn interlocking with the whole-tone segment D♭–F–G–B. After a series of transpositions of these interlockings, the whole-tone component is expanded as part of the growth process. The violins (from the middle of m. 68 to the middle of m. 69) unfold the first complete whole-tone collection, D–E–F♯–G♯–A♯–C, this time interlocked with diatonic segments. At the center of the development section (mm. 70ff.), the thirty-second-note scalar transformations of original idea a serve as a focal point in the movement for the realization of both complete whole-tone scales in continuous alternation.

Howell, in his Schenkerian foreground graph (see his Ex. 40) of this part of the development section (mm. 72ff.), interprets the successive transpositions of idea a (Lydian, or whole-tone tetrachordal cell) as forming "a complex chain of thirds, for example, C–D–F♯–E reduces to C–E."[33] In his graph, the cell transpositions, which unfold alternately in viola and violins (mm. 72ff.), are represented by their major-third boundaries: A♭–C (=A♭–B♭–D–C, viola), G♭–B♭ (=G♭–A♭–C–B♭, violins), C♭–E♭ (=C♭–D♭–F–E♭, viola), A–C♯ (=A–B–D♯–C♯, violin I), D–F♯ (=D–E–G♯–F♯, violin II), C–E (=C–D–F♯–E, violin I), and B♭–D (=B♭–C–E–D, violin I), etc. In this pattern of alternating whole-tone tetrachords, the last three transpositions (D–F♯, C–E, and B♭–D) belong to the same whole-tone collection, so the latter (WT 0) is extended to its complete form, i.e. transpositions D–E–G♯–F♯, C–D–F♯–E, and B♭–C–E–D, together produce G♯–F♯–E–D–C–B♭ locally. According to Howell, the motives "are designed to dilute, if not destroy, any sense of middleground diatonic or tonal progression." He infers, therefore, that "it seems pointless to attempt to discern (or impose) an underlying diatonic system as an explanation of the choice of pitch-classes for each motivic appearance when, by pursuing the system which Sibelius has set up so far in the piece . . . it seems more consistent and analytically appropriate at this stage to group them according to whole-tone allegiance."[34] Howell's graph can also be used to clarify a higher level of analysis, in which the two whole-tone collections intersect

[33] Howell, *Jean Sibelius*, p. 148. Howell's assertion regarding the primacy of the whole-tone conception is further supported by Sibelius's sketch of the movement (Howell's Ex. 41), in which the composer worked out whole-tone transpositions of the opening whole-tone motif.
[34] See ibid.

Ex. 10.2   Fourth Symphony, first movement, mm. 55ff., development, opening stretto

with the octatonic sphere. The actual motivic ordering of the notes in the two alternating whole-tone collections (i.e., Gb–Ab–C–Bb/A–B–D♯–C♯/C–D–F♯–E) implies the presence of a more background-level octatonic unfolding, i.e. as seen in the initiating dyads of the four-note segments, Gb–Ab .. /A–B .. /C–D .. [Eb–F], or the ending dyads, .. Bb–C/ .. C♯–D♯/ .. E–F♯/ .. [G–A]. This interpretation is supported by the earlier interactions (mm. 41–42 and 55ff.) between whole-tone (augmented triads) and octa-tonic scalar segments.[35]

Returning to the Exposition, the earlier ambiguous interlocking set segments continue to unfold. The series of short powerful brass crescendi at idea c in the transition (mm. 29–31), which is so characteristic of Sibelius's orchestral writing, leads to idea d of theme 2 in F♯ major. While the descending segment is clearly diatonic, the initial ascending segment, derived from idea a, outlines a whole-tone segment, A–B–[ ]–D♯, extended to A–B–D♯–C♯ by the second note of the descending segment. Not only do we get a thematic fusion here (ideas a, d, and the crescendo of c),[36] but the chromatic unfolding of tonalities to this point (C, A, and F♯, or Gb) suggests a background-level link to the octatonic rather than the diatonic spectrum. The new tritone boundary (A–D♯) of theme 2 is a local extension of this scheme (C–A–F♯–D♯) and is also the minor-third complement of the original C–F♯ boundary of idea a. (The recapitulation of theme 2, at mm. 87ff., cello, now bounded by the original tritone C–F♯, further bears out this complementary tritone relationship; the A tonic is

[35] The octatonic scale is realized in its complete form (C♯–D–E–F–G–Ab–Bb–B) only later, in the trio section of the second movement (mm. 263ff. and 296ff., low strings), where it appears in counterpoint with the trio's main whole-tone-colored modal theme, A♯–G♯–F♯–D–F♯–D/C♯–B. Transposition of the latter by the tritone, to E–D–C–Ab–C–Ab/G–F (mm. 273ff., ob./cl.), produces a long-range completion of the WT-0 collection (A♯–G♯–F♯–E–D–C). This transposition of the trio theme also produces a long-range octatonic extension of the original cadential notes, D/C♯–B, by the transposed cadential notes, Ab/G–F, to imply the presence of a six-note octatonic segment, [ ]–D–C♯–B–[ ]–Ab–G–F. This collection belongs to the same octatonic scale that unfolds against it. Thus, the whole-tone-colored modal theme and the octatonic set of the accompanying strings are linked by a common set segment (i.e. combined cadential elements, D–C♯–B/Ab–G–F).
[36] Laufer, "On the First Movement of

Sibelius's Fourth Symphony," pp. 137ff., also reveals motivic manifestations and transformations of the neighbor-note figure from the opening tritone motif (C–D–F♯–E) in the closing subject (mm. 41ff.) as well as theme 2 (mm. 31ff.). Beyond that, he shows that the "tritone-motive [his Ex. 13b] relates to the rising fifth-motive [his Ex. 13c] which is answered by the descending fifth (mm. 10–12): the rising and descending fifths then associate with the horn's fifth-motive [C–G] (m. 37) and the closing theme (mm. 41ff. and 50ff.)." To this we may add that the transformation of idea a in the solo clarinet and oboe (mm. 48ff.) of this theme group contracts the original tritone boundary to a perfect fourth to produce a more distinctly diatonic character. From these and other transformations of the tritone motif (see also his Ex. 14, which presents analytical sketches of the exposition), he deduces the metaphor: "struggle to victory, from nothingness to being," p. 138.

then held as a pedal in place of the F♯.)[37] While theme 2 is a relatively unambiguous diatonic focal point in the exposition, the closing material (mm. 41ff.), which returns to ideas a and b, is a preparation for the shift to the central octatonic and whole-tone interactions of the development section. Parallel fragments of idea b, which are ambiguously modal, whole-tone, and octatonic, initiate this closing section (Ex. 10.3). In anticipation of the development section, the first two segments of the viola (F♯–A♯–C and B–D♯–F) suggest representations of both whole-tone collections, respectively. At the same time, the alignment of each of these with the figure in the cello also implies two octatonic segments: F♯–A♯–C and A♯–C♯–E yield A♯–C–C♯–[ ]–E–F♯[ ]–[ ], while B–D♯–F and D♯–F♯–A produce D♯–F–F♯–[ ]–A–B; the linear progression of A♯–C♯–E and D♯–F♯–A in the cello implies an extension of the first octatonic segment to A–A♯–[ ]–C♯–D♯–E–F♯–[ ]. However, the remaining statements of this closing group establish the primacy of F♯ major, so the initial whole-tone and octatonic implications serve only as chromatic coloring within the diatonic spectrum here. The return of the closing section at the end of the movement establishes the key of A major, with some chromatic coloring. By the outset of the recapitulation (i.e. timpani, mm. 88ff.), the tonic note A already produces a sense of repose, whereas a similar occurrence of the A tonic (sustained in the timpani, mm. 77ff. of the development section) had served as a dissonant element, and, as Laufer observes, "the chromaticism of the exposition's a^1–b^1–$d♯^3$–$c♯^3$ is also revalued, now within a clear tonic."[38]

The second movement further develops these pitch-set interactions (diatonic, octatonic, and whole-tone) and modal colorings in a series of thematic unfoldings within the suggested traditional scherzo-trio form. The movement can be subdivided into scherzo, trio, scherzo (abridged):[39]

[37] Tawaststjerna, in *Sibelius*, p. 181, points out that this phenomenon, in which the larger tonal scheme of the Exposition – Dorian A minor (7ff.), leading to Lydian C major (25–27), then F♯ major (28ff.) – reflects the local intervallic (tritone) detail, similarly occurs in Nielsen's *Sinfonia espansiva*, composed in the same year as the Sibelius symphony.

[38] See Laufer, "On the First Movement of Sibelius's Fourth Symphony," p. 152 and his Ex. 21e (mm. 88–91, timpani roll, trombones, and lowest note of the trumpet).

[39] See Stedman, *The Symphony*, pp. 262–63. See also Howell's formal outline, which differs somewhat from Stedman's. As qualified by James, in *The Music of Jean*

Sibelius, p. 75, this movement is "a scherzo by repute rather than by nature." Similarly, Tawaststjerna, in *Sibelius*, p. 185, considers the movement beyond the interpretation of a classical or romantic scherzo, but acknowledges that Abraham, Layton, and Vignal recognize a trio section and "a cryptic allusion to the omitted reprise." Murtomäki, in *Symphonic Unity*, pp. 98–107, sees the central problem of this movement in the equivocal position of the trio. He analyzes the vast paradigmatic, melodically almost identical units of the dactylic section (letter B) and the *Doppio più lento* section (letter K, mm. 4ff.) to determine whether the trio begins from the one or the other of these two sections.

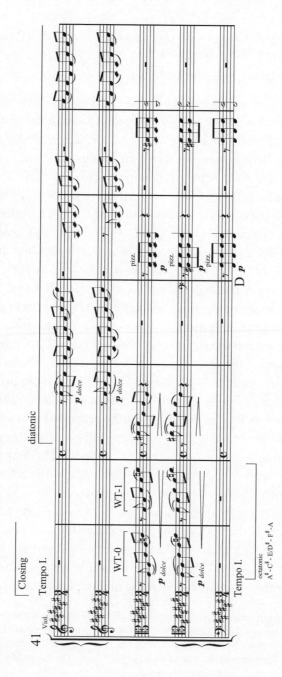

Ex. 10.3   Fourth Symphony, first movement, mm. 41ff., closing, return to ideas a and b

Scherzo (mm. 1–239); A (mm. 1–49) with five subsidiary ideas, a1
(mm. 2ff), a2 (mm. 13ff), a3 (mm. 21ff.), a4 (mm. 29ff.), a5 (mm. 39ff.);
B (mm. 50–123) with b1 (mm. 50ff.) and b2 (mm. 98ff.); a5 (mm. 152ff.);
C (mm. 163–68); a2 (mm. 169ff); C (mm. 177–85); A′ (mm. 186–239);
transition (mm. 240–262)

Trio (mm. 263–344): D (mm. 263ff.), E (mm. 281ff.), D (mm. 301ff.),
E (mm. 321ff.), D (mm. 340ff.)

Scherzo (A″ only, mm. 344–350)

Theme a1, a pastoral-like melody for oboe, is established in the F Lydian
mode above a static F–A ostinato. A local detail of this theme, F–A–B
(mm. 9–10), which suggests a transformation of idea a of the first movement, becomes more prominent in idea a3 (mm. 21–23). The F lydian
meaning of the segment is reinterpreted as part of a longer octatonic line
in violin I, F–[ ]–[ ]–A–B–C–D–Eb (mm. 21–26), the violin II ostinato
supplying one new note (Gb) to produce an expanded, exclusively octatonic segment (F–Gb–[ ]–A–B–C–D–Eb) at this point.[40] However, the
main focus at the cadence, in Bb major, is diatonic. In the next passage
(mm. 29ff., Ex. 10.4), nondiatonic intrusions into the modal sphere
become increasingly block-like and clearly defined. A sequence of tritones in the outer voices progresses by whole steps to produce a complete
whole-tone collection, E–F♯–G♯–Bb–C–D. The local tritone juxtaposi-
tions suggest the structure of the ambiguous Lydian segment (F–A–B) as
the source for this passage: between oboe and violin I, three-note adja-
cencies produce E–G♯–Bb and D–F♯–Ab as well as inverted forms. Once
again, the main focus at the cadence in F major (m. 39) is diatonic.

Section B (mm. 50ff.) repeats the process of moving from the F Lydian
mode, generated by the basic segment F–A–B to alternations of segments
from both whole-tone scales (mm. 64ff.). The first descending whole-
tone segment, A–G–F–Eb–Db–Bbb, ends with a form of the Lydian
segment (Bbb–Db–Eb), the next whole-tone segment exclusively based on
an inversion (Gb–Ab–C), and the third whole-tone segment, B–A–G–Eb,
ending with Eb–G–A, etc. This passage foreshadows the Trio theme (at
mm. 263ff.), in which the whole-tone descent (A♯–G♯–F♯–D) concludes
with D–F♯–G♯. In this case, the whole-tone structure is immediately
interpreted as part of B melodic minor, perhaps a distant reminder of the

---

[40] The gap between F and A (mm. 21–22)
initially implies the F Lydian mode, especially
when considering the cadential G to F in the
preceding measure; i.e. until the Gb appears in
violin II (m. 25), the suggested mode is
F–[G]–A–B–C–D–Eb. This nondiatonic
hybrid construction (a kind of Lydian mode
with flat seventh), which is exploited by
Bartók and other eastern European

composers, appears as Pattern 15 of Table 2 of
Bartók's Rumanian Folk Music, vol. IV, ed.
Benjamin Suchoff, trans. E.C. Teodorescu *et
al.* (The Hague: Martinus Nijhoff, 1975), p. 20.
Tawaststjerna, in *Sibelius*, p. 175, identifies
what he refers to as "the so-called Bartók scale
(the major scale with a sharpened Lydian
fourth and flattened Mixolydian seventh)" as
early as 1892 in the *Kullervo* Symphony.

Ex. 10.4   Fourth Symphony, second movement, mm. 29ff., nondiatonic intrusions

whole-tone/melodic-minor relationship established at the very opening of movement I. The trio theme in the oboe and clarinets is juxtaposed with the complete octatonic scale (C♯–D–E–F–G–A♭–B♭–B), which unfolds in the lower strings at this central focal point of the movement. The movement ends in F, the boundary tritone (F–B) of the basic F Lydian segment prominently sustained as a pedal.

The organic development of the symphony by means of thematic transformation and interaction of modal, whole-tone, and octatonic collections reaches its most intensive stage in the third movement. The sonata allegro form can be outlined as follows (with slight modification):[41]

> Exposition (mm. 1–27): themes A (mm. 1ff), B (mm. 9ff.), C (mm. 11ff.),
> D (mm. 12ff., cello), E (mm. 15ff., violins), closing (mm. 18–27), A
> (mm. 18ff., bass), B (mm. 22ff., viola), C (mm. 23ff., cello); Development

[41] See Stedman, in *The Symphony*, p. 264. Howell, in *Jean Sibelius*, pp. 166–169, analyzes this movement more specifically according to a rondo-type layout, but considers this formal conception "interpretative, even conjectural, rather than conclusive," the analytical enigma of which "arise[s] from the essential compositional precept of the work: *compression.*" According to James, in *The Music of Jean Sibelius*, p. 76, the third movement has been described as "rhapsodic," thereby suggesting that "its form is even more enigmatic than the others ... It is the primary distinction of Sibelius's use of motifs and themes that it is genuinely organic, an inner evolutionary process that constitutes the principle of true growth, rather than simple accumulation or complex mathematical combination."

Ex. 10.5   Fourth Symphony, third movement, mm. 1–2

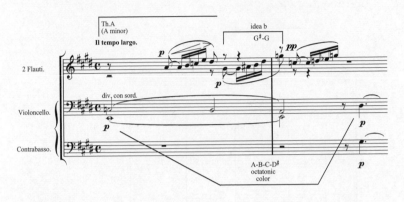

based on all themes (mm. 28–72): A (mm. 28ff.), D (inv.) or E (mm. 35ff.),
D′/B+C (mm. 38ff., cello), C (mm. 45ff.), D (mm. 47ff.), B+C (mm. 51ff.),
D/B (mm. 54ff., bass), A (mm. 57ff.), D/B+C (mm. 65ff.); Recapitulation
(mm. 73–87): A (mm. 73ff.), A/B+C (mm. 76ff.), A (mm. 77ff.), B+C
(mm. 82ff., anticipated in bass, m. 80); Coda (mm. 88–101): A1 (mm. 88ff.),
anticipation of A1 of Mvmt IV (mm. 92ff.)

Within the condensed form and transparent textures, the motivic elements and divergent pitch-set components of the preceding movements
now appear to be highly synthesized. The initial motive (theme A) for two
flutes suggests the A minor ascending contour of idea b from the opening
movement, the second flute segment of which is bounded by the same
major seventh (G♯–G, Ex. 10.5).[42] Embedded in the first flute statement is
the whole-tone segment (A–B–D♯), which suggests idea a of the first
movement, and the latter is explicitly manifested in notes 3, 2, and 4
(A–B–D♯) of the upper cello line. The larger linear outline of A–B–C–D♯
also suggests an octatonic coloring within the A minor contour of the
flute. The second flute statement, encompassed by the original conflicting
modal seventh degrees (G♯ and G) of idea b, supports this thematic association. As Jackson's graph suggests,[43] the chord A–C–E–G can be read as an
augmented sixth of C♯ (the notated key and key of the movement as a
whole), i.e., as A–C–E–F× resolving to G♯ in m. 3. The tonic C♯ is delayed
until m. 22, so that, as in the first movement, there is a large-scale auxiliary

[42] According to James, in *The Music of Jean
Sibelius*, p. 77, the initial flute theme of the
third movement gradually evolves into what
seems to be the main theme of this
movement (m. 51, cello I), an interpretation
which invokes the notion of an "emergent"
element (a specific tonality or thematic
idea), as expressed by Gow regarding

Bartók's music, in "Tonality and Structure,"
p. 259.
[43] See Timothy Jackson, "'The Maiden with a
Heart of Ice': 'Crystallization' and Compositional Genesis in Sibelius's *Pohjola's Daughter*
and Other Works," in *Sibelius Forum*, ed. Veijo
Murtomäki et al. (Helsinki: Sibelius Academy,
1998), pp. 253–4 (Ex. 3b, last system).

Ex. 10.6   Fourth Symphony, third movement, mm. 4–6

cadence. The interesting point here again is the superposition of collections – i.e. pitch-class sets – and tonal functions. While the diatonic properties of the flute theme are prevalent, the second statement is colored prominently by the augmented (whole-tone related) triad, B–D♯–G.

All three pitch sets (diatonic, whole-tone, and octatonic) are realized more fully in the spinning out of the flute theme and its counterpoint (at mm. 4–6, Ex. 10.6). The implied octatonic segment (B–C–D–E♭–F) is diatonicized by the next note, G, followed by two mutually exclusive whole-tone tetrachords (G♯–A♯–B♯–D and F–E♭–D♭–B). The latter whole-tone segment is extended to five notes in the low strings (B–C♯–D♯–E♯–G, in enharmonic spelling, B–D♭–E♭–F–G). In turn, the same whole-tone tetrachord in the flute is linearly overlapped by a six-note octatonic segment (B–C♯–D–E–F–G), again diatonicized by the next new note, A.

The Finale, although the longest and most varied of the four movements in terms of its thematic materials, is highly integrated by means of thematic transformation and is the most unified in terms of its modal-diatonic priorities.[44] Because of its complex formal structure,

[44] James's reference, in *The Music of Jean Sibelius*, p. 77, to the relation between the opening string theme of this movement and the opening oboe theme of the scherzo, and that between the ensuing solo cello theme (m. 32) and the string motive of the scherzo (letter A), brings to our attention long-range as well as local integration through thematic transformation. "But the most striking feature," according to James, "is the way in which Sibelius, while apparently adhering to the traditional four-movement symphonic form, in fact makes a number of significant moves towards total unification. The balance of movements is especially telling: if the second movement relates to the finale . . . the first and third are no less internally connected." He compares this tendency toward large-scale fusion with that in the symphonies of Beethoven and Brahms, a tendency already evident in the late classical sonata style.

interpretations of this movement have varied widely. In terms of the broad formal outline, Howell analyzes this movement as an arch-structure: Introduction (mm. 1–15); A (mm. 16–144): Transition I (mm. 32–48), Transition II (mm. 57–90), Transition I (mm. 114–144); B (mm. 144–218); C, which can be construed as the Development section (mm. 219–281); B (mm. 282–313); A (mm. 314–441); Coda (mm. 442–527).[45] For a more detailed breakdown into numerous thematic elements, Stedman outlines a more elaborate sonata allegro plan:[46]

Main exposition based on seven discrete ideas (mm. 1–46)
    A1 (mm. 1ff.), A2 (mm. 19ff., viola), A3 (mm. 21ff., bells), A4 (mm. 22ff., flute), A5 (mm. 23ff., violin I), A6 (mm. 25ff., violin I), A7 (mm. 32ff., cello)
Varied and abridged repetition of Exposition (mm. 47–55)
Development (mm. 56–313)
    parts 1–4 based on A ideas: part 1 (mm. 56ff.), part 2 (mm. 89ff.), part 3 (mm. 110ff.), part 4 (mm. 122ff.)
    part 5 based on new B ideas (mm. 138–217): B1 (mm. 143ff., winds), B2 (mm. 170ff.), B1 (mm. 179ff.)
    part 6 (mm. 218ff.)
    part 7 (mm. 251ff.)
Recapitulation (mm. 313–49)
Coda 1 (mm. 349–83)
    part 1 of Development varied (mm. 349ff.)
    new part 8 (mm. 385ff.)
Coda 2 (mm. 484–527)

Tawaststjerna sees the form as a less complex sonata rondo, in which the main section, A, alternates with B and C in a symmetrical scheme: A–B–A1–C–A2–C1–A3–B1–A4–Coda.[47] For Murtomäki, the arch form of the Finale becomes clear if one realizes that the central section (development and trio combined in his analysis), which differs significantly from the framing sections, is taken from the unfinished orchestral song,

[45] See Tim Howell, *Jean Sibelius*, p. 178, Ex. 45. Timothy Jackson's view of the form is close to Howell's. He regards the recapitulation as "reversed"; i.e., it begins in m. 281 with the second group. The first group is recapitulated in mm. 318 ff. For Jackson's analysis, see "Bruckner and Tragic Reversed Sonata Form," in *Bruckner Studies* (Cambridge: Cambridge University Press, 1997), pp. 201–203. Tawaststjerna, in *Sibelius*, compares (p. 197) his own formal view of the finale with that of Gerald Abraham in

Sibelius. A Symposium, ed. Gerald Abraham (London: Lindsay Drummond, 1947), p. 27.
[46] See Stedman, *The Symphony*, pp. 267–68. In his otherwise plausible formal outline, in which the detailed breakdown of thematic ideas is quite useful for descriptive purposes, Stedman's placement of the development section as early as m. 56 seems untenable.
[47] Erik Tawaststjerna, *Jean Sibelius. Vol. V* (Helsinki: Otava, 1988), p. 192; this outline appears on p. 197.
[48] See Murtomäki, *Symphonic Unity*, p. 122.

The Raven, to Edgar Allan Poe's poem.[48] For this genealogical reason, the development in his analysis begins at m. 138, the recapitulation at mm. 313/314, as confirmed by thematic, tonal, and stylistic features. He outlines the form as follows:[49]

Introduction: Ai (mm. 1–7), Bi (mm. 8–14)
First sonata rondo section=exposition: A1 (mm. 15ff.), B1 (mm. 31ff.), A2
    (mm. 48ff.), C1 (mm. 57ff.), A3 (mm. 91ff.)
Transition: d (mm. 103ff.)
Second sonata rondo section=trio and development combined:
    D (mm. 138ff.), A4 (mm. 215ff.), D/a (mm. 237ff.)
Third sonata rondo section=recapitulation: A5 (mm. 313ff.), B2
    (mm. 330ff.), A6 (mm. 339ff.), C2 (mm. 349ff.), A7 (mm. 388ff.)
Coda: d+c (mm. 432ff.)

Within this framework, whole-tone and octatonic intrusions into the primarily diatonic contexts are more isolated locally than in the preceding movements and, at the same time, are absorbed for the first time into a directed tonality that is increasingly reliant upon certain basic tonal functions. The opening theme is unambiguously in A major, with several chromatic tones embellishing certain diatonic degrees of the scale. The most significant is D♯ (m. 2) which, in contrast to its occurrence in the opening theme of the third movement, clearly emphasizes the dominant scale degree (E). At the same time, D♯ produces the basic motivic element (A–C♯–D♯) of the symphony as an isolated surface detail. The latter formation, in contrast to its ambiguous role at the opening of the first movement, has a clearly diatonic function; now the tritone is subsidiary to the perfect fifth. While pedal tones still serve to establish tonal areas, leading-tone functions become increasingly prominent. This is evident near the opening of Stedman's local idea A2 (mm. 19–20), where the fifth of the sustained tonic chord is emphasized by D♯, and at the cadence of Stedman's A6 (mm. 28–29), where the fifth of the E dominant seventh chord is emphasized by A♯. In both cases, the leading-tone forms part of a linearly outlined whole-tone tetrachord bounded by a tritone, but in this case the diatonic meaning is immediately evident.

In the first main cadential passage (mm. 79–88) of Howell's second transition, the basic tritone (A–D♯) of this movement emerges as a more

Considering Sibelius's fear of death from illness during the time he was writing the symphony, the connection with Poe's poem dealing with death would seem to have symbolic significance.

[49] See Murtomäki, *Symphonic Unity*, p. 119, in which his A4 (m. 215) is the "axis of symmetry" of the central section and the movement as a whole, while the coda breaks the symmetry.

prominent element within the tonal diatonic spectrum. The two-part texture is separated bitonally into A major in the strings and E♭ major in the winds. Each is part of a functional linear progression, the E♭–G of the woodwinds (mm. 79–81) as part of a V–I progression as it moves to A♭ (m. 89), the A pedal of the strings moving to its dominant-seventh chord, E–G♯–[ ]–D (m. 89). The latter also suggests a form of the basic motivic segment, D–E–G♯. This becomes more prominent in Stedman's idea A6 of Howell's second transition (mm. 110ff.), which begins with a D–E pedal against the initial G♯ of the viola theme (both pedal and theme together, D–E–G♯–F♯–D♯–E, suggesting a transformation of ideas a and d that opened theme 2 of the first movement, mm. 31–32, strings).

Within this primarily functional tonal context, the end of Howell's second transition and the modified return of his first transition (mm. 110–143) now experience increasing intrusions of whole-tone and octatonic segments (Ex. 10.7). The scale passage in Stedman's idea A7 of Howell's modified first transition (mm. 113–121) is based on continuously shifting modal segments, a complete octatonic scale (F♯–G♯–A–B–C–D–E♭–F) emerging as an intersection of segments in E major (D♯–E–F♯–G♯–A–B) and C minor (C–D–E♭–F–G). At the same time, the D–E pedal initiates a whole-tone descent (E–D–C–B♭–A♭), which is diatonicized by the opening notes of Stedman's idea A2 (m. 122). The ascending and descending scales of the winds (mm. 134–135) reassert the E♭–A tritone polarity, but once again in a primarily diatonic context. At the end of Howell's modified first transition (mm. 138ff.), which begins Murtomäki's development section, an A major chord is then presented in the woodwinds simultaneously against an E♭-dominant seventh chord in the remaining instruments. The bitonal combination (A–C♯–E and E♭–G–B♭–D♭) of these chords, which are separated by the tritone A–E♭, produces a composite six-note octatonic sonority (E♭–E–[ ]–G–A–B♭–[ ]–D♭).

Henceforth, perfect fifths dominate the texture, the final reiteration of the A–E♭ (or A–D♯) polarity occurring (mm. 435–436) just prior to the coda. Here, the A major triad (marked *fff*) is sustained against the D♯ of Stedman's idea A2 in the E trumpet, the D♯ resolving to the fifth degree (E). This resolution has been prepared in the rhythmically augmented statements of idea 2 in the winds at the opening of Howell's development (C) section (mm. 218–236), all in C major. With the establishment of this key, the original C–F♯ tritone polarity in the basic motivic cell C–D–F♯–E, which opened the first movement, is dissolved as the cell is reduced to C–D–E in the cadential bell figure of Stedman's idea A3 (mm. 230–237). Dominant–tonic progressions pervade the last measures of the movement. In spite of this resolution of the basic tritone polarity to the perfect

Ex. 10.7 Fourth Symphony, fourth movement, mm. 110–21

Ex. 10.7 (*cont.*)

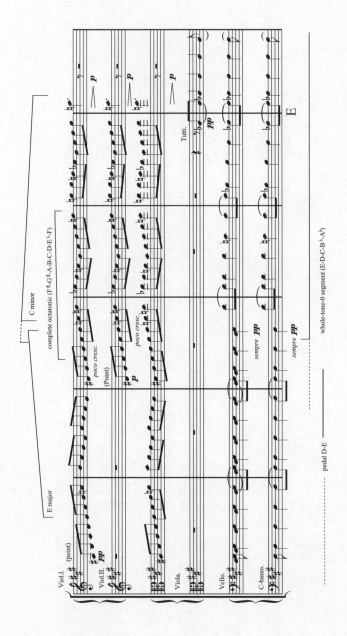

fifth, the tragic tone prevails in the Fourth Symphony; this was no doubt induced by the composer's fear of death from illness.[50] But the Fourth Symphony invokes a mood that seems to go beyond his "personal fears and depressions." It is perhaps "the expression of a particular kind of tragic stoicism; of broken faith seeking its point of identification in a hostile universe":

> There is not much joy here, anywhere; and what hint there is of it at the beginning of the finale is soon extinguished. At bottom, the Fourth Symphony of Sibelius is a stoical acceptance of a tragic world- and life-view in the face of inimical nature; and it analyzes the essence of those inimical forces with total integrity. Perhaps it is most truly seen in terms of the Hegelian tragedy of consciousness.[51]

The mood of the Fourth Symphony was also premonitory of the tragic events of World War I, after which, although Finland achieved its independence in the wake of the Bolshevik Revolution, conditions worsened as civil war broke out early in 1918. Due to Sibelius's artistic isolation in the following years, during which time he also became estranged from the newest European musical developments,[52] he produced only four major works after the war, including the Sixth and Seventh Symphonies (1923 and 1924), the incidental music to *The Tempest* (1925), and the tone poem *Tapiola* (1926). These late works, based on the most intensive synthesis and development of thematic materials, represent the culmination of his compositional evolution toward extreme formal concentration, which is most evident in the condensation of the traditional four-movement symphonic scheme into the one-movement form of the Seventh Symphony.[53] The Fourth Symphony may be considered an intermediary stage in the development toward that concentration. The interactions, extensions, and transformations of the non-traditional pitch sets (modal, whole-tone, and octatonic) are essential in the implementation of Sibelius's more concentrated, organic structure.

[50] In contrast to this notion of the prevailing tragic tone, Laufer's metaphor, in "On the First Movement of Sibelius's Fourth Symphony," p. 138, suggests "struggle to victory, from nothingness to being"; see n. 24 above.
[51] James, *The Music of Jean Sibelius*, p. 79.

[52] Robert Layton, "Sibelius," in *The New Grove Dictionary of Music and Musicians*, vol. XVII, 6th edn ed. Stanley Sadie (London: Macmillan, 1980), p. 283.
[53] Gerald Abraham, "The Symphonies," in *The Music of Sibelius*, pp. 35–36. See also James, *The Music of Jean Sibelius*, pp. 77–78.

11 Rotations, sketches, and the Sixth Symphony

James Hepokoski

I

One of the classic problems of Sibelius analysis is that of the strikingly original, highly concentrated forms of the late works, especially those in the last three symphonies and surrounding tone poems. Sibelius's shift away from traditional *Formenlehre* structures to differing architectural principles – what I have called "content-based forms" – was a conscious decision, as we know from several remarks in his diary from 1912. His entry from 8 May 1912, for example, stated the essential aim: "I intend to let the musical thoughts and their development determine their own form in my soul."[1] This pledge was as bold as it was fanciful: rather than actively fashioning material into more or less familiar shapes, he would now seek to curb the intervention of traditionalism into the compositional process. Instead, at least in principle, he was prepared to turn his musical sensibility, experience, and personality into a richly fertile, more passive matrix, a receptive medium within which, he believed, the "other" that was the musical idea could speak more elementally as it sought out its spiritually truer path.

Among the grounding axioms of this aspiration, we might suppose, was the by-passing of traditionally mediated thought and external control in favor of more potent, archetypal urges that were believed to strike more deeply than the schematic methods of an "artificial" rationality – the trusting embrace of the apparently mythic or pre-rational claims of intuitive impulse, blood, and nature (including raw sound itself). Such convictions were hardly unfamiliar to early twentieth-century cultural practice in Europe, and some of their incarnations, especially in Germany, were capable of taking on genuinely disturbing implications. For Sibelius this conceptual turn toward the pre-modern had been prepared throughout his career, and it was also now replicated in his increasingly isolated withdrawal with his family at his forest villa, Ainola, outside of Järvenpää.

[1] Quoted (with other relevant entries) in James Hepokoski, *Sibelius. Symphony No. 5* (Cambridge: Cambridge University Press, 1993), pp. 21–23. The passage also includes a discussion of "content-based forms."

Above all, it had privately mystical overtones that resonated with his own quasi-pantheistic nature meditations. Moreover, the composer's pre-modern stance was obliged to maintain an emphatic dialogue with the very modernity of symphonic practice itself, all of which presented dilemmas with whose contradictory demands he wrestled from that point onward. In the late works Sibelius strove to sidestep predetermined formal conventions in order to create freely coherent, intuitive, or *ad hoc* shapes. Such shapes, he recognized, were relatable only to the pre-existing formal category of free "fantasia," and some of his struggles were taxonomic: should he call his late multimovement or multisectional pieces "symphonies" or "fantasies"?[2]

Particularly challenging issues arose with the Sixth Symphony, completed in 1923 and published the following year. The Sixth marked an even more radical break from sonata-form practice than had the Fifth; it veered further away from sonata norms and scarcely seems in dialogue even with extreme sonata deformations. Shortly after its 19 February 1923 premiere Sibelius described the new work in the starkest of terms to a Swedish interviewer: the Sixth was "built, like the Fifth, on linear rather than harmonic foundations . . . [Its] four movements . . . are formally completely free and do not follow the ordinary sonata scheme."[3] Thus the Sixth has always posed a problem for analysts. This is especially true of its finale. In a recent analytical study of the Sibelius symphonies, for example, Veijo Murtomäki treated the Sixth's last movement under the subheading, "The Enigma of the Finale," and early on cited the puzzlement of both Gerald Abraham (who in 1947 had found the finale's form "peculiar") and Erik Tawaststjerna (who had concluded in 1988, in his five-volume study of Sibelius, that "the [finale's] structure follows no familiar pattern" and had proceeded to devise an *ad hoc* structure for it featuring a prominent "ritornello" and a "free recapitulation").[4] Faced with such difficulties, most analysts have tried to assimilate the finale into the psychology of pre-established norms – to reconcile what they have found with certain traditional structures: "free" sonata form, rondo

[2] On the "fantasia" question, see ibid., pp. 28, 29, 39–41, 57, 58.

[3] Quoted from Erik Tawaststjerna, *Sibelius. Vol. III*, trans. Robert Layton (London: Faber, 1997), p. 227. Cf. the earlier publication and Finnish translation in Tawaststjerna, *Jean Sibelius*, Vol. 5 (Helsinki: Otava, 1988), pp. 125–26, 368, which identified this as emerging from an interview with William Seymer published in the *Svenska Dagbladet*, 27 February 1923.

[4] Veijo Murtomäki, *Symphonic Unity. The Development of Formal Thinking in the Symphonies of Sibelius*, trans. Henry Baron and Veijo Murtomäki, Studia Musicologica Universitatis Helsingiensis 5 (Helsinki: University of Helsinki, 1993), pp. 226–27. See also Abraham, "The Symphonies," in *The Music of Sibelius*, ed. Abraham (New York: Norton, 1947), p. 33; and Tawaststjerna, *Jean Sibelius*, vol. 5, pp. 162–64.

form, ABA designs, bar form, expanded song form, and so on.[5] But the work has never been comfortably merged into these schemes. Indeed, the movement has been so puzzling that scholars have disagreed about even so fundamental an issue as whether the first forty-eight measures constitute the beginning of the formal design proper or whether they are merely introductory.

Because of the persistence of such problems – coupled with our awareness of Sibelius's pledge in 1912 – it would seem appropriate to complement Sibelius's compositional aims by asking to what degree such pieces as the Sixth's finale are capable of disclosing to us what their underlying logic might be. However momentarily – for we might wish to pursue different strategies at later stages of analysis – we might seek initially to suspend the workings of our normative formal terminology in order to listen to the works' unfolding of potentially unique structures and organizational principles. This procedure is not so free-floating as it might seem: like Sibelius, we bring to the enterprise a background of formal traditions and habitual expectations that can never be fully suppressed. Nor should they be: we, too, are aware of the habits of conventional symphonic practice, and Sibelius's new shapes are invariably heard against the background of what in many cases they no longer are. In a sense the old formal categories are still "there," still conceptually present through their conspicuous acoustic absence. That they were pushed to the sidelines, rendered apparently irrelevant, or even negated altogether is a central poetic aspect of the pieces at hand. The aesthetic impact of this relative freedom from traditional practice – the claim of a more "natural," untrammeled growth of musical units at all structural levels – is only perceptible, paradoxically, from a perspective that notices which customary compositional choices are *not* being made at any given point. Any seemingly new or *ad hoc* shape within these works is incapable of showing itself without remaining in some sense in dialogue with conventional organizational methods.

In addition, as I have suggested on several occasions, Sibelius's post-1912 conception of symphonic form does seem anchored in certain elemental architectural principles of ongoing musical process and cyclical reshaping that he had been developing throughout his career but that he was now encouraging to take center stage and operate with increasing independence from normative sonata- or rondo-practice.[6] Within smaller spans his main concern appears to have been to produce a non-schematic,

[5] A survey of analyses is provided in Murtomäki, *Symphonic Unity*, p. 227–28.
[6] For a fuller general discussion of this method, see my *Sibelius. Symphony No. 5*, pp. 19–30; pp. 58–84 demonstrate how the method may be applied to an entire work.

"natural" multiplication of interrelated musical cells, analogous to organic sprouting or (to change seasons) to the free multiplication of ever-varied ice crystals on a February windowpane. Within larger spans – building works as coherent, single-minded wholes – he came to rely on two principles that I have termed rotational form and teleological genesis. My present concern is to provide a brief discussion of these concepts and to show in some detail how they can be applied to the Sixth Symphony's "peculiar" finale, which may be regarded as a paradigm of this sort of musical construction.

By *rotational form* I mean a structural process within which a basic thematic or rhetorical pattern presented at the outset of a piece (the initial passing-through or "rotation" of thematic and harmonic materials) is subsequently treated to a series of immediate, though often substantially varied, repetitions. Rotational form may also be described as a set of rhetorical cycles or waves, in which the end of each rotation reconnects with (or cycles back to) its beginning – that is, to the beginning of the next rotation: hence the circular connotation of the term "rotation."[7]

One of Sibelius's underlying models for this method was surely that of folk-epic recitation-statement with varied repetitions (the Kalevalaic or typically Finnish procedure that he had admired and absorbed since the 1890s). More broadly, it may also have been that of organic growth or ramification – a traditionally romantic aesthetic principle carried out here in an idiosyncratic way. Even more to the point, though, the rotational idea was hardly new with Sibelius: it had been embedded not only as an *Ur*-principle in such familiar structures as strophic song and theme and variations but also as a motivating feature within the rhetorical aspects of

---

[7] Devising a term for a previously unlabeled but generally recognizable practice is not easy. I use "rotation" here in the familiar sense provided in definition 2a of the *OED*: "the fact of coming round again in succession; a recurring series or period." This meaning of the word is virtually identical with two of the *OED* definitions of "cycle": "a recurrent round or course (of successive events, phenomena, etc.); a regular order or succession in which things recur; a round or series that returns upon itself"; or "a round, course, or period through which anything runs in order to its completion; a single complete period or series of successive events." In the abstract, another (perhaps even more literally precise) term for rotational form would be "cyclical form." The problem here, of course, is that that term already means something different in formal analysis – a work in which important or motto themes from an initial movement return in later movements. The terms "rotation" and "rotational form" are uncontaminated with these prior denotations: it is true that the term "rotation" is used with a specific meaning in the analysis of serial practice and ordered musical sets, but that is an entirely different repertory, and an entirely different kind of discussion from the one in question here. Confusion between these two uses of "rotation" seems unlikely. Similarly, the term "strophic form" carries verbal/textual connotations not appropriate here; the term "theme and variations" implies a whole network of historical precedents that for the most part are largely irrelevant; and such terms as "varied repetitions" or "varied-repetitional form" seem both too bland and too cumbersome.

certain types of sonata form. From this perspective it is sometimes helpful to consider the exposition of eighteenth- or nineteenth-century sonata forms to function as an initial rotation, with the recapitulation serving as another: complementarily, it was possible (though by no means invariable) for developments – and even some codas – to refer referentially, as either complete or incomplete cycles, to the order of events laid out in the expositional rotation. For some later nineteenth-century composers – such as Bruckner, for example – such concerns became a generating principle of large-scale rhetorical coherence.[8] This is why some of Sibelius's more purely rotational structures may be understood as being simultaneously in dialogue with the principle of sonata form or sonata deformation.[9]

Rotational form is a concept that a composer may adapt with astonishing freedom, and, as one might expect, there are several differing treatments of it in Sibelius's works. In one subtype, for example – found in the finale of the Third Symphony, the outer movements of the Fifth Symphony, *Luonnotar*, *The Oceanides*, and several other pieces – the initial rotation is thematically differentiated and, consequently, substantial in length. Such a rhetorical pattern comprises at least two contrasting thematic modules articulated broadly on two separate tonal planes, and when it occurs, this pattern can recall the generically contrasting first and second themes of certain types of late nineteenth-century sonata expositions. Characteristically, however, the sonata analogy becomes strained or counterproductive once past the first rotation: more typically, the bi- or multithematic pattern is recycled (perhaps in free recastings) two or three more times throughout the rest of the piece, with harmonic, thematic, and textural variants, an eventual tonal resolution, and the like. In this subtype the specific order of the thematic modules (1, 2 or 1, 2, 3) is usually retained in

[8] See especially the illuminating treatment of Brucknerian rotations and rotational form in Warren Darcy, "Bruckner's Sonata Deformations," in *Bruckner Studies*, ed. Timothy L. Jackson and Paul Hawkshaw (Cambridge: Cambridge University Press, 1997), pp. 256–77. Such Brucknerian principles – although, as Darcy points out, they are not unique to that composer – provide the necessary backdrop within which Sibelius's "new forms" can be productively considered.

[9] This basic principle of the sonata, along with several others, will be treated in a forthcoming book by the present author in collaboration with Warren Darcy: *The Classic Sonata: Norms, Types, and Deformations*. On the term "sonata deformation" see my *Sibelius. Symphony No. 5*, pp. 4–8, as well as "Fiery-Pulsed Libertine or Domestic Hero? Strauss's *Don Juan* Reinvestigated," in *Richard Strauss. New Perspectives on the Composer and His Work*, ed. Bryan Gilliam (Durham, N.C.: Duke University Press, 1992), pp. 135–76; and my "Structure and Program in *Macbeth*: A Proposed Reading of Strauss's First Symphonic Poem," in *Richard Strauss and His World*, ed. Bryan Gilliam (Princeton, N.J.: Princeton, University Press, 1992), pp. 67–89. See also n. 8 above.

subsequent rotations (albeit with the possibility of variants, additions, and deletions).

A second, freer subtype is anticipated in such works as *Lemminkäinen's Return* and appears in *The Bard*, in the finale of the Sixth Symphony, and – most subtly of all – throughout the elusive Seventh Symphony, in which the freedom of the principle seems maximized. This subtype is characterized by a relatively brief first cycle followed by rotations of markedly differing length. Here the initial rotation normally consists of either a brief idea or a restricted set of differing compositional modules that generate relatively unconstrained expansions and accumulations in the succeeding rotations. ("I intend to let the musical thoughts and their development determine their own form in my soul.") Were such a principle of *crescit eundo* (growing as it proceeds onward) carried out consistently, each rotation would become both larger and freer, picking up variants and accumulations along the way. The compact initial rotation serves as a seed-idea, and each subsequent rotation reinterprets the previous pattern, enlarging or modifying it in some way. Such a procedure produces a concentrated meditative sway, which Sibelius probably regarded as relatable to certain kinds of spiritual nature meditation or mythic thinking: always in suspended motion through ever-elapsing time, one returns to the meditative object, re-contemplates it as it passes by, draws out different or deeper secrets from it in an elastic lingering on individual details or newly surfacing ideas, completes the cycle, returns again for another encounter, and so on. In this second subtype one can expect to find a half-dozen or more rotations, and each encompasses especially the possibility of accretions, newly produced musical branches or "blossoms," reorderings of inner material, recastings of mood, tempo, mode, or emotional content, momentarily stalled or fixed obsessions with single ideas, subrotations within rotations, and the like.

What is the larger principle governing the ordering of an entire set of rotations? In Sibelius's works, it is usually what I call *teleological genesis*: the gradual production and shaping of a cumulative goal (*telos*), which often arises as the culmination of a set of rotationally staged, cumulative pre-*telos* waves. Thus the rotational process of cycles – as they are reshaped and altered in successive presentations – is not arbitrary: the pattern repetitions proceed toward a goal. Taken together, the rotations may be understood as a gestational matrix supporting the generation of a peak moment at some climactic point in the piece. Nor is this a new concept within Sibelius: certainly by the late nineteenth century the symphonic practice of inexorable waves of intensification (*Steigerung*) was familiar from works by Liszt, Wagner, Bruckner (as Ernst Kurth would

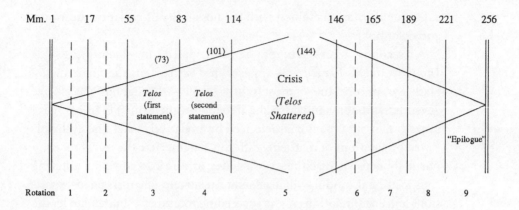

Figure 11.1

explicitly argue), Strauss, Mahler, and others.[10] When coupled with Sibelius's obsessively generative small cells, however – as well as with the complementary rotational method – the *Steigerung* principle took on a decidedly new accent and purpose.

Just as there are subtypes of rotational form, so too may we distinguish varieties of teleological genesis. In one of them, the cumulative goal or *telos* arrives at or near the end. This procedure may be found, for instance, in the finale of the Third Symphony and in the finale of the Fifth, both of which drive toward their final sonorities. In another subtype, the *telos* is sounded nearer the middle or shortly thereafter. In these instances, once this *telos* is produced, the general expressive ascent curve of the rotational process, its task fulfilled, turns toward expressive descent and decay, sometimes quite rapidly. Here the decline away from the peak is prolonged: it occupies a significant amount of time within the piece. Not surprisingly, in the decay phase the rotations may begin to shrink or suggest other signs of musical dissolution.

This ascent-descent model (or florification-decay model) is the one discernible in the nine-rotation finale of the Sixth Symphony. This structure can be represented as in Fig. 11.1, which includes my proposed rotation numbers for the movement (to be discussed later in this essay) along with an indication of the measure number at which each rotation begins.

[10] See, e.g., Ernst Kurth, *Bruckner*, 2 vols. (Berlin, 1925; rpr. Hildesheim: Olms, 1971), excerpts in *Ernst Kurth. Selected Writings*, ed. and trans. Lee A. Rothfarb (Cambridge: Cambridge University Press, 1991), pp. 151–207. Cf. Rothfarb, "Kurth's Concept of Form," in *Ernst Kurth as Theorist and Analyst* (Philadelphia: University of Pennsylvania Press, 1988), pp. 190–216; and also Stephen Parkany, "Kurth's *Bruckner* and the Adagio of the Seventh Symphony," *19th-Century Music* 11 (1988), 262–81. See also the discussion of "Steigerung" in Walter Werbeck, *Die Tondichtungen von Richard Strauss* (Tutzing: Hans Schneider, 1996), *passim*, but especially chap. 8, pp. 323–86.

Such a structure may invite a metaphorical hermeneutic in line with Sibelius's much-noted devotion to nature during this period. The model in Fig. 11.1 can suggest a natural cycle or meditative process that, I will argue, is directly relevant to that movement: 1) a gradual ripening or phenomenological Coming-into-Being;[11] 2) an attainment of a peak followed by an immediate overripening; 3) crisis, distortion, and decay.

How can we recognize the peak moment or *telos*? In most cases, this is an elementary matter: it typically announces itself through melodic fullness, articulation, climactic texture and dynamics, eruptions or outbursts, and so on. But it is especially convenient when sketch evidence helps to confirm our instincts. The peak of the Fifth Symphony's finale, for instance, was among the first ideas for the work that Sibelius jotted down.[12] In the case of the finale to the Sixth Symphony, similar evidence bolsters the hypothesis of expanding and contracting rotational structures coupled with a concern for teleological genesis. In what follows I shall first provide an overview of that evidence and then provide an analytical discussion and hermeneutic interpretation of the finale, which, again, I hear as subdividing into nine rotational sections.

II

Those who have dealt recently with Sibelius's late style are aware that one of the gateway documents into the period is a packed, forty-page sketchbook from 1914–1915 (now housed in the State Archives in Helsinki), fifteen important pages of which were published in facsimile in the fourth volume of Tawaststjerna's (Finnish-language) biography of the composer.[13] Here we find interrelated germinal ideas for the major late works: the sketchbook is both a revelation and a telling guide for interpretation. On page 18 one finds the first entry of a thematic complex in E♭ dorian/E♭ minor (transcribed in Ex.11.1a), at first conceived within the orbit of the Fifth Symphony.[14] But this entry, as both Tawaststjerna and Murtomäki have noted, was destined to become the D Dorian/D minor

---

[11] On the similarities of Sibelius's music and certain aspects of Husserlian and Heideggerian phenomenology, see Hepokoski, *Sibelius. Symphony No. 5*, p. 27.
[12] Ibid., pp. 33–38.
[13] Erik Tawaststjerna, *Jean Sibelius*, vol. IV (Helsinki: Otava, 1978): the photographs are situated between pp. 176 and 177. The photographs are available only in the Finnish-language original; they were not

reproduced in Robert Layton's abridged translation of this portion of the biography, *Sibelius. Vol. III*.
[14] I am concerned here only with the first two staves of the five on the page: the three additional staves not transcribed here – which may or may not be a continuation of the upper two – develop the concluding idea further, but in a way that seems unrelated to what would become the Sixth Symphony.

Ex. 11.1a   1914–15 Sketchbook, p. 18

Ex. 11.1b   1914–15 Sketchbook, p. 23 (or 27?)

Ex. 11.1c   1914–15 Sketchbook, p. 23 (or 27?)

idea that is introduced at m. 73 of the finale of the Sixth (Ex. 11.3, p. 336) – the moment, I shall argue, that provides the first presentation of the *telos*-idea.[15] Particularly notable in the Ex. 11.1a sketch is its chaining together of three successive ideas: the initial rise from $e\flat^1$ to $d\flat^2$ and back to $b\flat^1$; a middle link articulating a descent via triplets and coming to a brief pause on the half-note f^1; and a concluding, dotted-rhythm idea disposed in rising sequences but ultimately falling back toward the tonic.

Also available in the plates from the 1914–15 sketchbook in Tawaststjerna's vol. IV is a second, more provocative entry of the same idea – a version now cast in D Dorian/D minor. Although some of its

---

[15] Tawaststjerna, *Jean Sibelius*, vol. IV, p. 69;
Murtomäki, *Symphonic Unity*, pp. 198–99.

readings are difficult to decipher – particularly toward the end – I have provided a transcription (with uncertainties marked) in Ex. 11.1b.[16] Once again, despite some variants in thematic content, we may observe the same three links of the melodic chain, which in this case recycle back to the material of its beginning. Perhaps the most provocative aspect of this sketch entry is the Swedish word "mellantema" (literally, "between-theme," or, more comfortably, "connecting theme"), which Sibelius wrote directly beneath the second unit of the concluding, dotted-rhythm module (see Ex. 11.1b). The word's placement on the sketch as a whole, however, creates some ambiguity, and its precise referent cannot be determined unequivocally: it is also possible (but less likely) that "mellantema" refers to a separate theme provided on the staff directly below it (transcribed in Ex. 11.1c). Still, the word is placed much closer to the Ex. 11.1b theme, and with it Sibelius seems to have suggested some sort of transitional or connective status to that theme, which in the sketch does lead back to a recapturing of the first melodic idea. In other words, this dotted-rhythm/syncopation module is not the start of something new or the onset of a central thematic idea (it is not, for example, a "sidotema" or "sluttema" – second theme or closing theme within a sonata form – much less a "huvudtema" – first theme) but rather something that leads from one important idea to another, as a bridging melodic entity "in between" – as a "mellantema." As we shall see, the point of its relatively subsidiary status as an inner element of a larger melodic string is significant: most analyses of the Sixth's finale have mistakenly considered the idea into which Sibelius would transform the "mellantema" to be the head motive of a governing interior idea, largely,

[16] In Tawaststjerna, vol. IV, the sketch is reproduced as the fourth facsimile from the end (see n. 13 above). In that photograph, the last digit of the page number in the sketch book (upper right corner) is partially cut off: the page number may be either "23" or "27." The sketch itself is part of a theme table for a projected symphony (probably a Sixth, although the Fifth was still in the planning stage) – and the three staves transcribed in Exx. 11.1b–c are written under the rubric "III" or third movement. (The projected second movement, located directly above, cites a prominent melody from what would become the slow movement of the Fifth: this is transcribed in Hepokoski, *Sibelius. Symphony No. 5*, p. 40, Ex. 9.) The most uncertain aspect of my transcription in Ex. 11.1b concerns the sequentially descending music toward the end, which appears in the transcription as eight groups of four beamed eighth notes. Sibelius's notation at this point is unclear: the uppermost note of each four-note group could also be read as a "3" and the beam as a triplet-grouping (of three quarter notes). My own preferences between these two readings (triplets or four beamed eighth notes) have shifted back and forth. In the end, I have sided with the transcription of this passage as provided by Daniel MacGregor Grimley in his "Form and Tonality in Sibelius's Sixth Symphony" (typescript, King's College, Cambridge, 1994), p. 37. It might be added that Grimley also proposes a "rotational" reading of the finale of the Sixth. His analysis differs from the one presented here.

one supposes, on the basis of its abrupt first appearance in m. 49 (a point to which we shall return).

Because of the close layout of the sketch page (with its quickly scrawled, hand-drawn staves), it is unclear whether the immediately ensuing staff (Ex. 11.1c) follows directly after the music of Ex. 11.1b or whether it stands as a closely related but separate idea. Since the music of Ex. 11.1b seems to break off in the middle of the opening theme (sounded for the second time) and, consequently, because the end of Ex. 11.1b does not appear to lead directly into the beginning of Ex. 11.1c, I have considered the latter to be a separate, closely related sketch. (As mentioned above, it is also possible, though less likely, that this is the "mellantema.")[17] The thematic material on the first half of the staff – with the prominent double leading tones, c#^{1} and e♭^{1}, circling around d^1 and broken off with the letters "osv" written above (Swedish, "och så vidare": "and so on") – is readily recognizable: it would ultimately find its place in the Sixth Symphony finale, mm. 55ff., 83ff., and 114ff., where it also serves as a "connecting theme." In each case within the completed symphony this music directly follows the concluding link of the preceding sketch idea. In the Ex. 11.1c sketch the second half of the staff (after a strong vertical divider or barline and the "osv" to its upper right) seems to continue the idea more freely: notice especially the presence of the e♭^{1}–c#^{1} double leading-tone idea.

---

[17] The "mellantema" ambiguities are compounded by a second appearance of that word on the sketch-page – an appearance that is also unclear in its referent (does it label the theme above or below?). Directly below the concluding third of the sketch transcribed in Ex. 11.1c one may read the words "mellantema i h moll" ("connecting theme in B minor") followed by another word that is illegible. At first, one might think that the phrase would seem to refer to the last portion of Ex. 11.1c (lying above it), thus indicating that 11.1c (not the end of 11.1b) was the real "mellantema." But B minor, of course, is nowhere in evidence in Ex. 11.1c. However, on the staff directly below these words ("mellantema i h moll") is another staff and theme, now under the rubric "IV," for fourth movement. This theme is in D major (I have transcribed it in *Sibelius. Symphony No. 5,* p. 41, Ex. 10), and it breaks off mid-staff. The words "mellantema i h moll" are located directly over the remaining, empty portion of the staff – where the B-minor reference would make more sense, as something to which the D-major theme might reasonably lead – and in a separate, later entry below this staff Sibelius wrote "N'oubliez pas!" ("Don't forget!") In sum: the second reference to a "mellantema" seems to refer instead to the fourth-movement sketch-entry – as though Sibelius were planning to reintroduce the "mellantema" (from the end of Ex. 11.1b), transposed, into that projected fourth movement. One might only add – in a separate observation – that on the second staff of the fourth movement sketch we find one additional thematic reference to what would become part of the fourth movement of the Sixth Symphony. This is a brief chromatic descent (in three sequential cells) that correspond with the moment of "crisis" in the Sixth's finale: the melodic sketch encompasses the equivalent of the upper voice (violin 1) of mm. 136 and the first two beats of m. 137 (Hansen score, p. 78, mm. 3–4), although in the sketch the chromatic sequential figure begins a diminished seventh higher, on e♭^{2}.

At at least one later point in its compositional history Sibelius's verbal associations with the Ex. 11.1a–b theme extended beyond structural matters. (Here one must continue to bear in mind that the theme was not yet assigned to a "Sixth Symphony.") On p. 29 of a different set of sketches from a few years later – perhaps around 1919 (Pl. 11.1, HUL X/0395) – Sibelius jotted down a set of six fragmentary ideas and provided them with nature-animist descriptive labels.[18] Two of these fragments (Exx. 11.2a–b, obviously resembling each other) would turn up as prominent ideas in the Sixth Symphony. The first, on D Dorian, consists only of eight notes, lingering on the fifth, and written mostly without stems ($\hat{1}$–$\hat{2}$–$\hat{3}$–$\hat{4}$–$\hat{5}$—$\hat{7}$–$\hat{6}$–$\hat{4}$), which the composer labeled, in Finnish, as "Talvi?" ("winter?" – the question mark is Sibelius's). The fragment is intervallically relatable to the opening of the Ex. 11.1a–b idea in self-evident ways, but it is even more recognizable as virtually identical with what would become one of the main ideas of the *first* movement of the eventual Sixth Symphony, mm. 29–37 (see Ex. 11.5 below, where it is cited in the context of an overview of the motivic network grounding the whole piece). A second fragment from this c. 1919 period (Ex. 11.2b) is a fragmentary variant of the Ex. 11.1a–b theme, apparently on C Dorian (?), and Sibelius provided it with the Finnish label, written above it and circled, "Hongatar ja Tuuli" ("the [feminine] pine spirit and the wind").[19] At least at this pre-Sixth Symphony stage in the composer's conception of these themes, he was associating them with natural landscapes and, in the case of the crucial Ex. 11.1a–b theme, perhaps with the bending of pines under the strain of the wind – probably the winter wind. From such hints, and lacking any evidence to the contrary, we might suggest that

[18] General descriptions of the forty-three-page manuscript (No. A and X/0395) may be found in Kari Kilpeläinen, *The Jean Sibelius Musical Manuscripts at Helsinki University Library. A Complete Catalogue* (Wiesbaden: Breitkopf & Härtel, 1991), pp. 67, 412. Kilpeläinen suggests the dates 1915–23 for the entire document; a closer dating for this portion of the manuscript is suggested in Kilpeläinen, "Sibelius's Seventh Symphony: An Introduction to the Manuscript and Printed Sources," trans. and ed. James Hepokoski, in *The Sibelius Companion*, ed. Glenda Dawn Goss (Westport, CT: Greenwood, 1996), pp. 239–70; see n. 19 below. I am grateful to Docent Kilpeläinen for providing me with a photocopy of this sketch-manuscript.

[19] The label "Hongatar ja Tuuli" applies to all of Ex. 11.2b: it extends over both sketch-modules – over the interior double-bar. The last two pitches of the first half of Ex. 11.2b seem literally to be on the a^1 space. In the context of the preceding pitches, however – and given Sibelius's haste in scribbling down the notes – the reading of Ex. 11.2b seems to be the one intended. Directly below these two sketch modules appear two labels for yet another thematic fragment that is part of a complex that would eventually be fashioned into the trombone theme of the Seventh Symphony: "Kuutar ja pilvet" ("the [feminine] moon spirit and the clouds") and "Tähtölä" ("where the stars dwell"). For a study of the genesis of this theme over several years, see Kilpeläinen, "Sibelius's Seventh Symphony: An Introduction to the Manuscript and Printed Sources."

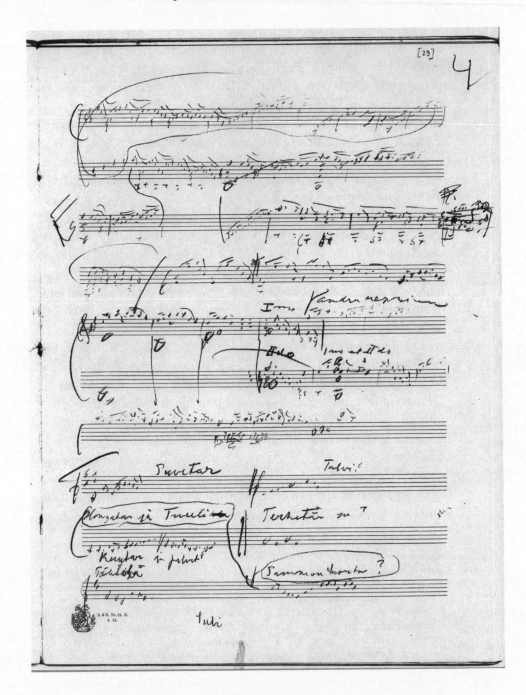

Plate 11.1   HUL X/0395/5, Sketchbook, p. 29 (fragmentary ideas used in the Sixth Symphony)

Ex. 11.2a   Sketch, Helsinki University Library, Kilp. A and X/0395/5, p. 29

Ex. 11.2b   Sketch, Helsinki University Library, Kilp. A and X/0395/5, p. 29

Sibelius might also have considered the Sixth Symphony to be a work that sought to represent – or even to become one with – the core of the isolated winter experience: a spiritual identification with winter, or a "northern winter symphony."

However we wish to extend our interpretations, the central musical idea behind all of this is the three-link complex shown in Exx. 11.1a and b. Example 11.3 shows this complex's point of first attainment in the fully realized piece, the finale of the Sixth Symphony, mm. 73–83 (rehearsal letter D is m. 72). In a larger context this Ex. 11.3 music is the concluding element of Rotation 3, itself prepared motivically, harmonically, and thematically by prior cycles.

In short, this "pine spirit and wind" (Hongatar ja Tuuli) musical statement is the contemplative object over which Sibelius brooded for years before producing the Sixth. From the evidence currently available to us, it appears that he privileged it – at least initially – over other ideas for the work, as a guiding idea around which other thoughts could be shaped, clustered, or understood. As such, it is likely that it is the *telos*-idea not only of the finale but also of the entire four-movement design – an analytical conclusion already anticipated by Murtomäki in 1993 (who did not, however, isolate the entire *telos* theme).[20] If so, then Sibelius constructed the whole work to grow into this Ex. 11.3 moment: here we have the wellspring of the motives, themes, harmonic strategies, and so on, of all the movements.

To demonstrate this gradual, four-movement preparation of the *telos* idea is not a difficult task, but it is a tedious one: drawing all of the relevant (and aurally obvious) motivic and harmonic connections would require

[20] Murtomäki, *Symphonic Unity*, p. 199. ("The central theme of the Finale, which is the starting point of the entire symphony . . . contains all the pitches which are characteristic of the work as a whole.")

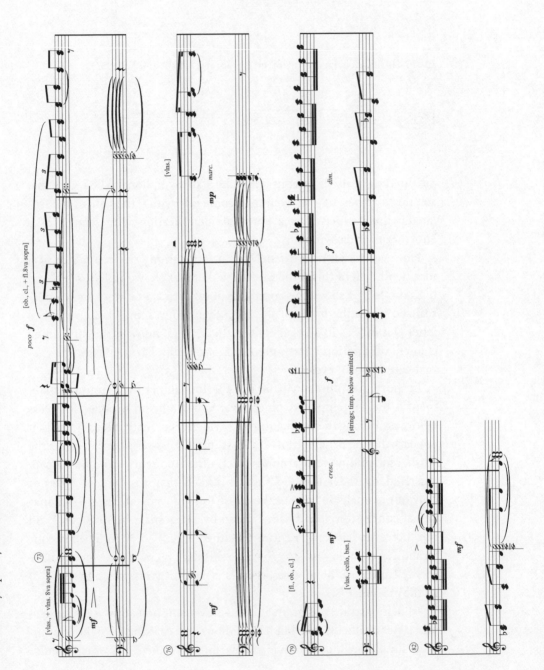

Ex. 11.3   Symphony No. 6, fourth movement, mm. 73–83

both space and patience that we need not invoke here. By attending instead to a revised conception of the larger, rotational shape of the finale – the main task of what remains of the present essay – we may readjust our conceptual frame for understanding that movement. Not only can this lead to a new way of hearing the finale, it can also direct us toward a heightened awareness of the phenomenological process that lies at the heart of Sibelius's late style.

Consider, for example, the finale's first *telos* moment shown in ex 11.3. Here we can easily distinguish its grounding motives. The first is the launch via the stepwise (modal) rising seventh (which Murtomäki sought to identify as the "basic motive" of the symphony),[21] followed immediately by a curling back from the top through the interval of a minor third (here, within a Dorian D, $\hat{7}$–$\hat{6}$–$\hat{5}$: c^2–b^1–a^1). A second motive is the prominent stepwise descending fourth in the horns, mm. 76–78, in this case reinforcing a new, compelling C major sonority and moving downward from c^2 to g^1. Sibelius reshaped this descending fourth into other patterns elsewhere in the *telos* passage. It appears, for example, as the background principle of the preceding woodwind triplet figure in mm. 74–76 (Tawaststjerna argued that this was the movement's "ritornello" idea, but notwithstanding its multiple resurfacings, that designation, with its multiplicity of connotations implicated in older formal categories, strikes me as misleading), and it also surfaces, with its descending fourth shape inverted, into the chattering ascending fourth pattern in mm. 81–82, where it provides the concluding idea for Rotation 3.

We might also notice the harmonic motion of this Ex. 11.3 peak moment: a D Dorian opening is momentarily pulled down by an undercurrent of C major (mm. 75–78); the music then sequences upward on a new figure (mm. 78–80) and re-descends on D minor (not D Dorian), with an added accidental B♭ (mm. 81–83). This sonority scheme, D

---

[21] Murtomäki, *Symphonic Unity*, pp. 198–202 (the section subtitled "The Dorian Basic Motive of the Symphony"). To clarify further: Murtomäki's "basic motive" consists only of the stepwise ascent through seven scalar notes, from d^1 to c^2. This is isolated as a motive in his Ex. 86 on p. 90. While I find much in Murtomäki with which to agree, my own reading differs from his in three principal ways. First, I view the leading idea of the work to be a thematic complex (shown in my Ex. 11.3), not any single motive. Second, I prefer to consider the Dorian rising-seventh fragment as being incomplete unless followed at once by a complementary descending third (for example, d–e–f–g–a–b–c–b–a, as in Ex. 11.3). Third, on p. 199 Murtomäki cites the published score (Copenhagen: Hansen), p. 65, m. 3 (finale, upbeat to m. 65), as an example of what appears to be the clearest statement of the basic motive. It is true, of course, that this presentation provides us only with the rising seventh (and no complementary third), but, as will emerge, my argument in the present essay is that this moment in the score (m. 65) is only a partial realization of (or "preparation for") the first statement of the *telos* proper, which emerges only with the upbeat to m. 73 – my Ex. 11.3 above.

Dorian / C major / D minor (with added flat), furnishes the main harmonic colors for the entire symphony. (The finale is notated without key signature for its first 164 measures, then – significantly – manages to "achieve" a one-flat signature with Rotation 7 at m. 165, letter K.)

The contemplative objects (musical motives) in Ex. 11.3 – and throughout the symphony – may be represented even more basically. Example 11.4 provides some illustrations of this, and they are given here to suggest that the whole symphony may be construed as a contemplation of the constituent elements of, primarily, the D Dorian scale – fortified by an additional contemplation of the neighboring C major and related D minor. The D scale can appear with or without B♭, and, similarly, the C scale can sometimes be modally inflected with a raised fourth scale step, F♯. Needless to say, the D Dorian scale is subdivisible into its own constructive elements (Ex. 11.4, system 2): first, the initial span from $\hat{1}$ to $\hat{5}$ (which Sibelius since the 1890s had argued was the characteristically Finnish pentachord), thus producing a grounding fifth; second, this fifth may expand upward with a complementary fourth, a to d (our fourth motive), or it may stretch upward only to the seventh scale step, c, and curl back through a motivic third, $\hat{7}$–$\hat{6}$–$\hat{5}$, c–b–a – the characteristic Sibelius "minor third ideogram" (also sounded as $\hat{3}$–$\hat{2}$–$\hat{1}$ in minor) that underpins so much of his work.[22] This move from D only to scale step C of course also suggests the potential for the realization of C major, A minor, and so on. The remainder of Ex. 11.4 suggests ways in which the contemplative objects may be expanded, filled in, inverted, unfolded in sequences, shadowed by underthirds, and the like.

Many of these interrelationships among the symphony's ideas are obvious. Example 11.5a–d shows a few instances – almost randomly selected – of how the idea of the rising modal seventh rounded off with the falling third (the launch-figure of the finale's *telos*) is pre-echoed in some of the earlier movements: Ex. 11.5a is from the first movement, mm. 29–37 (this is the final version of the motive that in a non-Sixth-Symphony context Sibelius, c. 1919 (?), had labeled "winter?"); Ex. 11.5b is also from the first movement, mm. 85–89 (beginning 2 mm. before letter C); Ex. 11.5c is a main idea of the third movement, mm. 9–13; Ex. 11.5d is the consequent phrase from the finale's incipit (mm. 5–8). Such instances reinforce the claim that the whole symphony is a growth toward the finale's peak moment. In his 1993 study of the Sixth, Murtomäki cited several other "basic motive" moments similar to those in Ex. 11.5.[23] Such interrelationships pervade the symphony, and they are easily multiplied.

[22] I have discussed the "minor-third ideogram" in the chapter, "Sibelius," in *The Nineteenth-Century Symphony*, ed. D. Kern Holoman (New York: Schirmer, 1997), pp. 417–49 (e.g., p. 425).

[23] Murtomäki, *Symphonic Unity*, p. 200. Note especially the helpful Exx. 85–90, indicating inversions, retrogrades, and so on.

Ex. 11.4 Scales, scalar segments, intervals, and chords central to the Sixth Symphony

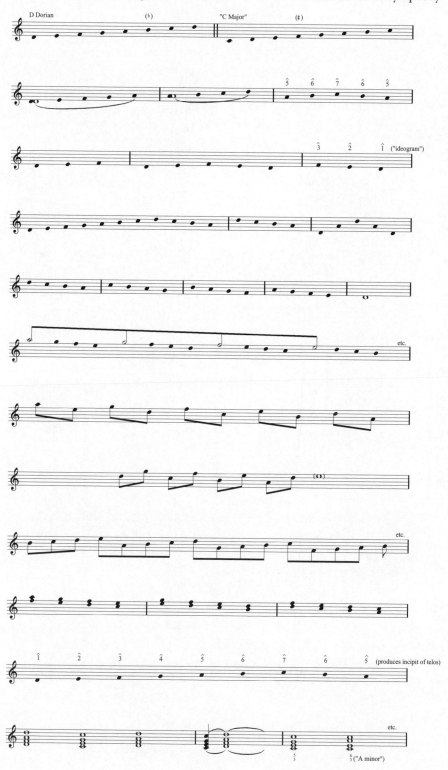

Ex. 11.5a   Symphony No. 6, first movement, mm. 29–37

Ex. 11.5b   Symphony No. 6, first movement, mm. 85–89

Ex. 11.5c   Symphony No. 6, third movement, mm. 9–13

Ex. 11.5d   Symphony No. 6, fourth movement, mm. 5–8

III

With the *telos*-idea and its motivic components in mind, we may now proceed to a more orderly discussion of the finale. While the mid-movement motivic ideas in Ex. 11.3 represent the first achievement of a conceptual fullness, those in Ex. 11.6, the opening of this finale, supply most of the raw materials for the peak moment, although they are not yet sounded in *telos* order. First among these is the c–g descending fourth in mm. 1–2, here heard an octave higher (c^3–g^2) than in its later *telos* presentation (Ex. 11.3, mm. 76–78). In measure 3 Sibelius introduced several ascending fourth leaps (inversions of the initial descending fourth), not yet filled in with passing notes as in the *telos*, but descending in stepwise sequences, just as they will do at the end of Rotation 3. We might additionally observe in Ex. 11.6 that the stepwise sequence of rising fourths in mm. 3–4 itself can suggest a larger (motivic) descending fourth, d^2–a^1. Measures 1–4 constitute a thematic antecedent (recalling the opening, introductory phrase of Tchaikovsky's *Serenade for Strings*) in the winds and upper strings.[24] Here the key is C major strongly colored by a virtually co-equal A minor shadow. Its consequent, a characteristically Sibelian antiphonal response in the lower strings, appears in mm. 5–8 and settles on C major. Led by the upper cellos, this consequent introduces (at least within this movement) what will become the motivic launch of the *telos* idea: the stepwise, rising modal seventh, a–b–c^1–d^1–e^1–f^1–g^1 (here Aeolian), followed in m. 6 by a descending minor third, here g^1–f^1–e^1.[25]

Should we consider Rotation 1 to end with the C major perfect authentic cadence in m. 8? The idea certainly arises, since what follows in mm. 9–16 is a recycling of the initial, periodic idea. My preference,

[24] The Tchaikovsky observation was suggested to me by Joseph C. Kraus. Was Sibelius aware of this allusion? And if so – and more to the point – was it one that he might have expected us to recognize? To be sure, clear evidence connecting Sibelius to the *Serenade* is lacking. Still, many other features of the sonic surface, color, and texture of the Tchaikovsky *Serenade* (from 1880) seem to foreshadow similar aspects in much of the Sibelius oeuvre. Compare, for example, the general texture, melodic contour, and musical "feel" of the opening of the third movement of the *Serenade* with portions of Sibelius's Seventh Symphony – e.g., with p. 12, mm. 4ff (beginning 7 mm. after E) of the orchestral score published by Hansen.

Sibelius's "Russian connection" has been a central point of debate in the past few years: see, for example, Malcolm Hamrick Brown, "Perspectives on the Early Symphonies. The Russian Connection Redux," in *Proceedings from the First International Jean Sibelius Conference. Helsinki, August 1990*, ed. Eero Tarasti (Helsinki: Sibelius Academy, 1995), pp. 21–30. For this reason, I hasten to add that such similarities apply to idiosyncratic string sonority (an attitude toward the immediacy of orchestral "sound itself"), local chordal and melodic detail, short-range voice leading, and the like – not to large-scale structure, in which respect, to be sure, Sibelius differs markedly from the Russian composers.

[25] This relationship has been noticed by other commentators as well. See, e.g., Murtomäki, *Symphonic Unity*, p. 227 (Ex. 109).

Ex. 11.6   Symphony No. 6, fourth movement, mm. 1–9

IV

however, is to view the initial eight-bar period and its slightly varied repetition (mm. 9–16) as a single rotation. In the first place, the second statement (mm. 9–16) complements the first – without significant expansion in length. In addition, Sibelius echoes and expands the repetitive pattern of mm. 1–16 as a whole (two statements of the antecedent and consequent) in mm. 17–55 (one statement plus enlarged restatement). Perhaps we might strike a balance between these two "rotational" views by considering mm. 1–16 to consist of two complementary subrotations 1a and 1b, each consisting of an antecedent–consequent pair, the second of which is already subject to reshaping and, hence, already displaying the potential for further germination. If one prefers, of course, what I am calling Rotations 1a (mm. 1–8) and 1b (mm. 9–16) may also be construed as two separate rotations.

In Rotation 2a–b (mm. 17–55, elided into Rotation 3) the antecedent–consequent pairs are recycled with variations and accretions: the rotations are starting to grow. This is particularly true of the second pair (2b, beginning in m. 25), which branches out remarkably. The first evidence of growth involves an evasion of the consequent–cadence (mm. 29–32) and a move away from the implied C major and toward the "shadow," A minor (beginning with the new flute–bassoon phrase, snowflake-gentle, at the upbeat to m. 34). After a varied repetition of this new phrase (mm. 38–40) we encounter the production of two more new limbs. The first is the double sounding of the woodwind triplet motive (based on fourths), mm. 41–44, 45–48, that will be heard again at the center of the *telos*. (This is what Tawaststjerna claimed as the "ritornello" idea; more properly understood, it is the second melodic link in the thematic sketches from 1915, as shown in Exx. 11.1a and b.) The last of the new limbs produced in the expanded Rotation 2b – and this will prove to be crucial to the present interpretation of this movement – is a new, sequentially scampering conclusion (beginning at rehearsal letter B, on the third beat of m. 49 and coming to rest only at m. 55), which renounces the momentarily tonicized A minor to move to the true tonic, D minor. This idea's consistent harmonic function (here and elsewhere) is to secure the "real" tonic of the movement, D Dorian/minor, within a movement that had begun off-tonic, on C. Thus Rotations 1a–b and 2a–b, taken together, represent a growth toward the actual tonic; harmonically they serve as an anacrusis or preparation for the tonic arrival at m. 55.

Recognizing this last-mentioned theme (mm. 49–55) as a continuation and concluding gesture is important, for the interpretive decision made about the implications of this thematic and harmonic event indelibly affects one's analysis of the rest of the movement. Prior analyses have stumbled, I think, in mistaking m. 49 for the opening of a new structural section, an interpretation that, in my view, runs into difficulties later in the movement. By the time that we reach m. 55 (which I regard as the beginning of Rotation 3) some commentators have placed us within a complementary central B section of a ternary form (usually one that had started in m. 49, letter B).[26] Such a perception of a "new, contrasting section" is not surprising: the sense of musical determination at m. 49, along with the changed texture and the rapid attainment of D minor, does contrast in important ways with the preceding music.

But we can be quite certain that Sibelius did not think of the idea at m. 49 as an opening gesture. As we have seen, his 1914–1915 sketch entries had placed it unmistakably as a sequential, "third-link" continuation to the music that precedes it (Exx. 11.1a and b), and in one of these sketches (Ex. 11.1b) he even seems to have labeled this dotted-rhythm/syncopated idea as a "mellantema" or "connecting theme" (literally, "between-theme"). Even apart from the "mellantema" designation (which, as discussed above, cannot be considered certain), the musical evidence in the sketches shows that Sibelius consistently conceived the sequential figure as the continuation and conclusion of a larger idea, not as the beginning of a new one on its own. Finally, we may also perceive that within the Sixth's finale this "mellantema" idea will serve the same concluding function in Rotations 3 (mm. 55–83) and 4 (mm. 83–114), as an idea rounding off the *telos* complex (mm. 78–83 and, varied and expanded, 108–114). In all cases the "mellantema" finishes one rotation and merges smoothly into the onset of the next one. The evidence, then, is clear: this figure is a rotation concluder, not a section opener, and for this reason the structural and conceptual divisions of this movement that I am proposing here deviate from all prior analyses of which I am aware.

So far, within Rotations 1a–b and 2a–b we have been concerned with a process of motivic ramification. The upcoming Rotation 3 (mm. 55–83) is most productively construed not as a large contrasting unit but as the continued growth and addition of further accretions to the motives established in Rotations 1a–b and 2a–b – along with, of course, a clear centering onto the *telos* key, D Dorian or D minor. Within Rotation 3 Sibelius reshapes the principle of the double antecedent–consequent into a double articulation of the *telos* idea. Rotation 3 unfolds in three phases. The first is a round of *preparation* and concretization of the "new" D tonic (mm. 55–64; this preparation idea, of course – with its prominent "Phrygian" $e\flat^1$ – is that found in the 1915 sketch transcribed in Ex. 11.1c).

---

[26] For example, Ernst Tanzberger, *Jean Sibelius. Eine Monographie* (Wiesbaden: Breitkopf & Härtel, 1962), pp. 130–32.

Characteristically, this idea, here and elsewhere, bridges the end of the preceding rotation to the more *telos*-related ideas that follow. The second phase is a thematic *anticipation* of the *telos* – especially its emphatic, vigorously articulated rising seventh *sul G*, suggesting, perhaps, that the *telos* idea is "about to flower" (beginning 5 mm. after letter C, mm. 65 [with upbeat]–72, presented in strong, descending sequences). The third phase articulates a full *statement* of the *telos*-theme-complex proper (beginning 1 m. after letter D, mm. 73 [with upbeat]–83) – once labelled in a separate sketch, we recall, as "the [feminine] pine spirit and the wind" (Ex. 11.2b; see also the sketches in Exx. 11.1a and b; the whole statement phase of Rotation 3 is transcribed in Ex. 11.3). This may be understood as the first uncovering of the central thematic block of the entire symphony, the first revelation of the core idea as conceived in the sketches.

But an even stronger climactic moment – a second "wave" leading to a fuller sonic disclosure of the guiding d–C–d idea – is reserved for Rotation 4 (starting 1 m. after E, mm. 83–114), which recycles and intensifies the material of Rotation 3. To be sure, this Rotation 4 *telos* is grandly produced, with more urgent momentum and a more impressive sonority, but it is not necessarily to be heard as a purely positive attainment: at the point of maximal strain – the *telos* phase, launched in the center of m. 100 (8 mm. after letter F, a more severe sweep of winter wind, straining the pine to the utmost? the spiritual revelation of the essence of wind itself?) – the initial rising seventh is lacking. What we experience here is the sudden absence of an important thematic strand (mm. 101–03). Instead of the rising-seventh figure one encounters a drop to *piano*, followed immediately by an immense crescendo gust, *piano* to *fortissimo*, whose thematic content encompasses only the descending-third portion of the *telos* idea.

In brief, this shuddering arrival of the *telos* complex is simultaneously marked by signs of its own liquidation – a fleeting, climactic presence marked disturbingly by a simultaneous absence. Even within the climactic moment of Rotation 4 the phase of dissolution or decay has set in. Here the initial *telos* launch figure is obliterated by a tidal wave of pure sonority – either an onrush of elemental, non-thematic *Klang* or a moment of sudden loss, a thematic void overcome only by sheer momentum and will power. We should also notice that in its expanded concluding figure (starting at letter G, mm. 108–114) Rotation 4 begins to spin off in different thematic directions, as if some decentering principle has deflected it away from the course of simple repetition.

All this is elided smoothly into Rotation 5, which now follows (7 mm. after G, mm. 114–146), and in many ways it continues the sonic accumulation begun in Rotations 3 and 4 – only now operating under the sign of overripeness or decay. The rotation begins as if trying to recover these *telos*-related ideas which were already beginning to slip away at the end of Rotation 4. In Rotation 5 the *telos statement* proper is no longer attainable: instead, Sibelius produces music that seems to struggle (in "developmental" fragments) to produce even its *anticipation* (which it finally does at letter I, mm. 130–36). But instead of ushering in the *telos* statement one more time, this anticipation spins off catastrophically in whole-tone and chromatic sequential decay and heavy imbalance (mm. 136–43),[27] all the while gathering energy in a powerful *molto crescendo*. By mm. 144–45 this produces a massive crisis of sonority and tonality. (Measure 144 is mistakenly labeled a second letter I, not the correct letter J, in some editions.) Here Sibelius leads us into a triple *fortissimo* arpeggiated B half-diminished seventh chord, motivically representing a shattering of the *telos* statement idea. This is immediately followed by a shattering of pulse itself with the sudden break at the first beat of m. 146 and the ensuing two bars of *poco rallentando* on an F–A dyad. (Compare this sonority with that which had begun the first movement, m. 1 – a wrenching reminder of the symphony's point of origin.) There can be no doubt: mm. 144–45 articulate the single point of maximal tension within the finale – and, correspondingly, within the entire symphony. The most compelling *telos* of this finale, it seems, is one of crisis, not one of affirmation. At this crisis point of shattered statement, the finale's musical processes lose once and for all what they had attained – the *telos* moments of the earlier "waves" in Rotations 3 and 4.

We are now in a position to suggest a hermeneutic interpretation of the finale. By mm. 144–45 we have encountered three moments of thematic and textural *telos* – in Rotations 3, 4, and 5 – each of which has become progressively more intense, more disturbing. The initial grasping of the "pine spirit and wind" *telos* idea in Rotation 3 (Ex. 11.3) is the most untroubled – and indeed, it is the statement that can be most closely related to Sibelius's early sketch ideas. The second production of the *telos* – within a thickened, more urgent Rotation 4 – may at first strike one as even more "splendid" sounding. But that splendor is simultaneously marked by the thematizing of absence and loss as the *telos* incipit suddenly (though momentarily) finds itself without a voice, in the midst of an even more vehement surge of wind. This loss persists with the continued accumulation of Rotation 5 – the crisis rotation. It is here that the positive features passed through in the earlier rotations drive to a negative textural *telos* marking the inevitability of decay and loss. The final

---

[27] This moment of chromatic decay was also among the earliest melodic ideas sketched for the work: see the final paragraph of n. 17 above.

and strongest *telos* of the succession of three – that of Rotation 5 – brings us past our once-splendid peaks to an over-ripened *telos* moment of self-destruction. With the crisis point of mm. 144–45 we are now past our high noon: from this point onward the shadows will fall in the opposite direction. The ability to grasp the *telos* is a thing of the past, and we now lie in its wreckage.

In Rotation 6a–b (beginning *poco rallentando* in mm. 146–47 with two bars of anacrusis followed by the rotation proper, *allegro molto*, mm. 148–165, elided at the end into the next rotation) the motives begin to disintegrate into their original constituent parts. Here we find no more *telos* music but rather the return of the incipit idea from Rotation 1, melodically and tonally distorted. In the first antecedent–consequent pair, for instance (mm. 148–54), we are now led from a "distorted F major" (more accurately, a six-three chord over an A bass in the cellos) to a weak-beat perfect authentic cadence on B♭ major (m. 154) and another momentary loss of pulse (the fermata at the end of the measure). Complementarily, the restatement, Rotation 6b (mm. 155–65), displays a deeply-shadowed antecedent (B♭ major/G minor) and decayed consequent (mm. 159–65), although that consequent does manage to reinstate the *telos* tonic, D minor, at the rotation's end (m. 165).

Sibelius's planting of the new key signature (one flat) at letter K, m. 165, marks an important moment of articulation. The composer is now preparing us for the symphony's eventual dissolution into silence. In the reading proposed here, Rotation 7 encompasses the block of music from mm. 165 to 189 (as usual, with elision into the next block). Harmonically, its crucial event is the decay of the tonic D minor into the "false comfort" of its major mediant, F major. The move to the major mode (for example, in mm. 169ff, surrounding letter L), along with a full-throated restatement of the finale's opening melody (nine measures after L, mm. 181–88), may superficially suggest a moment of renewed attainment or affirmation, but the point, surely, is that such an utterance is now both short-lived and permissible only outside the tonic. As such the thematic recurrence here may be understood more as a heartfelt farewell – within a general environment of dissolution – than as a sign of renewal.

In terms of its phrase rhetoric, Rotation 7, the music of letters K and L, is subdivisible into three parts: 8+8+(4+4) measures. With a thin, transparent orchestration (the eighth-note pulse in the harp recalls the preparatory, "positive" phases of Rotations 3 and 4 [mm. 55 and 83 – cf. Rotation 5, m. 115]), the first eight measures at first stabilize the sober D minor but immediately suggest its loss with a move toward F major in the concluding half. The next eight bars (letter L, mm. 173–180) take up the fragmentary incipit motive with more determination and energy (*Allegro assai*), all within a local context of accumulation and further preparation. Here the tonic is a confident F major at the outset, but that "false security" is immediately challenged by the non-diatonic contortions of an unsettling new triplet figure in the cellos. As a result, when the arrival point at m. 181 is reached – the *forte* restatement of the finale's original antecedent–consequent melody, though now with a consequent phrase that does not attain its cadence – the established F major is prominently shadowed by its submediant, D minor. Within the larger context of decline, the *telos* tonic, D minor, is being relegated here to subsidiary status. Its continued existence on its own terms is being called into question.

Rotation 8 (letters M, N, and the first part of O, mm. 189–221) recycles and expands the materials of Rotation 7 through immediate block repetition and dynamic and registral intensification. Thus mm. 189–96 correspond to mm. 173–80 within Rotation 7 (with undermining triplet figure), and the eight measures are immediately repeated an octave higher in mm. 197–204. The arrival point here, once again, is the *forte*, antecedent–consequent melody (F major shadowed by D minor, mm. 205–12), at first sounded with a non-cadential consequent (as in mm. 181–88). This is followed at once by a *mezzo-forte (dolce)/diminuendo* restatement (mm. 213–20), in which the consequent phrase is finally brought to a perfect authentic cadence on the "off-tonic" F major. The satisfaction provided by this major-mode cadence at mm. 219–20, the passing through a notational double barline, and the instant relaxation of the tempo into a *doppio più lento* on a reverberating F–A dyad (mm. 221–23 – once again, compare this with the opening of the first movement, m. 1) should not distract us from the structural significance of the moment at hand: by this point we have lost not only the themes of the unfurled *telos*, but also its forward-driving tempo, fullness of texture, and D minor tonic.

It is also important to recognize that in the latter half of Rotation 8 the thematic and chordal substance of mm. 205–20 correspond almost perfectly to that of mm. 1–16 – that is, to that of Rotation 1a–b. Setting aside matters of texture, the two principal differences between the corresponding passages are: in Rotation 8 the governing key is the "off-tonic" F major, not the initial "off-tonic" C major; and in Rotation 8 the first "consequent" phrase (mm. 209–12, beginning nine measures after letter N) is not yet brought to a perfect authentic cadence (as was the case in mm. 5–8). The unambiguous relationship between the two sixteen-measure sections is secured by Sibelius's return to the "Rotation 1b" variant of the antecedent melody in mm. 213–16 (beginning four meas-

Ex. 11.7a   Symphony No. 6, fourth movement, mm. 17–20

Ex. 11.7b   Symphony No. 6, fourth movement, mm. 224–26

ures before letter O; compare these measures with mm. 9–12). Thus the concluding portion of Rotation 8 (mm. 205–20) functions as a rhetorical (not a tonal) reprise of the whole of Rotation 1a–b (mm. 1–16). It would appear that achieving this moment of rhetorical–reprise correspondence, with its satisfying, though off-tonic, major cadence, was the central point of the post-crisis music from Rotation 6 (m. 146) onward.

Recognizing this attainment of a brief rhetorical reprise in mm. 205–20, surrounding letter O, not only helps us to grasp the music from Rotation 6 to Rotation 8, but it also sheds light on the *doppio più lento* conclusion that follows (mm. 221–56). This final section might be regarded as a dissolving Rotation 9, one of whose points is to demonstrate the valedictory abandonment of the rotational principle altogether. We might consider the compositional logic here along the following lines. The rhetorical reprise had brought back the ideas of Rotation 1a–b, and reprises in general, we might suppose, have a built-in drive to continue, to provide an even larger zone of rhetorical symmetry at the close of a movement. In other words, just as Rotation 1a–b had proceeded directly to Rotation 2 (beginning in m. 17), with its melodically undular variant of the antecedent melody in the oboe, we might suppose that the reprise in Rotation 8 would lead to the same figure at the onset of Rotation 9.

But this is just what this reprise cannot do amid so many signs of dissolution: the off-tonic cadence, the shrinkage of F major into a dyad, the enervated dynamics and texture, the shattering of the pulse back to *doppio più lento*, and so on. Instead of encountering the next link of the rotational series, the twisting oboe figure heard at mm. 17–18 (Ex. 11.7a), we find instead, at half-tempo, the free *inversion* of its incipit in mm. 224–25 (Ex. 11.7b).[28] Moreover, this opening leads not to a discernible tracking through the material of Rotation 2a–b but to the sounding of a relatively free, hymnic epilogue. Once past the inverted incipit figure, Sibelius seems to uncouple the music from the rotational principle, although it may be that he intended the figure in the flutes, mm. 240–42 – which presents a poignant shift downward into a fleetingly articulated C♯ minor (♯vii!), immediately "corrected" back to D minor – to recall dimly the flute figure in mm. 33–40 or the subsequent twisting figure in mm. 41–48. By and large, though, Sibelius rejects the "normal" rotational process here in favor of freely valedictory utterances. We might understand this as a farewell not only to the finale but also to the whole symphony, into whose first-movement, D minor textures this epilogue is reabsorbed at the end.

This final, *doppio più lento* section is something of a "twilight" epilogue: it features dying glimmers, individual memories, and strong emotional responses. And at the end it fades into the blackness of silence – a silence that Sibelius provided with its own fermata (m. 256, beat 4), surely as a sign of permanence.

IV

In the reading presented here, the finale of the Sixth Symphony is neither in significant dialogue with the sonata principle nor is it satisfactorily describable as some sort of rounded, symmetrical ABA′ ternary-block structure, even though certain features of statement and reprise are locatable within the movement. It is best understood, I think, as an experiential process, as a touchstone of Sibelius's late-style rotational structures, particularly as merged with the principle of teleological genesis – the rotational production (then loss, in this case) of a peak moment, perhaps identifiable here as a spiritualized representation of elemental Finnish landscape, a wintry struggle between two formidable pagan gods, "the [feminine] pine spirit and the wind." An awareness of compositional genesis is here taken to be one of the central clues guiding analysis and interpretation.

[28] This motivic relationship was first noted by Gerald Abraham, "The Symphonies," p. 34, with examples on p. 195. Rather than interpreting his observation, Abraham was content to note the relationship only in the abstract – presumably as a sign of concealed motivic interrelationships within the symphony. As he noted on p. 34, he was responding here to Cecil Gray who had argued in the 1930s that this concluding passage of the Sixth "appears to be an entirely fresh line of thought, bearing no relation to anything that has gone before." My exx. 11.7a–b essentially reproduce Abraham's examples on p. 195.

And finally, apart from the question of whether the details of the discussion here might or might not be individually persuasive – for surely other listeners to the work will have different dialogues with it – we at least hope that Sibelius might have been pleased for us to meditate upon the process structure of the Sixth's finale as a kind of elemental archetype: a natural cycle rising to a peak (and into a centered tonic, D Dorian), then declining into extinction, in the manner, perhaps, of a day, a season, a year, or a person's life. In thus contemplating the general shape of rise, full flowering, and inevitable decay, Sibelius, as nature-mystic, may have been inviting us to brood on the elemental cycles that structure our own lives. "These symphonies of mine" wrote Sibelius in 1918, "are more confessions of faith than are my other works."[29] Nowhere more, I would propose, than in the finale of the Sixth.

[29] Quoted in my *Sibelius. Symphony No. 5*, p. 55.

12 Continuity and design in the Seventh Symphony

Edward Laufer

The Seventh Symphony is widely regarded as Sibelius's greatest achievement.[1] "One might be tempted to describe it as the dome mounted on the granite structure of the earlier symphonies . . . It is the climax of his creative work and its music is a concentration of the essence of the other symphonies' best qualities."[2] The Symphony was first performed on 24 March 1924 at a concert conducted by Sibelius in a program that also included his First Symphony and Violin Concerto. He had completed the work earlier that month: "on the 2nd March, at night, as I entered in my diary, I completed *Fantasia Sinfonica* – that was what I at first thought of calling my Seventh Symphony in one movement."[3] The work had been many years in the making, and had undergone various changes of direction compositionally, for six years earlier the composer had clearly thought of the work as a *symphonic* composition, rather than as a *fantasia*: "The VIIth Symphony. Joy of life and vitality with appassionato passages. In three movements – the last an 'Hellenic rondo' . . . In regard to Symphonies VI and VII the plans may possibly be altered according to the development of the musical ideas. As usual, I am a slave to my themes and submit to their demands."[4] But the compositional evolution of the Symphony would entail a study in itself. My purpose here will be to consider the work in its final state: to consider its often noted unique formal layout and, through study of the underlying

[1] This chapter is based on a paper read at the First International Jean Sibelius Conference, at the University of Helsinki, Finland, on 24 August 1990.
[2] Simon Parmet, *The Symphonies of Sibelius*, trans. Kingsley A. Hart (London: Cassel, 1959), p. 121.
[3] Karl Ekman, *Jean Sibelius*, trans. Edward Birse (Helsinki: Holger Schildts Förlag, 1935), p. 254.
[4] Ibid., pp. 251–52. I am indebted to Veijo Murtomäki for pointing out that in the original Swedish edition of Erik

Tawaststjerna's *Sibelius*, vol. IV, pp. 270–72 (omitted in Robert Layton's English translation), Sibelius's own description of his plans for his Symphonies Five, Six, and Seven is quoted. According to his remarks, which date from 1918 – i.e. about six years before the Seventh Symphony was completed – the "Hellenic rondo" idea refers to his original conception of a third movement, corresponding to the section beginning at m. 285 of the final version, which I have termed "scherzo."

voice leading in order to reveal motivic continuity, association, and contrasts, to consider how single movements are linked together to form a complex whole. Indeed, with regard to the synthesis of continuity and contrast in a symphonic work, one may well note Hans Keller's astute observation that the essence of contrast in symphonic thought is not so much that between different themes, but rather that between *expositional* sections (stable, in a foreground sense) and *developmental* sections (unstable or modulatory, in a foreground sense).[5]

The large-scale formal design

Parmet refers to the design of the Symphony as overflowing with "a host of distinguished details, growing out of one another and complementary to one another, finally uniting to form a whole according to an ingenious and extremely complicated pattern."[6] However, a key to the extraordinary and altogether unique formal design of the Symphony may be perhaps, found in Sibelius's 1918 remark quoted above: "an Hellenic rondo." For although Sibelius was thereby referring specifically to the *third movement* as initially conceived, one might stretch a point and extend the rondo idea to the Symphony as a whole. In this sense (Ex. 12.1), the main section would correspond to the refrain of this quasi-rondo: the three occurrences of this refrain would be the main central sections towards and around which the other sections gravitate (the "expositional" sections in Keller's terms).[7] "Hellenic" would perhaps denote a noble severity: the classic Grecian simplicity and grandeur which characterizes this "rondo" refrain in particular, and indeed the Symphony in general.

The design mapped out in Ex. 12.1 obviously challenges traditional aspects of symphonic form. There is no sonata form, no opening allegro section, no second subject, and no development section as such. If one considers a classical rondo (as in a sense I have suggested) then it is extraordinary that, as a C section, there should be an entire scherzo movement enclosed.[8] Moreover, that this scherzo is in the tonic key creates an effect not of a *contrasting* C section within a vast rondo framework, but of a separate movement altogether – an effect altering the formal perception of the whole. A sense of a chain of individual movements is suggested thereby

[5] Hans Keller, "The State of the Symphony: Not Only Maxwell Davies's," *Tempo*, June 1978, pp. 6–11.
[6] Parmet, *The Symphonies of Sibelius*, pp. 127–28.

[7] Compare the design proposed by Parmet, ibid., p. 129.
[8] The last movement of Mozart's Piano Concerto in E♭, K.271, is perhaps somewhat similar.

Ex. 12.1

Formal Design

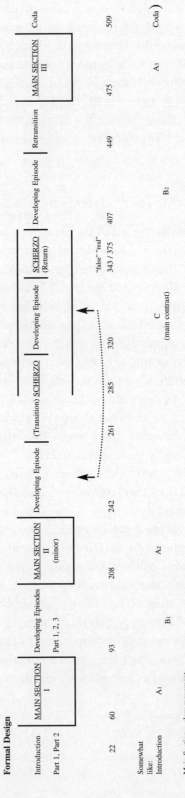

– not that of a single "rondo." But if the three main sections correspond to a rondo refrain, they also constitute, in character, a recurrent slow movement. The intervening developing episodes (compare Keller's "developmental" contrasts) correspond in character, but not in formal structure, to a fast movement which has been broken up and interspersed. One of these episodes (mm. 242ff.) is restated (mm. 320ff.) to become the middle section, or "quasi-trio," of the scherzo, binding the scherzo to the whole.

Consideration of this unique and highly original formal design gives rise to a number of questions as to the evolution of the "symphony" in the twentieth century. For one thing, a classical aspect of symphonic thought is that there would be at least two or three different characters, typically portrayed in the individual movements, such as allegro, adagio, scherzo. As noted, here the main section corresponds to a slow movement, the episodes to an allegro; and there is a scherzo as well. But while conserving these classical divisions, Sibelius intermingles and cross-cuts them in a bold refashioning of the classical design. Secondly, by redistributing the symphonic contrasts (the expositional versus the developmental – in Keller's terms) – that is, by *not* concentrating the developmental passages in one larger section as in a sonata form movement, but by placing them throughout so as to *introduce* and thereby enhance the expositional sections, a sense of continuous growth, cumulation, and completion of sections is achieved. Thus, the introduction leads to the main section I; the developing episodes (mm. 93ff.) to the main section II; the developing episode and transition (mm. 242ff.) to the scherzo I; the next developing episode to the scherzo II; and finally – the long delay creating a magnificent sense of arrival – the developing episode and retransition (mm. 407–74) lead to the final peroration, the main section III. Thus the effect of the formal design, with its synthesis of contrasts, is to create a single entity, one vast sweep, of cumulation, of renewal and completion. A voice-leading sketch of the Symphony as a whole will be shown in Ex. 12.27.

Main section I

Example 12.2 (p. 356) sketches the main section (mm. 60ff.), which may be regarded as providing the motivic basis and source for the whole Symphony. Certain motivic features are illustrated in Ex. 12.3. As in Ex. 12.3-1, the neighbor-note and fourth-figure (circled) is placed upon a middleground rising scale figure (Ex. 12.3-2). The fourth-figure is fulfilled, so to speak, just at the c^2 melodic high point, composed as a *filled-in* fourth (mm. 70–80, Exx. 12.3-1, 3-2, and 3-3). The rising scale figure

Ex. 12.2

Ex. 12.3

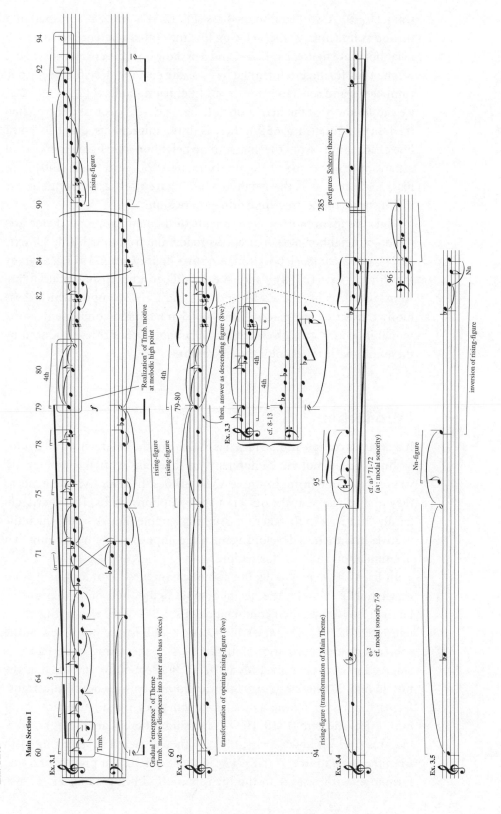

(mm. 60–79) is worked into the bass (Ex. 12.3-1, mm. 82–85); then into the top voice (mm. 90–91), closing the line with a reference to the d^2–c^2 neighbor-note figure. Ex. 12.3-4 and 3-5 show how the rising scale-figure will be transformed to form the basis of the ensuing developing episode (mm. 94ff.) and scherzo (mm. 285ff.). Returning to Exx. 12.2-1 and 2-2, we can follow how the neighbor-note figure d^1–c^1 becomes a third, then the fourth-figure (mm. 65ff.): there is thus a miraculous, point-to-point line of continuity from the unassuming neighbor-note figure to its broad expansion as the fourth-figure (mm. 80–92). And as is shown in Ex. 12.3-3, it is as if the neighbor-note figure itself came about as the closing notes of the preceding fifth-progression!

Thus the main motivic components of the main section's theme are: the d^1–c^1 neighbor-note figure; its broadening to a fourth (m. 80, Exx. 12.2-4 and 2-5); its elaboration as a turn-figure (mm. 71–73, shown by the brace, Ex. 12.2-4); and the middleground rising scale-figure (mm. 60–80, as in Exx. 12.2-4 and 2-5, and Ex. 12.3) upon which these motivic features are placed. Another characteristic component is the modal inflection to a♭, b♭, e♭, and f♯. The modal sonorities produced by these chromatic tones color the entire work.

Introduction

If an overall compositional idea has to do with the emergence and cumulation of these motivic components in the main section, one may ask where they came from. Example 12.4 outlines these motivic elements as they first appeared at the outset of the Symphony. In Ex. 12.4 they seem hardly "motives," but rather unassuming, simple figures from which the motives and themes develop: again, the compositional intent being that of cumulation and transformation.

In Ex. 12.4 we may note: the rising scale-figure, beginning as if from nowhere (Ex. 12.4-1); the neighbor-note figure, becoming the fourth-figures (Ex. 12.4-2); their combination (Ex. 12.4-4); the elaborating turn-figure (Ex. 12.4-5). Examples 12.4-7 and 4-8 illustrate only a few of the subsequent transformations: in Ex. 12.4-7, the rising scale-figure is enlarged to become mm. 14ff. and 22ff., subsequently simplified as the fifth in mm. 27 and 28; in m. 94 the developing episode beautifully transforms this rising figure; a free inversion gives rise to the motives at mm. 148ff. and mm. 154ff. How varied and different are these transformations, and yet how remarkably may they be heard as springing forth from the same source! And Ex. 12.4-8 suggests a similar process of transformation with respect to the turn-figure: following along Ex. 12.4-8,

Ex. 12.4

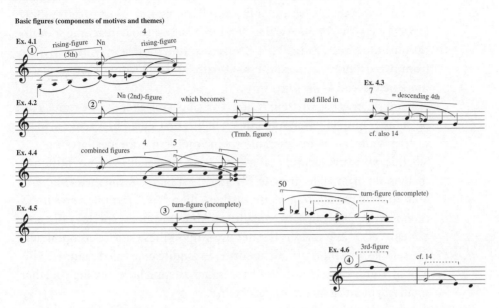

m. 148 can also be heard as a transformation of this turn-figure. A point to be noted is that there are only a few basic figures – just because these express a classic simplicity, they lend themselves to far-reaching modifications. Moreover, as Ex. 12.4-8 suggests, one motive may be derivable from two or more sources: it is as if paths starting from different places nonetheless lead to the same spot.

Santeri Levas has written: "Cecil Gray and a number of other musicologists after him have remarked that Sibelius first stated his thematic ideas in fragments, so as to assemble them into actual themes later on . . . Sibelius quite categorically said: 'That's not true at all. I do not build my themes out of small fragments.'"[9] As Ex. 12.4 suggests, the themes are not built out of small fragments: rather, they have certain *elements in common*. The basic figures constitute a kind of source repertory of components; all of the various themes draw upon these source components, reassemble and *transform* them, often in a quite concealed manner. This way of composing is not at all the same as somehow putting together small fragments to make longer themes.

Examples 12.5–12.8 sketch the introduction. Example 12.5-1 illustrates, step by step, the harmonic-contrapuntal basis of mm. 1–9. The top voice implies a neighbor-note motion d^2–c^2; as in Exx. 12.5-2 and 5-3, the neighbor-note figure d^2–c^2 is at first only implied (the high d^2 is not yet present), then explicitly stated (mm. 7–8), and then continues, to give rise to the descending fourth c^2–g^1 (mm. 8–13). This process exemplifies the compositional idea of gradual emergence, for, as shown in Exx. 12.5-4 and 5-5, extending the neighbor-note figure in this way gives rise, in concealed and artful manner, to the trombone motive of the main section (compare also Exx. 12.6-1 and 6-2)! This is quite astonishing: what a magical connection – that the trombone motive should underlie the opening, mm. 1–21, in this way! The modal component, already noted in the main section, is also foreshadowed (Exx. 12.5-1: $e\flat^1$; and 12.5-3: $e\flat^1$, $a\flat^1$, $b\flat^1$). If these are modal details here, they will later assume independence, as part of the principle of emerging and gradual realization. Example 12.6 sketches the introduction, part I, to m. 21, the top stave indicating how the trombone motive of the main section is magnificently prefigured, in enlargement, in the middleground.

An idea behind the second part of the introduction (Ex. 12.7), from m. 22 on, is to set the tone for the whole symphony by emphasizing an almost static slow tempo from which to gain momentum: the sense of

[9] Santeri Levas, *Sibelius. A Personal Portrait*, trans. Percy M. Young (London: Dent, 1972), p. 88.

Ex. 12.5

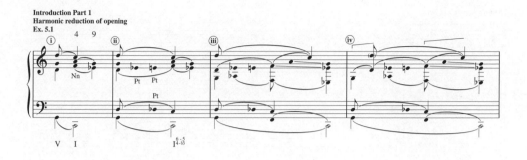

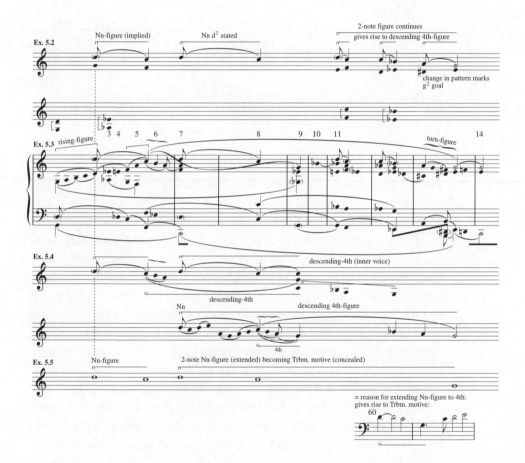

Ex. 12.6

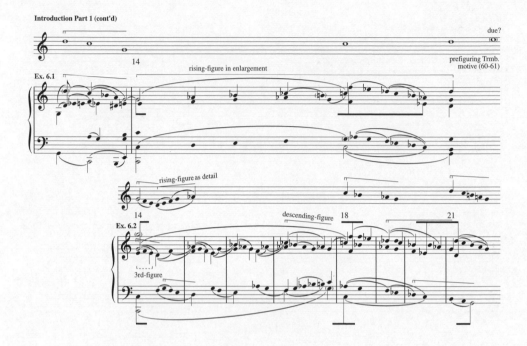

gradual emergence. This sense is also expressed in the slow rise from the lower to the higher register (m. 45) which will be picked up only in the final main section III (m. 500). The same principle is also present in the motivic aspect: the theme of the main section gradually appears, as in Ex. 12.7-3, and at m. 34, hidden in the second violin part! The rising scale-figure is shown in Exx. 12.7-1 through 7-4; Ex. 12.7-4 notes the preparation of the turn and neighbor-note figures, which will appear in the main section. Example 12.7-1 presents a foreground sketch of the passage.

As in Exx. 12.8-1 and 8-3, marking the melodic high point (m. 50), the opening neighbor-note figure is again expanded to become the descending fourth-figure, exactly as later in the main section (m. 80). The main top voice (g^2–f^2–e^2) does not close (to d^2 and c^2); instead, as noted (Ex. 12.2-3), the due notes d^2–c^2 become the initial notes of the trombone theme of the main section: an ingenious stream of continuity, the beginning of one section taking over the "completion" of the previous section.

Developing episode leading to the Scherzo

If the main section can be characterized as the central motivic and harmonic source, the ensuing developing episode (mm. 93–207) engages in a

Ex. 12.5

Introduction Part 1
Harmonic reduction of opening
Ex. 5.1

Ex. 12.6

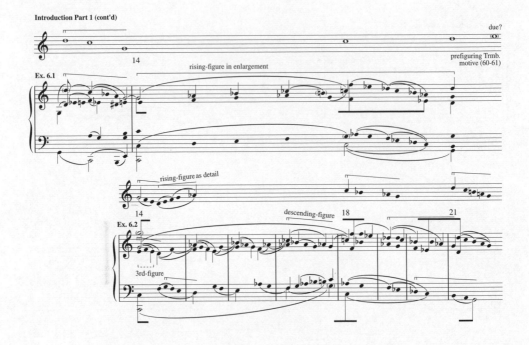

gradual emergence. This sense is also expressed in the slow rise from the lower to the higher register (m. 45) which will be picked up only in the final main section III (m. 500). The same principle is also present in the motivic aspect: the theme of the main section gradually appears, as in Ex. 12.7-3, and at m. 34, hidden in the second violin part! The rising scale-figure is shown in Exx. 12.7-1 through 7-4; Ex. 12.7-4 notes the preparation of the turn and neighbor-note figures, which will appear in the main section. Example 12.7-1 presents a foreground sketch of the passage.

As in Exx. 12.8-1 and 8-3, marking the melodic high point (m. 50), the opening neighbor-note figure is again expanded to become the descending fourth-figure, exactly as later in the main section (m. 80). The main top voice (g^2–f^2–e^2) does not close (to d^2 and c^2); instead, as noted (Ex. 12.2-3), the due notes d^2–c^2 become the initial notes of the trombone theme of the main section: an ingenious stream of continuity, the beginning of one section taking over the "completion" of the previous section.

Developing episode leading to the Scherzo

If the main section can be characterized as the central motivic and harmonic source, the ensuing developing episode (mm. 93–207) engages in a

Ex. 12.7

Introduction Part 2

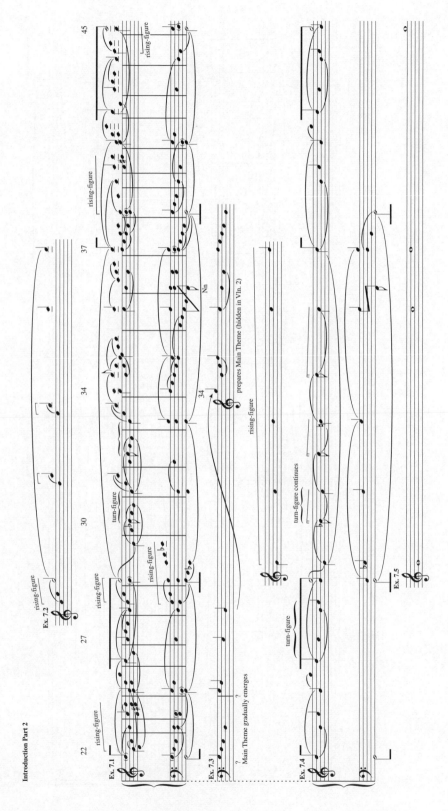

Ex. 12.8

Introduction Part 2 (cont'd)

remarkable recomposition of the motivic features of that main section. Example 12.3-4 had shown the amazing relationship of m. 94 (the episode's motive – the rising scale-figure) to the rising scale-figure of Ex. 12.3-2. Example 12.9-1 shows further foreground aspects of this figure. Examples 12.9-2 and 9-3 illustrate the developmental reworkings of the neighbor-note and turn-figures of the main section. Developmental also, in the sense of tonal instability at the foreground level, is the bass motion (Ex. 12.9-3) C–E♭–F♯–G. This modulatory aspect of the episode creates a transitional effect, of being on the way to something else. Along this way the modal inflections (E♭, F♯) from the main section are beautifully recomposed, and take on greater independence. Example 12.10 continues Ex. 12.9. Of special note (Ex. 12.10-3) are the rhythmic shifts, mm. 115–118, indicated by the slanted lines in the sketch, which bring forth the characteristic Sibelian ninth-chord sonorities. (These are only apparent ninth chords: Ex. 12.10-4 explains the underlying harmonic progression.) Measures 119–131 present a modified restatement of mm. 94–118, in which mm. 99–110 are omitted, thereby avoiding a mechanical restatement and, also by this foreshadowing, enhancing the sense of hastening forward. Examples 12.10-1 and 10-2 call attention to underlying motivic aspects.

Example 12.11 (p. 368) summarizes the entire Episode. Example 12.11-1 shows the underlying harmonic basis (mm. 93–107) in three stages of elaboration. If an exact sequence had been maintained, the progression would have arrived on a VI♯-chord (Ex. 12.11-1, 4); but the return to the tonic is marked by the recurring trombone motive (Ex. 12.11-1, 3, m. 107). This becomes clear as one compares Exx. 12.11-1, 3 (and the foreground readings, Exx. 12.11-2 and 12.11-3) with Ex. 12.11-4. These sketches reveal Sibelius's subtle logic in composing the developing episode as a transformation of the main section: from the main section he recomposes, here in the middleground, the rising fourth g^1–c^2 (mm. 93–107) of the rising scale-figure, the motivic neighbor-note figures decorating this fourth; the following descending fourth figure; and the continuation of this descending figure after m. 119. Moreover, the middleground neighbor-note motion g^2–$a♭^2$–g^2 (Exx. 12.11-2 and 11-3) is a vast expansion of this same foreground neighbor-note figure of the main section. This profound and organic way of composing assures cohesion even as the sound and character of the music are so modified!

Example 12.12 (p. 369) shows a reduction of the second part of the episode. Example 12.12-6 shows that the underlying bass motion c–G (mm. 133–149) once again recomposes the descending fourth c^2–g^1 of the main section (as in Ex. 12.12-7). The motivic neighbor-note figure g^2–$a♭$–g^2 (compare Exx. 12.11-1 through 11-3) is also recomposed.

Ex. 12.9

Ex. 12.10

Developing Episode, Part 1 (cont'd)

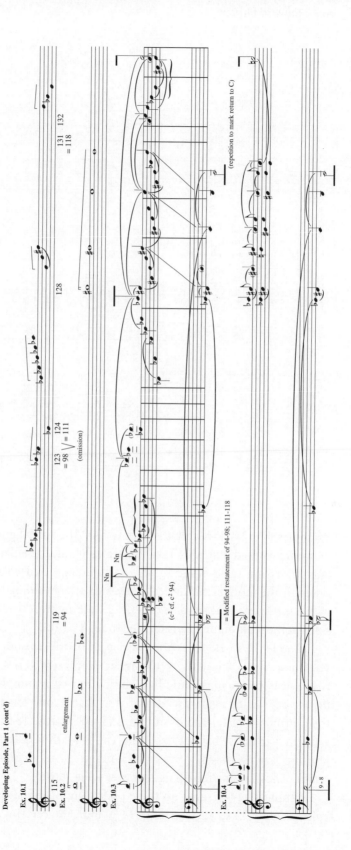

Ex. 12.11

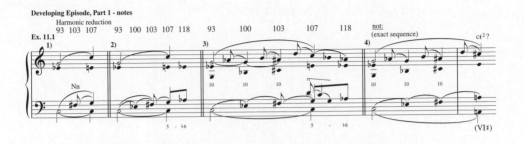

Examples 12.12-1 through 12-4 show how the turn-figure and rising-figure are worked in: Ex. 12.12-4 illustrates a fantastic enlargement of the opening rising scale-figure (g^1–d^2) in middleground enlargement, followed by the motive of mm. 152ff, revealed as combining the turn-figure with a freely inverted form of the rising scale-figure. Foreground expressions of the scale-figure are indicated in Ex. 12.12-3.

Example 12.13 sketches the third part of the episode, showing the same basic figures underlying the music. As presented in Ex. 12.13-3, the rising scale-figure in the middleground is at first incomplete, then complete – expressing again the idea of arrival at a goal. The motivation for the transposed restatement (of mm. 156–80) at mm. 181ff. (Ex. 12.13-1) was surely to arrive back at the bass G (m. 187): thus the overall bass progression (mm. 162–87, Exx. 12.13-1 and 13-4) expresses the main section's descending fourth figure in yet a new guise!

Example 12.14-1 sums up these points, in a general overview of the episode; and Exx. 12.14-2 and 14-3 indicate certain middleground

Ex. 12.12

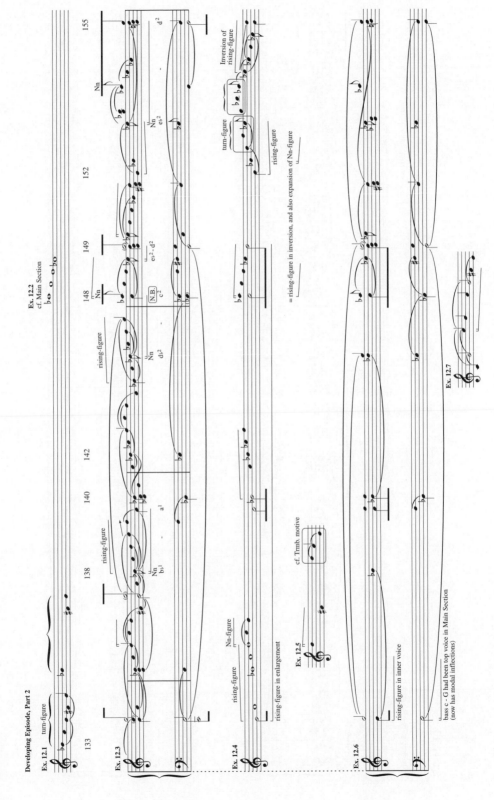

Developing Episode, Part 2

Ex. 12.13

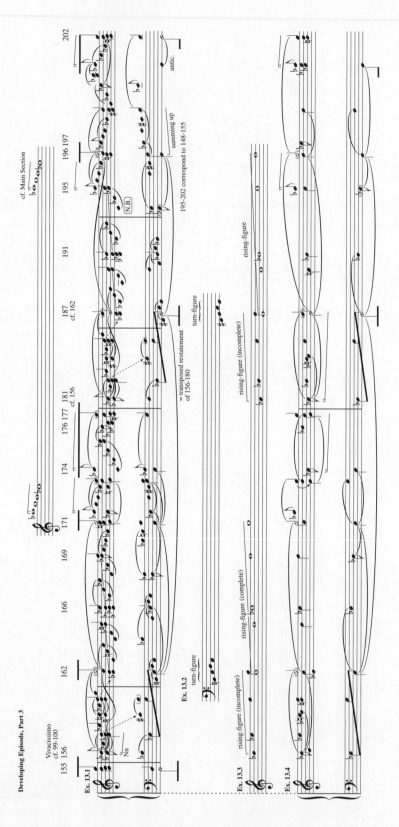

Developing Episode, Part 3

Ex. 12.14

Overview: Developing Episode,
Part 1

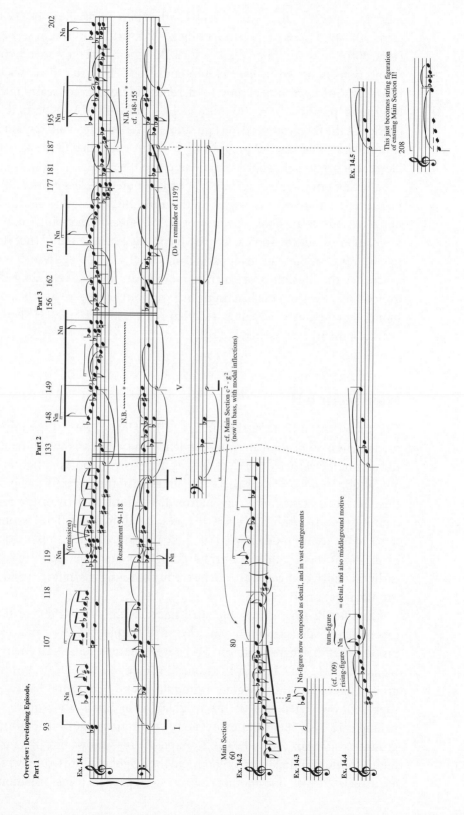

motivic aspects. Thus (Ex. 12.14-1) the bass motion c–B♭–A♭–G (mm. 130–49) is a recomposition of the c^2–g^1 fourth of the main section (mm. 80ff.), now with modal inflections. But one of the most wonderful connections is shown in Exx. 12.14-4 and 14-5. Here, the rising scale-figure (in the foreground at mm. 134ff.) emerges from its concealed middleground position (mm. 133ff., and later mm. 187ff.) to become – outright – the foreground string figuration of the ensuing main section II (mm. 208ff.). The sense of progressing from the concealed to the overt is like that of bright light appearing and bursting through!

A further point regarding Ex. 12.14 may be noted. A classical development section almost never begins on the tonic. But here, over this developing episode as a whole, Sibelius not only begins on the tonic (m. 93) but composes out the tonic over part I, and suggests the *sound* (but not the meaning) of the tonic over parts II and III (Ex. 12.14-1). In so doing, he creates the illusion of a separate movement. Indeed, extending the tonic all the way from the beginning brings about a sense of massiveness, monumentality, expansiveness – perhaps suggestive of the "Hellenic" character mentioned earlier.

Main section II

The main section II is sketched in Ex. 12.15. The purpose of the minor mode here is to give greater independence and emphasis to the modal features noted earlier – the e♭, a♭, b♭ – as if thereby to indicate that these are "wrong" notes, so to speak. That is, in terms of the larger formal plan, this section is transitory – an intermediate point of arrival: the real, definitive return, with the "correct" notes, is still to come. The "wrong" notes of the minor mode imply this, as does the incomplete presentation of the main theme and the unresolved *agitato* character, opposing the earlier serenity, as if calling for that serenity to return, as indeed it will in the main section III.

Example 12.16-1 shows the turn-figure with which the previous incomplete main section II had closed. Examples 12.16-3 and 16-5 propose that this turn-figure (m. 241) is now composed in a vast enlargement (mm. 242–61). Here is an astonishing compositional feat: the foreground figure becomes the guiding middleground line! Example 12.16-4 suggests how statements of the neighbor-note figure are worked in; Example 12.16-6 identifies expressions of the turn-figure in the foreground (e.g., mm. 244 and 246). Example 12.16-7 shows how the turn-figure, the descending fourth-figure, and the neighbor-note figure (which are associated with one another) become – by gradual transformation –

Ex. 12.15

Main Section II

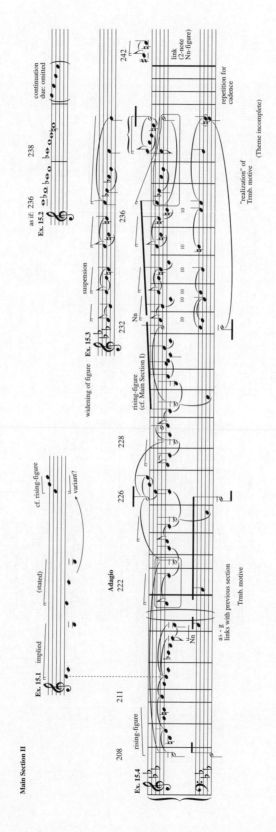

Ex. 12.16

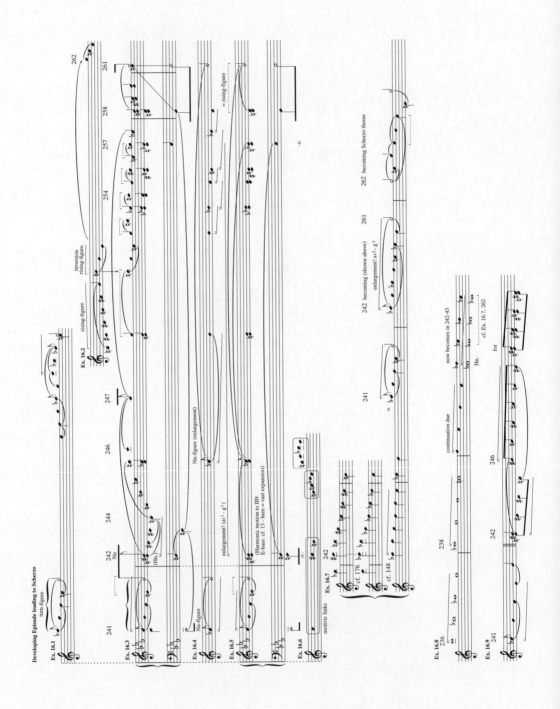

Ex. 12.17

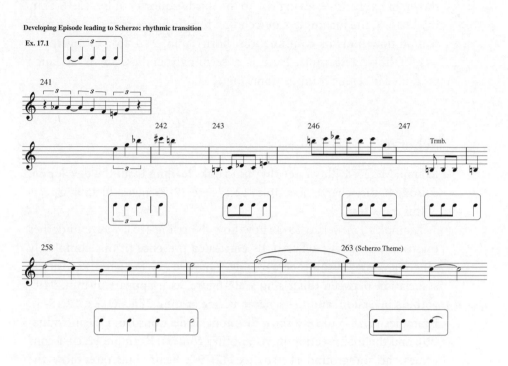

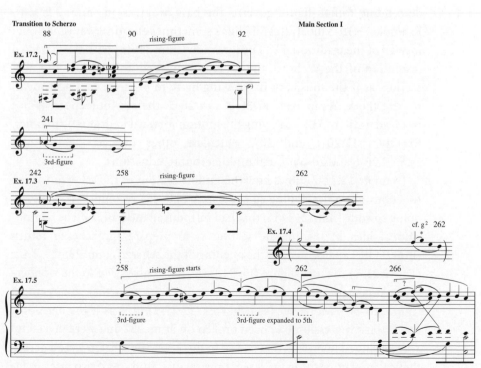

the scherzo theme (m. 262)! The thirds-sonority of the turn-figure is shown in Ex. 12.16-9, giving rise to the thirds-sonority of Ex. 12.16-5. In Ex. 12.16-8, the incomplete descending fourth-figure from the previous section now finds its continuation (horns, mm. 242–43): an ingenious way of linking sections. Here is a seemingly endless flight of fancy grounded in serene compositional logic!

Scherzo

Example 12.17-1 illustrates rhythmic links leading from the developing episode to the scherzo. Examples 12.17-2 to 17-5 suggest further aspects of this transition.

Examples 12.18-1 to 18-3 show how the rising scale-figure underlies the transition to the scherzo. Its concealed presence in this completely different context is quite remarkable. Example 12.18-4 suggests a subtle association between this rising scale-figure, as it appears in mm. 94ff., with its inversion, and the scherzo theme at mm. 285–86 (Ex. 12.18-5). Examples 12.18-5 to 18-8 show the modal inflections from the introduction and the main section in yet another context. Example 12.19-1 continues the foreground sketch; Ex. 12.19-2 again illustrates how the descending fourth-figure governs the bass progression (mm. 305–10). Example 12.19-3 illustrates Sibelius's sometimes elliptical way of writing: instead of the traditional V–I progression (mm. 310ff.) with the expected resolution of the V chord, the cadence is evaded, to lead into the next section, as if the music, in its growing haste to proceed, had no time to resolve the V. As in Exx. 12.20-3 and 20-5, the six-four chord is not resolved until m. 337 – carrying the motion forward in dramatic manner. Examples 12.20-1 and 20-2 elucidate other motivic details, and Exx. 12.20-5 and 20-6 present middleground reductions.

Example 12.21-2 shows how the middle section of the scherzo (which functions like a developing episode, mm. 320–42) recomposes the developing episode (mm. 242–84) that had introduced the scherzo. The compositional idea in the middle section is to prepare the scherzo return (mm. 343ff.) analogously to the opening of the scherzo (mm. 285ff.). Thus (Ex. 12.21-1) the turn-figure (m. 24), which had given rise to the wonderful enlargement (mm. 242ff.), now appears in a further enlargement (mm. 320–38). Moreover (as below Ex. 12.21-2), it is as if the harmonic and linear progression had been broken off at m. 257 and were picked up and continued in m. 322: that is, as if in this sense the scherzo were a parenthetical insertion within the larger musical direction – as if two interpretations, the continuous and the discontinuous, were superimposed. The

Ex. 12.18

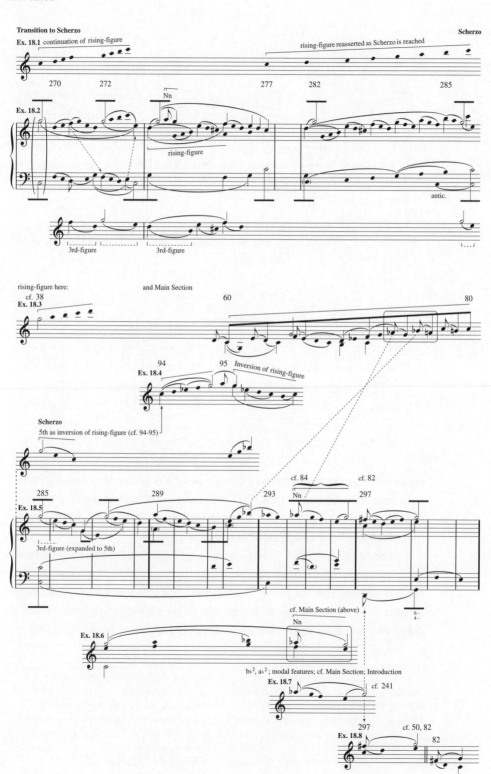

Ex. 12.19

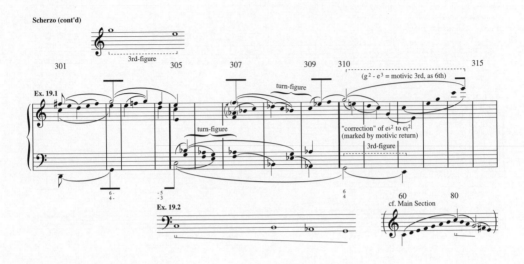

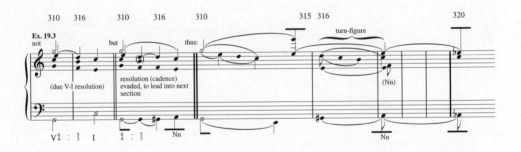

effect of this extraordinary way of composing is of binding together and enclosing disparate sections for continuity and cohesiveness, and of enhancing the overall sense of cumulation – as if the scherzo itself were a by-way along the grander, more fundamental path.

Examples 12.21-3 and 21-4 offer an explanation of the harmonic progression in mm. 334–43. Example 12.21-3, 1 shows the underlying diatonic meaning; Exx. 12.21-3, 2 and 3 elaborate this framework. A further elaboration, with a series of harmonic shifts and anticipations, is indicated in Ex. 12.21-3, 4.[10] Example 12.21-4 may now be understood in

---

[10] Such shifts and anticipations are a very characteristic Sibelian technique. For instance, in Ex. 12.2-4, m. 73, the top-voice g^1 belongs harmonically not with the bass F but with the G bass note which follows (as indicated by the slanting line), and in Ex. 12.2-5, at m. 80, the top-voice c^2 belongs with the bass c: the bass B♭ is technically a lower neighbor note. But what striking emphasis is accorded by this shift to the climactic high c^2! Another instance: Ex. 12.10-3, mm. 115 ff. See also places such as mm. 96–97 (bass and top parts); and overlappings, such as in mm. 363 ff.; and anticipations, such as in mm. 251ff. and mm. 338ff.

Ex. 12.20

terms of the preceding more basic versions. The harmonic shifts give rise to the complex, chromatic density: the compositional intent is to let the resultant chromatic, sharp dissonances set off the clarity of the tonic return (m. 343) as a point of arrival: an "unstable" to "stable" progression.

The return of the scherzo (m. 343), although in the tonic, must be read as a "false" return. To be sure, it is paradoxical that a "false" return should occur in the "correct" (tonic) key, while the "real" return should be delayed and placed over the lowered mediant, i.e., the "false" key of E♭ (mm. 375ff.). This interpretation – admittedly paradoxical – may be rationalized as follows. The key of E♭ now represents the arrival, fulfilment, and realization of all the previously noted e♭ modal inflections. Here at last, the e♭ fully attains its independence; no longer is it merely a chromatic alteration of another tone, but the main scale degree itself.

Ex. 12.21

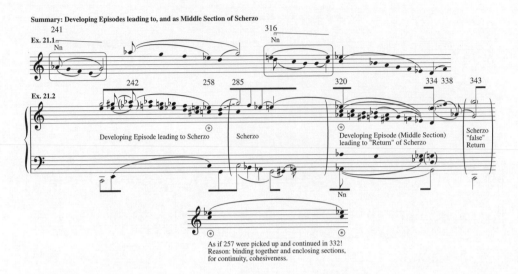

Furthermore, in Schenkerian terms, it is precisely at this point that the fundamental line begins its structural descent. The bass E♭ (m. 375) offers strong support to the top-voice e♭² as the ♭$\hat{3}$ of the fundamental line (see Ex. 12.27, m. 375). Here, at last, structural harmonic support marks a new, fundamental harmonic-contrapuntal direction – suggesting that, from this point, the symphony is heading towards its conclusion. Example 12.22-1 sketches this "false" return; the descending fourth-figure (Ex. 12.22-2) in the middleground clearly becomes the foreground

Ex. 12.22

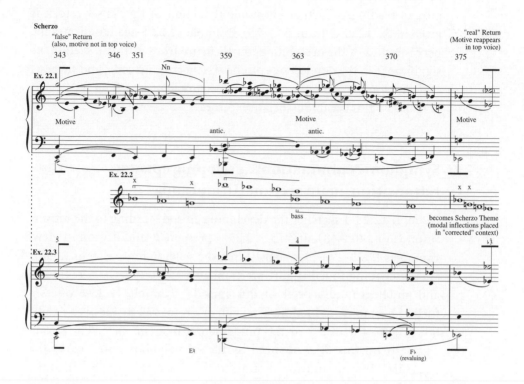

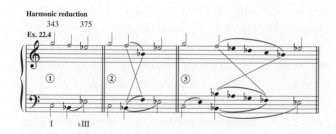

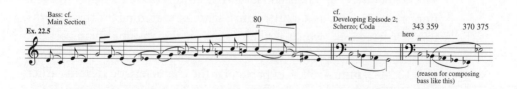

of the scherzo theme (mm. 375ff.). Example 12.22-3 shows a middle-ground reading. A further harmonic reduction of the "false" return is given in Ex. 12.22-4 (mm. 343–75). Example 12.22-5 again indicates the pervasiveness of the descending fourth-figure from the main section, its significance in the developing episode II, scherzo, and coda, and suggests that a reason for composing the fourth-figure here as well, in the bass, is to maintain this organic associative feature.

Symphonic culmination: developing episode, retransition, main section III, and coda

Example 12.23-1 sketches the developing episode leading to the retransition (mm. 407–48), and Ex. 12.23-5 presents a middleground view. Examples 12.23-2 to 23-4 suggest that the scherzo motive (mm. 285ff.) and descending fourth-figure are transformed to underlie foreground and middleground aspects of this episode. Example 12.23-6 offers a further harmonic reduction. The high $e\flat^3$ (mm. 422 to 438) is a neighbor note to the $d\flat^2$, $\flat\hat{2}$ of the fundamental line (m. 442). The strong emphasis on this $d\flat^2$, enhanced by the $e\flat^3$ neighbor note, marks the structural descent and the motion to the $\flat\hat{2}$ (instead of the diatonic, usual $\natural\hat{2}$).

The Retransition (Ex. 12.24) appears as a reminder and transformation of the introduction and its rising scale-figure: altogether, the retransition constitutes an extended upbeat to the final presentation of the main section, and in a number of ways combined, it serves to mark and highlight the concluding main section as the goal and climactic point of arrival, aimed for throughout the whole symphony. For instance, as in Exx. 12.24-1, 24-2, and 24-3, the massive expansion of the initial rising scale-figure leads forcefully to the main section, and (Ex. 12.24-1) the scale-figure is itself transformed into the trombone theme (mm. 475ff.). The deliberately "unbalanced" seven-bar groups (Exx. 12.24-2 and 24-4, mm. 449, 456, 463, and 470) create a sense of searching for their rhythmical "correction," which is then found in the ensuing main section, with a corresponding sense of arrival. The chromatic alterations (Ex. 12.24-2, mm. 456ff. – in particular the characteristic f♯ from earlier on) emphasize the contrast between "unstable" chromaticism and diatonic stability represented by the arrival of the main section. As in Ex. 12.24-4, harmonically, the retransition occurs over an extended dominant six-four chord; the delay in its resolution (at m. 475) further emphasizes the main section as a point of arrival. Moreover, the main section now reappears with heightened immediacy: the introductory

Ex. 12.23

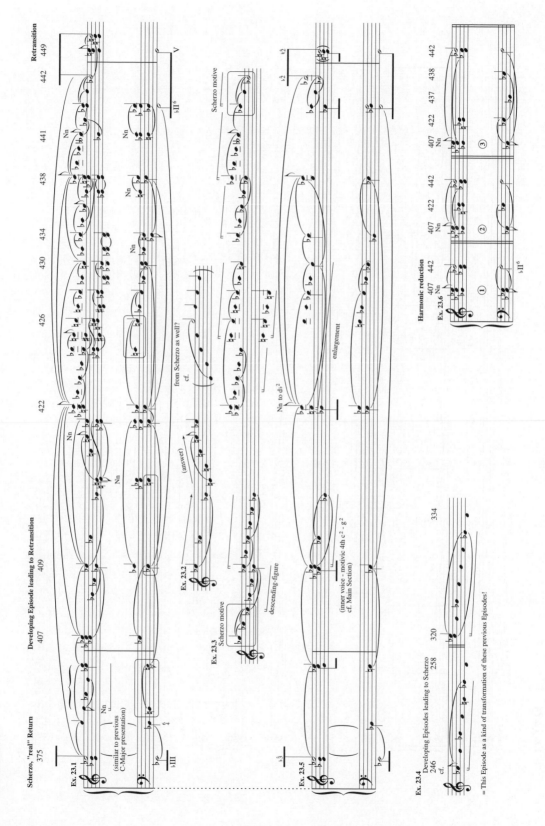

Scherzo, "real" Return   Developing Episode leading to Retransition   Retransition

= This Episode as a kind of transformation of these previous Episodes!

Ex. 12.24

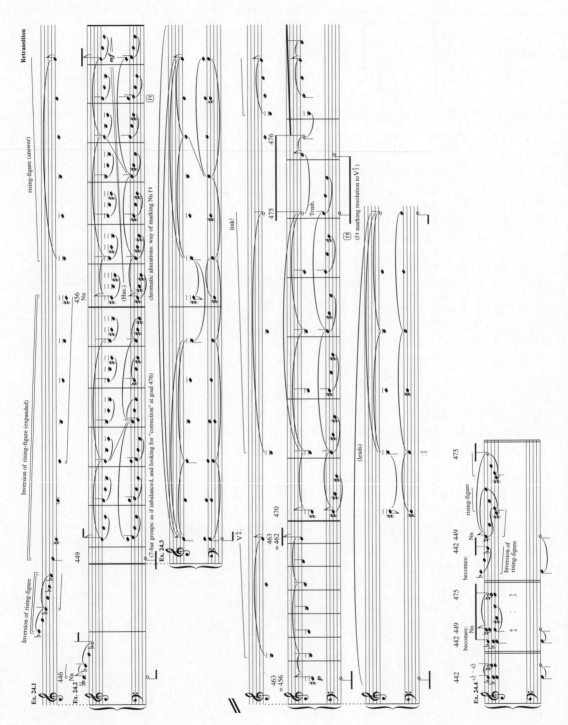

episodic material (mm. 22–59) which had led to the first main section does not reappear. The modally inflected top line's eb^3 to db^2 in the developmental episode leading to the retransition (mm. 422–42, Exx. 12.23-5 and 23-6) sets off the diatonic grandeur of the final peroration. Recall that the second main section (mm. 222ff., Ex. 12.15) had been incomplete and inconclusive, and in the minor mode: now in, Ex. 12.25 the *affettuoso* (mm. 506ff.) reasserts the opposing forces of the modal inflections, with the major mode overcoming these. The opposition of slow and fast movements is now also integrated, for the retransition had been the fastest section and its fast figuration is here boldly superimposed over the grandly slow main section, paradoxically combining fast and slow as if to reconcile these conflicting elements. It is as if the main sections throughout represented, programmatically, that which is permanent and unchanging – an "Hellenic" classicism – while everything else around them was in constant flux and transformation.

Ex. 12.25-1 indicates expressions of the descending fourth-figure underlying the foreground and middleground of the final main section (Exx. 12.25-2 and 25-4), while Ex. 12.25-3 calls attention to the rising scale-figure and its answer. The sonority in m. 500 (Ex. 12.25-2) sums up mm. 446–48. As in Ex. 12.25-2, earlier modal inflections are recalled as if, programmatically, to bring about a reconciliation.

Example 12.26 (pp. 387–88) shows the coda: Exx. 12.26-2 and 26-8 foreground and middleground, Ex. 12.26-1 the descending fourth-figure; and Ex. 12.26-4 a reminder of certain textures from the Introduction. Example 12.26-3 briefly sketches the preceding main section in order to place the coda in context: the eb^1 or eb^2 (Exx. 12.26-2, 26-8, and 26-9) are reminders of the eb^2 (m. 502, Ex. 12.26-3) of the final main section – in turn a reminder of the scherzo's Eb section (mm. 375ff.). The rising scale-figure c^1–c^2 from the first main section (mm. 60–80, Ex. 12.2) is summed up in the final gesture, Ex. 12.26-5. As in Ex. 12.26-9, the coda sums up, for the last time, the neighbor-note figure d^1–c^1 (compare Exx. 12.2-5 and 3-1): the chain of suspensions shown in Ex. 12.26-8 is continued for the primary tones $\flat\hat{3}$ and $\hat{2}$ and gives rise to the final 9-8 (d^1–c^1) suspension, so beautiful because of the motivic association with the d^1–c^1 neighbor-note figure.

Finally, Ex. 12.27 (p. 389) provides an overview of the whole symphony.

These analytical sketches will have indicated, from a technical viewpoint, something of the complexity and yet underlying background simplicity of this work. With its noble thematic material, ever-engaging formal design, characteristic and individual orchestral sonorities, its infinite richness in harmonic-contrapuntal procedures and "the profound logic that created an inner connection between all of the

Ex. 12.25

Ex. 12.26

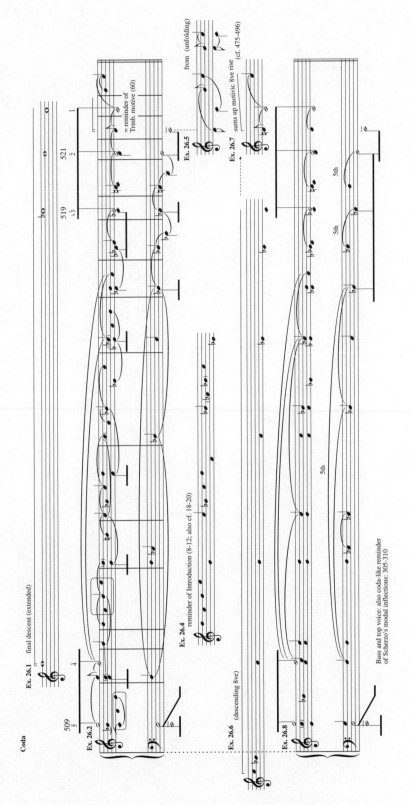

(continued)

Ex. 12.26 (*cont.*)

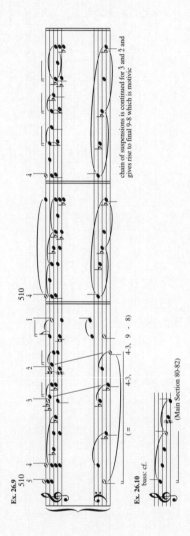

Ex. 12.27

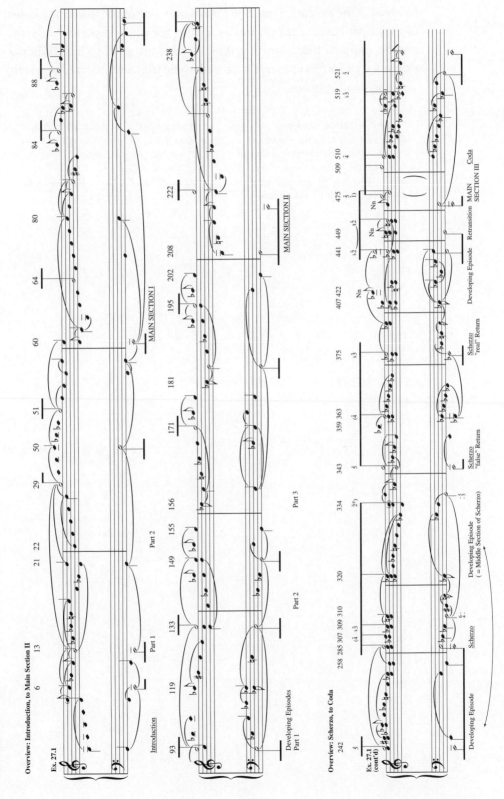

motives,"[11] the Seventh Symphony is not only one of the towering glories of twentieth-century music, but indeed of the whole repertory of symphonic composition altogether. For, as Sibelius "used to say: 'When a work of art which is intuitively created is scientifically analyzed it reveals amazing requirements.'"[12]

[11] "When our [Mahler's and my] conversation touched on the essence of symphony, I said that I admired its severity and style and the profound logic that created an inner connection between all the motives. This was the experience I had come to in composing. Mahler's opinion was just the reverse. 'Nein, die Symphonie muß sein wie die Welt. Sie muß alles umfassen.'" Ekman, *Jean Sibelius*, p. 191.

[12] Levas, *Sibelius. A Personal Portrait*, p. 83.

Index